Russia's Long Twentieth Century

Covering the sweep of Russian history from empire to Soviet Union to post-Soviet state, *Russia's Long Twentieth Century* is a comprehensive yet accessible textbook that situates modern Russia in the context of world history and encourages students to analyze the ways in which citizens learned to live within its system and create distinctly Soviet identities from its structures and ideologies.

Chronologically organised but moving beyond the traditional Cold War framework, this book covers topics such as the accelerating social, economic, and political shifts in the Russian empire before the Revolution of 1905, the construction of the socialist order under Bolshevik government, and the development of a new state structure, political ideology, and foreign policy in the decades since the collapse of the Soviet Union. The authors highlight the polemics and disagreements that energize the field, discussing interpretations from Russian, émigré, and Western historiographies and showing how scholars diverge sharply in their understanding of key events, historical processes, and personalities.

Each chapter contains a selection of primary sources and discussion questions, engaging with the voices and experiences of ordinary Soviet citizens and familiarizing students with the techniques of source criticism. Illustrated with images and maps throughout, this book is an essential introduction to twentieth-century Russian history.

Choi Chatterjee is Professor of History at California State University, Los Angeles. She is the author of *Celebrating Women: Gender, Festival Culture and Bolshevik Ideology, 1910–1939* (2002), co-author of *The Twentieth Century: A Retrospective* (2002) and co-editor of *Everyday Life in Russia Past and Present* (2015) and *The Russian Experience: Americans Encountering the Enigma, 1890 to the Present* (2012).

Lisa A. Kirschenbaum is Professor of History at West Chester University. She is the author of *Small Comrades: Revolutionizing Childhood in Soviet Russia, 1917–1932* (2001), *The Legacy of the Siege of Leningrad, 1945–1991* (2006), and *International Communism and the Spanish Civil War* (2015).

Deborah A. Field is Professor of History and Director of Women's and Gender Studies at Adrian College, Michigan. She is the author of *Private Life and Communist Morality in Khrushchev's Russia* (2007) and winner of the Adrian College Teaching Excellence Award.

Russia's Long Twentieth Century

Voices, memories, contested perspectives

Choi Chatterjee, Lisa A. Kirschenbaum, and Deborah A. Field

Routledge
Taylor & Francis Group

LONDON AND NEW YORK

First published 2016
by Routledge
2 Park Square, Milton Park, Abingdon, Oxon OX14 4RN

and by Routledge
711 Third Avenue, New York, NY 10017

Routledge is an imprint of the Taylor & Francis Group, an informa business

© 2016 Choi Chatterjee, Lisa A. Kirschenbaum, and Deborah A. Field

The right of Choi Chatterjee, Lisa A. Kirschenbaum, and Deborah A. Field
to be identified as authors of this work has been asserted by them in
accordance with sections 77 and 78 of the Copyright, Designs and Patents
Act 1988.

British Library Cataloguing-in-Publication Data
A catalogue record for this book is available from the British Library

Library of Congress Cataloging-in-Publication Data
A catalog record for this book has been requested

ISBN: 978-0-415-67036-4 (hbk)
ISBN: 978-0-415-67037-1 (pbk)
ISBN: 978-1-315-62184-5 (ebk)

Typeset in Sabon
by Keystroke, Station Road, Codsall, Wolverhampton

Contents

Figures

Maps

Publisher's acknowledgments

The publishers would like to thank the following for their kind permission to reproduce textual material:

The Slavonic and East European Review; Nathaniel Knight; W.W. Norton & Company, Inc.; University of Pittsburgh Press; Princeton University Press; Yale University Press; Oxford University Press, Yad Vashem Holocaust Resources; John Wiley & Sons, Inc.; Ludmilla Alexeyeva and Paul Goldberg; Henry Holt and Company, LLC; AB – Die Andere Bibliothek GmbH & Co.; East View Press; Rowman & Littlefield Publishers, Inc., and Melville House Publishing, LLC.

We would also like to thank the estate of Sir Martin Gilbert for permission to reproduce eight maps from *The Routledge Atlas of Russian History*.

In some cases we have been unable to trace the owners of copyright material. We would appreciate any information that would enable us to do so, and any omissions brought to our attention will be remedied in future editions.

An introduction for students and instructors

As professors in regional institutions of higher education, we have spent many years teaching students who hail from diverse backgrounds and possess vastly different levels of preparation. We wrote this book for our students, and its structure and approach are a result of what they have taught us.

We had two primary goals in writing this text. First, we wanted to emphasize that studying history does not mean simply accumulating facts, but is, rather, a process of asking questions and seeking answers, of looking for meaning. To that end, we have not written a textbook that strives to be comprehensive (many of these already exist). Instead, we have adopted an inquiry-based structure. Our second goal was to convey our own interest in Russian history and to encourage students to delve more deeply into the topics and issues we introduce here.

How this book is structured: an inquiry-based approach

A central problem for us in approaching this book was that students often seem to understand history textbooks as the work of a Great and Powerful Oz, an all-knowing disembodied head spouting Truth. In some cases, textbook authors encourage this view, assuming a tone of omniscience and final authority largely absent in their more specialized books for other historians. But the real problem seemed to us the genre itself. Outside of a short list of "guiding principles" tucked away in the introduction, textbooks do little to explain how the ostensibly comprehensive, neutral volume students hold in their hands came to be. Even when authors are careful to include excellent and lively surveys of historians' debates and disagreements, students, in our experience, still approach the history textbook as a unified true story to be learned "for the test."

We aimed to create a different kind of textbook, one that, like Dorothy's pesky little dog, pulled back the curtain to reveal how (and why) historical narratives get made. At the controls in this case readers will find three women who completed PhDs at large public universities in the mid-1990s, and whose careers since have combined research and a great deal of undergraduate teaching. At the outset of this project, we asked ourselves: How can a textbook help students to understand history not as a received narrative, but as an act of creation?

Our answer has been to construct chapters that in their very structure call attention to the questions, sources, and priorities that shaped them. We introduce each chapter with a short vignette that we hope sparks students' curiosity. We follow the vignette with a series of "Chapter Questions." Questions, of course, are a fairly typical textbook feature; however, here they are fully integrated into the text—not seques-tered in a "box" at the beginning of the chapter or relegated to a "test your under-standing" exercise at the end. We use the Chapter Questions to specify our concerns and approach. They can be used to structure class discussions or suggest essay topics.

Our Chapter Questions are not meant to be comprehensive, but they are meant to be provocative. They offer a reminder that "all written history is partial," both because it covers "only a tiny *part* of what really happened" and because "it inevitably takes sides, by what it includes or omits."[1] Instructors may find themselves disagreeing with our selection of themes and questions, disputing our interpretations or omissions. We urge you to share your disagreements with students and to encourage them to argue with our text or to propose alternative questions.

Coming at the beginning of the chapter and structuring the sections that follow, the Questions allow us to help students to understand history as a process of inquiry. We encourage students to read the chapter with an eye toward constructing their own answers. To this end, we explicitly re-raise questions throughout the chapter as we detail the varied perspectives of historical actors and historians.

Mini-biographies included in each chapter expose students to multiple perspectives and raise questions about whose perspectives matter. We include "ordinary" people alongside well-known figures, the so-called great men of history, and ask students to consider what distinguishes the "great" from the "ordinary." Thus our chapter on World War II includes not only Joseph Stalin but also Sofia Ivanovna Sherevera, a teenager who enlisted in the Red Army. In many cases, students can trace the develop-ment of a single individual's perspective over time. For example, we introduce Mikhail Gorbachev not in 1985, when he became secretary general and undertook the reforms that ended in the collapse of the Soviet Union, but some twenty years (and two chapters) earlier, when he was an idealistic young apparatchik inspired by Nikita Khrushchev's reforms.

We have departed somewhat from textbook convention by allowing each chapter to reflect its author's distinctive voice: Choi Chatterjee is the primary author of chapters 1–2 and 11–12; Lisa Kirschenbaum of chapters 3–4 and 6–7; and Deborah Field of chapter 5 and chapters 8–10. We have also included endnotes rather than extensive lists of "additional readings." These decisions reflect our commitment to showing how our text was made. They also allow us to model good historical prac-tice: We want our students to develop their own distinctive voices and to cite their sources. Additionally, the endnotes offer a starting point for further investigation. Our choices are not, it is worth repeating, meant to be comprehensive. We emphasize recent, accessible sources in English that we have found useful and thought provok-ing. We have also worked to keep the book short enough that instructors will be able to assign primary sources, scholarly articles, or monographs in addition to the text.

Each chapter ends with a selection of primary sources that provides a kind of laboratory for students to try out their answers to the Chapter Questions. Although they come at the end, they are not an afterthought. We reference them throughout the chapter, encouraging students to think about how they support, complicate, or challenge the interpretations and perspectives described in the text. Questions specific to each source help students to identify its perspective and its connections to other sources; we have chosen sets of sources for each chapter that allow students to construct tentative answers to the Chapter Questions (see guidelines for reading primary sources below). As students draw on these sources (and others) to build interpretations, we hope that they come to see history not as an immutable chronicle that explains why the world must be as it is, but as a multiplicity of contingent and shifting interactions to which a wide range of interdependent actors contribute.

A post-Cold War history: our historical approach

Twenty-five years after the fall of the Soviet Union, the Cold War continues to cast a long shadow. Thus historians still have a tendency to tell Russia's twentieth-century history as a moralizing tale of utopian/dystopian Bolshevik visions, a catalog of failed state policies and massive repression initiated from above—a story dominated by elite politics and personalities. Yet our students are often unaware of Cold War politics, modernization theories, and the triumphalism implicit in both of these paradigms. Today's undergraduates, for the most part, are multicultural citizens of a global world who are interested in Russia not as a cautionary tale of failed modernization nor as the site of a misguided experiment in Marxism—although some come to class interested in both of those things—but as a dynamic society that embarked on its own path to development.

To make Russian and Soviet history relevant to the post-Cold War generation, we have structured it around the vital concerns of the present: globalization, inequality, and identity. Russian and Soviet history has often been treated as an aberrant story of peculiar national development. In contrast, we situate this history in world time and explain how the Russian empire intersected with other nations and empires. While Russia has long been compared with the West, we develop a broader comparative framework that integrates contemporary developments in non-European areas of the world. This transnational approach integrates the stories of nationalities and ethnicities that coexisted in the multinational Russian/Soviet empire. We also include the voices of international visitors and outsiders: American journalists, French communists, African university students. The impact of race, ethnicity, and nationality on historical experience within Russia and the Soviet Union features prominently in this text.

We also make gender and generation an integral part of the history of the Russian empire. Without minimizing the "traditional" questions of state power and state repression, we have tried to highlight the perspectives of the "ordinary" people whose voices were often silenced in Cold War narratives. The Bolshevik revolutionaries were unusual for their time in having a coherent program for women's and also children's liberation, one that included normative codes both for the conduct of everyday life and for the formation of gendered subjectivity. We can discern the long-term effects of these policies in the strong feminist and emerging gay rights movements in post-Soviet Russia.

Recognizing that most of the students using this book know little about Russia, we have worked to communicate our own fascination with the complex and vibrant array of cultures that compose Russian society. We hope that this textbook will encourage students to undertake further and deeper investigations into the history and culture of Russia, and replenish the ranks of scholars in the field of Slavic Studies.

A very brief guide to reading primary sources

Each chapter ends with a selection of primary sources that students can use (perhaps in conjunction with additional primary sources and scholarly articles) to propose answers to the Chapter Questions. While we have provided specific questions for each primary source, the following procedures provide a starting point for all primary sources. However, not all questions will apply to all cases.[2]

1   Sourcing: What do you know about when, where, by whom, and for what purpose this source was created? Is this a memoir written long after the fact? A transcript of a meeting? A poem? What can (and can't) the source tell us about the time in which it was written (or the time it is writing about)?

2   Contextualizing: Where do you find evidence of the larger context in which the source was written? How can the larger context help you to understand the source? What people, events, and places mentioned in the text might offer clues to the world in which it was produced? What are the key concepts used in the source? Does the author's use of them differ from contemporary usages? It is often useful to pay attention to anything that seems strange, surprising, or even immoral from our perspective; such dissonances can offer a sense of how the author's worldview differs from our own.

3   Close reading: Here you want to pay attention to not only what the author says, but also how she or he says it. What does the source suggest about the author's assumptions, priorities, etc. or about the system in which he or she is embedded?

4   Corroboration: How does the source agree with, complicate, or challenge other sources? What is unique about the source's perspective? What does it reveal about a situation that other sources don't? What does it omit or suppress?

5   Interpretation: How does the source help you to answer the overarching question?

Notes

1   Emphasis in original. Howard Zinn, "The Use and Abuse of History," in Zinn, *Declarations of Independence: Cross-Examining American Ideology* (New York: Harper Perennial, 1990), 51.

2   For a fuller introduction, see Miriam Dobson and Benjamin Ziemann, eds., *Reading Primary Sources: The Interpretation of Texts from Nineteenth and Twentieth Century History* (New York: Routledge, 2008).

1 Empire and modernization

INTRODUCTION

In May of 1896, the handsome and dashing American reporter Richard Harding Davis arrived in Moscow to witness the coronation of Tsar Nicholas II at the Assumption Cathedral in the Kremlin. The court officials were determined to keep representation from the press corps, whose journalists lacked the requisite social manners to attend these aristocratic ceremonies, to a basic minimum. This provoked furious competition among those vying to enter the imperial arena, but Richard Davis worked the social networks of tsarist officialdom with aplomb and brilliance. His good looks brought him the approval and help of high ranking ladies of the Russian court, and through their kind intercession Davis was allowed to attend both the coronation and the numerous other social events that followed.[1]

The grand coronation ceremonies that marked the ascension of the twenty-six year old Nicholas II and his young German bride, Alexandra, were marred by the tragedy at the Khodynka Fields, located five miles to the north of Moscow. Large crowds of patriotic revelers and merry makers had gathered to celebrate the new monarch, hoping to feast on pretzels and sausage, and receive keepsake enamel mugs of the coronation. They also hoped to see the handsome young tsar who was supposed to attend the event. But rumors of a food shortage led to a stampede during which more than a thousand people were crushed to death and many more were injured. The poor preparations on the field and the ineptitude of the authorities compounded the confusion. Although the tsar paid compensation to the families of the victims and visited many in hospital, his attendance at a glittering reception at the French embassy later that evening was considered to be in poor taste. Subsequently, the Khodynka Field tragedy has been interpreted as an ominous omen for the doomed regime. In 1894 few, including Richard Davis, would have prophesied that the long lasting Romanov dynasty would come to an inglorious end in 1917. But the presence of a commoner at these imperial ceremonies signaled that change was imminent in autocratic Russia.

CHAPTER QUESTIONS

In this opening chapter we will cast a wide net over the history of the Russian empire and focus on the last two decades before the Revolution of 1905. We will consider the role that geography, imperialism, and competitive modernization played in accelerating social, political, and economic changes. Why was imperialism central to the formation and identity of Russia? How did autocracy evolve based on an alliance with the nobility? Was tsarist autocracy compatible with industrialization and modernization, and if so what would society look like in the aftermath? Who would lead the country toward global modernity, and what role would workers, peasants, and the new middle class play in shaping these epochal transitions?

VOICES, MEMORIES, CONTESTED PERSPECTIVES

Russian imperialism: autocracy and nobility

As in the case of other empires, such as the British, the French, and the Ottoman, the Russian autocrat and the ruling class viewed the Russian state as an imperial formation, and many, both among the upper and lower classes, believed that they were destined to rule one of the largest contiguous empires in world history. Russians also believed they had inherited the mantle of the Byzantine civilization, and as such had preserved the essence of the Christian faith that had been deformed by the Reformation and Counter-Reformation in Europe. Russia was destined to bring spiritual comfort and philosophical sustenance to a materialistic and decadent West. In the late nineteenth and early twentieth centuries some Russian intellectuals even considered themselves to be youthful Scythians, or Asiatic barbarians who would revolutionize European modes of art and culture, reconstruct politics, and create new ways of imagining one's selfhood and one's relationship with the community.

Russian civilization, which had begun around Kiev in the ninth century, the capital of present day Ukraine, had been dominated by the Mongol overlords from the twelfth to the fifteenth centuries. Russian tsars prospered as tax collectors for the Great Khan and over time gathered the resources to emerge as a serious competitor to the Mongols in the north. But intermittent wars between the tsars and grand noble families stunted the growth of Muscovy and frustrated its imperial ambitions. Incursions from the north and west by Swedes, Poles, and Lithuanians also weakened nascent state formation. The Muscovite heartland, where the Romanov dynasty was centered, had poor soil and a relatively short growing season. Due to the prolonged winter Russia could not sustain an agricultural system productive enough to support a large population. But it was conveniently located on a riverine system complemented by lakes that facilitated trade, travel, and military excursions.

Starting from the seventeenth century, the Romanov dynasty managed to consolidate and centralize power. They then used the fruits of imperial expansion to harness an influential caste of warrior nobles to the defense of an autocratic state. The nobility derived enormous privileges from this alliance in terms of huge land grants, monetary wealth from tax farming contracts, and powerful positions in a rapidly expanding armed forces and bureaucracy. Finally, the nobility also secured the services of a servile peasantry that was increasingly bound to the land by a system of state-enforced serfdom from the seventeenth century onward. Romanovs justified their autocratic monopoly on power because of the insecure frontiers with bellicose European powers in the north and the west, military threats from the Ottoman and Persian empires to the south and the southwest, and competition with China over the domination of Asia. They also pointed to the divisions within the nobility and warned that, without a strong hand at the center, Russia would descend into civil war, chaos, and anarchy.

In early eighteenth century, Tsar Peter the Great conjured up the stately city of St. Petersburg on the banks of the steely waters of the Neva. The construction of St. Petersburg served as a calling card to Western Europe in the early eighteenth century; that a new empire had emerged on the world scene and was ready to play its part in Europe, the Middle East, and Asia. It was a city built by the back-breaking labor of hundreds and thousands of serfs who perished while they hauled giant blocks of granite to build the city of stone surrounded by water. Serfs brought to life the plans of an array of Russian, French, and Italian architects who designed buildings that added grace, form, and functional embellishments to Peter's famous Venice of the north. During the eighteenth century St. Petersburg became a city of parade grounds, stately avenues, imperial palaces, and monumental government buildings. Exquisite mansions of the nobility, fountains, parks, canals, and promenades created memorable architectural ensembles throughout the city. Above all St. Petersburg stood for order, hierarchy, and military control, notions derived both from the European Enlightenment and Russian autocratic traditions.

According to Dominic Lieven, the Russian nobility, a cosmopolitan, polyglot, multi-ethnic elite that included representatives from both the Russian upper classes and those from the colonized areas, had a vested interest in imperial expansion.[2] The Romanov dynasty cannily drew talented administrators from every major ethnic group in the empire; thus, for example, the Baltic nobility were very well represented in the upper reaches of the imperial army once these lands were conquered. Immigrant Germans came at the express invitation of the German princess Catherine the Great in the late eighteenth century and dominated large sections of the army as well as the universities. The Russian aristocracy assimilated Tatar, Polish, Finnish, Georgian, and even Chechen noble families, and their sons joined the imperial administration.

Their presence added to the luster and provided an exotic tone to the court at St. Petersburg. But assimilation was a double edged sword and sometimes elites switched sides by responding to calls of ethnic particularism, religious solidarity, and nationalism. The tug of war between loyalty to the Russian empire and to one's own chosen group, whether based on politics, philosophical inclinations, or claims of ethnicity, was a constant theme throughout Russian history. During times of trouble, elites from different parts of the empire sought freedom and self-determination, but during good times they benefited greatly from their association with the Russian imperial administration.[3] Is it possible to belong to more than one political formation and have more than one civic identity?

Looking south and then east, Russian imperialists secured the grain production of the southern steppes of New Russia, and the wheat, beet sugar, and iron and coal of the Ukrainian lands. They believed that they were bringing the fruits of a superior Western and Christian civilization (science, progress, law, commerce, and bureaucratic administration) to the lesser races that dwelt in the enormous and resource-rich Siberia and the Arctic tundra, the mountains of the Caucasus, and the vast lands of Central Asian Khanates despite the opposition of the indigenous peoples. The fighting in the Caucasus was particularly vicious as the populations put up a spirited resistance under their charismatic leader Imam Shamil, and the Russian imperial forces took many decades of the nineteenth century to brutally subdue the Chechens, Ossetians, Circassians, and other mountain peoples that lived in independent communities and nominally subscribed to forms of Islam. As the nineteenth century ended, Russia had successfully brought these regions under its direct control, in addition to ruling Finland, the Baltic states, Poland, Ukraine and Bessarabia in the west, and Siberia in the east.

Russia had long considered the Balkans as its natural arena of expansion, because of their similar language and religious beliefs, but after the humiliating defeat in the Crimean War (1856) the Russian imperial gaze turned toward Asia; by the end of the century it had formally incorporated the territory of the Khanates of Khiva, Kokand, and Bukhara.[4] Russian penetration into these areas threatened the British empire that sought unsuccessfully to create a buffer zone in Afghanistan to protect its richest colony, India. From the 1860s, Central Asian lands, especially modern day Uzbekistan, were used to grow cotton to feed the textile mills of Moscow and also served as a market for Russian manufactured goods. In the Far East, Russia won considerable territorial concessions from the weak Chinese empire during this period, and extended its territory to the Pacific. In 1860, Vladivostok was founded as one of the new imperial port cities on the Pacific. This brought Russia into competition with other powers such as Japan, the United Kingdom, France, and the United States who all fought for access to the vast markets of China and the lucrative trade in the Indian Ocean. Russian bureaucrats believed that their empire, the extraordinary land mass that lay between Asia and Europe, was destined to completely reorient global interactions in the twentieth century.

Like the British and French colonial authorities, the Russians devised many, sometimes contradictory, colonial policies depending on context and chronology. The Ukrainian, Baltic, Finnish, and Georgian nobility was incorporated into the Russian imperial order. Even as Poland was brutally Russified after the 1863 uprising, and thousands of nobles were sent to Siberian exile, Polish nobles continued to appear at the court in St. Petersburg. Central Asian Muslims, called inoverstsy or people of a different faith, were allowed to practice their religion and customary law, even though racial hierarchies separated the colonial administration from the native parts of town in Uzbekistan. In the former Tatar areas of the middle Volga region, especially in Kazan, Orthodox clergy tried with limited success to convert Tatar Muslims to Christianity and assimilate them into the mainstream.[5] But the enormous expansion of the Russian empire meant that, according to the 1897 census, the Russian-speaking population in the empire constituted a slight majority only with the addition of Ukrainians and the Belorussian populations whose languages were similar to Russian. The administration of the empire brought advantages in terms of land, resources, and taxable subjects, but it also led to imperial overstretch brought about by the need to defend endless borders and control restive border populations that were always susceptible to persuasion by other empires.

Unlike the English nobility that fought against the efforts of an absolutist Stuart monarchy to centralize the authority of the king in the seventeenth century, or the French nobility that led the fight against Bourbon centralization in the eighteenth century, the Russian nobility secured a strong alliance with the Romanovs and with few exceptions served loyally in the army, navy, and many imperial bureaucracies until 1917. As late as the early twentieth century, even liberal and progressive members of the nobility could scarcely imagine a Russian imperium bereft of autocratic rule. They depended on the tsarist order to defend their privileged position in society and their unequal access to land, employment, capital, and educational systems. Conservative thinkers such as Konstantin Pobedonostsev, who served as an influential tutor to Nicholas II, were convinced that parliamentary representation led not to democracy and self-rule but to the irresponsible misuse of state power against the interests of the people. The fight in Russia between a traditional autocratic order and a more representative political system was being replicated in many parts of the globe.

Industrialization and problems of modernization

The Crimean War of 1853–1856 was a big shock to the Russian autocracy that had effortlessly dominated European politics after triumphantly defeating Napoleon's army in the war of 1812. After initially winning a war against the Ottoman empire during the campaign in Crimea, the Russian army and navy were badly beaten by a coalition of British and French forces. Seeking to preserve their control of naval routes to Asia, Western powers wanted to prevent Russian domination of the Black Sea by propping up the weak Ottoman empire, and by destroying Russia's fledgling navy that was being built in the Crimean Peninsula. During this war the British and French used modern artillery, rifles, railroads, telegraphs, and trench warfare, while Russia struggled to provision its army in the Balkans via bumpy and muddy roads. Realizing that it was falling behind the Western European powers, Russia embarked on a course of modernization that was going to have decidedly mixed results for the autocracy and the nobility.

Tsar Alexander II abolished serfdom in 1861, and freed peasants were given legal rights, privileges, and a stake in the land markets. But emancipation did not bring peace, as peasants lost access to the vast acreages that they had traditionally farmed under serfdom. Unlike the American slaves who were freed two years later, serfs in Russia did receive a portion of the land under the terms of the Emancipation Settlement. However, they resented having to compensate landowners for the land that they received and felt that they received lands of inferior quality. The government, fearing an exodus of free and landless peasants from villages, strengthened the authority of the peasant commune at the expense of the individual by authorizing it to collect and pay taxes on behalf of the peasantry. Peasants remained a separate estate with their own law courts and subject to the jurisdiction of the local police and the gentry. But despite formal restrictions peasant entrepreneurs rented and bought land from their former owners, many of whom were unable to transform themselves into successful commercial farmers and compete in the competitive global grain markets.

Reforms that accompanied the emancipation overhauled the law courts and permitted trials by jury. The educational system expanded and Russian universities started producing significant numbers of graduates in science, engineering, law, and medicine. The state eased press censorship, and a lively public media was formed that fought ceaselessly against policies of censorship. From the 1890s, Russian industrialization grew significantly, creating three new social classes of capitalists, factory workers, and a middle class that was uncertain about its identity, political mission, and values.

Modernization was an uneven and protracted phenomenon, concentrated in the cities and leaving immense areas in the empire mired in poverty and subsistence agriculture. The tsarist state was itself ambivalent about the nature and outcomes of modernity. It coveted the fruits of modernization in terms of enhanced state power, and the greater financial and military resources that modern methods of taxation could yield, but the bureaucracy was very afraid of the social and political repercussions that such a transition would necessarily entail.

Figure 1.1 Three generations of workers. Courtesy of the Library of Congress Prints and Photographs Division, Prokudin-Gorskii Collection (LC-DIG-prok-02044).

Notice the differences in appearances among the workers. What does that suggest about social and generational change?

Members of the ruling class were aghast at the emergence of a vociferous civil society with its new talk of civil rights, political representation, and a constitution limiting the powers of autocracy. Factory workers who wanted better pay, better working conditions, and unionization were more assertive, more vocal, and better organized than the traditionally servile peasantry who only erupted periodically. The transition from a paternalistic feudal system, where individualism was subordinated to the needs of the community, to a new social system, equally unequal but based on civil liberties, political rights, and the primacy of private property, was threatening to both the autocracy and the nobility. The middle class in the peripheries added national self-determination to its repertoire of demands, further threatening the imperial order.

Russian politics had a third rail: revolutionaries of all stripes, including feminists, anarchists, socialists, religious sectarians, and artists who dreamed of building state-less utopias of equality, based on the communalization of property.[6] The Russian intelligentsia, who styled themselves as moral guardians and representatives of the dispossessed, came from many classes, including scions of the nobility, clergy, former serfs, workers, peasants, and children of industrialists and wealthy farmers. While the Marxists were pro-modernization and hailed the advance of capitalism and industrialization as a step toward socialism, many others were committed to building a stateless society of communes, cooperatives, and other decentralized and self-governing communities. Russia in 1894 was at a historic crossroads, torn apart by influential groups representing various social classes ranging from the peasantry to the highest circles of the nobility. They offered competing visions for the road forward and sought to influence the tsar using modes of persuasion that ranged from advice, to literature, to political tracts, to revolutionary uprisings, and even assassination attempts. In the chapter that follows we will analyze the leading oppositional ideologies of the period that led to the Bolshevik revolution of 1917.

Nicholas II was a kind father, a supportive husband, and a ruler who believed until his dying day that he had the best interests of his people at heart. But he lacked the courage and vision to reshape autocracy in accordance with the demands of capitalism and modernity. Both history and historians have been uniformly unkind in their assessment of Tsar Nicholas II. He has been characterized as an incompetent and ill prepared ruler dominated first by his conservative tutor, Konstantin Pobedonostsev, and later by his German born wife, the Empress Alexandra. However, a recent study argues that Nicholas II was not opposed to popular representation per se, but believed that while a parliamentary body could exercise legislative initiative, it should not curtail autocratic privilege in any meaningful way.[7] Many leading thinkers and politicians at that time believed that the preservation of an autocratic system of government offered the best guarantees against the perceived corruption and flaws of Western democracies. Russians had memories of protracted periods of terrible political instability and feared that the dilution of centralized power would lead to anarchy and civil war.

Like Otto von Bismarck, the Iron Chancellor of Germany, the leading statesmen of Russia believed that an autocratic tsar and a strong state were necessary to govern, modernize, protect, and expand the vast expanses of the Russian empire in search for scarce resources, adjudicate fairly between various factions of the multiethnic and fractious elite, and defend the interests of the peasantry and the workers from the agrarian nobility, the merchants, and the industrialists. Nicholas II took his role as the paternalistic father figure very seriously and believed that the peasants, who made up the vast majority of the imperial populations, would be duped, cheated, and oppressed by elites as well as the irresponsible liberals, radicals, and other members of the intelligentsia, if they ever did come to power. While Nicholas II failed to realize that the only way Russia could maintain and extend its empire was through investing in industrialization and modernizing the army, he was astute enough to understand that any system of political representation would undermine the absolutist state that he had inherited. Do you think that it was possible for Nicholas both to defend his patrimony, the Russian empire, and to preside over its transformation?

Industrialization and the creation of new social classes

By the late nineteenth century a new world system was coming into effect, one in which the rate of industrialization was going to determine the wealth and military might of empires, in addition to the possession of land, natural resources, gold, and exploitative systems of labor. Although industrialization had started in England in the early part of the nineteenth century, it was slow to spread to other parts of the world. But by the late nineteenth century warfare became increasingly mechanized and armed forces needed railways and navies to move troops rapidly across the world. Countries such as the United States, Germany, Mexico, and Japan raced to stabilize their finances and convert their currency to the gold standard. Governments realized that only vast infusions of international capital could allow them to develop mines, create factories and systems of communications, expand ports, and build roads and railroads to transport soldiers, raw materials, and finished goods. This era of globalization saw the rise of a cohort of ruthless and brilliant entrepreneurs worldwide who built their fortunes by investing their money in modern industry and agriculture, and modern systems of banking, finance, and communications.

In the Russian empire, talented ministers such as Nikolai Bunge and Ivan Vyshnegradsky had already laid the basis for the development of heavy industry in Russia when Sergei Witte was appointed the Minister of Finance in 1892.[8] Although a descendant of the old noble family of Dolgorukys on his mother's side, and born into privileged surroundings in Tiflis, Georgia, Witte fancied himself as a self-made man. In his autobiography he emphasized the fact that his success was due to hard work and talent and extraordinary prescience. An excellent student, Witte had originally planned to study mathematics in Odessa but was dissuaded from pursuing an academic career by his noble relatives. Instead, during the 1870s and 1880s Witte worked in various railroad companies in Ukraine, finally serving as the Director of Russian Railways for the Finance Ministry. In 1892 he was appointed the Minister of Finance.

Having learned the intricacies of administrative politics within the railroad system, Witte realized that, without an expansive and efficient railway system, Russia could neither hold together its imperial domains nor muster up sufficient strength on European battlefields. Under the Witte system, both direct and indirect taxes levied on the peasantry, coupled with the proceeds from the government monopoly on the sale of alcohol, were used to fund the industrialization of Russia. This approach was not unusual. Industrialization across the world was funded by exploiting the agrarian sector, and armies of slaves and indentured laborers working in plantations in Asia, Africa, North and South America, had helped fund earlier waves of European modernization.

Witte's conservative monetary policies attracted the attention of European capitalists, especially French bankers who invested heavily in Russian bonds. His greatest achievement was the expansion of the Trans-Siberian Railway, one of the largest railroad systems in the world linking the Russian heartland with the city of Vladivostok on the Pacific coast. The railroad was built with multiple objectives, notably to facilitate Russian expansion into Asia, especially Manchuria and Korea, and to secure Russian control over the resources of Siberia and Central Asia. By the nineteenth century, much of the valuable fur-bearing animals such as ermine and sables had been depleted by relentless hunting and trapping, but Siberia had endless forests and vast mineral resources that were going to prove invaluable for Russian industrialization.

The Trans-Siberian Railway helped in the migration of four million Russian peasants to Siberia, easing population pressures in Central Russia. Despite incompetence, mismanagement, and corruption, this large scale railroad was completed in 1916.[9] The railroad helped bring cheap Siberian grain to Russian markets, and provided an outlet for products from Russia's developing heavy industry. Like the Transcontinental Railroad in the United States, Russian engineers started work on both ends of the railroad and created a huge multinational labor force to complete the grandiose project. As the expansion of the American colonies to the Pacific coast led to the decimation of the Native Americans in the Great Plains and in the West, similarly the Russian advance through Siberia took a catastrophic toll on the native populations, already displaced by centuries of heavy-handed colonial policies and ruthless resource extraction.[10]

The development of Russia's heavy industry was aided by the infusion of international capital, technology, and expertise.[11] Gigantic coal, iron, metal processing, and chemical works were built in the Urals, St. Petersburg, the Baltics, Poland, Ukraine, and Moscow. Moscow also saw the development of a textile and consumer goods industry, while a significant oil industry developed around Baku in the Caucasus. After the Revolution of 1905, the rate of Russian industrialization was in some sense comparable to that of both Germany and the United States, and Russian industry, in addition to fulfilling government contracts, also exported to countries in Asia and the Middle East. Russia's industrial and commercial elite were beginning to develop a modern identity, a lifestyle that was similar to that of Westernized nobles, and separate themselves from their more traditional brethren in the merchant community who continued to live secluded lives and follow the Old Believer faith. Russian entrepreneurs came from many different classes and, as in the United States, included a significant number of foreigners and members of the Jewish community.[12]

Many of the Russian bourgeois families such as the Tretiakovs, like their counterparts the Vanderbilts, Rockefellers, and Carnegies, became major philanthropists, patrons of higher education, art collectors, and passionate devotees of the ballet and theater. Pavel Tretiakov acquired one of the largest collections of Russian icon paintings at the world famous Tretiakov Galleries, one that survived the Bolshevik revolution. Savva Mamontov, a wealthy industrialist, created a colony for artists on his beautiful estate Abramtsevo, where he tried to revive the traditional Russian arts of painting, carving, and woodwork by providing scholarships and employment for artists. Like their fellow noblemen, Russian entrepreneurs and merchants patronized the arts as a way to gain social legitimacy and acceptance into high society.

Savva Morozov founded the Moscow Arts Theater, and its directors Konstantin Stanislavsky and Vladimir Nemirovich-Danchenko influenced theater productions throughout the world. The Morozovs were a family of Old Believers who had made their money in the textile industry over the course of three generations. Unlike his grandfather, a gifted businessman who started life as an illiterate peasant, young Savva studied physics, mathematics, and engineering, first at the prestigious Moscow University and then at Cambridge University. A sophisticated man of the world, in addition to being a successful businessman, Morozov also had a social conscience and provided cultural enlightenment to his many workers by building a library, theater, schools, and choirs. But unlike his peers across the world Morozov's brand of politics became increasingly socialist. He came into contact with radical Russians through his affair with the actress Maria Andreevna. Under her political guidance, Morozov funded the Bolsheviks and contributed money to political prisoners sent to exile in Siberia. His family not surprisingly feared for his sanity and removed him from the management of the factories when he threatened to introduce a profit-sharing scheme for workers. In 1905, Savva Morozov shot himself at a hotel in Cannes, France. Although the official cause of his death was suicide, we still know little about this talented and complex millionaire, a man devoted to the arts who tried to combine his interest in worker welfare with his quest for profits.

Russian middle class?

Until recently, scholars believed that Russia was different from the West in so far as it had a weak bourgeoisie and lacked a middle class, a class of educated professionals such as lawyers and doctors, service sector employees, teachers, professors, engineers, statisticians, and others. Although numerically far smaller than its Western counterparts, at the turn of the century the emerging middle class in Russia was educated and based in both the great metropolitan areas of the empire and the provincial capitals and towns.[13] Russia had twelve major universities in cities such as Odessa, Kiev, Moscow, St. Petersburg, Kharkov, Saratov, and Kazan, the easternmost of all the universities and the former seat of the Mongol overlords. Many of the new members of the middle class were sons of the clergy, released from service on their estates by the clerical reforms of the 1860s. No longer forced to serve in the clerical order, these well-educated sons of clerics flooded into the modern professions of law, journalism, medicine, engineering, academia, and even revolutionary politics. But while their education helped the new middle class adjust to the new social order, at the same time many retained an earlier ethos of disdaining materialism and believed that ascetic behavior and self-sacrifice for the sake of the greater social good was more important than individualism.[14]

From the middle of the nineteenth century, access to education determined much of the social mobility in the Russian empire. The government, although deeply suspicious of the political proclivities of both students and faculty, and prone to regulate curriculum, student politics, and faculty research with an insensitivity and heavy handedness that infuriated everyone, nonetheless expanded the reach of educational centers through much of the empire. The creation of the *zemstvos* and city councils in the 1860s, self-governing assemblies at the district and county levels that were in charge of education, road maintenance, fire brigades, economic development, veterinary medicine, and public health, led to an extraordinary expansion of elementary schools. Peasants themselves realized the value of a modern education, literacy, and numeracy, and even young peasant women received some schooling. Government-run teacher training institutions trained hundreds and thousands of prospective teachers, many of them women who came from either clergy families or declining noble families. Russia had far higher rates of girls being educated in secondary schools than France or Germany, and women physicians in Russia dramatically outnumbered their counterparts in Europe by the early twentieth century.[15]

Russian women were affected by the winds of globalization and modernity. As the price of grain declined in world markets in the latter part of the nineteenth century due to global overproduction, noble estates lost much of their monetary value and the noblemen rented out more and more of their landholdings to their former serfs. Noblewomen, who had been gently raised by governesses and servants themselves, entered the job market and became teachers, pharmacists, doctors, and even lawyers. Women fought for the right to higher education and entrance to Russian universities. Many of them went abroad to Switzerland and received medical degrees. Sofia Kovalevskaia was the first woman in all of Europe to receive a doctorate in mathematics from the University of Göttingen in Germany. Although she was refused a faculty position in Russia and had to teach in Sweden, ultimately the Russian Academy of Sciences accepted her as a member. While a disproportionate share of women within higher education tended to be from noble families, at the lower end of the social ladder many women became schoolteachers and nurses.[16]

Formally, Russia remained an estate-based society until 1917, but in reality the imperial divisions between the four castes of nobility, clergy, peasantry, and townsmen was increasingly getting blurred thanks to urbanization, industrialization, and social mobility. Economists, geographers, doctors, sports enthusiasts, and philanthropists, among others, despite government suspicions about the transfer of power to civil society, formed a variety of associations in which members were identified by their training, education, and culture rather than birth. These included the Pirogov Society of Physicians, the Free Economic Society, and the Royal Geographic Society, among many others. Civic associations, research bodies, and professional unions came together in the spirit of public service in numerous cities and provincial towns. They were interested in the dissemination of scientific knowledge to an educated public, and the gathering of data about the various physical, biological, and human resources of the Russian empire.[17]

In the provinces, civil associations were formed whose members believed that modern scientific education could be used to revitalize their societies. The Jadids in Turkestan, a modernizing group of cultural figures, inspired by Crimean Tatar intellectuals such as Ismail Gasprinki, tried to reform traditional religious-based education in local schools by adding sciences to the curriculum. They translated a variety of scientific and social science texts, imported textbooks from the Ottoman empire, the Arab world, and India, and produced works of literature to spread their message of modernity. In Ukraine, a sophisticated literati and intelligentsia promoted Ukrainian nationalism based on a corpus of modern literature, poetry, and history. Did people educated in modern institutions form a middle class across the empire?

Russian peasants and workers

Peasant life was hard, mired in back-breaking labor, and most peasants used traditional methods of agriculture that severely limited productivity. As in most premodern societies, crop failures and aberrational weather patterns led to periodic famines, the most severe being that of 1891. But across the world spectrum the Russian peasant fared no worse than his counterparts in either the Ottoman or the British empire and in many cases had a better diet, less onerous taxations, and relative autonomy from absentee landlords. Millions of Indian peasants died in the famines between 1870 and 1900 in British India. While some of these famines were caused by bad weather conditions, many were compounded by high taxation and imperial pressure to grow commercial crops for export rather than for subsistence.

Like other social classes, peasants helped in the expansion of Russian imperialism, both voluntarily and involuntarily. They migrated to different parts of the empire, intermarrying with local populations, and farmed the dry steppe lands with their distinctive forms of agriculture.[18] Fugitive peasants who joined Cossack communities of military settlers sometimes worked as the advance guard of imperialism as they streamed into borderlands. As the Russian military built garrisons, monks their monasteries, and noblemen were given land grants to secure border areas, they moved large numbers of peasants to work the soil and provide labor for construction. The advance of the peasantry eased population pressures at the center but also led to extreme pressures on the nomadic populations of Central Asia and Siberia, many

Figure 1.2 Southern part of the village of Nyrob and entrance into the village. View from the bell tower in 1910. Courtesy of the Library of Congress Prints and Photographs Division, Prokudin-Gorskii Collection (LC-P87- 4420).

of whom suffered catastrophic population losses. Often peasants in imperial border-lands had greater privileges than their counterparts in Russia. Thus there was no serfdom in Siberia, the rates of taxation were significantly lower, and immigrant peasants in Central Asia were free from military conscription.

Peasants located in the central parts of Russia suffered more from low agricultural productivity and increasing populations than from either state taxation or land redemption payments.[19] As a result, peasants coveted the lands of large landowners and the demand for land galvanized peasant uprisings throughout this period. In areas such as Ukraine and the Northern Caucasus, agricultural productivity rose remarkably on large estates that relied on cheap migrant workers to harvest the fields. Many former peasants such as the father of the socialist Lev Trotsky worked hard to acquire significant land holdings from profligate noblemen. But Trotsky was appalled at the way his notoriously frugal father exploited migrant workers. His socialist consciousness formed as a result of his observations and early experiences in the countryside.[20]

Independent peasant households in Siberia exported prodigious quantities of butter, dairy products, and wheat in the early part of the twentieth century. While peasant villages in the central provinces retained the old communal system as a safety network, at the same time they responded positively to market penetrations. Farms located near railway lines around Moscow and St. Petersburg became enmeshed in modern business practices. Young men and women from villages migrated to the cities in vast numbers, fleeing rural poverty and also chasing dreams of consumer culture and modern lifestyles in the city.[21] From the late nineteenth century, peasant women streamed into cities to work in the factories and workshops. Many worked in the textile industries and formed a significant part of the workforce. Women also found employment in stores, as servants, in laundries, and in tailoring establishments but too often were forced into prostitution because of low wages. Their monetary independence had led to the waning power of the joint family system in the villages.[22]

Work in the factories was arduous, back-breaking, and for the most part conducted in poorly ventilated premises with machinery that often led to loss of life and limbs. Across the industrializing world, from the United States to Japan, the early factory system savagely exploited peasants from the countryside, paying them poor wages, arbitrarily cutting short employment, and providing little in the way of social or health insurance, pensions, or compensation for accidents. Not surprisingly, the relations between labor and management were combative and marked by episodic violence.

Apartment buildings, department stores, tramcars, and theaters were constructed in St. Petersburg and Moscow to accommodate the new middle class, while the newly arrived peasant and workers huddled in dank basements, crowded tenements, and barracks located in suburbs outside the city. Some journalists, novelists, and social commentators viewed the urban poor as new specimens of humanity.[23] Famous novelists such as Dostoevsky and Gorky described the poverty and desperation of the urban poor, who often had to turn to crime and prostitution in order to survive the city. But within the tenements, the spread of education and radical ideas provided new forms of identity and selfhood. Maxim Gorky came from what he called rather memorably the "Lower Depths" (title of a play from 1902) of society. Orphaned at an

Figure 1.3 Maxim Gorky, a famous Russian writer, in 1910. Courtesy of the Library of Congress Prints and Photographs Division, Bain Collection (LC-B2-1034-2).

How is he dressed? What do his clothes suggest about his background and identity?

early age, Gorky was sent out to earn his keep by a cruel grandfather at the age of eight. He worked a variety of jobs to keep body and soul together, and sailed down the Volga as a dishwasher on a barge. He lived in different parts of the empire, including Kazan and Tiflis, and became an internationally beloved novelist and playwright. While Gorky chose to write about the hardships of the poor people of Russia, especially the factory workers in his famous novel *Mother*, his life and literary success exemplified the fact that education was the key to upward mobility in the Russian empire. An autodidact, Gorky's love of learning was to be a lifelong passion, but like the sons of the clergy, and industrialists such as Savva Morozov, he never forgot that it was important to use his art in the service of the people.

Gorky's upward mobility notwithstanding, workers had little reason to believe that life would improve in the factories, and throughout Russia in the 1890s and the 1900s labor violence was an endemic part of the industrial landscape. The tsarist authorities learned from the German government that the best way to deal with the labor problem was to set up a system of comprehensive legislation that guaranteed workers' rights, benefits, and social welfare. While a system of factory legislation that imposed limits on working hours and conditions, especially relating to child workers, was instituted, often factory inspectors failed to enforce these codes. Despite the policies of certain socially conscious capitalists, for the most part labor relations were tense and few were surprised when the Russian revolution broke out in 1905.

Revolution of 1905

Imperial aggrandizement, which had served the Russian ruling class as well as the peasantry well in the preceding centuries, was going to prove more problematic in the age of industrial warfare. Tsar Nicholas II, an avid imperialist, continued to believe that a large army and a loyal officer corps drawn from the flower of the nobility would allow the empire to expand as it had done so successfully in the past centuries. He was also persuaded by the famous explorer Nikolai Przhevalsky that Europeans were destined to prevail in any encounter with decadent and weak Asians.[24] He was irritated with Witte's strictures about the need to avoid further imperial ventures in the Far East, especially in Korea and Manchuria. The tsar, anticipating Witte's objections, moved him from the Ministry of Finance to a largely ceremonial post in the Council of Ministers before embarking on what he hoped would be a successful war in the Pacific.

The Revolution of 1905 revealed the incompatibility of imperial war and modernization. Witte was alarmed that the court circles were considering war with Japan in order to press their advantage on the Korean Peninsula. He suggested that the state cancel peasant tax arrears and believed that, by advancing them low interest loans, peasants would become owners of land as well as consumers for Russian factory goods. He firmly believed that in the long run the fruits of industrialization would trickle down to the lowest levels of Russian society. But Witte's influence on Nicholas II was beginning to fade as the tsar embarked on a ruinous course of action in Asia.

The Japanese had initially agreed to accept Russia's special position in Manchuria in return for recognition of Japan's special interests in Korea, but negotiations broke down in 1904 as Russia sought a warm water port on the Pacific both for its navy and for its growing international maritime trade in the region. Port Arthur, leased from the Chinese, formed the basis of Russian expansion. But on 8 February 1904 an unexpected

Japanese naval attack on the Russian eastern fleet in Port Arthur resulted in a stunning victory for an Asiatic power over a European empire, sending shock waves through much of the colonized world. Although the war ended in September 1905 with few Russian territorial losses, Russia suffered numerous defeats both on land and at sea. Witte's excellent diplomatic skills saved Russia from too many territorial losses, but the Russo-Japanese war was a major defeat for Russia. Perceived Russian weaknesses emboldened Germany to pursue a free hand in reshaping southern Europe, especially the Balkan Peninsula where Russia had long posed as the champion of the Christian populations.

The war was unpopular at home and this manifested itself in uprisings, protests, and demonstrations. The revolution began inadvertently on Bloody Sunday, 9 January 1905, when a peaceful procession of unarmed workers holding portraits of the tsar marched to the Winter Palace in St. Petersburg to demand better pay and working conditions.[25] They were led by the charismatic Father Gapon who had built a working class organization with the patronage of the Russian police. The soldiers of the Imperial Guard, in a costly miscalculation, fired at the crowds, leaving almost a thousand people dead and wounded. Thereafter the Russian core as well as the empire was rocked by a series of working class strikes, peasant uprisings, middle class political demonstrations, and even isolated incidents of mutiny among the armed forces and the navy. In Finland, Poland, and the Baltic provinces there were calls for national independence.

During 1905, workers got their first taste of political power in the working class neighborhoods of St. Petersburg. Led by the fiery socialist orator Lev Trotsky, workers organized soviets or ultra-democratic representative councils composed of workers elected from the factory floor. The soviets took over the running of the factories in addition to dealing with the local government. The soviets organized a general strike in St. Petersburg that spread through much of the empire. In the working class districts of Moscow workers even built barricades to prevent the entry of armed forces, but the uprisings ended with many dead and parts of the city devastated.

CONCLUSION AND FURTHER QUESTIONS

The Revolution of 1905 brought to a head decades of vociferous civic and political activity both in the cities and in the provinces. Civil society tried to participate in the art of self-governance by forming unions and political parties such as the Constitutional Democrats, better known as the Kadets, and the Octobrists. The lifting of censorship shone light on the many inefficiencies of imperial government, and associations and civic assemblies rushed to fill the gap. Feminist groups led by activists such as Maria Pokrovskaia not only fought for the right to vote, but tried to create cross-class coalitions to ameliorate the plight of the urban poor through philanthropy, civic engagement, the creation of educational centers, and cultural activities.[26] Many even flirted with revolutionary politics and made donations to various socialist parties. Russia's path to modernity was jagged and strewn with explosives.

This cross-class coalition came to an end when the tsar reluctantly granted the October Manifesto in 1905. Under Witte's prodding, the autocratic state guaranteed citizens of the empire the rights of personal inviolability, and freedom of conscience, assembly, speech, and association. The tsar also promised to call a Duma, an elected parliament that would approve legislation and supervise the legality of government institutions. Political groups, with a few exceptions such as the Bolsheviks, put their faith in parliamentary rule and eagerly fielded candidates even as the state tried to control and manipulate elections and promote pro-tsarist candidates. Despite many setbacks this system stayed in place until 1917. But Trotsky was prescient when he called the 1905 Revolution the dress rehearsal for 1917. As the war with Japan came to an end, the Russian government was able to use imperial troops to crush the uprisings of workers and peasants as well as mutinies. But in 1917 the tsarist state was unable to simultaneously field millions of soldiers for World War I as well as engage in mass repression at home. The Romanov dynasty had excelled at imperial conquest for many centuries and created a gigantic empire that straddled Europe and Asia. But they failed to bind their restive populations as the old social bonds of deference and fear gave way to new ideas of individualism, private property, and political representation. A new social order based on the modern class system challenged the claims of noble birth, aristocratic precedence, and absolutism, but the fight was going to be long, protracted, and bloody.

PRIMARY SOURCES

Use the questions to analyze the content, context, and significance of each primary source. Then synthesize the primary sources and the material in the chapter to formulate a response to the primary chapter questions: Why was imperialism central to the formation and identity of Russia? Was tsarist autocracy compatible with industrialization and modernization?

Document 1.1   Excerpts from Konstantin Pobedonostsev, "On Parliamentary Democracy"

Questions for analysis

1   Identify three arguments that Pobedonostsev advances against a democratic system. Do you believe that he was justified in his critique?
2   What are Pobedonostsev's views on human nature and social class?
3   Construct a response to Pobedonostsev's ideas about autocracy by outlining a clear defense of a democratic and parliamentary system. Be as precise and eloquent as Pobedonostsev was!

What is this freedom by which so many minds are agitated, which inspires so many insensate actions, so many wild speeches, which leads the people so often to misfortune? In the democratic sense of the word, freedom is the right of political power, or, to express it otherwise, the right to participate in the government of the State . . . Forever extending its base, the new Democracy now aspires to universal suffrage—a fatal error, and one of the most remarkable in the history of mankind. By this means, the political power so passionately demanded by Democracy would be shattered into a number of infinitesimal bits, of which each citizen acquires a single one. What will he do with it, then? How will he employ it? In the result it has undoubtedly been shown that in the attainment of this aim Democracy violates its sacred formula of "Freedom indissolubly joined with Equality." It is shown that this apparently equal distribution of "freedom" among all involves the total destruction of equality. Each vote, representing an inconsiderable fragment of power, by itself signifies nothing; an aggregation of votes alone has a relative value . . . In a Democracy, the real rulers are the dexterous manipulators of votes, with their henchmen, the mechanics who so skillfully operate the hidden springs which move the puppets in the arena of democratic elections. Men of this kind are ever ready with loud speeches lauding equality; in reality, they rule the people as any despot or military dictator might rule it . . . The history of mankind bears witness that the most necessary and fruitful reforms—the most durable measures – emanated from the supreme will of statesmen, or from a minority enlightened by lofty ideas and deep knowledge, and that, on the contrary, the extension of the representative principle is accompanied by an abasement of political ideas and the vulgarization of opinions in the mass of the electors . . .

Source: K. P. Pobyedonotseff, *Reflections of a Russian Statesman*, trans. R. C. Long (London: Grant Richard & Co., 1898). Revised by Nathaniel Knight and available at http://academic.shu.edu/russianhistory/index.php/Konstantin_Pobedonostsev,_Reflections_of_a_Russian_Statesman (accessed 27 May 2015). Used by permission of Nathaniel Knight.

Document 1.2   Excerpts from the petition prepared for presentation to Nicholas II, 9 January 1905 (Bloody Sunday)

Questions for analysis

1   Does this document present only the demands of workers or does it also reflect the interests of other classes?
2   Are the demands moderate and compatible with a modern democratic order, or do they represent a trend toward socialism?
3   If you were the tsar, how would you respond to this document? What actions would you undertake?

We, workers and inhabitants of the city of St. Petersburg, members of various *sosloviia* (estates of the realm), our wives, children, and helpless old parents, have come to you, Sovereign, to seek justice and protection. We are impoverished and oppressed, we are burdened with work, and insulted. We are treated not like humans [but] like slaves who must suffer a bitter fate and keep silent. And we have suffered, but we only get pushed deeper and deeper into a gulf of misery, ignorance, and lack of rights. Despotism and arbitrariness are suffocating us, we are gasping for breath. Sovereign, we have no strength left. We have reached the limit of our patience. We have come to that terrible moment when it is better to die than to continue unbearable sufferings . . .

But no single measure can heal all our wounds. Other measures are necessary, and we, representing all of Russia's toiling class, frankly and openly speak to you, Sovereign, as to a father, about them.

The following are necessary:

I   Measures against the ignorance of the Russian people and against its lack of rights

   1   Immediate freedom and return home for all those who have suffered for their political and religious convictions, for strike activity, and for peasant disorders.

   2   Immediate proclamation of the freedom and inviolability of the person, of freedom of speech and of the press, of freedom of assembly, and of freedom of conscience in matters of religion.

   3   Universal and compulsory public education at state expense.

   4   Accountability of government ministers to the people and a guarantee of lawful administration.

   5   Equality of all before the law without exception.

   6   Separation of church and state.

II   Measures against the poverty of the people

   1   Abolition of indirect taxes and their replacement by a direct, progressive income tax.

   2   Abolition of redemption payments, cheap credit, and the gradual transfer of land to the people.

   3   Naval Ministry contracts should be filled in Russia, not abroad.

   4   Termination of the war according to the will of the people.

III Measures against the oppression of labor by capital

1 Abolition of the office of factory inspector.
2 Establishment in factories and plants of permanent commissions elected by the workers, which jointly with the administration are to investigate all complaints coming from individual workers. A worker cannot be fired except by a resolution of this commission.
3 Freedom for producer–consumer cooperatives and workers' trade unions— at once.
4 An eight-hour working day and regulation of overtime work.
5 Freedom for labor to struggle with capital—at once.
6 Wage regulation—at once.
7 Guaranteed participation of representatives of the working classes in drafting a law on state insurance for workers—at once . . .

Georgii Gapon, priest
Ivan Vasimov, worker.

Source: Translated by Daniel Field and available at http://academic.shu.edu/russian history/index.php/Workers%27_Petition,_January_9th,_1905_%28Bloody_Sunday% 29 (accessed 29 May 2015). Used by permission of Nathaniel Knight.

Document 1.3   Excerpts from the Manifesto of October 17th, 1905

Questions for analysis

1 What civil rights and liberties did the tsar grant his people under the October Manifesto?
2 Does this document indicate that the Russian empire was moving to a constitutional system?
3 Could autocracy survive if all legislative power was vested in the Duma? Is autocracy compatible with a representative political system?

We, Nicholas II, By the Grace of God Emperor and Autocrat of all Russia, King of Poland, Grand Duke of Finland, etc., proclaim to all Our loyal subjects:

Rioting and disturbances in the capitals [i.e., St. Petersburg and the old capital, Moscow] and in many localities of Our Empire fill Our heart with great and heavy grief. The well-being of the Russian Sovereign is inseparable from the well-being of the nation, and the nation's sorrow is his sorrow. The disturbances that have taken place may cause grave tension in the nation and may threaten the integrity and unity of Our state . . .

We require the government dutifully to execute Our unshakeable will:

1 To grant to the population the essential foundations of civil freedom, based on the principles of genuine inviolability of the person, freedom of conscience, speech, assembly and association.
2 Without postponing the scheduled elections to the State Duma, to admit to participation in the Duma (insofar as possible in the short time that remains before it is scheduled to convene) all those classes of the population that now are completely deprived of voting rights; and to leave the further development of a general statute on elections to the future legislative order.

3   To establish as an unbreakable rule that no law shall take effect without confirmation by the State Duma and that the elected representatives of the people shall be guaranteed the opportunity to participate in the supervision of the legality of the actions of Our appointed officials.

We summon all loyal sons of Russia to remember their duties toward their country, to assist in terminating the unprecedented unrest now prevailing, and together with Us to make every effort to restore peace and tranquility to Our native land.

Given at Peterhof the 17th of October in the 1905th year of Our Lord and of Our reign the eleventh.

Source: Translated by Daniel Field and available at http://academic.shu.edu/russian history/index.php/Manifesto_of_October_17th,_1905 (accessed 28 May 2015). Used by permission of Nathaniel Knight.

Notes

1 Richard Davis, *A Year from a Reporter's Notebook* (New York and London: Harper Brothers, 1903).
2 Dominic Lieven, *Empire: The Russian Empire and Its Rivals* (New Haven, CT: Yale University Press, 2001).
3 Mikhail Khodorkovsky, *Bitter Choices: Loyalty and Betrayal in the Conquest of the Caucasus* (Ithaca, NY: Cornell University Press, 2014); Willard Sunderland, *The Baron's Cloak: The History of the Russian Empire in War and Revolution* (Ithaca, NY: Cornell University Press, 2014).
4 Jeff Sahadeo, *Russian Colonial Society in Tashkent* (Bloomington: Indiana University Press, 2010).
5 Robert Geraci, *National and Imperial Identities in Late Tsarist Russia* (Ithaca, NY: Cornell University Press, 2001).
6 Richard Stites, *Revolutionary Dreams: Utopian Visions and Experimental Life in the Russian Revolution* (New York: Oxford University Press, 1991).
7 Valery Stepanov, "An Autocrat at the Crossroads: Nicholas II between Pobedonostsev and Bunge," *Russian Studies in History*, 50, no. 4 (Spring 2012): 7–32.
8 Frank Wcislo, *Tales of Imperial Russia: Life and Times of Sergei Witte, 1849–1915* (Oxford: Oxford University Press, 2011).
9 Steven Marks, *The Trans-Siberian Railroad and the Colonization of Asian Russia* (Ithaca, NY: Cornell University Press, 2001).
10 Yuri Slezkine, *Arctic Mirrors: Russia and the Small Peoples of the North* (Ithaca, NY: Cornell University Press, 1996).
11 Peter Gatrell, *The Tsarist Economy, 1850–1917* (London: Palgrave Macmillan, 1986).
12 Thomas Owen, *Capitalism and Politics in Russia: A Social History of the Moscow Merchants, 1855–1905* (New York: Cambridge University Press, 1981).
13 Wayne Dowler, *Russia in 1913* (DeKalb, IL: Northern Illinois University Press, 2010).
14 Laurie Manchester, *Holy Fathers, Secular Sons: Clergy, Intelligentsia and the Modern Self in Revolutionary Russia* (DeKalb, IL: Northern Illinois University Press, 2008).
15 Ben Eklof, *Russian Peasant School: Officialdom, Village Culture and Popular Pedagogy 1881–1914* (Berkeley: University of California Press, 1990).
16 Barbara Clements, *A History of Women in Russia: From the Earliest Times to the Present* (Bloomington: Indiana University Press, 2012).
17 Joseph Bradley, *Voluntary Associations in Tsarist Russia: Science, Patriotism and Civil Society* (Cambridge, MA: Harvard University Press, 2009); Catherine Evtuhov, *Portrait of a Russian Province: Economy, Society and Civilization in Nizhnii Novgorod* (Pittsburgh, PA: University of Pittsburgh Press, 2011).
18 David Moon, *The Plough That Broke the Steppes: Agriculture and Environment on Russia's Grasslands, 1700–1917* (New York: Oxford University Press, 2014).

19 Yanni Kotsonis, *States of Obligation: Taxes and Citizenship in the Russian Empire and Early Soviet Republic* (Toronto: University of Toronto Press, 2015).
20 Leon Trotsky, *My Life: An Attempt at an Autobiography* (New York: Dover Publications, 2007).
21 Jeffrey Burds, *Peasant Dreams and Market Politics: Labor Migration and the Russian Village, 1861–1905* (Pittsburgh, PA: University of Pittsburgh Press, 1998).
22 Barbara Engel, *Between the Fields and City: Women, Work and Family in Russia, 1861–1914* (New York: Cambridge University Press, 1996).
23 Mark Steinberg, *Petersburg, Fin de Siècle* (New Haven, CT: Yale University Press, 2011).
24 David Schimmelpenninck van der Oye, *Toward the Rising Sun: Russian Ideologies of Empire and the Path to War with Japan* (DeKalb, IL: Northern Illinois University Press, 2001).
25 Abraham Ascher, *Revolution of 1905: A Short History* (Stanford, CA: Stanford University Press, 2004).
26 Rochelle Ruthchild, *Equality and Revolution: Women's Rights in the Russian Empire* (Pittsburgh, PA: University of Pittsburgh Press, 2010).

2 Modernity, war, and revolution

In December of 2012 President of Russia Dmitry Medvedev and Prime Minister Vladimir Putin unveiled a statue of Peter Stolypin in Moscow, to commemorate his 150th birthday. The ceremony was odd as, during his lifetime and for many decades after his untimely death, Stolypin was hated and reviled by many from both ends of the political spectrum. Nicholas II disliked him immensely, as did the conservative monarchists who feared that Stolypin was bent on destroying autocracy through the adoption of liberal principles. The liberal members of the Kadet Party and the Octobrists, meanwhile, blamed Stolypin for increasing the representation of landed nobles and propertied classes in the Duma. Vladimir Lenin described Stolypin contemptuously as the arch-hangman, and Leo Tolstoy, novelist, historian, and philosopher, publicly excoriated Stolypin for forcefully suppressing the Revolution of 1905–1907, during the course of which many thousands were executed and many more imprisoned and exiled.

Stolypin's tenure as the prime minister of Russia was stormy and his end was bloody and tragic. After surviving numerous assassination attempts, in 1911 he was killed in a theater in Kiev, the capital of Ukraine, in the presence of Nicholas II. Stolypin died as stoically as he had lived. He had refused to wear a bulletproof vest despite the many previous attempts on his life. It was widely rumored that the assassin, twenty-four year old Dmitry Bogrov (born Mordechai Gershkovich), a left-wing revolutionary, was in the pay of the Russian government and had been allowed to enter the theater even though he had a gun. A judicial inquiry into the conditions of Stolypin's death was quickly ended, and subsequently Stolypin's reputation was further sullied in the Soviet Union. In the 1980s, Alexander Solzhenitsyn, Nobel Laureate and chronicler extraordinaire of Bolshevik concentration camps, rehabilitated him in his monumental novel *The Red Wheel*. Today Putin considers Stolypin, as a promoter of nationalism and modernization, as a worthy role model for his own administration.

Who was Stolypin and what did he represent? Did he unwittingly become the target of the many fears and apprehensions that Russians experienced during this exciting decade of transition? Why is historical change so easily visible in hindsight but so difficult for populations to endure, experience, or even imagine?

CHAPTER QUESTIONS

In this chapter we will examine some of the hopes about the future and fears about a rapidly changing society as expressed by the citizens of the Russian empire.

During this pivotal period, which started with the Russo-Japanese War of 1905 and ended with the fall of the Romanov dynasty in February 1917 and the Bolshevik revolution in October later that year, imperial subjects faced both unprecedented challenges and received enormous opportunities to shape the future of the Russian empire.

What were the stumbling blocks on the road to modernity within the Russian empire? How did various groups, such as bureaucrats, intellectuals, revolutionaries, peasants, workers, and officials, respond to modernizations? Depending on their political inclinations, historians characterize this decade as either marking the final failure of the old tsarist order that made the Bolshevik revolution inevitable or constituting a period when the Russian empire was modernizing at an impressive rate and had the potential to evolve into a constitutional monarchy. However, we will never know how the story of tsarist modernization would have ended as World War I intervened too soon for it to be possible to fully analyze the impact of the reforms from the last decade.

VOICES, MEMORIES, CONTESTED PERSPECTIVES

Stolypin's reforms

The post-1905 government led by Stolypin, a talented, imaginative, but dictatorial prime minister, tried to build on the processes that Witte's reforms had set in motion.[1] Like Witte, Stolypin had one foot in the past and one in the future, and he sincerely believed that tsarist absolutism could become a force for modernization. On the one hand, Stolypin, a scion of a wealthy landowning family and used to wielding autocratic measures, authorized the execution of three thousand extremists and peasant rebels during the period between 1906 and 1911, and he sent many more into exile to end the revolutionary uprisings of 1905–1907. On the other hand, he created one of the boldest agrarian reforms attempted since the abolition of serfdom in 1861.

Stolypin had a degree in agriculture from St. Petersburg University and had served in numerous elected and administrative positions, including as the governor of Saratov province. He understood quite clearly that Russian modernization would only be complete when millions of peasants, who currently held land jointly through their communes, became individual property holders with a vested interest in upholding the laws of the land. Stolypin admired the peasant homesteads that he had seen in the Baltic state of Lithuania and hoped to bring some of the values of individualism to the communal heartland of Russia.

Stolypin's reforms were intended primarily to reduce the power of the repartitional peasant commune (*mir*) in village society that had been strengthened by the Emancipation of 1861 in order to reduce peasant mobility and facilitate tax collection. He wanted to encourage wealthy peasants to consolidate their land holdings so as to increase their agricultural productivity. Stolypin also set up the Peasant Land Bank, which was designed to advance peasants easy credit, and more than two million peasants took advantage of his system to emigrate to Siberia and Central Asia. At the same time, Stolypin also feared the penetration of market forces into the Russian countryside and worked to safeguard peasants from exploitation and expropriation. Therefore he sought to restrict sales of peasant lands exclusively to other peasants.

Stolypin died before he could institute a system of primary and universal education, a comprehensive package of accident insurance, and disability and pension systems for workers. Like their counterparts in Germany, many Russian bureaucrats believed that the state was above class interests and its policies should be aimed at enhancing universal welfare. Could an autocratic state become a vehicle of economic modernization and limited political democracy?

Meanings and consequences of "modernization": peasants into workers

Despite the many progressive and benign meanings attributed to the innocuous term modernization, the experience of modernity in every society has been painful, alienating, and in many instances even catastrophic. Some countries such as England and France experienced the process of modernization over many decades. Millions of peasants from small villages, where they eked out subsistence from agriculture, trade, or artisanal work, moved to work in factories, retail, and domestic service in European or colonial urban centers over a long period. But in the Russian empire, as in Germany, Japan, or Mexico, the time frame of the migration was telescoped so

Figure 2.1 Village of Paltoga, 1909. Courtesy of the Library of Congress Prints and Photographs Division, Prokudin-Gorskii Collection (LC-P87-5290).

How does the appearance of the church contrast with the peasant homes?

abruptly that a generation of urban migrants had little chance to adjust to arduous factory work or the rhythms of city life.

Daily life in the city challenged peasant beliefs about religion, patriarchy, gender, consumption practices, and leisure. New immigrants had to change even their personal notions of hygiene and cleanliness as spitting sunflower seeds or expectorating on pavements was frowned upon. Peasants, who through centuries had forged a meaningful attachment to the soil, measured time through nature's cycles, and conducted religious rituals within close knit communities, now had to learn to be individuals among a multiethnic urban population and to consume city goods and services in newly prescribed ways.[2]

Recent arrivals to the city rebelled against urban manners and against the hostile deadening work in factories. They erupted on to streets in spontaneous protests; sometimes they harassed passersby through acts of hooliganism and later, as we will see, through carefully organized strike actions.[3] The Russian empire, despite its fearsome image abroad, was in many ways a weak empire that lacked the police forces as well as the management skills necessary to deal with restive populations in towns and countryside, unmoored from social bonds. As customary relationships were being frayed by population transfers in different parts of the country, many areas, such as Ukraine, Poland, the Baltic states and parts of the Caucasus and Central Asia, prepared to break away from the empire. Throughout this decade the Russian armed forces were overwhelmed by having simultaneously to keep peace at home and fight wars in the extremities of empire.

Fearful that industrialization and urbanization would destroy centuries of agricultural knowledge, culture, and community, many political organizations were formed clandestinely to stop government policies of modernization. The party of Socialist Revolutionaries (SRs), along with anarchist groups of various stripes, dreamed of creating a harmonious society of small peasant producers and cooperatives that engaged in mutual aid and exchanges.[4] In the 1870s and 1880s, thousands of university students streamed to the Russian countryside hoping to foment peasant uprisings against the tsarist state.

Ekaterina Breshko-Breshkovskaia, one of the leading members of the SRs, was internationally renowned as Babushka, or the Little Grandmother of the revolutionary movement. Although a member of a noble family, she sacrificed her life, her marriage, and her home for the well-being of the peasants. The tsarist government imprisoned her, sentenced her to hard labor in the mines, and exiled her for many years to Siberia. But the punishment only strengthened her determination. Her personality and demeanor won her many followers throughout the world, and influential Americans greatly admired Babushka for her tireless antitsarist crusades. In a conversation with a famous American journalist, George Kennan, Breshkovskaia said, "Mr. Kennan, we may die in exile, and our children may die in exile, and our children's children may die in exile, but something will come of it at last."[5]

The SRs believed that the peasants were natural socialists and that without the interference of the state and corrupt landowners, and without the intrusion of private property and capitalistic ideas of profit, peasants could live in communal harmony. They also believed that communal ownership of land would allow the importation of science, technology, and education, and that modern knowledge would end endemic peasant poverty. While they shunned capitalism and industrialization, the SRs wanted to participate in a just and modern world.

The SRs claimed to represent the majority of the empire's peasantry and believed that the best way to stem the tide of industrialization was to assassinate bureaucrats and high-ranking tsarist officials in order to spark a revolution. They thus initiated the first wave of terrorism in modern history, killing thousands of officials in the first decade of the twentieth century. Some members of the SRs, such as the young Maria Spiridonova who shot G. N. Luzhenovsky, a member of the Tambov Provincial Council and an advocate of the brutal suppression of peasant uprisings, were motivated by good intentions. Many of these revolutionaries were venerated for their asceticism and dedication to the well-being of the people. On the other hand, many members of the SRs became advocates of terrorism pure and simple. The actions of the SRs inspired many others in places as far away as India and the Balkans, where groups were also fighting against colonial rule.[6] Do you believe that one can use violent means in pursuit of a good cause?

Modernity and its discontents

Many Russian thinkers, scholars, artists, and intellectuals had serious doubts about the unfettered individualism of modern spaces such as anonymous boulevards, cafes, and shopping centers replacing what seemed to be in retrospect the social conviviality of the village community. While modernization promised an increase in material possessions and resulted in upward mobility, it also tempted men with drink and the brothel (strongly associated with sexually transmitted disease). It was feared that women would forget their virtue in the search for urban pleasures in shopping arcades, music halls, theaters, and cabarets. Educated society was apprehensive and ambivalent about the shape and texture of the future.[7]

At one end of the political spectrum, Russian Marxists, an inconsequential group before the 1917 Revolution, realized that the societies of the future were going to be based on the industrial economy and that the chimera of harmonious peasant socialism that the SRs advocated was just that: a utopian project that was doomed to failure. They took heart in the fact that the impoverished masses of teeming tenements and slums in major Russian cities were fleeing rural poverty in the millions. Marxists looked forward to the growing strength of the Russian factory workers, known as the proletariat in their parlance. Intellectuals such as Georgi Plekhanov and Vera Zasulich courageously turned from the peasant politics of the populists and SR terrorism, and came to accept the new social and economic reality of industry that was changing the face of the globe in unimaginable ways. But they were a minority in an ocean of voices on both the right and the left who believed that the real Russia could only be found in the countryside.[8]

As we saw in the last chapter, Nicholas II believed that as long as he kept the loyalty of the peasants and the aristocratic elite, his throne would be safe. He never shared the views of Witte and members of the Russian bourgeoisie who saw industrialization as the only way to strengthen the Russian state. Even large landowners who profited handsomely from the global trade in grain, and invested extensively in stocks and bonds, extolled the virtues of paternalistic feudalism and autocracy. They also tried to sabotage Stolypin's program of extending local self-government in the countryside through the adoption of the zemstvos in the southwestern regions. They interpreted Stolypin's attempts to strengthen the bureaucracy as an affront to the power of landed interests.

Even the newly emerging middle classes, themselves products of modernization, were deeply ambivalent about the transition from a rural society to one of cities and factories.[9] Many feared that the emotional bonds of deference and gratitude, customs and mutual obligations that defined both tsarist society and the patriarchal family would be replaced by contractual relationships. Individualism and materialism would lead to a shallow and emotionally impoverished society regulated by desire for individual profit rather than the good of the commonweal. They were concerned about turning honest Russian peasants into faceless and vice ridden workers in the city. Even the Kadets, who called for a constitutional monarchy and civil liberties in true English style, believed that all agricultural land should be socialized and turned over to the peasants, tillers of the soil and natural custodians of the land.[10]

Intellectuals in the Russian empire continued to believe that the fate of the peasants was central to the Russian empire. Members of the old landed nobility, the literati, and the intelligentsia were troubled by the anonymity and loneliness of urban existence, one they personally experienced after moving to the city in both the empire and in the West. Nobleman turned anarchist Peter Kropotkin, who spent the majority of his life in exile in European cities, never really adjusted to urban living and the bourgeois lifestyle and until the end of his life romanticized the democratic life of the peasant communities that he had witnessed on his father's estates. Until his death in Bolshevik Russia in 1921, Kropotkin believed that individual liberty must be balanced by the well-being of the community.[11]

Alternative visions: Tolstoy, nonviolence, and the search for community

Count Leo Tolstoy, Russia's most beloved and famous novelist, was another individual who spent his life seeking to create the perfect community as a viable alternative to the loneliness and alienation of both aristocratic and modern society. Tolstoy had been deeply troubled by his experiences as an army officer in the Caucasus and refused either to romanticize imperial conquest or to legitimize it as a civilizing mission that was undertaken to uplift downtrodden and backward peoples.[12] Tolstoy in his masterpiece *Hadji Murad* (published posthumously in 1912) wrote about the many ways that imperialism degraded both the conqueror and the conquered. In this short story, Tolstoy presents the protagonist, Hadji Murad, a Muslim tribal leader, as a complex human being, rather than a "fanatical Muslim." We see Hadji Murad worry about the well-being of his family, suffer heartbreak as a father, a brother, and a son, and experience emotions common to all humanity.

Tolstoy's fiction presented a new way to understand colonized people that was very different from the inarticulate savage or fanatical purveyor of unfamiliar customs and manners that was standard in European literature about Asia and Africa of that time. Tolstoy wrote sarcastically:

> But one has only to free oneself from the superstition that justifies violence to be horrified at all these crimes which have been committed and are being committed ceaselessly by some nations against others, and still more to be horrified at the national moral stupidity resulting from that superstition, according to which the English, the Russians, the German, the French, and the Americans can talk— in the face of the frightful crimes they have committed and are still committing

in India, Indo-China, Poland, Manchuria, and Algeria—can talk not only about the threats of violence confronting them, but the need to protect themselves against these threats.[13]

Figure 2.2 Leo Tolstoy in Iasnaia Poliana in 1908, a bitter critic of the Russian empire and a global celebrity. Courtesy of the Library of Congress Prints and Photographs Division, Prokudin-Gorskii Collection (LC-DIG-prok-01971).

What do his pose, clothing, and beard suggest about the image he was trying to convey?

Tolstoy developed a powerful critique of the state as the progenitor of infinite violence, and sought answers in a radically simplified version of Christianity, shorn of the church and the priests, and the frugal and shared culture of the Russian village. He believed that nonviolence was the only response to the modernizing state that demanded endless sacrifices in its endless quest for power and violence. Tolstoy advocated that man should spend part of his day engaged in "bread labor," or producing that which he consumed in order to escape from the modern curse of alienation from nature, and indeed Tolstoy spent part of his day on the estate where he was born, Iasnaia Poliana, performing menial tasks around the farm. Jane Addams, a young visitor to the estate in 1896 and later a famed social activist of the Progressive era in the United States, was so impressed by Tolstoy's example that she too spent part of her busy day working in the bakery of her famous Hull House settlement in Chicago.[14]

Tolstoy believed that modern people lacked the ability to create authentic human relationships with each other and suffered intensely because they lived for material and sensual pleasures alone. Tolstoy, in his travels in the Caucasus and among the Cossacks, and observing the Russian peasants on his estate, realized that members of premodern rural societies often experienced true happiness because their life of labor was conducted within a close knit community that was saturated by genuine human relationships. They also took sparingly from nature, rather than plundering its bounties.

Tolstoy's efforts to create a viable commune on his estate of Iasnaia Poliana as an alternative to the loneliness and anonymity of city life resonated with audiences worldwide. As a young man in London, Mohandas Gandhi, the future leader of the movement for Indian independence, read Tolstoy's works with deep interest as he struggled to formulate his vision of *satyagraha* or his struggle for a politics of truth and nonviolence. Tolstoy believed that man's estrangement from nature was the root cause of the modern epidemic of violence. And he spoke in concert with other major thinkers such as Henry David Thoreau and Ralph Waldo Emerson in the United States, William Morris and John Ruskin in England, Rabindranath Tagore in India, Jamal al-din al-Afghani in the Middle East, and Liang Qichao in China. These intellectuals were all troubled by the rampant modernization that threatened to destroy ecosystems and sweep away centuries of accumulated culture and knowledge, and the fine mesh of social relationships.[15]

Unlike our modern tolerance for the impoverished industrial and urban landscape, in the late nineteenth century people were horrified by the degradation of the environment. Bewildered peoples watched as rivers filled with chemical effluents from textile dyes, canals choked with industrial waste, and wetlands, forests, farmlands, and commons were paved over to accommodate roads, trams, railways, and suburbs. Many around the world who were experiencing the full onslaught of industrialization, including those who profited handsomely from it, were appalled at the unleashed juggernaut of capitalism and believed that they should hold the line against its overwhelming reach. This was the epochal fight between subsistence agriculture, a lifestyle nurtured through historical time, and industrial capitalism that promised to increase material wealth at an astronomical rate but impoverished and exploited millions of human beings on the path to the promised land. While experiences in Europe held out the promise that industrialization would eventually lead to higher standards of living over the course of several generations, many thoughtful people in Russia were unable to see the light at the end of the tunnel. We see similar processes unfolding today in different parts of the world as modernization sparks riots, protests, agrarian uprisings, and in some cases even revolutions, and weak states, like the tsarist regime, use horrendous violence in attempting to contain these movements.

Alternative visions: Semen Kanatchikov and the workers' movement

The path from the village to the city could also be exciting and energized by the novelty of breaking the bonds of religion and patriarchy. However, it also entailed loneliness, disorientation, fear, and anxiety. The search for community, the desire to embed oneself in a network of like-minded peers who shared one's political and moral concerns, symbolic universe, and cultural references, was omnipresent both among the educated classes and the newly arrived peasants from the provinces who were bewildered by the noise and speed of tramcars, and the uncaring masses that thronged the city's byways.

Semen Kanatchikov, a peasant turned worker revolutionary, recounts during his exile in Saratov and Siberia his many attempts to form close emotional communities while working in factories in Moscow and St. Petersburg.[16] While Kanatchikov quickly transitioned from a peasant to a skilled worker in the factory, he hungered for learning and education, the currency of the city. Although he was repelled by the self-assurance and the patronizing ways in which well-meaning Russian intellectuals treated him, he needed their help as he struggled to understand literature, mathematics, science, and political economy.

Rather than use literacy as a tool to advance his material self-interest, Kanatchikov was increasingly drawn to the socialist ideas that he heard in workers' educational circles. In urban learning centers organized by well-intentioned university students, liberals, and members of the intelligentsia, workers were exposed to European factions and political thought. While Kanatchikov struggled to read the classic works of Marxist theory and economics, he was able to grasp—by means of passionate conversations and arguments in his close circle of friends and enemies and informal seminars and tutorials, in jail and in Siberian exile—the essential ideas about the inevitability of proletarian revolution and the abolition of private property.

Revolution was a lived experience in conspiratorial circles and in the workers' movement, and few had an intellectual grasp of abstract theory. This was one of the hallmarks of the Russian revolutionary movements, and as a result activists tended to venerate intellectuals who had actually read the socialist texts written by Plekhanov, Vladimir Lenin, and Lev Trotsky. Participation in the revolutionary underground was also a ticket to upward mobility, and a means of gaining self-respect from a bourgeois Russian society that secretly admired the conspirators' capacity for self-sacrifice and ability to endure the rigors of prison life and Siberian exile.

From his personal experiences in the countryside, Kanatchikov knew that the peasants did not dream of communism but of improving their personal standing within the welfare system that the peasant commune provided. He, like the writer Maxim Gorky, found the peasants to be avaricious, grasping, and petty—but shrewd businessmen. Repelled by the idiocy of rural life and the inability of the peasants to understand his politics, Kanatchikov found a like-minded group of workers among the Social Democrats.

Founded in 1898, the Russian Social Democratic Workers' Party was committed to Marxism and proletarian revolution, rejecting the peasant revolution at the heart of the Socialist Revolutionaries' program as utopian. In 1903, the party split into two factions, the Bolsheviks (from the word for majority) led by Lenin, who advocated a tightly organized party of "professional" revolutionaries, and the Mensheviks (minority), a looser, actually bigger, faction around Lenin's old comrade Iulii Martov that stood for a mass party and a more orthodox variant of Marxism emphasizing the need for a long phase of capitalism before the eventual and inevitable proletarian revolution.

Kanatchikov ultimately became a Social Democrat and was persuaded by Lenin's arguments that Russia was already a capitalist society and that the unjust and oppressive tsarist state was incapable of modernizing Russia.[17] Unlike the SRs, however, he was an advocate of a humane and just system of industrialization. Having witnessed firsthand how the factory system exploited and underpaid the workers, Kanatchikov dreamed of an industrialized society where a government of workers would administer factories and distribute the wealth and profits to all, rather than just the wealthy few. Like Witte, Kanatchikov dreamed of quickening the tempo of industrialization in Russia, but, unlike Witte, he believed that a proletarian state could build the industrial world of the future. Kanatchikov was inspired by Leninist maximalism, which demanded that the Bolsheviks come to power sooner, and opposed the Mensheviks, the more traditional Marxists, who believed that the proletariat would come to power after the stage of political democracy and economic modernization.

Alternative visions: the culture of the future

The Bolsheviks' fascination with modernization and industry was also reflected in the contemporary artistic obsession with the shapes, forms, and visual representations of the future. Groups of Russian artists, poets, playwrights, and designers experimented with various ways of representing the cities of the future. Artists of all descriptions alternately shocked and frightened the educated public with their decadent literature, outré art exhibitions, outrageous theater productions, and transrational poetry— poetry motivated by sound rather than sense. They drew inspiration from artistic experimentations in France and Italy, places that they actually visited, and from an America that they imagined as the epitome of the modern industrial civilization: built on money, technology, and accelerated time.

Roaring machines, fast railways, roads and bridges, speeding cars, and buildings that touched the sky provided exciting fodder for artworks. Some of the youthful artists and poets, including Vladimir Mayakovsky, wanted to escape the weight of Russia's literary and artistic past and craft a new aesthetic that celebrated the destruction of the old world. Their manifesto entitled "A Slap in the Face of Public Taste" declared: "*We* alone were the *face* of *our* Time. Through us the horn of time blows in the art of the world. The past is too tight. The Academy and Pushkin are less intelligible than hieroglyphics. Throw Pushkin, Dostoevsky, Tolstoy, etc., etc. overboard from the Ship of Modernity."[18]

They dreamed of new cities built on linear principles, shorn of medieval and baroque architecture that prevented transparent communal living. Crooked and ancient alleys would be torn down and replaced by broad avenues down which ranks of organized labor dressed in utilitarian clothing could march to new melodies of the future. Centers of industrial design would create new furniture, clothes, and china that were stylish, utilitarian, and democratically accessible to all. They would transform art from something designed to amuse, educate, or inspire the select few who could afford it into a mighty iconoclastic arm of the revolution, smashing cultural hierarchies and social differentiation, and elevating the worker as the true subject of history and culture.[19]

Who would be the New Man and Woman of this socialist civilization? How would they eat, drink, sleep, reproduce themselves, raise children, engage in productive labor and community politics? Artists, novelists, writers of science fiction, architects, designers, art critics, philosophers, and intellectuals all tried to provide content for this imagined dreamscape, and their collaborations, epic battles, and artistic quarrels over the definition of meaning gave birth to an extraordinarily fertile period of Russian art.[20]

Lyubov Popova, drawing on the techniques of cubism that were being developed in France, created mesmerizing images of the human form forced from natural or aesthetic modes of representation into odd geometrical shapes such as cubes, cylinders, straight lines, and angles, colored in with metallic shades of gray and black. Her ideas were visible in her 1915 painting of her brother entitled *Portrait of a Philosopher.* Popova, who was born into a wealthy bourgeois family of textile merchants, received a broad artistic education in classical painting and traveled extensively in Western Europe. She worked with some of the leading Russian artists, such as Olga Rozanova, Vladimir Tatlin, and Kazimir Malevich. While she called her style painterly architectonics, she also wanted to create the new material reality of a revolutionary world. After 1917, she embraced the Bolshevik revolution and designed books, textiles, and posters, created sets for the theater, and taught design at Vkhutemas (Higher Art and Technical Studio) that was founded by the Soviet government in 1920. The Bolshevik commitment that women should participate in the public sphere appealed to many feminists as well as socialists.

Figure 2.3 Portrait of a Philosopher by Lyubov Popova, 1915.
© DEA/E. LESSING/De Agostini/Getty Images.

What is avant garde about this painting?

World War I and the February Revolution

The twentieth century began with one of the most horrifying wars known to humankind. As the death toll mounted into the tens of millions during World War I, among the casualties were many dynasties: the Romanovs in Russia, the Habsburgs in Austria-Hungary, the Ottomans in the Middle East, and the Hohenzollerns in Germany. The British, French, and Dutch empires survived for another few decades in severely weakened condition thanks only to the timely intervention of the Americans.

While the Russian empire was severely divided over politics and modernization, educated society was united around the tsar as he continued to pursue imperial dreams in the Balkans and along the Black Sea coast. Indeed some historians have questioned the conventional wisdom that assigns primary blame for the conflict to the German empire, arguing that it was Russia's historic desire to control the Black Sea and the Turkish straits that led to war with the Central European Powers.[21] Russia had long dreamed of annexing Constantinople and controlling the Black Sea and felt that it was the legitimate defender of the many Slavic peoples of Orthodox faith in the Balkans against a Muslim Ottoman empire. Thus when Austria annexed Bosnia and Herzegovina, territories that Serbia legitimately regarded as theirs, Russia as the self-styled protector of Serbia encouraged it to challenge the Austro-Hungarian empire. When a Serbian revolutionary assassinated Archduke Franz Ferdinand, heir to the Habsburg throne, in June 1914, and in response Austria delivered an ultimatum to Serbia that threatened its very sovereignty, Russia decided to intervene militarily on Serbia's behalf.

The war started with unprecedented unity among the Russian public as it cheered the mobilization of almost six million men. The British and French governments promised Russia control of Constantinople and the Turkish straits in the aftermath of battle. While the Russian army was successful in the war against the Turks in the Caucasus, cemented its position in northern Persia, and looked forward to the dismemberment of the Ottoman empire, on the western front the Russian forces were unable to withstand the German assaults. In 1914, at the Battle of Tannenberg, the Germans beat the Russians decisively and took almost 100,000 prisoners. The Russian economy geared up for military production but in 1916, although the supply of rifles and artillery shells was increased greatly, it proved to be inadequate. In the offensive led by General Brusilov in 1916 Russia captured Galicia and Bukovina from Austria, but overall, despite a few military victories, the war exacted a terrible toll on the imperial army. Millions of Russian soldiers were killed, taken prisoner, or rendered unfit for service because of aggravated war wounds. The casualty rates among Russian officers in the army was so extraordinarily high that by 1917 many Russian junior officers with little if any formal education had to be hurriedly pressed into service after scanty preparation.[22]

As the war ground on remorselessly without victory on Russia's western front, the military effort hampered by poor military leadership, transportation bottlenecks, and inadequate production of war materials, the initial patriotic euphoria turned to disgust and anger. Nicholas II's decision to personally command the Russian army did not endear him to the forces at the front. At home, civil society was aghast at the way Tsarina Alexandra and her religious advisor, the peasant mystic Gregory Rasputin, interfered in politics and dismissed ministers considered insufficiently servile to them. The political situation did not improve even after a patriotic group of nobles and members of the Duma assassinated Rasputin in December 1916. Nicholas continued to block civil participation in government affairs even after coalitions of businessmen, zemstvos, worker organizations, and the War Industries Committee showed how effectively they could ramp up industrial production for the army.[23]

The military failures at the war front were compounded by food shortages, low wages, and inflation at home, leading to sporadic food riots and expressions of worker discontent. Other combatants in World War I such as France and Britain faced similarly tense domestic situations, but the unexpected loyalty of their colonial populations in Southeast Asia, India, and Africa, who suspended their demands for freedom and national sovereignty during the war, helped these empires survive the carnage at the war front. Colonial territories supplied almost a million soldiers for the European war effort, as well as raw materials and finished goods. In Russia, on the other hand, the German forces easily detached Poland, Latvia, and Lithuania from the Russian empire. Although Ukraine provided loyal troops to the imperial army, significant numbers of soldiers fought on the side of the Austro-Hungarian army in the hope of creating an independent Ukraine. Many nationalities within the empire used the war situation in order to agitate for freedom and secession. Finland claimed independence as early as February 1917. Uzbeks, Kazakhs, and Kyrgyz populations broke out in violent demonstrations at the possibility of being drafted into the Russian army. Troops had to be sent to pacify parts of Central Asia. The mighty forces of imperialism had set the course of Russian destiny and autocracy for almost six centuries, but the final Romanov venture ended with the ignominious collapse of tsarist Russia in February 1917.

Historians have dated the start of the revolution that toppled the tsar to Women's Day (23 February, or 8 March on the calendar in use in the West) in Petrograd, as St. Petersburg was renamed during the war. Women in textile factories downed their tools and decided to take to the streets to protest against the shortages of bread, coal, and other daily necessities.[24] They formed alliances with housewives standing in bread lines in front of bakeries and persuaded male workers to march to the center of town to demand bread from the city duma. They also prevailed upon Cossacks and soldiers of the Volhnyian regiment stationed in the local garrisons to allow workers to demonstrate peacefully on the streets. By 27 February, there were hundreds of thousands of people on the streets of Petrograd, openly supported by military units that feared deployment to active duty.

Unable to find troops loyal to the tsar in the city or to bring troops back from the front, the army's generals persuaded the tsar that his abdication was the only way to calm the demonstrations, and perhaps save the monarchy in some form. However, rather than abdicating in favor of his young son, who suffered from hemophilia, Nicholas II abdicated in favor of his brother Michael, who quickly decided on 3 March to renounce the throne. After more than three hundred years, the Romanov dynasty's rule of Russia had come to an end.

The relatively bloodless end of the old regime produced a sense of euphoria. Lenin, who returned from Swiss exile in April of 1917, deemed Russia the "freest country in the world." Crowds attacked jails, prisons, and courthouses. Prisoners were freed in record number, jail records were burned, and many erstwhile members of the tsarist police force fled the capital and the bands intent on vigilante justice. The new government instituted wide ranging civil liberties, freed political prisoners, who returned in large numbers from Siberia and from exile, and under pressure from feminist groups even gave women the right to vote in July. Discrimination against ethnic and religious minorities was abolished. Was this political modernization or political breakdown?

Arriving in the fall of 1917, Louise Bryant and John Reed, American journalists, described the excitement on the streets of Petrograd as the population exercised democratic rights for the first time in the history of the city. Bryant wrote about the intense discussions, arguments, and political assemblies in factories, cafes, military barracks, and on street corners. Everyone was debating the unexpected turn of events, the collapse of the Romanov dynasty, and the future of Russia. Even though the price of bread rose and it became harder to acquire the daily necessities of life, Petrograd hummed with political activity as radicals of every stripe, along with common citizens, strove to put their imprint on the revolutionary events unfolding.[25]

From February to October

The question of who would rule in the wake of the fall of the monarchy remained an open and contested one until the October Revolution. Immediately after the tsar's abdication, two centers of power emerged in the capital. On 2 March, liberal members of the Duma established a Provisional Government that promised to call a Constituent Assembly to write a new constitution. Several days earlier in the same building, the Tauride Palace, the workers of Petrograd organized a soviet (council) based on the model established during the 1905 Revolution. The Petrograd Soviet of Workers' (and later Soldiers') Deputies was, as its name suggests, a local authority. As prominent members of the various revolutionary parties returned from prison or exile, they created, with the support of workers, soldiers, and sailors, an alternative to the Provisional Government. Moreover, as in 1905, socialist activists all over Russia soon organized soviets of delegates elected from factories and military units and from the countryside. Workers set up trade unions, people's militias, and cultural organizations; they began to implement "workers' control" in their factories, sometimes carting out unpopular foremen in wheelbarrows to dump them in the river. In the countryside peasants met in congresses and hurried to Petrograd to air their demands for the total expropriation of all noble land.

The situation that developed after the February Revolution came to be known as "dual power." Russia in effect had two governments: on one side, the official Provisional Government, recognized by Russia's allies, the middle classes, and the officer corps; on the other, the soviets represented the so-called revolutionary democracy— urban workers, peasants, and rank-and-file soldiers and sailors. The Provisional Government saw itself as a caretaker government and was reluctant to undertake serious political or economic reform before elections to a Constituent Assembly could be held. It was thus unable to address the peasant appropriation of land in the countryside, the shortages of food and goods, or the slowdown of industrial production in the face of widespread strike actions and rising prices. Most fatally, it ignored the fact that the Romanov dynasty had fallen thanks to its military defeats during the course of World War I. The Provisional Government, under heavy pressure from its Anglo-American allies, pledged to honor Russia's commitments to its wartime allies and even sought to gain additional territories.

The soviets for their part were also in a holding pattern. Their socialist leaders showed little inclination to take over power and contented themselves with criticizing the ineptitude of the Provisional Government. However, even before the Provisional Government was officially constituted on 2 March, the Petrograd Soviet began, perhaps unwittingly, to undermine its authority and particularly its ability to continue Russia's involvement in the world war. Responding to demands made by the Petrograd garrison, the Petrograd Soviet issued "Order No. 1," which called on soldiers and sailors to elect committees of the lower ranks to take control of "all kinds of arms, such as rifles, machine guns, armored automobiles" and to ensure that they "in no case be turned over to officers, even at their demand."[26] Further undermining traditional military discipline, the order also abolished the practice of addressing officers as "Your Excellency" or "Your Honor," substituting "Mister General" or "Mister Colonel," and mandated that officers address their men in the formal "you" (*vy*) rather than the informal "thou" (*ty*).

When Lenin returned to Petrograd in April 1917, after crossing the war zone with German help, he called for an immediate end to cooperation with the Provisional Government. His "April Theses" shocked his fellow Bolsheviks, who had generally endorsed the orthodox Marxist view that the time was not yet ripe for proletarian revolution. Lenin, by contrast, demanded an end to dual power and the transfer of "all power to the Soviets," the representatives of the "whole people." In Marxist terms, he argued that the "present situation in Russia is that the country is *passing* from the first stage of the revolution—which, owing to the insufficient class consciousness and organization of the proletariat, placed power in the hands of the bourgeoisie—to the *second* stage, which must place power into the hands of the proletariat and the poorest sections of the peasants."[27] He proposed radically reorienting the Bolshevik political program around demands for "peace, land, and bread," a powerful and simple message that resonated widely. By late October, when the Second All-Russian Congress of Soviets met in Petrograd, the Bolsheviks constituted the majority party in the Petrograd Soviet and many others.

Historians have long debated the contentious questions about the nature of the Bolsheviks' victory and whether their seizure of power should be considered as a social revolution or a coup d'état. For those who emphasize high politics and political leaders, Lenin looms large as the mastermind of a carefully engineered power grab that he legitimized by the demand to transfer "all power to the Soviets." For those historians who emphasize social and economic structures, the Bolsheviks and Lenin rode a wave of worker and peasant radicalism grounded in the hardships of modernization and war. During the Cold War, these historiographical views took on great importance. Scholars on the right, who saw the Soviet Union as an evil and fundamentally illegitimate empire, tended to characterize the October Revolution as a coup. Those on the left, who favored a softer line in the foreign policy of the United States, emphasized radicalism in the town and country and argued that the Soviet government enjoyed popular support, at least at its origin.

By the summer of 1917, the initial postrevolutionary euphoria had faded. But the Provisional Government's decision that same month to launch a military offensive in Galicia further alienated workers, soldiers, and sailors from the Provisional Government and the socialist parties that supported it. Minister of War Alexander Kerensky, a socialist who had joined the Provisional Government in its first days as the minister of justice and who ultimately became prime minister, hoped that a quick victory would boost the morale of the army and might even bring peace. However, tough German resistance led to retreat and further demoralization at the front.

Insubordination, riots, and mutinies became common occurrences, and authoritarian officers were harassed and in many instances even murdered. Tens of thousands of peasant soldiers deserted the army, eager to join in the expropriation of land being carried out in the countryside.

Popular discontent in the wake of the failed offensive also fueled another round of mass protests in the streets of the capital, the so-called July Days. Armed demonstrators—factory workers, soldiers from the Petrograd garrison, and sailors from the nearby naval base on Kronstadt Island in the Gulf of Finland—surrounded the Tauride Palace to demand that the Soviet take power. They briefly seized Victor Chernov, the SR minister of agriculture in the Provisional Government, demanding: "Take power, you son-of-a-bitch, when it is offered to you." The Bolsheviks, who had been making the same demand since April, hesitated. The more cautious, with the example of the French Revolution in mind, feared stirring up the forces of counterrevolution and conjuring a Russian Napoleon. Ultimately, the protest was dispersed by both Provisional Government troops and charges that Lenin, who had relied on German assistance to return to Petrograd in April, was in fact a German agent. The government shut down the Bolshevik newspaper *Pravda*; Lenin fled in order to avoid arrest. Were the people responding to Bolshevik demands for "peace, land, and bread" or more radical than the Bolsheviks themselves?

The Bolsheviks' political fortunes shifted again in August, when the feared counterrevolution seemed to have finally arrived. General Lavr Kornilov, who had been appointed Supreme Commander of the Russian armed forces in July, orchestrated a military operation that aimed to dissolve the Soviet. The attempted coup failed miserably, as workers and soldiers stopped his troops before they could enter the capital. The entire episode further compromised Kerensky, who appeared to have endorsed the plot, and delegitimized further the Provisional Government. Due to the Bolsheviks' radical and clearly articulated program, the party claimed some 23,000 members in early 1917 had risen to perhaps 200,000 by August. The Bolsheviks did not constitute the majority in the Second All-Russian Congress of Soviets scheduled to meet in Petrograd in late October, but they had the support of many left-wing SR delegates, who, unlike the more moderate SRs, favored immediate land reform.

However, Lenin urged the party to seize power in advance of the congress. Thus historians often emphasize that the October coup was largely the result of Lenin's determination—and the effective local leadership provided by Trotsky, who became a Bolshevik in August of that year. As head of the Military Revolutionary Committee, a committee organized by the Soviet to defend the city, Trotsky won support in the local garrisons for the Bolshevik plan and coordinated the occupation of key strategic points in the city—rail stations, the telephone exchange, the telegraph office, and finally the Winter Palace where the Provisional Government ministers were meeting.

CONCLUSION AND FURTHER QUESTIONS

Why did the Provisional Government fall? Why was it unable to mobilize military and popular support on that fateful 25 October (7 November according to the Western calendar adopted by the new regime in 1918)? Some historians emphasize that, for all Lenin's prodding, it was only the threat of counterrevolution, Kerensky's decision to shut down the radical press, that finally made an "armed uprising of the kind envisioned by Lenin feasible."[28] Others conclude that "Bolshevik policy, alone among the political programs, corresponded to and reflected the aspirations and perceived interests of workers, soldiers, and sailors in Petrograd. Even without much direct participation in the October Days, the workers acquiesced in and backed the seizure of power by the soviets."[29] Does this acquiescence suggest popular support? Did common people realize that socialist democracy would become the dictatorship of the Bolshevik party? Finally, how did the Bolsheviks interpret the mandate of modernity that they had championed so eagerly in the preceding decades? In the following chapters we will analyze Bolshevik attempts to institute their vision of equality and anticapitalist modernization in the reconstituted Russian empire.

PRIMARY SOURCES

Use the questions to analyze the content, context, and significance of each primary source. Then synthesize the primary sources and the material in the chapter to formulate a response to the primary chapter questions: What were the stumbling blocks on the road to modernity within the Russian empire? How did various groups, such as bureaucrats, intellectuals, revolutionaries, peasants, workers, and officials, respond to modernizations?

Document 2.1   Translation of Stolypin's speech to the Duma on 18 December 1908

Questions for analysis

1   Describe the key elements of Stolypin's vision for peasant Russia. Do you think that his ideas were practical?
2   What ideology animated Stolypin's plans? Which social class was he trying to appeal to?
3   If World War I had not intervened, do you think that his plan would have speeded Russia's transformation into a capitalistic society?

Having enacted the law of 22 November 1906 under the provision of Article 87, the government relied not on the weak and the drunk but on the solid and strong. And in a short time there appeared of the latter about half a million heads of families who obtained the private ownership of over 8,640,000 acres of land. Do not paralyze the further progress of these people, gentlemen, and remember, while legislating, that these people, these strong people represent the majority of peasants in Russia ... And how much, gentlemen, a strong individual landowner is needed for the reorganization of our realm, for its reorganization on solid monarchical foundations, and how much he represents a barrier against the spread of the revolutionary movement, can be seen from the resolutions of the latest congress of the socialist-revolutionary party held in London in September of this year ... This, among other matters, is what it resolved: "Having suppressed the attempt at open revolt and forcible seizure of land in the villages, the government set as its aim the breaking up of the peasantry through the intensive fostering of individual private property or homestead ownership. Any success of the government in this direction represents a serious blow to the cause of revolution." And further: "From this point of view the present situation in the villages demands from the party first of all an unwavering criticism of private ownership of land, a criticism devoid of any compromise with various individualistic tendencies."
... One should not, gentlemen, formulate a law having in mind exclusively the weak and the feeble. No, in the world struggle, in the competition of nations only those of them can occupy a position of honour who reach the full concentration of their material and moral power. Therefore all efforts of the lawmaker as well as of the government must be aimed at raising the productive forces of the source of our well-being, the land ...

Source: From Leonid I. Strakhovsky, "The Statesmanship of Peter Stolypin: A Reappraisal," *Slavonic and East European Review*, 37, no. 89 (June 1959): 348–370. Used by permission of the *Slavonic and East European Review*.

Document 2.2   Lenin's Proclamation of 7 November 1917

Questions for analysis

1   Describe the key elements of Lenin's plan. Do you think that these were practical policies that could be implemented in a revolutionary Russia?

3   What ideology underpinned Lenin's plans? Do you think it was designed to win the hearts and minds of people?

3   If Russia had not plunged into civil war or if foreign powers had refrained from military intervention, do you think that a just and peaceful society could have been built on the principles of socialism?

We have deposed the Government of Kerenski, which rose against the revolution and the people. The change which resulted in the deposition of the Provisional Government was accomplished without bloodshed. The Petrograd Council of Workmen's and Soldiers' Delegates solemnly welcomes the accomplished change and proclaims the authority of the Military Revolutionary Committee until the creation of a Government by the Workmen's and Soldiers' Delegates.

Announcing this to the army at the front, the Revolutionary Committee calls upon the revolutionary soldiers to watch closely the conduct of the men in command. Officers who do not join the accomplished revolution immediately and openly must be arrested at once as enemies.

The Petrograd Council of Workmen's and Soldiers' Delegates considers this to be the program of the new authority:

First – The offer of an immediate democratic peace.
Second – The immediate handing over of large proprietorial lands to the peasants.
Third – The transmission of all authority to the Council of Workmen's and Soldiers' Delegates.
Fourth – The honest convocation of a Constitutional Assembly.

The national revolutionary army must not permit uncertain military detachments to leave the front for Petrograd. They should use persuasion, but where this fails they must oppose any such action on the part of these detachments by force without mercy.

The present order must be read immediately to all military detachments in all arms. The suppression of this order from the rank and file by army organizations is equivalent to a great crime against the revolution and will be punished by all the strength of the revolutionary law.

Soldiers! For peace, for bread, for land, and for the power of the people!

Source: Available at www.firstworldwar.com/source/lenin_25oct1917.htm (accessed 5 June 2015).

Document 2.3   Excerpts from chapter 8 of Rosa Luxemburg's *The Russian Revolution*, 1918 (Luxemburg was an important political theorist and revolutionary, and founded the German Communist Party in 1918.)

Questions for analysis

1   Describe the key elements of Luxemburg's vision. Do you think that Lenin should have accepted her criticism?
2   How does Luxemburg define socialist democracy and how is it different from political democracy?
3   What do Luxemburg's writings tell us about the character and nature of the international left within this period?

The basic error of the Lenin–Trotsky theory is that they too, just like Kautsky, oppose dictatorship to democracy . . . Lenin and Trotsky, on the other hand, decide in favor of dictatorship in contradistinction to democracy, and thereby in favor of the dictatorship of a handful of persons, that is, in favor of dictatorship on the bourgeois model. They are two opposite poles, both alike being far removed from a genuine socialist policy. The proletariat, when it seizes power, can never follow the good advice of Kautsky, given on the pretext of the "unripeness of the country," the advice being to renounce socialist revolution and devote itself to democracy. It cannot follow this advice without betraying thereby itself, the International, and the revolution. It should and must at once undertake socialist measures in the most energetic, unyielding and unhesitant fashion, in other words, exercise a dictatorship, but a dictatorship of the *class*, not of a party or of a clique—dictatorship of the class, that means in the broadest possible form on the basis of the most active, unlimited participation of the mass of the people, of unlimited democracy . . .

But socialist democracy is not something which begins only in the promised land after the foundations of socialist economy are created; it does not come as some sort of Christmas present for the worthy people who, in the interim, have loyally supported a handful of socialist dictators. Socialist democracy begins simultaneously with the beginnings of the destruction of class rule and of the construction of socialism. It begins at the very moment of the seizure of power by the socialist party. It is the same thing as the dictatorship of the proletariat . . .

Source: Available at www.marxists.org/archive/luxemburg/1918/russian-revolution/index.htm (accessed 6 June 2015).

Notes

1   Abraham Ascher, *P.A. Stolypin and the Search for Stability in Late Imperial Russia* (Stanford, CA: Stanford University Press, 2001).
2   Mark Steinberg, *Proletarian Imagination: Self, Modernity and the Sacred in Russia, 1910–1925* (Ithaca, NY: Cornell University Press, 2002).
3   Joan Neuberger, *Hooliganism, Crime, Culture, Power in St. Petersburg, 1900–1914* (Berkeley: University of California Press, 1993).
4   Maureen Perrie, *The Agrarian Policy of the Russian Socialist Revolutionary Party from Its Origins to the Revolution of 1905–1907* (Cambridge: Cambridge University Press, 1976).
5   George Kennan, *Siberia and the Exile System* (New York: Century Company, 1991), vol. 2, 121–122.

6   Steven Marks, *How Russia Shaped the Modern World: From Art to Anti-Semitism from Ballet to Bolshevism* (Princeton, NJ: Princeton University Press, 2003); Anthony Anemone, ed., *Just Assassins: The Culture of Terrorism in Russia* (Evanston, IL: Northwestern University Press, 2010).

 7   Louise McReynolds, *Russia at Play: Leisure Activities at the End of the Tsarist Era* (Ithaca, NY: Cornell University Press, 2003); Jeffrey Brooks, *When Russia Learned to Read: Literacy and Popular Literature, 1861–1917* (Princeton, NJ: Princeton University Press, 1985).

 8   Leopold Haimson, *Russian Marxists and the Origins of Bolshevism* (Cambridge, MA: Harvard University Press, 1955).

 9   Laura Engelstein, *The Keys to Happiness: Sex and the Search for Modernity in Fin-de-Siècle Russia* (Ithaca, NY: Cornell University Press, 1992).

10   Melissa Stockdale, *Paul Miliukov and the Quest for a Liberal Russia, 1880–1918* (Ithaca, NY: Cornell University Press, 1996).

11   P. A. Kropotkin, *Memoirs of a Revolutionist* (Boston, MA: Houghton Mifflin and Co., 1899).

12   Susan Layton, *Russian Literature and Empire: Conquest of the Caucasus from Pushkin to Tolstoy* (Cambridge: Cambridge University Press, 1994).

13   Leo Tolstoy, "The Law of Violence and the Law of Love," in James Edie, James P. Scanlan, and Mary-Barbara Zeldin, eds., *Russian Philosophy* (Chicago, IL: Quadrangle Books, 1965), vol. 2, 232.

14   Jane Addams, *Twenty Years at Hull House with Autobiographical Notes* (New York: The Macmillan Co., 1923).

15   Pankaj Mishra, *From the Ruins of Empire: Intellectuals Who Remade Asia* (New York: Farrar, Strauss and Giroux, 2012).

16   Reginald Zelnik, ed. and trans., *A Radical Worker in Tsarist Russia: The Autobiography of Semën Ivanovich Kanatchikov* (Stanford, CA: Stanford University Press, 1986).

17   Robert Service, *Lenin: A Biography* (Cambridge, MA: Harvard University Press, 2000).

18   Available at www.marxists.org/subject/art/literature/mayakovsky/1917/slap-in-face-public-taste.htm (accessed 8 June 2015).

19   Camilla Gray, *The Great Experiment: Russian Art 1863–1922* (New York: Abrams, 1962).

20   Richard Stites, *Revolutionary Dreams, Utopian Visions and Experimental Life in the Russian Revolution* (New York: Oxford University Press, 1989).

21   Sean McMeekin, *The Russian Origins of the First World War* (Cambridge, MA: Belknap Press of Harvard University Press, 2011).

22   Alan K. Wildman, *The End of the Russian Imperial Army: The Old Army and the Soldiers' Revolt (March–April, 1917)* (Princeton, NJ: Princeton University Press, 1980), 96–97.

23   Peter Gatrell, *Russia's First World War: An Economic and Social History* (New York: Routledge, 2005).

24   Choi Chatterjee, *Celebrating Women: Gender, Festival Culture and Bolshevik Ideology* (Pittsburgh, PA: University of Pittsburgh Press, 2002).

25   Louise Bryant, *Six Red Months in Russia* (New York: George H. Doran Co., 1918); John Reed, *Ten Days That Shook the World* (New York: Boni and Liveright, 1919).

26   Order No. 1, 14 March 1917, available at www.marxists.org/history/ussr/government/1917/03/01.htm (accessed 7 January 2016).

27   Vladimir Lenin, "The Tasks of the Proletariat in the Present Revolution," in Robert C. Tucker, ed., *The Lenin Anthology* (New York: W. W. Norton, 1975), 296.

28   Alexander Rabinowitch, *The Bolsheviks Come to Power: The Revolution of 1917 in Petrograd* (1976; reprint, Chicago: Haymarket Books, 2004), 314.

29   Ronald Grigor Suny, "Toward a Social History of the October Revolution," *American Historical Review*, 88, no. 1 (February 1983): 50.

3 Constructing the socialist order

INTRODUCTION

On the night of 26 October 1917, less than twenty-four hours after the Provisional Government fell, Vladimir Lenin addressed the Second All-Russian Congress of Soviets. American journalist John Reed described the Bolshevik leader "gripping the edge of the reading stand, letting his little winking eyes travel over the crowd as he stood there waiting, apparently oblivious to the long-rolling ovation, which lasted several minutes. When it finished, he said simply, 'We shall now proceed to construct the socialist order!' Again that overwhelming human roar."[1] Lenin then moved immediately to proposing "practical measures" for accomplishing one of the Bolsheviks' chief priorities: peace.

Lenin and his comrades hoped and expected that the Russian revolution's call to end the bloody world war would spark revolutions in economically "advanced" states, and that those revolutions would in turn safeguard the revolution in "backward" Russia. Their expectations were soon disappointed. In March 1918, the Soviet state signed a separate and punishing peace with Germany that precipitated a brutal civil war on multiple fronts against multiple internal and external enemies. Marxism offered little guidance to the embattled revolutionaries, who increasingly relied on centralized and militarized control of the economy—policies later dubbed "war communism"—as the best means of fighting the war and laying the groundwork for the construction of socialism.

By early 1921, Soviet power reigned over much of the territory of the former Russian empire. But the new state had not managed to "construct the socialist order." Facing an economy in ruins and mounting social unrest, Lenin advocated a change of course, a New Economic Policy, that allowed a temporary return of private trade and private property, but not of political pluralism, as a means of rebuilding the economy and preparing to build the socialist order.

CHAPTER QUESTIONS

This chapter raises questions about how state and party leaders, rank-and-file Bolsheviks, workers, and peasants conceptualized and worked between 1917 and 1927 to build (or oppose) a proletarian state. What was "the socialist order" to look like, and how did one go about constructing it? Could workers be trusted to build socialism or did they need to be disciplined and guided by the party? What did it mean to construct a "workers' state" in "backward," predominately peasant, Russia? In answering these questions, to what extent did leaders rely on Marxist ideology? To what extent were their decisions dictated by circumstances—foreign intervention, almost three years of fierce civil war, economic collapse, famine, peasant uprisings? How do we as historians explain the increasingly authoritarian character of the Bolshevik government?

VOICES, MEMORIES, CONTESTED PERSPECTIVES

Bolshevik expectations: workers and the dictatorship of the proletariat

Bolsheviks and other Marxists often turned to a Marxist-inflected reading of the past to try to make sense of the present and prepare for the future. Lenin's pamphlet "State and Revolution," completed in the heat of the revolutionary moment in August and September 1917, provided one picture of the transition to socialism as both violent and spontaneous.

In "State and Revolution" (see document 3.1) Lenin emphasized Marx's dictum that the workers' revolution must violently "smash" the bourgeois state, replacing it with a transitional "dictatorship of the proletariat." He imagined this "dictatorship" as a direct workers' democracy: a commune state managed by "the armed vanguard of all the exploited and working people." In Lenin's telling, the destruction of the bourgeois state would allow workers with "knowledge of the four rules of arithmetic" to take over the management of the infrastructure created by the capitalist system— factories, railways, telephone services—while technical experts remained at their jobs. Ultimately, the state would "wither away" entirely as people "freed from capitalist slavery ... will become accustomed to observing [the elementary rules of social intercourse] without force, without coercion, without subordination, without the special apparatus for coercion called the state."[2]

As a long line of Western scholars have noted, Soviet realities quickly diverged from the democratic, egalitarian, simple-to-administer "dictatorship of the proletariat" imagined in "State and Revolution."[3] Still, Lenin's blueprint for a future that was never built offers a useful starting point for the analysis of early Soviet efforts to imagine and construct a workers' state. On the eve of the October Revolution, Lenin envisioned workers as agents of a revolution that would naturally give birth to new, liberated, and self-disciplined people capable of building and living in a new world. But Lenin also reserved an important educational role for the party, which he mentioned only once in "State and Revolution." The party, as the "vanguard of the proletariat," assumed the task of "*leading the whole people* to socialism, of directing and organizing the new system, of being the teacher, the guide, the leader of all the working and exploited people."[4] Here Lenin articulated, but did not call attention to, a fundamental ambivalence, if not contradiction, in Bolshevik representations of workers, whom leaders at once celebrated as natural, spontaneous revolutionaries and deemed in need of guidance, enlightenment, and cultivation. Even as Lenin himself moved decisively away from the belief in the spontaneous emergence of socialism, this dual vision of workers produced important tensions among leading Bolsheviks.

Building a new order: origins of the one-party state

When in the early morning hours of 26 October the Bolsheviks claimed power, they did so in the name of the Congress of Soviets and the "revolutionary class." However, by the time Anatoly Lunacharsky made the announcement to the gathered delegates, the Mensheviks, the right wing of the Party of Socialist Revolutionaries, and other moderate socialists had walked out of the Congress to protest the Bolsheviks' "military conspiracy." They were seen off by Trotsky's famous advice: "Go where you belong from now on—into the rubbish-can of history."[5] Thus the Congress that constituted the new government included relatively few representatives of the "revolutionary class" who were not Bolsheviks.

The Soviet state's first decrees committed it to the speedy delivery of two key Bolshevik demands: peace and land. The Decree on Peace called for an immediate armistice and a general peace "without annexations or indemnities."[6] The Decree on Land, which largely coopted the program of the Socialist Revolutionaries, ratified actions already taken by the peasants, authorizing the seizure of landed estates as well as crown and church lands without compensation to the previous owners.

In the early morning hours of 27 October, the Congress also constituted a new government, the Council of People's Commissars. Technically, this was a provisional government, ruling only until the Constituent Assembly met. The very name "Council of People's Commissars" signaled a break with bourgeois forms. Undertaking a revolution in the language of state, the Bolsheviks abbreviated the names of new institutions, creating a mass of sometimes inelegant but self-consciously revolutionary neologisms. In this case the Council of People's Commissars was known as the Sovnarkom (*Sovet Narodnykh Komissarov*).

In addition to rejecting "ministers" in favor of "commissars," the decree mandated the incorporation of workers into the new state structure. Each commissariat was to be administered by a committee or collegium that included workers, soldiers, sailors, peasants, and other employees. Thus, as the diplomat Ivan Maisky recalled in 1923, the workers' collective at the Commissariat of Foreign Affairs, down to and including the janitors, "attempted" in the first euphoric days after the October Revolution "to arrogate to itself the right to conduct the foreign policy of Russia."[7] At the Commissariat of Labor, the commissar, former metalworker and long-time Bolshevik Alexander Shliapnikov, worked, not always amicably, with a collegium that included representatives from the trade unions.[8]

For all its formal commitment to including workers, the new Council of People's Commissars can also be understood as the one-party state in embryo. The slogan "All Power to the Soviets" had been taken by most, including many Bolsheviks, to mean a multiparty government of all the representatives of the "toilers." However, from the beginning Lenin, equating the Bolshevik party with the workers' interests, sought a Bolshevik monopoly on power. As initially constituted, the Council of People's Commissars was exclusively Bolshevik. Notable appointments included Lenin as chair of the Sovnarkom, Trotsky as commissar of foreign affairs, and Joseph Stalin as commissar of nationalities. Only the threat of a railway strike in December induced the Bolsheviks to add six commissars from the Party of Left Socialist Revolutionaries to the government.

Other early decrees also signaled a tendency to conflate workers' revolution with Bolshevik power. A 27 October decree on "hostile newspapers" (see document 3.2) banned the "counterrevolutionary press of all shades" and made clear that the Bolsheviks considered all opposition counterrevolutionary. In December, the Sovnarkom expanded the scope of repression, establishing an "Extraordinary Commission for Combating Counterrevolution and Sabotage" (known by the abbreviation Cheka). Its primary weapons against "saboteurs, strikers, and the Socialist-Revolutionaries of the Right" were initially nonviolent: "confinement, deprivation of [food] cards, publication of the names of the enemies of the people."[9]

By the summer of 1918, both the Bolsheviks and their opponents were increasingly turning to violence. Here separating the effects of ideology and circumstance is tricky. For revolutionaries contemptuous of "rotten" liberalism, "terror" was at once legitimate and necessary. The 30 August 1918 assassination attempt on Lenin prompted the Sovnarkom to authorize the Cheka to "shoot without fail" all "counterrevolutionary scoundrels."[10] Fania Kaplan, the former anarchist loosely affiliated with the SRs, who shot Lenin as he emerged from a Moscow factory meeting, was executed four days later. During the Civil War, the Cheka and other security forces executed hundreds of thousands of alleged class enemies, from the tsar to rebellious peasants.

Despite their allegedly "extraordinary" status, state control of the press and the political police became permanent features of the Soviet state. The Cheka was succeeded by a series of secret police organizations, including the GPU (1922–1923), the OGPU (1923–1934), the NKVD (1934–1943), the MGB (1943–1954), and the KGB, all of whose agents were colloquially known as "Chekists." Agents of the post-Soviet FSB (Federal Security Service of the Russian Federation) are also often referred to as Chekists. The question of why the Soviet and post-Soviet regimes developed in this authoritarian direction is one we will return to throughout this book. What did institutions such as the political police suggest about the Bolshevik approach to guiding workers in the construction of socialism?

Many historians cite the Bolshevik decision to dissolve the Constituent Assembly in January 1918 as a watershed in the development of a Bolshevik dictatorship. Before taking power, the Bolsheviks, along with all the revolutionary parties, had clamored for the assembly's convocation. Two weeks after the October seizure of power, the new government permitted elections to that body. Although the Bolsheviks polled quite well among urban industrial workers, soldiers, and sailors, they won only 24 percent of the more than forty million votes cast. The Socialist Revolutionaries, whose lists did not distinguish between SRs and Left SRs (allied with the Bolsheviks), won about 40 percent of the vote, the Mensheviks 3 percent, and the liberal Kadets less than 5 percent. The rest was split among various national parties, some with a socialist orientation. If the socialist idea had a clear electoral mandate, the Bolsheviks did not.

The Bolsheviks permitted the assembly to meet on 5 January 1918 but forbade public demonstrations of support for it, a ban enforced by Bolshevik troops who fired on marchers. When the assembly convened, the Bolshevik and Left SR delegates insisted it endorse the Sovnarkom government. The motion failed, and the Bolsheviks and their Left SR allies walked out. The rest of the delegates continued to meet into the small hours of the morning, until the sailors "guarding" the delegates complained that they were tired and sent them home. The next day the returning delegates found the doors to the Tauride Palace barred.

Even more important than the suppression of the Constituent Assembly may be the way the Bolsheviks justified their action as a revolutionary necessity. In a 6 January speech before the All-Russian Central Executive Committee of Soviets, Lenin argued that all opposition was essentially counterrevolutionary, asserting that the slogan "'All Power to the Constituent Assembly!' masks the slogan 'Down with Soviet power!'" Not yet ruling a one party state, the Bolsheviks had to make their case before a mixed audience of Mensheviks and SRs.

For their part, the SRs tried to paint the Bolshevik state as the return of tsarism. SR newspapers emphasized the massacre of peaceful demonstrators on 5 January—a date that they attempted to tie to "Bloody Sunday," 9 January 1905, when tsarist troops fired on peaceful petitioners (see chapter 2). Their efforts seemed to stem less from a genuine fear that the Bolsheviks might restore autocracy than from a desire "to exploit the historically and emotionally charged vocabulary of the radical movement."[11] However, because the Bolsheviks had already begun peace negotiations (see next section) and acceded to peasant land seizures, they could plausibly represent themselves as defenders of revolution. Indeed many peasants who voted for the SR label may have intended to elect the more radical Left SRs.

By contrast, Bolshevik charges that a "monstrous plot lurked behind the whole effort to convene the Constituent Assembly" seemed to carry more conviction, or in any event to tap into the "mass consciousness of 1917" that explained "everything as a grandiose and overarching 'bourgeois conspiracy.'"[12] *Pravda* colorfully and inventively characterized the SRs as "lickspittles of the bankers, capitalists, and landlords . . . slaves of the American dollar, backstabbers . . . evil enemies of socialism."[13] By "exposing" vast and improbable conspiracies, the Bolsheviks cast themselves as the only true revolutionaries. This sort of binary thinking, the insistence that there were only "two camps" and that moderate socialists, liberals, bankers, and monarchists all stood together on the "counterrevolutionary" side of the barricades, became, as we shall see, a crucial element of the Civil War. What does such binary thinking suggest about the origins of Bolshevik authoritarianism?

Revolution and peace

The drawn-out peace negotiations with Germany that began in December 1917 and ended with the Treaty of Brest-Litovsk in March 1918 underscored the tensions between the Bolsheviks as world revolutionaries and as state builders. At the heart of the Bolshevik approach to peace stood the conviction that the revolution in Russia would set off workers' revolutions in the capitalist West. Given that Europe had suffered three years of mass slaughter, that mutinies had shaken the French army, that there were signs of unrest in the German navy and waves of strikes in Vienna, Budapest, and Berlin, this was perhaps more than a vain hope. However, by early January 1918, the more realistic, or perhaps more pessimistic, among the Bolsheviks, first and foremost Lenin, worried that world revolution would not come soon enough to save Russia with its thoroughly demoralized army from the German war machine. Because the Allies refused to enter into peace negotiations, the Soviets were left to bargain on their own for a separate peace, a situation which raised the question of whether defending the "socialist fatherland" meant compromising revolutionary principles and hopes.

When the peace negotiations began on 9 (22) December 1917, it soon became clear that the settlement would include both annexations and indemnities. Generously, if disingenuously, endorsing the Bolshevik commitment to "self-determination of peoples," the Germans proposed "independence" for non-Russian territories of the former Russian empire then under German occupation: Russian Poland and the Baltic provinces. Later, Ukraine would be added to the list of nominally independent states. Two weeks later, Trotsky took over as head of the Soviet delegation. His main task was to spin out the negotiations. The Bolsheviks wanted to allow time for revolution to break out in Germany and to avoid adding to the political crisis around the dissolution of the Constituent Assembly with news of a failed negotiation or a humiliating agreement. Trotsky successfully prolonged the negotiations, and the talks recessed just as the assembly met for the first and only time.

Back in Petrograd, the Bolshevik leadership split over the proper response to the harsh German terms. Lenin favored accepting whatever terms they could get, as the Soviet army was no match for the Germans. The majority of the leadership and perhaps of the rank and file, with Nikolai Bukharin as their most prominent champion, favored refusing the offered terms and resuming the war, this time as a "revolutionary war" that they felt sure would win the support of the Russian and German masses. Trotsky prevailed in the debate with a sort of middle course, neither accepting the peace terms nor continuing the war. He, too, assumed that the German troops would not advance when word of the Soviet position reached the German lines.

Shortly after the peace talks resumed on 17 (30) January 1918, Trotsky sprung his "no peace, no war" formula. The initially flummoxed German high command responded with a renewal of hostilities. The German army advanced at a fantastic pace—in some places covering 150 miles in five days—against Russian forces that could not manage an orderly retreat. On 21 February, by which time the Germans were closing in on Petrograd and Lenin had finally persuaded a scant majority of his comrades to agree to accept German terms, the Soviet government issued a desperate plea that marked a step away from dreams of world revolution: "Until the time when the German proletariat rises and conquers, it is the sacred duty of the workers and peasants of Russia to defend the Republic of the Soviets against the hordes of the bourgeois-imperialistic Germany . . . The Socialist Fatherland is in danger! Long live the Socialist Fatherland!"[14]

Without immediate word that the Germans would agree to negotiate, the Bolsheviks contemplated the possibility of accepting Allied aid in the event that they had to continue the war. Bukharin passionately opposed such a move as an unconscionable violation of revolutionary principle. Lenin, who was not at the meeting, sent a note requesting that his comrades "add my vote in favor of taking potatoes and ammunition from the Anglo-French imperialist robbers." Trotsky recalled that at the end of the meeting Bukharin burst into tears.[15]

The eventual German terms were more punishing than those Trotsky had rejected in early February, undoing more than two hundred years of tsarist expansion in the west. Only Lenin's threatened resignation forced party leaders to go along with them. Russia lost the Baltic provinces (Courland, Lithuania, Livonia, Estonia), as well as much of Belorussia and Ukraine. (These territories were restored to Soviet control in 1945.) Because the Germans remained dangerously close to Petrograd, the Bolsheviks moved their government to Moscow, the old Russian capital, in early March 1918.

Still hoping to spark world revolution, the Bolsheviks accepted the Brest treaty as a necessary means of preserving Soviet power, thus rendering "the best and most powerful support to the proletariat of all countries."[16] However, as the Bolsheviks were sharply aware, their state remained embattled, "encircled," as they liked to emphasize, by hostile capitalist powers. Moreover, the treaty added to their enemies at home. The Left SRs proclaimed the treaty with Germany "a betrayal of the international program and of the Socialist Revolution begun in Russia."[17] They resigned from the Sovnarkom and soon took up arms against the Soviet state. For the Bolsheviks, this made them counterrevolutionaries, in league with the capitalist enemies of the socialist fatherland.

World war and civil war(s)

The Russian Civil War defies straightforward narration. Usually dated from mid-1918 to early 1921, the Civil War marked both the last gasp of the tsarist empire and the emergence of a consolidated Soviet state. Multiple actors—troops from more than half a dozen foreign nations, former tsarist officers and aristocrats, would-be military dictators, Cossacks, liberals, moderate socialists, nationalists seeking independence from Russia, and peasant armies—challenged Bolshevik power in a multitude of largely independent struggles that raged across the former empire from Finland in the west to Vladivostok on the Pacific coast.

Given the diverse regions and belligerents involved, some historians have argued for conceptualizing the Russian Civil War as "a series of overlapping civil wars and national conflicts."[18] These "wars" can be understood as occurring on three broad fronts: the south (Ukraine, the territories of the Don and Kuban Cossacks between the Black and Caspian Seas, the North Caucasus); the east (the Volga basin, the Urals, and Siberia); and the northwest (Poland and the Baltic). This approach has the analytical advantage of calling attention to the fluidity and complexity of local political alignments and their intersections with larger movements. However, it is also important to keep in mind that at the time "Russians understood themselves to be living through a 'civil war,' not 'civil wars,'" a perception that shaped their analysis of and responses to events.[19]

On the Volga and in Siberia, as in other theaters of the war, both the world war and the revolution shaped events. In response to the Brest-Litovsk treaty, the SRs resolved to move from peaceful efforts to elect their own delegates to local soviets to armed resistance to the Bolshevik regime. They viewed the treaty as evidence that the Bolsheviks had sold out the revolution to German imperialism. The SRs began planning for an uprising in the Volga region that aimed to oppose the Bolsheviks and, even more urgently, to prevent counterrevolution by renewing the war against Germany.

One of the stranger episodes linking the world war and Civil War came in May and June 1918 when the Czechoslovak Legion aided the SR uprising. In early 1918, the Bolshevik government agreed to give the Czechoslovak Legion safe passage out of Russia; the Legion was established in 1914 and numbered by late 1917 perhaps fifty thousand troops—mainly Czech and Slovak POWs and deserters from the Habsburg military who wanted the chance to fight against the empire and for Czechoslovak independence. The Legionnaires planned to cross Russia via the Trans-Siberian Railroad, then, departing from the port of Vladivostok, to circumnavigate the globe, transiting the US, in order to rejoin the war on the western front. Instead, a series of clashes with Bolshevik troops along the railroad escalated into a full-blown insurrection of the Czechoslovaks, who in July 1918 managed to take control of the railway from Samara on the Volga through Siberia to Irkutsk. The British and French, still furious about Brest, saw the Czechoslovak troops as a possible means of reopening the eastern front along the Volga. The SRs took advantage of the situation to push out local Bolsheviks and ultimately claim authority as the Committee of the Constituent Assembly (Komuch). In August 1918, with the aid of its own volunteer troops and the Legion, Komuch captured Kazan from the Bolsheviks. This development caused alarm in Moscow as it marked a substantial widening of the war and brought the Bolsheviks' opponents within striking distance (800 kilometers, 500 miles) of the capital.

Committed to restoring the Constituent Assembly and fighting both the Germans and the Bolsheviks, the SRs tried to position themselves as a "third force" in the Civil War. One might even say that they tried to characterize the violence consuming the former empire as overlapping struggles for revolution and national independence—rather than a Manichean battle between Red and White. Tellingly, Komuch flew the red flag, as had Kerensky's Provisional Government, a practice that alienated the local propertied classes. This sort of positioning was critical for the SRs as they stood for revolution but against what they considered the Bolsheviks' surrender to German imperialism.

The Bolsheviks, by contrast, promoted the red–white binary precisely because it delegitimized, even denied the possibility of, socialist or lower class opposition to Bolshevik rule. Bolshevik propaganda put the SR leader Victor Chernov along with his purported allies, a French officer with a sack of money, a White general, and a fat-cat *burzhui* (slang for bourgeois), all in the same rickety boat with a tattered sail emblazoned "Constituent Assembly."[20] Insisting more and more on purely Bolshevik organs of government, in June 1918 the Bolsheviks expelled Mensheviks and SRs from the Central Executive Committee of the Congress of Soviets.

The Bolsheviks' White opponents also represented the Civil War as an apocalyptic struggle between two irreconcilable forces. General Lavr Kornilov, one of the commanders of the Volunteer (or White) Army in the Don (the same Kornilov who led the attempted coup in August 1917), made no distinction between the German and Bolshevik enemy, declaring that "Russia has fallen into the hands of political adventurers who, under the flag of social revolution, are doing the Great-German work of destroying the military might of the country."[21] Like the Bolsheviks, he saw the world in terms of conspiracies and "masked" actors.

Ultimately, the SR effort to chart a middle course failed. A November 1918 coup overthrew Komuch's successor, the Provisional All-Russian Government, and replaced it with a military dictatorship under the former commander of the Black Sea fleet Alexander Kolchak. By then, the world war had ended, voiding the Brest-Litovsk treaty and removing the threat of German-backed counterrevolution that had motivated the SRs to take up armed struggle against the Bolsheviks. In any event, they preferred to support revolution, even with the Bolsheviks, than to risk opposition that might aid counterrevolution. But neither side had much use for the SRs, who were executed or exiled by the Whites and put on trial by the Bolsheviks. (In 1922, the Bolsheviks stayed the executions of those sentenced to death; most were killed in the Stalinist terror of the 1930s.)

Red and White terror

In the summer of 1918, when the SR seizure of Kazan produced a crisis for the Bolsheviks, the Reds perpetrated the war's most infamous act of terror. On the night of 16–17 July, Cheka agents executed the former tsar and tsarina, their five children, the family doctor, and three servants in the basement of a house in Ekaterinburg. The Provisional Government had sent the tsar's family to Siberia in July 1917, both to protect them from leftists eager to extract revolutionary justice and to thwart rightists intent on restoring the monarchy. A year later the local Bolsheviks—whether on their own initiative or at the behest of Moscow remains an open question—summarily executed the imperial family as a means of keeping them out of the hands of the anti-Bolshevik forces threatening Ekaterinburg. The Soviet press announced only the execution of the tsar, noting that with the murder "the will of the revolution has been fulfilled."[22] The Bolsheviks thus publicly justified the killing of the king—but not his family—as a revolutionary necessity.

Across Eurasia the struggle between the Bolsheviks and their opponents was marked by often unprecedented levels of violence, most of it lacking the symbolic veneer of the regicide. All told, at least one million civilians and soldiers died in the conflict, victims of combat or terror. The question of why the Russian Civil War was so brutal, even in comparison to other violent civil conflicts, has generated much historical debate that, like the historiography of the October Revolution, bears the imprint of the Cold War. Emphasizing the role of Marxist ideology or the Russian revolutionary tradition in generating violence, some historians argue that the Bolsheviks, who endorsed the "unsanitized brutality" of peasant and soldier rebellion, initiated "the cycle of atrocity" to which their opponents regretfully but necessarily responded in kind.[23] Other historians emphasize the linkages between the Civil War and the world war's legitimization and normalization of mass violence, particularly violence directed against civilian populations. (In World War I, civilian dead and wounded accounted for some 63 percent of total losses; in the Russian Civil War, the equivalent figure was 91 percent.)

Some of the Civil War's most shocking atrocities occurred in the western borderlands, where pogroms in 1919 and 1920 targeted civilian Jewish populations. All belligerents, including the Red Army, engaged in anti-Jewish violence to some extent. However, whereas Bolshevik commanders and commissars (political instructors in the army) understood soldiers' involvement in pogroms as a failure of political education, for their opponents anti-Semitism constituted a means of mobilizing support.

The most widespread violence against Jews occurred after the end of World War I, when the Germans evacuated Ukraine and the Bolsheviks invaded. In January 1919, retreating Ukrainian nationalist forces, with the encouragement of their commanders, engaged in the mass killing of Jews, whom they viewed as enemies of Ukrainian independence. In 1919 and 1920, the high command of the Volunteer (White) Army under General Anton Denikin in Ukraine fostered systematic anti-Semitic violence on a scale surpassed only during the Holocaust. While "Jews were occasionally shot" by the Volunteers, they "were more often hanged, trampled by horses, dismembered, and buried alive."[24] The total number of Jewish victims is difficult to determine; historians offer estimates ranging from 50,000 to 200,000 dead, of whom perhaps half were victims of the Volunteer Army, and tens of thousands "maimed, raped, and robbed."[25]

The anti-Jewish pogroms raise in particularly sharp form the question: In what ways and to what extent did ideology or practices that transcended ideology shape the violent course of the Civil War? White officers' "pathological" and murderous anti-Semitism can be understood in ideological terms; they equated Bolshevism and Judaism as a means of explaining "why the revolution had occurred" by blaming "the alien Jews."[26] While not ignoring this ideological dimension, other historians argue that the Civil War pogroms constituted the "culmination of anti-Jewish violence" that began in 1914, with the tsarist army's ruthless expulsion of "unreliable" Jews from the war zone, and continued in 1915 with the army's instigation of pogroms.[27]

The expulsions can also be understood more broadly as part of a pan-European "epoch of violence" spanning the years 1905 to 1921. Both White and Red forces employed the modern (and often violent) "state practices" such as forced population transfers, hostage taking, and summary executions that European states had developed in their colonies and turned against one another during World War I. From this perspective, what set the Bolsheviks apart from other groups was not the willingness to resort to violence, but rather "the extent to which they turned tools originally intended for total war to the new ends of revolutionary politics."[28] One important and arguably "revolutionary" Bolshevik innovation was women's involvement in combat (see document 3.4). At least 73,500 women served in the Red Army, 1,854 of whom were wounded or killed and 55 of whom were awarded the Order of the Red Banner.[29]

War communism and the making of the Soviet state

As the Bolshevik state battled White armies, national independence movements, supporters of the Constituent Assembly, and foreign troops on its peripheries, it also faced opposition behind the shifting lines. In the countryside, Bolshevik demands for conscripts, grain, horses, and other supplies essential to the war effort stirred up widespread and often intense resistance. Entrusted with feeding the Red Army and industrial workers, the Commissariat of Food Supply was, after the Commissariat of War, the new state's most powerful institution. It employed force and arrests to take grain from the peasants. These coercive practices incited peasant uprisings and generated complaints from provincial soviet officials.

Focusing on this critical internal front makes it possible to approach the Civil War less as a military operation than as an "exercise in mass mobilization and state-building."[30] From this perspective, the crucial questions are: How did the Bolsheviks manage to build the state institutions and mobilize the people and resources necessary to win the war? Did winning the war require sacrificing revolutionary dreams and ideological principles to pragmatic calculations? Why were the Bolsheviks' opponents unable to take advantage of the disillusionment of workers and peasants with the purported workers' and peasants' state?

The Red Army, the largest and arguably most important and efficient institution created by the early Soviet state, stood at the center of mobilization and state building efforts. In early 1918, as negotiations with the Germans stalled and White forces began to organize on the peripheries, Sovnarkom established a Worker–Peasant Red Army that resembled the "workers' militia" envisioned in "State and Revolution;" made up of class-conscious volunteers, the Soviet army banned the death penalty and allowed the rank and file to elect their own officers. By mid-1918, however, "the exigencies of civil war forced the regime to retreat from its socialist principles in the direction of a standing army."[31] Trotsky, who became commissar of war in March 1918, was the chief advocate and architect of the return of discipline and former tsarist officers (known euphemistically as "military specialists") whose loyalty was guaranteed by the assignment in April 1918 of political commissars to each unit. The victories of the Czechoslovak Legion in May prompted the move from a volunteer to

Figure 3.1 In an undated photograph (perhaps around 1918), Trotsky addresses the Red
   Guard. Courtesy of the Library of Congress Prints and Photographs Division, Bain
   Collection (LC-B2-5580-6).

*Pay careful attention to who is in the photograph and how they're dressed. Does this look
like a "workers' militia"?*

a conscript army. By 1920, the Soviet state had a standing army of perhaps five million
troops, 75 percent of whom were peasants by birth, led by former tsarist officers who
reinstituted "drill-sergeant discipline" and the death penalty for desertion.

   If building a standing peasant army was practical and necessary, it was also risky.
Peasants initially responded to call ups with extensive and often effective resistance.
Most commonly, peasants simply failed to appear at muster points. In June and July
1918, only about 40,000 of an expected 275,000 rural recruits reported; such draft
dodgers were labeled "deserters." The military turned to terror and coercion to round
up conscripts—methods that often stirred up popular rebellions against military and
state authorities. Where the military succeeded in conscripting peasants, it often
lacked the officers necessary to train them; the lack of adequate food, uniforms, boots,
weapons, and housing often set off another round of desertions. Returning to their
home regions, deserters in some cases formed "green" armies—a label apparently
derived from their forest refuges—to resist conscription by attacking state institutions
and local Communist Party (as the Bolsheviks renamed themselves in 1918) members.

   By late 1918, the Soviet state was not only conscripting peasants but also imple-
menting new and coercive grain collections, a core policy of what came to be known
as war communism. As the name suggests, the state's policies can be understood as a
pragmatic response to the war emergency and as an effort to put ideological principles
into practice. The regime implemented a system of assessments (*razverstka*), which

required districts to provide a set amount of grain (and other supplies) based not on actual surpluses but on centrally determined needs. The system aimed to suppress private trade. Whatever might be left over after the assessment was to be sold only to the state at fixed prices. For some communists the resulting curtailment of the market and the replacement of monetary transactions with barter signaled a leap into the revolutionary future—despite the fact that, due to the scarcity of manufactured goods, illegal trade flourished. In many cases, however, nothing was left over after state grain collections, as the quotas routinely exceeded peasant production. Food brigades seized grain necessary for the peasants' own subsistence as well as seed grain, generating both efforts by village groups to seek redress through the organs of the Soviet state and peasant uprisings.

How then to explain the fact that the Bolsheviks ultimately had greater success than their opponents in mobilizing peasants for military service? Families of Red Army recruits were promised (but did not always receive) exemptions from grain requisitions. Bolshevik propaganda countered peasant resistance with warnings that a White victory meant a return of the landlords, who would reclaim their estates. After all, the Whites, too, seized grain, conscripted peasants, and terrorized civilians; what distinguished them was their opposition to land reform and, in the non-Russian borderlands, their efforts to restore Russian imperial power. Warnings of a restoration of the old order resonated with peasants, especially in regions that had experienced White rule, for example along the Volga near Kazan, which the expanding and increasingly professional Red Army retook in September 1918. There peasant "deserters," who feared losing newly acquired land, enlisted in large numbers. The clear threat of White victory in the summer of 1919 likewise brought the "return" of thousands of peasants to the Red Army. At that moment, Moscow faced advancing White forces in the south (the Volunteer Army now under General Denikin), Kolchak's forces advancing from Siberia, and General Nikolai Yudinich's forces, which had reached the outskirts of Petrograd. The crisis prompted so many peasants to enlist that the army was unable to supply them all with uniforms and rifles. In fall 1919, the Red Army had the forces to launch a counteroffensive that by the end of the year had turned the tide on all fronts. By the end of 1920, Kolchak had been executed and the Whites defeated. War with Poland continued into 1921, and the last Japanese forces left the Russian far east in 1922.

Peasants', sailors', and workers' opposition: origins of the New Economic Policy

As the war wound down in 1920, the Bolsheviks faced devastating economic breakdown (*razrukha*) and mounting internal opposition. Even as peasants joined the Red Army to protect their revolutionary gains, they resisted state grain assessments by reducing sown acreage—from about 214 million acres in 1916 to about 133 million in 1922. As fears of a return of the landlords receded, resistance intensified. A series of massive rebellions erupted in the Caucasus, the Volga, and western Siberia in late 1920 and early 1921. The best known is the revolt in Tambov province, where the Bolsheviks faced a peasant army of 20,000 troops under the command of Alexander Antonov, a former Socialist Revolutionary and onetime collaborator with the Bolsheviks.[32] Only in spring 1921 did the Red Army, by employing methods borrowed from the world war, including the use of chemical weapons, manage to suppress the insurgency.

In the cities, too, war brought economic collapse and political opposition. The labor unrest that had helped to bring down the old regime continued as the Civil War exacerbated the problems caused by the world war: inflation, shortages of the fuel and materials needed to keep factories running, unemployment, and, most explosive of all, near famine conditions in many cities. The violent repression of hungry housewives and workers demanding bread, as occurred in early May 1918 in Kolpino, a suburb of Petrograd, became more common, and workers responded with increasing numbers of strikes demanding both economic and political reform. Workers also left the cities in droves to join the Red Army or to return to the countryside in search of food, threatening to make the Bolsheviks, as Shliapnikov quipped in 1921, the "vanguard of a nonexistent class."

Most threatening from the Bolshevik perspective was a mutiny in early 1921 at the Kronstadt naval base near Petrograd, long a Bolshevik stronghold. Just days before the Tenth Party Congress met in Moscow, the sailors at Kronstadt, an island fortress in the Gulf of Finland, went into open rebellion, calling for a Soviet government without Bolsheviks. The sailors' demands included freedom of speech and assembly; the release of all socialist and working class political prisoners; equal rations for all workers, with no privileged access for communists; and the end of grain requisitioning. Arresting and imprisoning the Bolshevik leaders of the local soviet, the sailors took control of the island. The Bolshevik leadership responded, as they did to the peasant insurgencies, with overwhelming force. The Red Army shelled the base from Petrograd, and Trotsky assembled a force of 45,000 to assault Kronstadt across the frozen gulf. By mid-March, the Red Army had crushed the rebellion, at the cost of hundreds of lives. The incident can be understood in terms of the Bolsheviks' declining trust in workers' ability to build socialism, as the sailors demanded an end to Bolshevik "guidance" and the Bolsheviks forcefully asserted their right to "discipline" and "lead" the masses.

Initially, many Bolsheviks proposed responding to dire economic conditions, as they did to rebellion, with the tools that seemed to have won the war: militarization, centralization, and regimentation. For them, the Civil War was a "formative experience"[33] that made certain sorts of responses to circumstances seem particularly feasible or desirable. Trotsky, a primary proponent of militarized socialism, proposed the victorious Red Army as a model for other Soviet institutions. Together with Lenin he endorsed replacing workers' control with one-person management in industry (largely nationalized by summer 1918) and expanding the use of technical (bourgeois) "specialists." In September 1920, enthusiasm for the "militarization of labor" reached its peak with the Ninth Party Congress's endorsement of the conversion of military units into labor armies (engaged in industries such as mining and shipbuilding) and the application of military discipline to industrial and railroad workers.

Ultimately, however, the Bolsheviks retreated from the decision to respond to the economic collapse that followed the Civil War by extending wartime policies. Having put down rebellions by force, the Bolsheviks took the arguably pragmatic step of making peace with the peasants. The New Economic Policy (NEP), proposed by Lenin at the Tenth Party Congress while the Kronstadt rebellion was still in progress, ended forced grain requisitions, replacing the hated centrally determined collection targets with a tax in kind. NEP also eased restrictions on private trade and permitted small scale private enterprise and manufacturing, although the state retained control of the "commanding heights" of heavy industry. Lenin disavowed the policies he now termed "war communism," arguing that "so long as there is no revolution in other countries, only agreement with the peasantry can save the socialist revolution in Russia."[34] Bukharin, who three years earlier had led the opposition to peace with Germany on ideological grounds, now emerged as an enthusiastic proponent of NEP, often called the "peasant Brest." Lenin called it a "breathing space" and a "strategic retreat" without specifying how long it might last.

The congress did not, however, make any concessions to more explicitly ideological opposition: the condemnation of regimentation and militarization as inimical to the revolution's promise of workers' empowerment. Led by Shliapnikov, the former commissar of labor, and Alexandra Kollontai, a woman of noble birth who had gravitated toward Marxism in the late 1890s and who is best known for her advocacy of women's emancipation (see chapter 4), the Workers' Opposition called for a return to the original emancipatory goals of October—communism made by and for the workers themselves—and rejected the party leaders' fixation on discipline and productivity. At the congress, the Workers' Opposition lost both its case for workers' control of industry and the right to challenge the party leadership. Concessions to the peasantry were thus accompanied by a renewed emphasis on the party's role as leader, organizer, and educator of the toiling masses and a rejection of the vision of self-activated workers as agents of revolution.

The ban on factions became a deadly political weapon only in the 1930s. For the moment, it diminished but did not eliminate opposition within the party. Shliapnikov, who viewed NEP as giving too little attention to industrial development, continued to participate in opposition groups, eventually siding with Stalin's opponents. In 1935, he was arrested in one of the first waves of the Stalinist terror; he was shot in 1937.[35]

NEP: "breathing space" or betrayal?

Advocating the New Economic Policy turned out to be Lenin's last major political act. In May 1922, he suffered the first of a series of debilitating strokes that largely sidelined him until his death in 1924. Lenin's prestige was such that there was no question but that the congress would approve NEP. Few doubted that, given the reality of economic collapse and widespread armed rebellion, some kind of change was necessary. But few shared Bukharin's enthusiasm for the new policy, and even Lenin himself was ambivalent, sometimes suggesting, as he did at the Eleventh Party Congress in 1922, that perhaps the retreat had gone too far, sometimes arguing, as he did in brief notes written in early 1923, that NEP offered a gradual path to socialism. Thus the succession struggle that began even before Lenin's death in 1924 and ended six years later with Stalin's ascendancy was both an often nasty and personal battle for power and a contest over how best to build a modern socialist order.

In the countryside, NEP did not offer immediate relief. On the contrary, a massive famine centered on the Volga basin gripped the country by mid-1921, the result of drought and three years of policies that had given the peasants little incentive to produce more grain. In the spirit of moderation and compromise that marked NEP, the state permitted novelist Maxim Gorky to appeal for foreign aid. The American Relief Administration led by Herbert Hoover fed millions; nonetheless, perhaps five million people died of starvation and disease. The famine also exacerbated the problem of homeless and abandoned children (*besprizorniki*), who by 1922 numbered close to seven million (see chapter 4).

By 1923, agricultural production had recovered, but industrial production lagged. Thus although NEP allowed a free market in grain, peasants could find few manu-factured goods—and those at high prices—for which to exchange their produce. Unsurprisingly, peasants began withholding their grain from the market. In line with the new commitment to a truce with the peasants, the state intervened to lower prices of manufactured goods in order to close the gap that opened—like a pair of scissors—between the rising prices of manufactured goods and the price of agricultural goods.

Although welcomed by peasant producers, closing the "scissors crisis" meant cost cutting, layoffs, and higher bread prices for industrial workers. From the perspective of workers and many rank-and-file party members, especially those for whom the Civil War had been a formative experience, the policy benefited only the *kulaks* (rich peasants) and the burzhui or NEP men (entrepreneurs involved in trade and small manufacturing) whom the workers' revolution had aimed to expropriate. They joked bitterly that NEP stood for "New Exploitation of the Proletariat." For many the ostentatious return of the market, jazz cafes, and fashionably dressed NEP men and women was a betrayal of revolutionary dreams and sacrifices.

CONCLUSION AND FURTHER QUESTIONS

A decade after 1917, the Soviet state was a long way from the "socialist order" Lenin had promised to build at once. The practical needs of establishing and consolidating power and of winning a brutal civil war seemed to rule out the vision that Lenin had offered in "State and Revolution" of a socialist future in which workers with basic skills in reading and math managed an advanced economy. But was the program of "war communism," with its militarized, authoritarian approach to economic and political problems—state control of trade and industry, suppression of newspapers, and political terror—notably more practical? If it was "utopian" for "State and Revolution" to suggest that the socialist order would emerge spontaneously from the ruins of the old world, was it any less utopian to believe that the socialist order could be built through force, expertise, and strict discipline?

Arguably NEP, with its emphasis on slow, consumer-centered growth and its efforts to make peace with the peasants, offered a more "practical" route to the socialist future. Such, in any case, was the argument made by the so-called rightists, most prominently Bukharin, who agreed with leftists such as Trotsky that a modern socialist state had to industrialize but rejected Trotsky's idea of "primitive socialist accumul-ation," that is the policy of exploiting the peasants (through taxes, not forced collectivization) in order to raise funds for industrialization. Instead, Bukharin argued that the way to accumulate capital for industrial investment was by encouraging the peasants to "enrich" themselves.[36] Yet the rightists' ostensibly pragmatic solutions had little appeal for people who joined the party during the Civil War and who equated building the socialist order with militarized and "heroic" action against class enemies. We are left with the question: To what extent did the methods of mobilization developed and employed during the war shape later Soviet institutions and practices?

PRIMARY SOURCES

Use the questions to analyze the content, context, and significance of each primary source. Then synthesize the primary sources and the material in the chapter to formulate a response to the primary chapter questions: What was "the socialist order" to look like, and how did one go about constructing it? Could workers be trusted to build socialism or did they need to be disciplined and guided by the party?

Document 3.1   Vladimir Lenin, "The State and Revolution" (1917)

Questions for analysis

1   What are the most striking or surprising aspects of Lenin's vision of the "workers' state"?
2   Why does Lenin emphasize so strongly that the Bolsheviks are not "utopians"? What about the conditions in 1917 might have made this plan seem practical? To what extent is it shaped by Marxist ideology?

We are not utopians, we do not "dream" of dispensing *at once* with all administration, all subordination. These anarchist dreams, based upon incomprehension of the tasks of the proletarian dictatorship, are totally alien to Marxism, and, as a matter of fact, serve only to postpone the socialist revolution until people are different. No, we want the socialist revolution with people as they are now, with people who cannot dispense with subordination, control and "foremen and accounts."

The subordination, however, must be to the armed vanguard of all the exploited working people, i.e., to the proletariat. A beginning can and must be made at once, overnight, to replace the specific "bossing" of state officials by the simple functions of "foremen and accountants," functions which are already fully within the ability of the average town dweller and can well be performed for "workmen's wages."

. . . A witty German Social-Democrat of the seventies of the last century called the *postal service* an example of the socialist economic system. This is very true. At present the postal service is a business organized on the lines of a state-*capitalist* monopoly. Imperialism is gradually transforming all trusts into organizations of a similar type, in which, standing over the "common" people, who are overworked and starved, one has the same bourgeois bureaucracy. But the mechanism of social management is already to hand. Once we have overthrown the capitalists, crushed the resistance of these exploiters with the iron hand of armed workers, and smashed the bureaucratic machine of the modern state, we shall have a splendidly-equipped mechanism, free from the "parasite," a mechanism which can very well be set going by the united workers themselves, who will hire technicians, foremen, and accountants, and pay them *all*, as indeed *all* "state" officials in general, workmen's wages. Here is a concrete, practical task which can immediately be fulfilled in relation to all trusts, a task whose fulfillment will rid the working people of exploitation, a task which takes account of what the [Paris] Commune had already begun to practice (particularly in building up the state).

To organize the *whole* economy on the lines of the postal service so that the technicians, foremen and accountants, as well as *all* officials, shall receive salaries no higher than "a workmen's wage," all under the control and leadership of the armed proletariat—this is our immediate aim. This is the state and this is the economic foundation we need. This is what will bring about the abolition of parliamentarism and the preservation of representative institutions. This is what will rid the laboring classes of the bourgeoisie's prostitution of those institutions.

Source: Vladimir Lenin, "The State and Revolution," in Robert C. Tucker, ed., *The Lenin Anthology* (New York: W. W. Norton, 1975), 344–346. Copyright © 1975 W.W. Norton & Company, Inc. Used by permission of W.W. Norton & Company, Inc.

Document 3.2   Decree on the Suppression of Hostile Newspapers, 27 October [9 November] 1917

Questions for analysis

1   How did the decree justify the control of the press?
2   In what ways and to what degree does this decree respond to circumstances? To what degree to ideology?

In the serious decisive hour of the revolution and the days immediately following it the Military-Revolutionary Committee was compelled to adopt a whole series of measures against the counterrevolutionary press of all shades.

Immediately on all sides cries arose that the new socialistic authority was violating in this way the essential principles of its program by an attempt against the freedom of the press.

The Workers' and Soldiers' Government draws the attention of the population to the fact that in our country behind this liberal shield there is practically hidden the liberty for the richer classes to seize into their hands the lion's share of the whole press and by this means to poison the minds and bring confusion into the consciousness of the masses.

Everyone knows that the bourgeois press is one of the most powerful weapons of the bourgeoisie. Especially in this critical moment when the new authority, that of the workers and peasants, is in the process of consolidation, it was impossible to leave this weapon in the hands of the enemy at a time when it is not less dangerous than bombs and machine guns. This is why temporary and extraordinary measures have been adopted for the purpose of cutting off the stream of mire and calumny in which the yellow and green press would be glad to drown the young victory of the people.

As soon as the new order will be consolidated, all administrative measures against the press will be suspended; full liberty will be given with the limits of responsibility before the laws, in accordance with the broadest and most progressive regulations in this respect.

... General rules on the press.

1   The following organs of the press shall be closed: (a) those inciting to open resistance or disobedience towards the Workers' and Peasants' Government; (b) those sowing confusion by means of an obviously calumniatory perversion of facts; (c) those inciting to acts of a criminal character punishable by the penal laws.
2   The temporary or permanent closing of any organ of the press shall be carried out only by a resolution of the Council of People's Commissaries.

3   The present decree is of a temporary nature and will be revoked by special *ukaz* when the normal conditions of public life will be reestablished.

Chairman of the Council of People's Commissars
  Vladimir Ulianov (Lenin)

Source: "Decree on Suppression of Hostile Newspapers," in Robert V. Daniels, ed., *A Documentary History of Communism in Russia: From Lenin to Gorbachev* (Lebanon, NH: University Press of New England, 1993), 65–66.

Document 3.3   Socialist Revolutionary response to Treaty of Brest-Litovsk, May 1918

Questions for analysis

1   On what basis did the Socialist Revolutionaries oppose the Bolsheviks?
2   How did they define "revolution"? How did they imagine the socialist future?

The complete capitulation of Bolshevism in the face of German imperialism nullifies not only the conquests of the revolution. It also simply turns the peoples of Russia over to the victor for looting. The peace accepted by the Council of People's Commissars destroys the independence of the Russian republic and may lead, in the present international situation, to its simple partition by the great powers . . . Taking the point of view of class, fighting for the interests of the toilers, defending the principles of progress, peaceful coexistence and intercourse between nations and their cultures, the PSR [Party of Socialist Revolutionaries] is obliged unswervingly and decisively to strive for the destruction of the agreement between the Council of People's Commissars and the German coalition and to organize resistance to the plundering of Russia and the possessions of its peoples. The slogan, "the Defense of the Country," designating simultaneously the defense of the revolution, is at the present time the most fundamental slogan of our political activity and should become our most effective slogan. The defense of democratic Russia against enslavement by international imperialism is at the same time a struggle for the International [organization of socialist parties] against bourgeois reaction, for labor against its full subordination to capital, for the freedom of nations against militarism, for the principles of revolution against international reaction, and for culture against barbarism.

Source: Scott B. Smith, *Captives of Revolution: The Socialist Revolutionaries and the Bolshevik Dictatorship* (Pittsburgh, PA: University of Pittsburgh Press, 2011), 37. Used by permission of University of Pittsburgh Press.

Document 3.4   Zinaida Patrikeeva recalls her time as a "cavalry boy" in the Red Army during the Civil War, 1938

Questions for analysis

1   How does Patrikeeva characterize the relationship between the Red fighters and the peasants? In what ways and to what extent do the peasants support the revolution?

2   What seem to be her primary motivations for fighting?
3   What does her story (published in 1938) suggest about visions of the socialist future?

In this excerpt, Patrikeeva describes events in 1918 after she fled Ekaterinoslav (present day Dnepropetrovsk) with a group of men from the factory where she worked, escaping the advancing Ukrainian nationalist army.

Tired and hungry, we reached the next village and asked the peasants for something to eat. They asked us: "Are you Bolsheviks or Whites?"—"We are for the Bolsheviks, and we are running away from the Whites."

Then they gave us some cabbage and potatoes. The peasants did not have any bread. We walked like this for many days, obtaining food in the villages. The peasants often stopped me: "What are you doing with them, young lady?" They would invite me to stay with them. But I would refuse and continue eastward with my detachment.

At one point we met up with another partisan group like ours. We joined forces and continued on to the Donbass. They were also from Ekaterinoslav. Their leader was an old Bolshevik, a foreman of the Rupaner factory. He treated me as if I were his own daughter. Seeing that I could stand any privation and was not afraid of partisan life, he started giving me serious assignments. Every time we would approach a village, the commander would send me first: "Go and find out who's there. But be very careful." So I would enter the village, find out everything we needed to know, and come back with a report.

At that time I was still wearing a skirt—the wide peasant kind. I must have looked strange to the peasants—they were not used to seeing women fighters. Some of them would laugh at me, while others said: "Don't go with them, you'll be killed. Stay here with us. That's a man's job, not a woman's." I never answered. I would just spur my horse and gallop ahead, to catch up with my comrades.

[Patrikeeva's group eventually joined the famed cavalry commander Semen Budenny's detachment. Budenny saw to it that she received a better horse, and reproached the men:]

"What, you think that just because she's a woman you can give her the worst mare? Don't think of her as a woman—think of her as your comrade-in-arms." . . .

Right then and there they brought me a wonderful horse—black, tall, fast, and well-saddled. I mounted my new horse and became not Zina, but the fighter Zinovy. I cut my wide skirt up the middle, sewed on some buttons, and made something resembling pants, an outfit convenient for riding a horse. I was also given a greatcoat, a tall sheepskin hat, and boots. After that I looked like a cavalry boy, a fighter during battle and a sister of mercy afterward . . .

I was given a Maxim machine gun. I attached it to my saddle and always carried it with me. As soon as the fighting began, I would dismount and shower those White bastards with bullets.

Source: Sheila Fitzpatrick and Yuri Slezkine, eds., *In the Shadow of Revolution: Life Stories of Russian Women from 1917 to the Second World War* (Princeton, NJ: Princeton University Press, 2000), 119–121. Used by permission of Princeton University Press.

Notes

1 John Reed, *Ten Days That Shook the World* (1919; reprint, New York: Bantam, 1987), 93.
2 Vladimir Lenin, "The State and Revolution," in Robert C. Tucker, ed., *The Lenin Anthology* (New York: W. W. Norton, 1975), 343, 345, 341, 383, 374.
3 Robert V. Daniels, "The State and Revolution: A Case Study in the Genesis and Transformation of Communist Ideology," *American Slavic and East European Review*, 12, no. 1 (February 1953): 22–43; Rodney Barfield, "Lenin's Utopianism: State and Revolution," *Slavic Review*, 30, no. 1 (March 1971): 45–56; Alfred B. Evans, "Rereading Lenin's *State and Revolution*," *Slavic Review*, 46, no. 1 (Spring 1987): 1–19; Mel Rothenberg, "Lenin and the State," *Science & Society*, 59, no. 3 (Fall 1995): 418–36.
4 Lenin, *State and Revolution*, 328, original emphasis.
5 Leon Trotsky, *History of the Russian Revolution*, trans. Max Eastman (1932; reprint, Chicago, IL: Haymarket Books, 2008), 846, 849, 843, 845.
6 "Second All-Russian Congress of Soviets, Decree on Peace," 8 November (26 October) 1917, available at www.marxists.org/archive/lenin/works/1917/oct/25-26/26b.htm (accessed 18 December 2015).
7 As quoted in Adam B. Ulam, *Expansion and Coexistence: Soviet Foreign Policy, 1917–73*, 2nd ed. (New York: Praeger, 1974), 83.
8 Lara Cook, "Collegiality in the People's Commissariats, 1917–1920," *Revolutionary Russia*, 26, no. 1 (2013): 10–18.
9 "Decree on Establishment of the Extraordinary Commission to Fight Counter-Revolution," 8 (20) December 1917, in Robert V. Daniels, ed., *A Documentary History of Communism in Russia: From Lenin to Gorbachev* (Lebanon, NH: University Press of New England, 1993).
10 "Order for Intensified Red Terror," 4 September 1918, in William Henry Chamberlin, *The Russian Revolution, Volume II: 1918–21* (1935; Princeton, NJ: Princeton University Press, 1987), 475–476.
11 Scott B. Smith, *Captives of Revolution: The Socialist Revolutionaries and the Bolshevik Dictatorship* (Pittsburgh, PA: University of Pittsburgh Press, 2011), 11.
12 Smith, *Captives*, 13; Boris I. Kolonitskii, "Antibourgeois Propaganda and Anti-'Burzhi' Consciousness in 1917," trans. Kurt S. Schultz, *Russian Review*, 53 (April 1994): 195.
13 As quoted in Smith, *Captives*, 13.
14 "The Socialist Fatherland Is in Danger," *Pravda*, 21 February 1918, available at www.marxists.org/archive/lenin/works/1918/feb/21b.htm (slight changes in translation; accessed 7 January 2016).
15 As quoted in E. H. Carr, *The Bolshevik Revolution, 1917–1923* (1953; reprint, New York: W. W. Norton, 1985), vol. 3, 46.
16 As quoted in Carr, *Bolshevik Revolution*, 56.
17 "The Socialist Revolutionaries of the Left Repudiate Ratification," in James Bunyan and Harold Henry Fischer, eds., *The Bolshevik Revolution, 1917–1918: Documents and Materials* (Stanford, CA: Stanford University Press, 1934), 533.
18 Peter Holquist, *Making War, Forging Revolution: Russia's Continuum of Crisis, 1914–1921* (Cambridge, MA: Harvard University Press, 2002), 143. Also, Vladimir N. Brovkin, ed., *The Bolsheviks in Russian Society: The Revolution and Civil Wars* (New Haven, CT: Yale University Press, 1997); Jonathan D. Smele, *Civil War in Siberia: The Anti-Bolshevik Government of Admiral Kolchak, 1918–1920* (New York: Cambridge University Press, 1996), 1.
19 Scott, *Captives*, xvi.
20 "Uchreditel'noe sobranie," Image ID: 1216219, New York Public Library Collection of Russian and Ukrainian posters, 1917–1921, digitalgallery.nypl.org.
21 As quoted in Leonid Heretz, "The Psychology of the White Movement," in Brovkin, ed., *The Bolsheviks*, 111.
22 As quoted in Lisa A. Kirschenbaum, "Scripting the Revolution: Regicide in Russia," *Left History*, 7, no. 2 (2000): 29.
23 Heretz, "Psychology," 115, 116.

24 Oleg Budnitskii, *Russian Jews between the Reds and Whites, 1917–1920*, trans. Timothy J. Portice (Philadelphia: University of Pennsylvania Press, 2012), 218; Stephen Brown, "Communists and the Red Cavalry: The Political Education of the *Konarmiia* in the Russian Civil War, 1918–20," *Slavonic and East European Review*, 73, no. 1 (January 1995): 85–88; Peter Kenez, "Pogroms and White Ideology in the Russian Civil War," in John D. Klier and Shlomo Lambroza, eds., *Pogroms: Anti-Jewish Violence in Modern Russian History* (New York: Cambridge University Press, 1992), 294.

25 Oleg Budnitskii, "Jews, Pogroms, and the White Movement: A Historiographical Critique," trans. Eugene Budnitsky, *Kritika*, 2, no. 4 (Fall 2001): 751.

26 Kenez, "Pogroms," 293, 310.

27 Budnitskii, *Russian Jews*, 225; Eric Lohr, "The Russian Army and the Jews: Mass Deportation, Hostages, and Violence during World War I," *Russian Review*, 60, no. 3 (July 2001): 406, 415–416.

28 Peter Holquist, "Violent Russia, Deadly Marxism? Russia in the Epoch of Violence, 1905–21," *Kritika*, 4, no. 3 (Summer 2003): 640, 651.

29 Richard Stites, *The Women's Liberation Movement in Russia: Feminism, Nihilism, and Bolshevism, 1860–1930* (Princeton, NJ: Princeton University Press, 1978), 317–322.

30 Orlando Figes, "The Red Army and Mass Mobilization during the Russian Civil War, 1918–1920," *Past and Present*, no. 129 (November 1990): 173.

31 Mark von Hagen, "Civil–Military Relations and the Evolution of the Soviet Socialist State," *Slavic Review*, 50, no. 2 (Summer 1991): 271.

32 Erik-C. Landis, "Waiting for Makhno: Legitimacy and Context in a Russia Peasant War," *Past and Present*, no. 183 (May 2004): 208, 213, 214.

33 Sheila Fitzpatrick, "The Civil War as Formative Experience," in Abbott Gleason, Peter Kenez, and Richard Stites, eds., *Bolshevik Culture: Experiment and Order in the Russian Revolution* (Bloomington: Indiana University Press, 1985), 57–76.

34 Quoted in John Eric Marot, *The October Revolution in Prospect and Retrospect: Interventions in Russian and Soviet History* (Leiden: Brill, 2012), 36.

35 On Kollontai and Shliapnikov's relationship, see Barbara Allen, "'A Proletarian from a Novel': Politics, Identity, and Emotion in the Relationship between Alexander Shliapnikov and Alexandra Kollontai, 1911–1935," *Soviet and Post-Soviet Review*, 35, no. 2 (2008): 163–191.

36 As quoted in Robert Conquest, *Harvest of Sorrow: Soviet Collectivization and the Terror-Famine* (New York: Oxford University Press, 1986), 64.

4 Making a new world and new people

INTRODUCTION

To celebrate International Women's Day on 8 March 1927, women throughout Uzbekistan participated in a dramatic public mass unveiling. Thousands of Muslim women tore off their paranji (the body-length horsehair and cotton garment Uzbek and Tajik women were expected to wear in public) and tossed them into bonfires. Although the organizers from the Women's Department of the Communist Party (Zhenotdel) were mainly Russian, Jewish, and Ukrainian newcomers to Central Asia, the *hujum* (attack) on patriarchy won the support of a small but influential indigenous urban elite, who even before the revolution had supported reforms aimed at ending women's seclusion. Rahbar-oi Olimova, an Uzbek woman (born in 1908) who unveiled on Women's Day in Tashkent, recalled both how difficult it was to do with "everyone" watching and how "happy" the act of liberation made her.[1]

The *hujum* was part of the Bolsheviks' larger effort to revolutionize everyday life (*byt*) and create a New Soviet Person. While the campaign against the veil was specific to Central Asia, it resembled other Bolshevik projects to "civilize," "modernize," and "liberate" the oppressed and "backward" masses—variously represented as workers, peasants, women, children, and national minorities. The Bolsheviks understood the modern, socialist order as necessitating and creating a new everyday life (*novyi byt*) in every detail, remaking family and sexual relationships, living arrangements, leisure time, even fashion, "right down to the last button on your vest," as Vladimir Mayakovsky promised in his 1917 poem "Revolution." Fedor Panferov, a younger and more traditional writer than Mayakovsky, imagined the glorious future in terms of the destruction of *meshchansky byt*, a phrase which might be rendered as "petty-bourgeois everyday life," but that in Russian carries more negative connotations. His list of petty-bourgeois practices and idols to be thrown off the ship of revolution included "official marriage, weddings, christenings, curtains (especially lace curtains), carpets, irons and so on."[2]

Such projects, as Rahbar-oi's enthusiasm for unveiling suggests, might appeal to the people that the Bolsheviks were seeking to emancipate and uplift. They could also generate resistance. In Central Asia, the backlash against unveiled women was massive and violent. Thousands of women who removed their veils in the main years of the campaign, 1927–1929, were murdered, raped, and mutilated, sometimes by local men in the party. Historians have understood this violence both as a brutal means of restoring patriarchal authority (akin to lynching as a means of enforcing racial hierarchy in the US) and as anticolonial resistance to the imposition of the foreign, atheistic norms.[3] In any case, such violence suggests the importance of Bolshevik efforts to revolutionize everyday life.

CHAPTER QUESTIONS

Focusing on what historians often describe as the most "utopian" of early Soviet projects—making world revolution; emancipating national minorities; remaking gender, family, and private life; and raising the children of October—this chapter asks: How did diverse understandings of the "revolution" shape Bolshevik policy? Were Bolshevik efforts to revolutionize everyday life primarily focused on "liberation" or "modernization" and "enlightenment"? Could these aims be reconciled? While all of these projects arguably required more resources than the Soviet state could muster, were they necessarily "utopian"? Or is it possible to see something "pragmatic" in efforts to take the first step to the new world?

VOICES, MEMORIES, CONTESTED PERSPECTIVES

World revolution: ideology and state interest

When the Bolsheviks seized power in October 1917, they understood their revolution as the spark that would set off socialist revolution throughout Europe and eventually the world. As noted in chapter 3, they counted on revolutions in more "advanced" countries to guarantee the success of revolution in "backward," largely peasant Russia. For the Bolsheviks, this sense of impending world revolution was not mere wishful thinking; it drew on Vladimir Lenin's analysis of imperialism as the "highest stage of capitalism," a system of international capitalist rivalries destined to breed wars and ultimately revolutions (see document 4.1). The revolution had begun in Russia—a weak link in the international capitalist system—but, the Bolsheviks were sure, it must soon spread. When, at the end of World War I, revolution erupted in Germany, Lenin enthused that "the international revolution has come so close in *one week* that it has to be reckoned with as an event of the *next few days*," and he urged the immediate organization of military aid to German workers.[4]

Historians have understood early Soviet engagement with the world as driven both by an ideological commitment to world revolution and by a pragmatic effort to preserve a revolutionary state in a hostile, capitalist world—an effort for which Marxist ideology provided little guidance. In some cases, as during the so-called Red Years of 1917 to 1920, the two goals seemed to overlap and reinforce one another. After 1920, the relationship between ideology and the practical interests of the Soviet state became more complicated. Promoting revolution was largely incompatible with the NEP policy of developing commercial relationships with capitalist states. Why, then, even as the prospects of revolution dimmed, did the Soviet state maintain, at least sporadically, its support of world revolution? This is a question that returned in the post-World War II period, when decolonization and the Cold War revived hopes of world revolution.

In the first years after October 1917, Germany stood at the center of Bolshevik hopes for world revolution. The November 1918 revolution that had so excited Lenin failed to produce the international revolution he expected. Instead it brought to power a government of moderate socialists who, far from supporting the cause of revolution, cooperated in the suppression of an uprising in January 1919 that aimed to establish a soviet republic in Germany. Communists blamed the socialists for the murder of the uprising's leaders, Rosa Luxemburg and Karl Liebknecht. However, even this grim result did not prompt the Bolsheviks to abandon the allegedly scientific certainty of world revolution.

In March 1919, the conviction that the revolution in Russia constituted the prelude to international socialist revolution took the institutional form of the Third or Communist International (Comintern). In the Soviet press, the Comintern's founding congress in Moscow overshadowed the second anniversary of the February Revolution and the fall of the tsar. It was, however, a rather unassuming affair. Only nine of the fifty-one delegates had managed to breach the Allied blockade; the rest were already resident in Russia, and most lacked credentials from their home parties. These largely self-designated representatives of the revolutionary proletariat met, as the French delegate Jacques Sadoul remembered, in one of the Kremlin's "most modest" halls, which had been outfitted with "flimsy chairs," "rickety tables obviously borrowed from some café," and heaters that "blew terrible gusts of frigid air" at the shivering delegates. Such, Sadoul noted, were the "inconveniences" of "Soviet life."[5]

While Sadoul's account can be understood as highlighting the contrast between grand Bolshevik aims and miserable Soviet realities, neither the material hardships nor the lack of representatives from beyond Soviet Russia tempered the congress's revolutionary optimism. The Manifesto written by Lev Trotsky and adopted by the congress proclaimed the Comintern "the International of revolutionary realization, the International of the deed," which had already won the "first great victories" in the struggle to overthrow "bourgeois world order" and to erect "in its place the edifice of the socialist order."[6]

In the spring of 1919, revolutions in Munich and Budapest, the only places outside of Russia where workers' councils (soviets) briefly held power, seemed to validate the First Comintern Congress's predictions of world revolution. However, by August the revolutions in both places had collapsed amid substantial violence and bloodshed. These failures led to a rethinking of the best means of making revolution, but not to an abandonment of the conviction that world revolution was both necessary and likely. In advance of the Second Comintern Congress, which was held in the summer of 1920, Lenin emphasized the "historical inevitability of a repetition, on an international scale, of what has taken place in our country."[7]

The more than two hundred delegates from thirty-seven countries who attended the second congress met in Moscow as the Red Army's drive into Poland renewed expectations of imminent world revolution. What had begun in April 1920 as a Polish invasion of Ukraine had by June turned into a Soviet advance that Lenin hoped would not only deter the Western powers from attacking Russia through Poland but also spark a revolution there which might spread to Germany. In Germany, communists "were actively learning Russian, and were even designing welcoming banners."[8] As it turned out, the Poles stopped the Red Army outside of Warsaw in August, and the 1921 Treaty of Riga transferred much territory in Belorussia and Ukraine to the new Polish state. But during the Comintern congress, hopes of world revolution once again ran high.

The setbacks of 1919, along with the apparent triumphs of 1920, strengthened the belief that Bolshevik tactics—a violent uprising coordinated by a disciplined, militarized, centralized party—constituted a tested and effective route to revolution. This conviction led the congress to adopt the "twenty-one conditions" for membership in the Comintern. The conditions explicitly required national parties to follow the Bolshevik model, to become "chemically pure Bolshevik parties overnight."[9] Any party "wishing to join the Communist International" had to "consistently and systematically remove reformists and centrists from all positions of any responsibility in the workers' movement."[10] Such directives often stripped would-be member parties of many of their best cadres. Moreover, the rules enshrined the special status of the Soviet state, as they required member parties to abide by the decisions of the (Soviet-dominated) executive committee. But many foreign communists eager to follow the Soviet example welcomed such control. Agents and gold dispatched from Moscow also constituted important means of enforcing the Comintern line and, when circumstances appeared ripe, instigating local uprisings. Thus in 1921 Comintern emissaries promoted the so-called March Action, an armed insurrection in Germany—an uprising that ended in complete defeat.

The failure of the March Action, coupled with the implementation of NEP and the signing of the first Soviet commercial deal with a major capitalist state—the Anglo-Soviet trade agreement (see document 4.3)—suggest that 1921 marked a key watershed in the Bolsheviks' turn away from revolution as the best means of ensuring the future of the Soviet state. In 1922, the Treaty of Rapallo gave the German military (which had been severely limited by the Treaty of Versailles) access to bases in Russia, allowed the exchange of military plans and instructors, and opened the way for German arms manufacturers to build factories in Soviet Russia, with the output shared by the two states. It seemed to some contemporary observers that in the cold light of NEP the "policy of world-revolution began to reveal itself not only as a failure, but as an embarrassment to the Soviet state."[11] Increasingly the leadership counted not on revolution but on agreements with capitalist powers as the best means of defending revolutionary gains in Russia. From this perspective, the Bolsheviks, for all their utopian dreams, were ultimately realists.

But if the retreat from a program of world revolution constituted part of a "pragmatic" effort to rebuild the Soviet economy, it was also partial and contested, at least when "revolutionary" circumstances presented themselves. The Russian leaders of the Comintern saw just such a revolutionary opportunity in 1923, when the French and Belgian occupation of the Ruhr, a response to Germany's failure to make the reparations payments demanded by the Treaty of Versailles, produced an economic and political crisis in the Weimar Republic. Hopes again ran high for a "German October." The Soviet government initially supported the German government against the occupation, but ultimately encouraged a communist bid to take power. Once again, the revolution failed to materialize. It took two days for police and army units to put down a poorly coordinated and poorly armed rebellion in Hamburg.

The failed 1923 uprising in Germany came in the last months of Lenin's life. It immediately became entangled in the struggle to succeed Lenin, who had suffered a series of debilitating strokes in 1922 and 1923; a massive stroke ended his life in January 1924. This struggle was both about power, as personal rivals maneuvered against one another, and about how to build the socialist order, as the leadership debated industrial policy (chapter 3) and the prospects and need for world revolution.

Stalin apparently drew the conclusion that the Soviet state did not need to rely on assistance from revolutions in advanced countries. In a May 1925 article in *Pravda*, he advanced the controversial idea of "socialism in one country," arguing that a "complete socialist society" could be constructed in isolated, peasant Russia even in the absence of world revolution. At the same time, Stalin affirmed that the ultimate goal was not socialism in Russia alone; only when capitalist encirclement was replaced by "socialist encirclement"—a term he left vague but that suggested the global spread of revolution—could the final victory be assured.[12]

Even as the idea of "socialism in one country" gained adherents, world revolution remained for many Bolsheviks an article of faith. Speaking at the Fifth Comintern Congress in June 1924, Grigory Zinoviev, the head of the Comintern, empathized with his audience's frustrations: "We are all dissatisfied . . . We expected the German Revolution: it failed to come. Sometimes one gets the feeling that it is a wretchedly slow process." "But," he assured the delegates, "objectively speaking, I believe that the march of events really is not so slow. It is said that when a fly is sitting on a large mill-wheel and the wheel is turning very rapidly, the fly feels as though the wheel is standing still. The same is true with us. The wheel of world history is turning very rapidly."[13]

After 1923, as revolution in the West came to seem a more remote possibility, many Bolsheviks concluded that the best hopes of revolution lay in the East. There the Bolsheviks imagined revolutions more like their own, attacks on the weak links of the imperialist system that would catalyze revolution in the more advanced states. The most serious effort to support a national liberation movement against Western imperialism occurred in China. The Comintern directed the Chinese Communist Party, founded in 1921, to form a united front with Sun Yat-sen's Nationalists. Despite the misgivings of local communists, the Comintern supported the policy of subordinating socialist revolution to national independence and sent the Nationalists thousands of military and political advisors. However, in 1927 Sun's successor, Chiang Kai-shek, turned on his erstwhile partners, massacring communist cadres in the streets of Shanghai. (In 1934, still under attack by Chiang's troops, communists led by Mao Zedong undertook the Long March to a remote base in northwest China, from which a larger, reinvigorated, more rural party emerged.)

The debacle in China, like the failure of the German uprising in 1923, quickly became an issue in the struggle to succeed Lenin. It contributed to a war scare in 1927 that was also fed by the British government's decision to break diplomatic relations with the Soviet Union (in part over Comintern meddling in areas of British colonial interest), the assassination of a Soviet minister in Warsaw, and the collapse of trade negotiations with the French. The threat of war, dramatically played up in the Soviet press, became a powerful weapon in Stalin's attack on Trotsky, whom he accused of undermining the unity of the Soviet state. The war scare may also have added to the appeal of Stalin's idea of building "socialism in one country" as the best means of strengthening Soviet defenses and controlling potentially unreliable peasants.[14] But the outcome in China did not sour the mood of the Comintern, now led by Stalin's new ally Nikolai Bukharin, on world revolution; indeed the "Theses on the Revolutionary Movement in the Colonial and Semi-Colonial Countries" adopted at the Comintern's Sixth Congress in 1928 called on communists in China to begin "preparing for and carrying through armed insurrection as the only way to . . . overthrow the power of the imperialists, landlords, and national-bourgeoisie."[15]

Throughout the 1920s, hopes for world revolution were closely tied to efforts to revolutionize life at home. "Socialism in one country" became party orthodoxy only at the end of the decade in the wake of Stalin's defeat of "the left." Before that, many Bolshevik leaders believed that only world revolution would ensure the success of the revolution in "backward" Russia. As hopes for revolution in the West faded, Soviet efforts to revolutionize their own "East"—Central Asia, Siberia, the Caucasus—with policies such as the *hujum* potentially offered a means of appealing to revolutionaries in the colonized world.

Anti-imperialism and the Soviet empire

The Bolsheviks had long understood the "national and colonial questions"—national self-determination and anti-imperialism—as fundamentally linked. For Lenin, as he emphasized in a 1914 pamphlet, the right of national or ethnic minorities to self-determination was part and parcel of proletarian opposition to all forms of privilege; the proletarians of an "oppressor nation," for example ethnic Russian (Great Russian) workers within the Russian empire, had to endorse the national demands of the oppressed, for example ethnic Ukrainians or Jews. The "Theses on the National and Colonial Questions" that Lenin drafted for the Second Comintern Congress in 1920 extended this logic to the colonial world, arguing that it was the duty of workers who belonged to "oppressor" nationalities or resided in colonizing states to "render direct aid to the revolutionary movements among the dependent and underprivileged nations (for example, Ireland, the American Negroes, etc.) and in the colonies."[16]

This tendency to treat the colonial and national questions together became more complicated after October, when the Bolsheviks found themselves running, in the name of the working class, a multinational state that most hoped to keep in one piece, ideally voluntarily but by force if necessary. Lenin continued to maintain that extending rights to national minorities was the best means of persuading minorities both at home and abroad of the emancipatory intentions of the Russian proletariat. As both Finland and the Baltic states (Estonia, Latvia, Lithuania) gained their independence, the Soviet state seemed to make good on the promise of liberating nations that had been "imprisoned" in the Russian empire.

During the Civil War, the Soviet state maintained its commitment to anti-imperialism abroad, while it increasingly came to resemble an empire at home, reclaiming imperial territories that had declared their independence. In April 1920, the Red Army marched into Baku, a major source of oil for Russia, and made Azerbaijan, which had been independent since 1918, a Soviet republic. Just five months later, in September 1920, the city hosted the Congress of Toilers of the East that brought together nearly two thousand delegates representing twenty-nine nationalities from both within and beyond the Soviet state. At the first session, Zinoviev insisted that the "greatest potential for revolutionary change now existed in the East," and called for a "holy war" against British imperialism (see document 4.2).[17] In the meantime, the Red Army continued to gather former Russian imperial lands. Independent Armenia fell in late 1920, and the Soviet war with Poland spelled the end of independent Ukraine. In February 1921, the Red Army marched into Georgia, overthrowing an independent Menshevik-led state that had been established in 1917—and recognized by the Soviet state in 1920. In October 1917, local, mainly Russian, socialists in Central Asia organized the Turkestan Soviet Republic, with its capital in Tashkent; however, only the Red Army's intervention completed the integration of the region into the Soviet state.

How these new republics should be integrated into a union of Soviet republics proved a divisive question. Lenin, more tolerant of nationalism than many of his comrades, argued for a union of equals. Stalin, the commissar of nationalities, advocated a more centralized plan: making Ukraine, Belorussia, Armenia, Azerbaijan, and Georgia autonomous republics within the Russian Soviet Federated Socialist Republic (RSFSR). Many party members, perhaps a majority, had little sympathy for concessions to national minorities. In 1923, Zinoviev paraphrased their analysis: "Isn't it written somewhere in the Communist Manifesto that the proletariat has no fatherland, workers of the world unite, etc.?"[18] Nonetheless, Stalin's highhanded treatment of Georgian nationalists, along with his insulting attitude toward Lenin's wife, Nadezhda Krupskaia, prompted an already ill Lenin to call for Stalin's removal from high office. In a "testament" dictated in 1922, Lenin reiterated the need to distinguish between "the nationalism of the oppressor nation and that of the oppressed nation," accused Stalin, without explicitly naming him, of being a "vulgar Great-Russian bully"—a Russified Georgian who outdid the Russians—and opined that he was "too rude" to continue as general secretary.[19] Lenin's old comrades did not act on or publicize his testament, which damned them all with faint praise and remained secret until the Twentieth Party Congress in 1956.

Ultimately, Stalin's vision of a more centralized union prevailed. While the 1924 constitution that established the Union of Soviet Socialists Republics (USSR) officially granted each republic the right to secede, in reality the policy of "indigenization" (*korenizatsiia*) allowed national republics only limited leeway to develop national culture, to teach native languages, and to employ national minorities in local government. The Soviet Union was to be "national in form" but "socialist in content," a formula that in practice meant real authority remained in Moscow, even as it encouraged ethnic or linguistic minorities to identify themselves in national terms.

Whether or not Soviet control of the non-Russian borderlands made the USSR an "empire" in the same sense as the British empire, the Soviet project shared with Western imperialism an emphasis on the triumph over backwardness. Zinoviev was hardly alone among the Bolsheviks in understanding the "toilers of the east"—a category that included the Soviet state's own national minorities—as "very backward" and thus in need of the aid of the "more civilized" workers of Europe and America. Even if one emphasizes—as many scholars have—the fundamental differences between Soviet campaigns to eradicate "backwardness" and Western imperial civilizing missions, there were clear "similarities in the rhetoric used by Russian Bolsheviks and Western European colonizers." The policies differed as the Soviet discourse of backwardness, unlike that of British and French colonizers, aimed not simply to justify European rule, but to "raise all parts of the Soviet Union to the same level of socialist modernity." Nonetheless, Soviet policies in Central Asia were often "imperial in effect," as "'modernity' and 'socialism' in the Soviet Union seemed to require giving up one's identity and capitulating to outsiders."[20] A recent study of Soviet efforts to reconcile anticolonial ideology with the realities of empire somewhat jokingly proposes that the Soviet Union often seemed to promote "imperialism as the highest stage of socialism."[21]

At the same time, many indigenous people appreciated the new opportunities provided by the Soviet state and both embraced and adapted for their own purposes the Soviets'—perhaps utopian, perhaps imperial—project of enlightenment and modernization. In Kyrgyzstan, for example, modernization included both attacks on

Figure 4.1 A Central Asian woman in a paranji, *c.* 1905–1915. Photograph by Sergei
Prokudin-Gorskii. Courtesy of the Library of Congress Prints and
Photographs Division, Prokudin-Gorskii Collection (LC-P87–8011A).

Was unveiling emancipatory or "imperial in effect"?

nomadism and the introduction of Western high culture—theater, opera, and ballet.
Often fusing "indigenous culture and artistic traditions of the West," performances
resonated if not with audiences, then with the Soviet-educated artists, who cherished
the training they received in Moscow and delighted in bringing Shakespeare to Central
Asia.[22] Similarly, as highlighted in the introduction to this chapter, many Central Asian
women chose to participate, often at great risk to themselves, in efforts to establish
"modern" gender relations.

Revolutionizing marriage and family

The Bolsheviks—along with other Russian Marxists, populists, and European socialists generally—had long assumed that revolution would open the way to women's
emancipation. Bolsheviks understood the so-called woman question, as they did the
national and colonial question, in terms of both modernization and liberation.
Hostile to feminism, which they defined as a movement that promoted the rights of
privileged women rather than economic justice for all, the Bolsheviks promised to free
women from the onerous double shift of wage labor and housework imposed by capitalism. To accomplish this sort of emancipation, they embraced the solution favored

by most socialists: some form of modern, professionalized, socialized housekeeping and childcare.

For the rationalizers and modernizers, notably Lenin to the degree he weighed in on these matters at all, collectivizing traditional women's work offered a means of enhancing the reproductive and productive capacities of socialist society. By contrast, liberationists—those focused on liberation from oppression—most famously Alexandra Kollontai, the Soviet state's first commissar of social welfare (and only female commissar), linked gender equality and women's economic independence to a revolution in private life (see document 4.4). Both agreed that the bourgeois family oppressed women. Lenin railed against what he called "old household drudgery and dependence on man." Kollontai declared the "separation of kitchen from marriage" a "reform no less important than the separation of Church and State," and predicted that "in a workers' state . . . it is doubtful whether you would find many volunteers for stooping over a stove to win a husband's approval."[23] But while Lenin had little patience for "discussions on how one loves and is loved" and urged women to direct their thoughts and energies "towards the proletarian revolution," Kollontai looked forward to a "new world" in which the "recognized, normal and desirable form of communication between the sexes probably will rest on a healthy, free, natural attraction (without perversions and excesses)."[24]

The Bolsheviks' linkage of women's emancipation and the eventual withering away of the bourgeois family animated efforts to socialize and professionalize childrearing (discussed in the next section) as well as legislation designed to end the legal oppression of women (and also children) in marriage. The original "Code on Marriage, the Family and Guardianship" ratified in October 1918 constituted "a compromise between utopian ideals and pragmatic considerations."[25] Because the code aimed to take the first steps toward utopia, it is often difficult to discern where the utopian ideal ended and the pragmatic compromise began. Did efforts to end practices deemed "backward" constitute sensible modernization or unrealistic overreach? For example, the establishment of civil marriage, which stripped the church ceremony of legal significance, can be understood as a moderate alternative to demands that the code abolish marriage altogether, a practical means of curtailing the church's influence, or a revolutionary, if not utopian, attack on patriarchal and religious authority. Potentially utopian, revolutionary, or modernizing provisions of the code included simplified divorce and the elimination of the category of illegitimate children. The code permitted married couples to adopt the husband's name, the wife's, or a joint surname. A wife was no longer required to accompany her husband if he changed residence. In the mid- and late 1920s, separate legislation in the Central Asian republics banned child marriage, bride-price, and polygyny. These were radical transformations, but Bolsheviks promoted them as "expressions of modern common sense."[26]

Perhaps the 1918 code's most obvious compromise was the decision to retain alimony and child support. By retaining alimony the Bolsheviks acknowledged "the persistence of the family as the primary form of social organization and security."[27] The provision constituted a clear admission that, in the period of "transition" between capitalism and socialism, the state lacked the resources to fully socialize childcare and to provide adequate social welfare programs. The law's gender-neutral language, which provided alimony for a "spouse" in need, to some degree masked the assumption that women remained economically dependent on men, although the law's framers were clear that their intention was to protect women. However, alimony and child support did not turn out to be particularly pragmatic solutions, as they proved difficult for women to collect.

The 1920 legislation decriminalizing abortion can be understood as grounded in a similar impulse to protect women from the social and economic hardships of the "transition" to socialism. The statute began with the recognition that the "difficult economic conditions of the present still compel many women to resort to" abortion, and noted that the criminalization of abortion succeeded only in driving "the operation underground" and making "the woman a victim of mercenary and often ignorant quacks." Thus the Commissariats of Health and Justice permitted doctors to perform abortions in Soviet hospitals as a means of protecting women's reproductive health. As promulgated, the law did not express a commitment to reproductive rights, although the women involved in its drafting, Krupskaia and Inessa Armand, the first head of the party's Women's Department (Zhenotdel), appeared to emphasize that the control of fertility was essential to women's personal freedom. The state did not widely publicize the decriminalization of abortion and in fact worked to combat "this evil"—via propaganda, not by making contraception readily and widely available.[28]

Another little-publicized shift in the criminal code, the 1922 decriminalization of sodomy (same sex relations between men), similarly appears grounded as much in a commitment to secularization, modernization, and the medical control of sexuality as to advancing the cause of personal freedom. The logic behind the decriminalization was not made explicit in the 1922 or 1926 criminal codes, which simply omitted a ban (present in the tsarist code) on consensual same-sex relations. However, the law's modern and medical language suggests an effort to "deprive sexual crime statutes of any pretense of safe-guarding religious ... morality and to thrust such offenses squarely into the remit of the guardians of public health and order."[29]

Almost as soon as the 1918 marriage code was ratified, critics began agitating for its revision. The 1926 revision responded to the concerns of both jurists concerned with liberating the law from prerevolutionary morality, who objected to the retention of "bourgeois" registered marriage, and their more moderate colleagues, who feared that divorce, far from liberating women, put them and their children at risk.[30] The new code provided what might be understood as a more radical definition of marriage, treating registered and unregistered (common law) marriages as equivalent. Moderate proponents of the 1926 law justified the more radical definition of marriage as necessary for the protection of women and children; by recognizing common law marriage, the code made it possible for unregistered spouses to sue for alimony and child support. Moreover, the code, while recognizing unregistered marriage, promoted registered marriage by the somewhat paradoxical means of a further simplification of divorce. The practice that became known as "postcard divorce" allowed either spouse to present themselves at a civil registry office (ZAGS), petition for divorce, and have the other spouse notified by mail. Some opponents of these changes agreed that women and children were vulnerable, but objected to offering unregistered spouses, imagined as "dandies and spongers," the same protections as ostensibly more worthy and traditional registered spouses.[31] Liberationist critics, most prominently Kollontai, questioned what they regarded as the un-socialist practice of relying on alimony, calling instead for more children's homes and expanded social welfare programs. Despite the objections, the new code extended alimony to unregistered spouses, the gender-neutral language again masking the stated intention of safeguarding women.

A number of leading female Bolsheviks undertook to make legal emancipation a lived reality for Soviet women. The Zhenotdel, established in 1919, grew out of the work of Kollontai, Armand, Krupskaia, and others to inform women of their new rights and obligations and to mobilize them not only to support and build new institutions such as kindergartens, daycares, and communal dining rooms, but also to challenge traditional patriarchal norms. To reach women in cities and villages, Zhenotdel activists organized literacy courses and produced a newspaper for women workers. Ultimately, the Zhenotdel worked to support the creation of the "new woman," a "strong, free citizen, not inferior to man in anything."[32] The department's leaders aimed to expand the number of women in the party; a paltry 8 percent of the membership in 1922, women constituted 12 percent of party members in 1927.

Many women defied convention in order to embrace the new rights and protections offered by the Soviet state. As divorce became more common, the percentage of cases involving claims for alimony and child support increased, from almost zero in 1918 to about 45 percent in 1924. Many of the women suing for child support were unmarried mothers who went to court despite the stigma still attached to illegitimacy. One 1925 survey of courts in Moscow city and province found that although men contested paternity in about one-third of the cases, women won child support 99

Figure 4.2 A 1924 Soviet advertising poster by Alexander Rodchenko for Gosizdat publishing house depicts actress Lili Brik, muse of the poet Vladimir Mayakovsky, shouting out the word "books"—"in all branches of knowledge." © ITAR-TASS Photo Agency/Alamy.

To whom might the poster have appealed?

percent of the time. Such outcomes relied on judges who were willing and able to adjudicate claims on the basis of the best interests of children and mothers, without reference to traditional moral criteria. For example, in the case of a woman who had sexual relations with three men but sued only one for child support, the judge responded to his objections by ordering all three to pay three rubles a month until the child reached the age of eighteen.[33]

Even as women and some Soviet officials embraced new norms, opposition to women's emancipation and a revolution in everyday life (*byt*) was widespread. Many advocates of the new code supported it precisely as a means of discouraging immorality (defined in terms of multiple partners or sex outside of marriage) and divorce, and of encouraging the formation of stable traditional families. The persistence and power of traditional attitudes, assumptions, and behaviors were perhaps clearest in Central Asia, where more than 200 unveiled women were murdered in a six month period in 1927–1928. The threat of violence prompted thousands of women to reveil.

Raising the children of October

The first years of Soviet power were often tragic ones for children. Both World War I and the Civil War removed, often permanently, the primary male breadwinner from countless families. Hurried and poorly managed evacuations from war zones also separated many children from their parents. The food shortages that plagued urban areas throughout the war and Civil War and culminated in the massive famine of 1921 further undermined parents' ability to care for their children. By 1922, there were at least seven million *besprizorniki* (literally unsupervised children, but usually translated as waifs or orphans), displaced or abandoned in the successive crises.[34] They fled the famine zone, hitching rides on the railroad, and crowded into Russia's cities and train stations. Begging, stealing, and selling their bodies, the *besprizorniki* constituted one of the most visible, heartbreaking, and intractable problems facing the new regime.

Despite the magnitude of the problem, many within the Soviet leadership initially saw the *besprizorniki* as both a challenge and an opportunity—a generation of children liberated from presumptively backward or oppressive parents. Acknowledging the often bitter realities of urban homelessness, the "visionaries" among the Bolsheviks pictured the children of the streets as "embryonic" collectivists, the independent, adaptable, resourceful, and bold constructors of the revolutionary future.[35]

Such assessments chimed with the outlook of progressive educators who in these years saw their central task as creating rich and nurturing environments in which children could essentially raise themselves, free of the prejudices and values of the bygone bourgeois era. The ideal children's home operated on an open-door basis and aimed, as a 1922 guide to child welfare issues expressed it, "to create a cosy corner that children like . . . so that they drop in every day."[36] The United Labor School that in 1919 replaced tsarist elementary and secondary schools emphasized hands-on learning and self-government. Relying on pupils' enthusiasm for creative labor and collective work, the labor school substituted work on interdisciplinary "themes" for traditional subjects and did away with exams, rote learning, and strict discipline. Soviet preschools (for children aged three to seven) adopted radically child-centered programs. In 1921, Dora Lazurkina, the head of the Commissariat of Education's preschool department, exhorted kindergarten teachers to avoid giving their charges excessive advice. Since the child, as "the future builder of life after us," would have to do "without our instructions or help . . . he must above all become accustomed to independent activity."[37]

Teachers implemented a wide range of programs in early Soviet schools and preschools, and emancipatory approaches, while privileged, were always contested. Even among the most progressive educators, the conception of children as "future builders" coexisted and sometimes competed with a desire to "civilize," "modernize," and discipline the rising generation. Proper hygiene was something of a Bolshevik obsession; everywhere schools and preschools strove to impress upon children the importance of clean clothes and hands and to get children to transform their parents' (presumptively slovenly) habits. Most fundamentally, any school project that took account not only of the child's present interests but also of the future needs of the Soviet state entailed some measure of enlightenment, control, or indoctrination.

By the mid-1920s, as the spontaneous emergence of socialist society seemed increasingly unlikely and faith in the liberationist model of revolution faded, the Soviet state abandoned the dream of raising children in "free" environments outside the family. The shift can be understood as a response to profound scarcity. Unable to provide adequate care even for orphans, the state had to make its peace with family upbringing.

Along with this move away from the vision of the child as a liberated, self-directed builder came an emphasis on instilling modern, disciplined habits. Was this combination "practical"? By 1927, programs in schools and children's homes reflected a growing fondness for order, discipline, and political indoctrination. The standardization of preschool and school curricula that began in 1924 appealed to many hastily trained and overworked teachers, who preferred ready-made and approved lessons to admonitions that they carefully study each child's needs and capacities and develop appropriate materials. Parents and teachers alike hailed the return of discrete subjects and exams as a practical means of inculcating the skills and work habits necessary to a modern socialist society. However, the new emphasis on political indoctrination that became increasingly urgent after Lenin's death—for example encouraging school children to read Lenin and Karl Marx—was not always clearly workable or age-appropriate.

New decrees mandated that wards of children's homes no longer be allowed to come and go as they pleased, a change that effectively eliminated the need to create cozy institutions that would attract street children. The new ideal was Anton Makarenko's children's colony, which had been roundly criticized by progressive educators like Krupskaia earlier in the decade. The inspiration for the popular 1931 film *The Road to Life,* Makarenko's colony emphasized self-discipline and collective living along with manual labor, military-style drills, uniforms, games, and firm punishment (see document 4.5). Here a utopia of disciplined productivity seemed to replace the progressive educators' utopia of creative chaos.

Soviet youth and sexual revolution

The early years of Soviet power produced a sexual revolution that young people in particular embraced as liberation from the constraints and hypocrisy of bourgeois society. In the brutal and uncertain period of the Civil War, the prototypical communist was a "crass commissar in a leather jacket, who swore, spat, drank heavily, and engaged in casual sex."[38] Such visions of revolutionary toughness outlasted the war, and in the 1920s both young men and young women, tens of thousands of whom had served at the front, equated romance, monogamy, and sexual restraint with *meshchantsvo* (vulgar, narrow-minded, petty-bourgeois values). Kollontai offered a sympathetic portrait, though not an endorsement, of such attitudes and behavior in her 1923 story *Love of Three Generations*. Zhenia, the daughter of a Bolshevik of Kollontai's generation, asks her mother for advice on how to arrange an abortion, ultimately revealing that she is having an affair with her mother's common law husband; that he or perhaps another young man had made her pregnant; and that she loves neither. When her mother responds with shock and despair, Zhenia argues back, emphasizing her own commitment to the revolution, and asking, "If I were a boy, your 20-year-old son who had been at the front and is used to leading an independent life, would you also be horrified if he lived with the women he likes? . . . No? Well then, why should you stand aghast at my 'immorality'?"[39]

For their part, Bolshevik traditionalists saw *meshchanstvo* or even a total lack of civilization in precisely the behaviors that young people associated with revolution. An interview with Lenin supposedly conducted in 1920, but published by German communist Clara Zetkin only after his death in 1925, quoted him admitting that the "so-called 'new sexual life' of the youth" seemed to him simply vulgar debauchery, "an extension of bourgeois brothels."[40] Sofia Smidovich, a prominent Bolshevik who had headed the Zhenotdel, complained in *Pravda* in 1925 that Soviet youth viewed "everything which goes beyond the primitive conception which might be suitable for a Hottentot" as "something characteristic of the petty bourgeoisie, a bourgeois attitude toward the sexual problem."[41]

In 1925, at roughly the same moment that the press was filled with debate on the proposed new marriage code giving unregistered marriage the same legal status as registered marriage, *Pravda* devoted sixteen columns to readers' letters on the sex question. A letter from a young woman protesting Smidovich's attack on the alleged immorality of youth presented her generation as the real revolutionaries: "Not only is a girl who abstains [from sex] bourgeois but one who destroys her youth in the name of prejudices of the past." As in the marriage code debate, much of the discussion revolved around the image of the female victim. Smidovich emphasized that the male worker-student characterized sexual abstinence as "bourgeois" in order to pressure the woman worker-student into a sexual affair that carried much more serious consequences for her than for the "tomcat boy" looking to "satisfy his sexual desires." Both men and women contested this image of weak women, emphasizing that women "themselves seek satisfaction" and that women were fully capable of telling tomcat boys to "go to hell."[42]

While the communist Smidovich hinted that there was something at least vaguely counterrevolutionary in seeking to "satisfy" sexual desires, the young letter writers suggested a more tolerant, if not supportive, attitude. Many young people were simply "indifferent to the revolutionary project, pursuing popular pleasures like flapper dress or the foxtrot." Others "actively resisted" communist efforts to define and control revolutionary youth.[43] Anxieties about sex, pleasure, and consumption were central to debates about what Soviet young people and the Soviet Union ought to be.

CONCLUSION AND FURTHER QUESTIONS

Neither the marriage code debate nor the debate on the sexual question mapped neatly onto the contemporary debates on industrialization and world revolution more closely associated with the political struggle to succeed Lenin. However, taken together the debates may shed light on the larger question of how the Bolsheviks imagined the process of revolutionary transformation after almost a decade in power. The debates can be understood as structured in similar ways. On one side stood a varied group of liberationists who looked forward to spontaneous emancipation from bourgeois institutions that they viewed as oppressive and that were in any case often disintegrating under revolutionary conditions: the family, the schoolroom, moral codes, empire. On the other side stood modernizers or rationalizers concerned with building an orderly, productive socialist state, who hoped to impose disciplined, "socialist" norms of behavior and reshape even intimate relationships.

Viewing the watershed years that followed Lenin's death in 1924 through the lens of the efforts to reshape *byt* foregrounds not political intrigues or the polemics of the industrialization debate but the problem of how to make revolutionary change and raise new people. The debates of the mid-1920s, including the industrialization debate, raise the question of how a state could be "revolutionary" and suggest how difficult it was for Bolsheviks in power to agree on a proper and effective revolutionary course of action.

PRIMARY SOURCES

Use the questions to analyze the content, context, and significance of each primary source. Then synthesize the primary sources and the material in the chapter to formulate a response to the primary chapter questions: Were Bolshevik efforts to revolutionize everyday life primarily focused on "liberation" or "modernization" and "enlightenment"? Could these aims be reconciled?

Document 4.1 Excerpt from Vladimir Lenin, "Preface to the French and German Editions," *Imperialism, the Highest Stage of Capitalism* (1920)

Questions for analysis

1 How did Lenin define imperialism?
2 Why did he believe the world war would lead to revolution?

. . . Capitalism has grown into a world system of colonial oppression and of the financial strangulation of the overwhelming majority of the population of the world by a handful of "advanced" countries. And this "booty" is shared between two or three powerful world plunderers armed to the teeth (America, Great Britain, Japan), who are drawing the whole world into *their* war over the division of *their* booty.

. . . The tens of millions of dead and maimed left by the [First World] war—a war to decide whether the British or German group of financial plunderers is to receive the most booty—and those two "peace treaties" [Brest-Litovsk and Versailles] are with unprecedented rapidity opening the eyes of millions and tens of millions of people who are downtrodden, oppressed, deceived, and duped by the bourgeoisie. Thus, out of the universal ruin caused by the war a world-wide revolutionary crisis is arising which, however prolonged and arduous its stages may be, cannot end otherwise than in a proletarian revolution and in its victory.

Source: "Imperialism, the Highest Stage of Capitalism," in Robert C. Tucker, ed., *The Lenin Anthology* (New York: W. W. Norton, 1975), 206–207. Copyright © 1975 by W. W. Norton & Company, Inc. Used by permission of W. W. Norton & Company, Inc.

Document 4.2 Excerpt from Grigory Zinoviev's speech, First Session, Baku Congress of Peoples of the East, 1 September 1920 9:40 pm

Questions for analysis

1 How does Zinoviev's vision of revolution in the colonial world connect to Lenin's analysis (document 4.1) of imperialism as the highest stage of capitalism?
2 How would you characterize Zinoviev's tone and program? Does he think that colonized people are capable of making revolution on their own?

We know that the working masses of the East are in some places, through no fault of their own, very backward: illiterate, ignorant, they are sunk in superstition and believe in spirits, they are unable to read newspapers, they do not know what is going on in the world at large, they do not understand the most elementary principles of hygiene. Only the lackeys of imperialism can mock them for all this . . .

The task of the more civilised, more literate, more organised workers of Europe and America is to help the backward toilers of the East . . . to extend the hand of aid to them, . . . so as to help the peasant of the East to take the land for himself, to help him carry further that great revolution which the Russian peasants have started, after such heavy labours . . .

. . . From the moment that even just one country has broken away from the chain of capitalism, as Russia has done, from the moment that the workers have put the question of the proletarian revolution on the agenda, from that moment we can say that in China, India, Turkey, Persia and Armenia it is possible and necessary to begin fighting directly for a Soviet system. The workers of Europe will use their power, of course, not in order to plunder Turkey, Persia and other countries, but to help them.

. . . Comrades! Brothers! The time has now come when you can set about organising a true people's holy war against the robbers and oppressors. The Communist International turns today to the peoples of the East and says to them: 'Brothers, we summon you to a holy war, in the first place against British imperialism!' [Tumultuous applause, prolonged shouts of 'Hurrah'. Members of the Congress stand up, brandishing their weapons. The speaker is unable to continue for some time. All the delegates stand up and applaud. Shouts of 'We swear it'.]

. . . Long live the fraternal alliance of the peoples of the East with the Communist International! May capital perish, and long live the reign of labour! [Burst of applause.]

Chairman: Please calm down and resume your seats. Comrade Buniat-Zade will translate Comrade Zinoviev's speech.

Buniat-Zade translates into Turkic and another interpreter translates into Persian.

Source: Available at www.marxists.org/history/international/comintern/baku/ch01.htm (accessed 7 January 2016).

Document 4.3   Anglo-Russian Trade Agreement, 1921

Questions for analysis

1   How does the agreement address British concerns about the Soviet Union?
2   How does this source connect to the discussion of foreign policy in the chapter and Zinoviev's speech (document 4.2)? Did the Soviet Union fulfill the pledges made here?

The present treaty is conditioned upon the fulfillment of the following: both sides will refrain from hostile acts or measures against the other party as well as from introducing into its territory any official, direct, or indirect propaganda against the institutions of the British Empire or the Russian Soviet Republic . . . [The Soviet government pledges that] it will refrain from any attempt or incitement through military, diplomatic, or any other ways of any Asiatic nation to activities hostile to British interests or those of the British Empire . . . and especially in the case of India and Afghanistan.

Source: *Documents of the Foreign Policy of the USSR* (Moscow, 1959), 3: 608.

Document 4.4   Alexandra Kollontai, *Communism and the Family*, 1920

Questions for analysis

1   According to Kollontai, how will communist society make life better and happier for families? How will communism liberate women?

2   Are her proposals practical, utopian, or both? Would the changes she imagines revolutionize everyday life?

. . . Instead of the working woman cleaning her flat, the communist society can arrange for men and women whose job it is to go round in the morning cleaning rooms. The wives of the rich have long since been freed from these irritating and tiring domestic duties. Why should the working woman continue to be burdened with them? In Soviet Russia the working woman should be surrounded by the same ease and light, hygiene and beauty that previously only the very rich could afford. Instead of the working woman having to struggle with the cooking and spend her last free hours in the kitchen preparing dinner and supper, communist society will organise public restaurants and communal kitchens . . .

The working woman will not have to slave over the washtub any longer, or ruin her eyes in darning her stockings and mending her linen; she will simply take these things to the central laundries each week and collect the washed and ironed garments later. That will be another job less to do. Special clothes-mending centres will free the working woman from the hours spent on mending and give her the opportunity to devote her evenings to reading, attending meetings and concerts. Thus . . . housework . . . [is] doomed to extinction with the victory of communism. And the working woman will surely have no cause to regret this. Communism liberates the working woman from her domestic slavery and makes her life richer and happier.

But even if housework disappears, you may argue, there are still the children to look after. But here too, the workers' state will come to replace the family, society will gradually take upon itself all the tasks that before the revolution fell to the individual parents . . . Under capitalism children were frequently, too frequently, a heavy and unbearable burden on the proletarian family. Communist society will come to the aid of the parents . . . We already have homes for very small babies, creches [daycares], kindergartens, children's colonies and homes, hospitals and health resorts for sick children, restaurants, free lunches at school and free distribution of text books, warm clothing and shoes to schoolchildren. All this goes to show that the responsibility for the child is passing from the family to the collective . . .

Communist society has this to say to the working woman and working man: "You are young, you love each other. Everyone has the right to happiness. Therefore live your life . . . Do not fear marriage, even though under capitalism marriage was truly a chain of sorrow. Do not be afraid of having children. Society needs more workers and rejoices at the birth of every child. You do not have to worry about the future of your child; your child will know neither hunger nor cold." . . . Society will feed, bring up and educate the child . . . Communist society will take upon itself all the duties involved in the education of the child, but the joys of parenthood will not be taken away from those who are capable of appreciating them. Such are the plans of communist society and they can hardly be interpreted as the forcible destruction of the family and the forcible separation of child from mother.

Source: Available at www.marxists.org/archive/kollonta/1920/communism-family. htm (accessed 7 January 2016).

Document 4.5   A. S. Makarenko describes how work is organized at the Gorky Children's Colony, 1925

Questions for analysis

1   What does Makarenko's description suggest about the atmosphere and aims of the children's colony? Why might he use military terminology (detachment, commander)?
2   How did Makarenko's program compare to other educational experiments described in the chapter? Does it seem more or less practical? What makes it "communist"?

The mixed detachment is a temporary detachment, organized for not more than a week at a time and receiving short, definite tasks, such as weeding potatoes in a particular field, ploughing a particular allotment, sorting a consignment of seeds, carting a certain amount of manure, sowing a definite area, and so on.

Each assignment demanded different numbers of workers—in some mixed detachments, only two persons were required, in others five, eight, or even twenty. The work of the mixed detachments also varied as to the time it required. In the winter, while school was being attended, the boys worked either before or after dinner, in two shifts. When school was out, a six-hour day was introduced, with everyone working simultaneously, but the necessity for exploiting to the full both livestock and inventory led to some boys working from six a.m. to noon, and others from noon to six p.m. Sometimes there was so much to do that working hours had to be increased.

All this variety of work as to type and length of time, caused a great variety in the mixed detachments themselves. Our network of mixed detachments began to look something like a railway schedule . . .

The Commanders' Council endeavoured to make all members of the colony in turn—with the exception of the most glaringly unsuitable—mixed detachment commanders. This was quite fair, since the command of a mixed detachment entailed great responsibility, and a lot of trouble. Thanks to this system, most of the colony members not only took part in work assignments, but also shouldered organizational functions. This was extremely important, and exactly what was required for communist education. And it was thanks to this system that our colony distinguished itself in 1926 by its striking ability to adapt itself to any task, while for the fulfilment of the various tasks there was always an abundance of capable and independent organizers, and proficient managers—persons who could be relied upon . . .

This created an extremely intricate chain of subordination in the colony, in which it was impossible for individual members to become unduly conspicuous, or to predominate in the collective.

The system of mixed detachments with its alternation of working and organizational functions, its practice in command and subordination, in collective and individual activities, keyed up the life of the colony and filled it with interest.

Source: A. S. Makarenko, *The Road to Life*, Volume 1, Ch. 25: Regimental Pedagogics, available at www.marxists.org/reference/archive/makarenko/works/road1/ch25.html (accessed 7 January 2016).

Notes

1 As quoted in Marianne Kamp, *The New Woman in Uzbekistan: Islam, Modernity, and Unveiling under Communism* (Seattle: University of Washington Press, 2006), 157–158.
2 Fedor Panferov, "Chto takoe kommunizm," *Oktiabr'*, no. 1 (1960): 103.
3 For the former view, see Kamp, *New Woman*, 201; for the latter, see Douglas Northrop, *Veiled Empire: Gender and Power in Stalinist Central Asia* (Ithaca, NY: Cornell University Press, 2003), 27.
4 As quoted in Fernando Claudín, *The Communist Movement: From Comintern to Cominform. Part I: The Crisis of the Communist International*, trans. Brian Pearce (New York: Monthly Review Press, 1975), 53, original emphasis.
5 Quoted in John Riddell, ed., *Founding the Communist International: Proceedings and Documents of the First Congress, March 1919* (New York: Anchor Foundation, 1987), 19, 20.
6 "Manifesto of the Communist International to the Workers of the World," available at www.marxists.org/archive/trotsky/1924/ffyci-1/ch01.htm (accessed 7 February 2013).
7 Cited in Kevin McDermott and Jeremy Agnew, *The Comintern: A History of International Communism from Lenin to Stalin* (Basingstoke: Palgrave Macmillan, 1996), 16.
8 Aleksander Vatlin, "The Testing-Ground of World Revolution: Germany in the 1920s," in Tim Rees and Andrew Thorpe, eds., *International Communism and the Communist International, 1919–1943* (Manchester: Manchester University Press, 1998), 119.
9 Claudín, *Communist Movement*, 109.
10 John Riddell, ed., *Workers of the World and Oppressed Peoples, Unite! Proceedings and Documents of the Second Congress, 1920* (New York: Pathfinder Press, 1991), vol. 1, 291.
11 Historian E. H. Carr, writing in 1937 as quoted in Jonathan Haslam, "E. H. Carr and the History of Soviet Russia," *Historical Journal*, 26, no. 4 (December 1983): 1025.
12 Erik van Ree, *The Political Thought of Joseph Stalin: A Study in Twentieth-Century Revolutionary Patriotism* (London: Routledge Curzon, 2002), 90, 210.
13 *Fifth World Congress of the Communist International: Abridged Report of Meetings Held at Moscow June 17th to July 8th, 1924* (London: Communist Party of Great Britain, [1925]), 38–39.
14 John P. Sontag, "The Soviet War Scare of 1926–27," *Russian Review*, 34, no. 1 (January 1975): 66–77; Hugh D. Hudson, Jr., "The 1927 Soviet War Scare: The Foreign Affairs–Domestic Policy Nexus Revisited," *Soviet and Post-Soviet Review*, 39, no. 2 (2012): 145–65.
15 In Jane Degras, ed., *The Communist International, 1919–1943: Documents* (London: Frank Cass, 1971), vol. 2, 543.
16 "Communism in the East: Theses on the National and Colonial Questions," in *The Lenin Anthology*, 622.
17 Grigory Zinoviev's speech, First Session, Baku Congress of Peoples of the East, 1 September 1920, 9:40 pm, available at www.marxists.org/history/international/comintern/baku/ch01.htm (accessed 22 May 2013).
18 As quoted in Terry Martin, *The Affirmative Action Empire: Nations and Nationalism in the Soviet Union, 1923–1939* (Ithaca, NY: Cornell University Press, 2001), 20.
19 V. I. Lenin, *Collected Works*, 4th ed. (Moscow: Progress Publishers, 1966), vol. 36, 594, 610–611.
20 Adrienne Edgar, "Bolshevism, Patriarchy, and the Nation: The Soviet 'Emancipation' of Muslim Women in Pan-Islamic Perspective," *Slavic Review*, 65, no. 2 (Summer 2006): 256, 257, 265, 272, 270.
21 Yuri Slezkine, "Imperialism as the Highest Stage of Socialism," *Russian Review* 59 (April 2000): 227–234.

22 Ali İğmen, *Speaking Soviet with an Accent: Culture and Power in Kyrgyzstan* (Pittsburgh, PA: University of Pittsburgh Press, 2012), 102, 103 (quotation), 111.
23 Clara Zetkin, "Women, Marriage and Sex," in *Reminiscences of Lenin* (New York: International Publishers, 1934), 58; "Excerpts from the Works of A. M. Kollontay," in Rudolf Schlesinger, ed., *Changing Attitudes in Soviet Russia: The Family in the USSR* (London: Routledge and Kegan Paul, 1949), 49.
24 Zetkin, "Women, Marriage, and Sex," 46; Alexandra Kollontai, "Make Way for the Winged Eros (1923)," in Vassiliki Kolocotroni, Jane Goldman, and Olga Taxidou, eds., *Modernism: An Anthology of Sources and Documents* (Chicago, IL: University of Chicago Press, 1999), 235.
25 Lauren Kaminsky, "Utopian Visions of Family Life in the Stalin-Era Soviet Union," *Central European History*, 44 (2011): 65.
26 Douglas Northrop, "Subaltern Dialogues: Subversion and Resistance in Uzbek Family Law," *Slavic Review*, 60, no. 1 (Spring 2001): 119.
27 Wendy Z. Goldman, *Women, the State and Revolution: Soviet Family Policy and Social Life, 1917–1936* (New York: Cambridge University Press, 1993), 133.
28 "Decree on Legalization of Abortions of November 18, 1920," in Schlesinger, ed., *Changing Attitudes,* 44; Elizabeth A. Wood, *The Baba and the Comrade: Gender and Politics in Revolutionary Russia* (Bloomington: Indiana University Press, 2000), 107–110.
29 Dan Healey, *Homosexual Desire in Revolutionary Russia: The Regulation of Sex and Gender Dissent* (Chicago, IL: University of Chicago Press, 2001), 122.
30 Goldman, *Women, the State,* 185–186.
31 "Discussion of the Draft of the Code," in Schlesinger, ed., *Changing Attitudes,* 95.
32 *Petrogradskaia pravda,* 31 December 1918, as quoted in Barbara Evans Clements, "The Utopianism of the Zhenotdel," *Slavic Review,* 51, no. 3 (Autumn 1992): 487.
33 Goldman, *Women, the State,* 133–136.
34 Alan Ball, *And Now My Soul Is Hardened: Abandoned Children in Soviet Russia, 1918–1930* (Berkeley: University of California Press, 1996), 1.
35 Ball, *And Now My Soul,* xiii, 40, 80.
36 As quoted in Catriona Kelly, *Children's World: Growing Up in Russia, 1890–1991* (New Haven, CT: Yale University Press, 2007), 202.
37 As quoted in Lisa A. Kirschenbaum, *Small Comrades: Revolutionizing Childhood in Soviet Russia, 1917–1932* (New York: Routledge, 2001), 72.
38 David Hoffmann, *Stalinist Values: The Cultural Norms of Soviet Modernity, 1917–1941* (Ithaca, NY: Cornell University Press, 2003), 60.
39 "Excerpts from A. M. Kollontay," 74.
40 Zetkin, "Women, Marriage, and Sex," 49.
41 As quoted in Richard Stites, *The Women's Liberation Movement in Russia: Feminism, Nihilism, and Bolshevism, 1860–1930* (Princeton, NJ: Princeton University Press, 1978), 359.
42 As quoted in Gregory Carleton, *Sexual Revolution in Bolshevik Russia* (Pittsburgh, PA: University of Pittsburgh Press, 2005), 32–33, 31, 32.
43 Anne E. Gorsuch, *Youth in Revolutionary Russia: Enthusiasts, Bohemians, Delinquents* (Bloomington: Indiana University Press, 2000), 2.

5   Revolution from above

INTRODUCTION

A series of explosions rang out across Moscow on a December day in 1931. The government was blowing up the Cathedral of Christ the Savior. Designed to honor the 1812 Russian victory over Napoleon, the cathedral had been consecrated in 1883 after decades of construction. It stood on the bank of the Moscow River and dominated the surrounding landscape. The interior was lavishly decorated with paintings and sculptures and could hold over 7,000 people. For Soviet officials, such a looming

Figure 5.1 The Cathedral of Christ the Savior. Courtesy of the Library of Congress Prints and Photographs Division, Photochrom Prints (LC-DIG-ppmsc-03844).

Describe the architectural style of this building. What elements do you think most offended Soviet architects?

monument to the religion and the power of the tsars was incongruous in the capital of a revolutionary state, and after demolition they planned to replace it with a Palace of Soviets, an immense skyscraper topped by a statue of Lenin three times the size of the Statue of Liberty. Construction began on the new building in 1935, but water kept seeping into the foundation and slowing progress. The outbreak of World War II halted further work, the building was abandoned, and in 1960 the foundation was turned into the world's largest outdoor heated swimming pool. After the collapse of the Soviet Union, the new government began to construct a replica of the old cathedral on the same site and it was completed in 2000, just as Vladimir Putin took office.

In many ways, the cathedral's destruction is emblematic of the period between 1928 and 1932, a time of renewed revolutionary fervor and of violence justified through the rhetoric of class conflict. The architect who designed the Palace of Soviets described the destruction of the cathedral in just these terms: "The proletarian revolution is boldly raising its hands against this cumbersome edifice which symbolized the power and the taste of the lords of old Moscow."[1]

CHAPTER QUESTIONS

Between 1928 and 1932, the Soviet state initiated a series of policies that, like the razing of the Cathedral of Christ the Savior, were intended to obliterate the old and replace it with the new; the most important of these were the collectivization of agriculture and an ambitious economic plan for rapid industrialization called the First Five-Year Plan. Borrowing Stalin's terminology, historians commonly describe these policies as generating a "revolution from above." In this chapter, we will examine the applicability of this designation. What was revolutionary about the events and campaigns of this period? To what extent were policies motivated and implemented "from above" (i.e., by the state)? What was the role of ordinary people, especially young people, in advancing change "from below"?

VOICES, MEMORIES, CONTESTED PERSPECTIVES

Stalin's mentality and the revolution from above

As we have seen in the previous two chapters, party leaders disagreed about how to construct the new state, and their policy differences became entangled with a power struggle over who would replace Lenin as supreme leader. Stalin's post as general secretary put him in charge of party appointments and he was able to amass the backing of many rank-and-file communists, who owed their positions to him. Over the course of the 1920s he drew on this support to defeat his rivals and impose his vision. Initially, Stalin supported NEP and advocated for "socialism in one country." He allied with other leaders to oppose Trotsky, Lev Kamenev, and Grigory Zinoviev (the "left"), who advocated greater investment in industry at the peasants' expense and who insisted that the ultimate success of revolution in Russia depended on revolutions in more "advanced" countries. Stalin succeeded in ousting Trotsky from the Central Committee in 1927 and then exiling him from the Soviet Union in 1929.

However, the future of NEP was increasingly precarious. Many party members were dissatisfied with the compromises it required, and in 1927 and 1928 rumors of war and the threat of food shortages imperiled the Soviet Union's fragile stability. The low prices set by the state and a shortage of manufactured goods discouraged peasants from selling their grain; they would not make much of a profit and there was nothing to buy with the proceeds, so they stored their surplus grain or fed it to their livestock instead of bringing it to market. In the cities, food prices shot up and rationing was reintroduced. Stalin and his sometime allies on the "right" disagreed about how to deal with this problem. Bukharin advocated importing grain to meet immediate needs and then raising the price for it in the future, but over the next year Stalin eliminated Bukharin from power and began to implement some of Trotsky's ideas, which he had condemned a few years earlier. Under Stalin's leadership, the state jettisoned NEP's mixed economy, seized grain by force, began to collectivize agriculture, and embarked on a plan for rapid industrialization.

By 1930, Stalin and his associates controlled the Soviet state. Stalin had not yet amassed all of the dictatorial powers he would assume later in the decade; Politburo members such as Viacheslav Molotov, Lazar Kaganovich, and Sergei Kirov had some autonomy and did their best to forward the interests of the commissariats and regional party organizations that they ran. Nonetheless, Stalin dominated his allies, mediating disputes among them, isolating potential rivals, and initiating important policies, including the collectivization of agriculture and rapid industrialization.[2] Thus, Stalin's personality and mentality shaped the revolution from above.

Stalin was born as Iosif Vissarionovich Dzhugashvili in 1878 in Gori, Georgia, an area in the Caucasus that had been incorporated into the Russian empire during the first half of the nineteenth century. His parents had been born serfs and young Soso, as he was nicknamed, grew up poor, bright, and rebellious. Soso's mother wanted him to become a priest, but he dropped out of the seminary to become a Marxist revolutionary. While in exile in 1913 he adopted the pen name "Stalin," which means "man of steel."

Stalin was physically unprepossessing: short of stature with a face that had been pockmarked by smallpox and a left arm permanently bent from a childhood accident. He was not a sophisticated theoretician or inspiring orator, and during the 1920s his rivals had underestimated his abilities. However, Stalin possessed a retentive memory, a practical intelligence, and a keen understanding of how to manipulate other people. Despite his complete ruthlessness, he could be charming when it suited his ends. Averell Harriman, who served as the American ambassador to the Soviet Union from 1943 to 1946, described "his high intelligence, that fantastic grasp of detail, his shrewdness and the surprising human sensitivity that he was capable of showing . . . At the same time, he was, of course, a murderous tyrant."[3]

Stalin was married twice and had three children. His first wife died at a very young age and his second wife, Nadezhda Alliluyeva, committed suicide in 1932. Accounts differ as to whether the cause was primarily depression, Stalin's rudeness, or despair over his policies. Certainly, Stalin was not a model family man. His daughter Svetlana described him as living for politics alone: "He gave himself fully to political interests and emotions, leaving too little room for everything else a man lives by . . . Human feelings in him were replaced by political considerations."[4] Stalin identified himself completely with the Soviet state. Once, berating his son for trying to make use out of his famous name, Stalin told him: "You're not Stalin and I'm not Stalin. Stalin IS

Soviet power. Stalin is what he is in the newspapers and the portraits, not you, not even me!"[5] Consequently, anybody who expressed opposition to Stalin's policies became, by definition, an enemy of Soviet power.

Stalin pretended to be a down-to-earth, modest man of the people, but he cared deeply about his image. According to his daughter, he had a habit of pacing around his Kremlin apartment smoking his pipe and occasionally spitting on the floor. One day his pet parrot mimicked his spitting. Enraged at this imitation of an embarrassingly vulgar habit, he hit the parrot with his pipe, killing it with one blow.[6] Over his years in power, Stalin became increasingly concerned with developing his persona, and he eventually developed a full-scale personality cult.

Modern personality cults, like the ones centered on Stalin and Hitler, use mass media to exalt the leader and thus inspire loyalty to the state. The glorified leader personifies popular sovereignty on a symbolic basis while eliminating actual democracy.[7] Stalin's personality cult surfaced in 1929 in celebration of his fiftieth birthday, when an entire issue of *Pravda* was devoted to articles praising his leadership and accomplishments. After abating during the difficult years of 1930–1932, the cult was revived in 1933 and employed a wide variety of media: paintings, newspaper articles, plays, songs, and films. Visual portraits of Stalin were pervasive and depicted him as invariably calm and authoritative, often gazing thoughtfully outward, presumably into the future, and without pockmarks or a bent arm. Stalin represented the epitome of masculine power and he was portrayed as the great patriarch of the entire Soviet Union. For example, a song described meeting Stalin in distinctly paternal terms:

> You, whose name has reached the stars,
> With the glory of the first wise man,
> Were attentive, affectionate, simple
> And dearer to me than my own father.
> For the joyous, fatherly reception in the Kremlin
> Stalin, my sun, I thank you.[8]

This image of Stalin as the ultimate father became commonplace enough to merit mockery. A joke describes a man applying to the Communist Party who is questioned about his parentage: "Who is your mother?" "Our Soviet Motherland." "Who is your father?" "Our great leader, Comrade Stalin." "And what is it you hope to become?" "An orphan!"[9]

Stalin played an important role in directing his own cult and he personally approved or rejected many of his portraits.[10] However, he pretended to dislike the cult, grudgingly acceding to it only because it expressed the Soviet people's devotion to him, and he periodically scolded those who sought to glorify him. It is likely that he enacted this charade of modesty because the glorification of the leader represented such a blatant contradiction of Marxism's collectivist tenets.

In the past, scholars have disputed Stalin's relationship to the ideas of Marx and Lenin. Conservatives tended to interpret Stalin's policies as the natural outgrowth of Leninist Marxism and therefore as evidence of its immorality. Those on the left, by contrast, saw Stalin as abandoning or perverting Marxist ideas rather than fulfilling them. Recent work provides a synthesis that acknowledges both ideological continuities and the influences of historical contingency. Stalin's personal correspondence indicates that he took Marxism seriously and continued to employ its concepts and terminology even in private letters to his closest allies.[11] It is also clear that Stalin emulated Lenin's willingness to adapt ideology to circumstance; he identified himself as a "creative" rather than "dogmatic" Marxist. But the legacy of Marx and Lenin was filtered through Stalin's own personality and experiences, especially that of the Civil War, and what resulted was less a consistent ideology than, in the words of one historian, a "style of thought, a tendency to see things in a peculiar light, a set of core assumptions making certain decisions less likely than others . . ."[12] The elements of this mentality included a distrust of market forces as dangerously uncontrollable; opposition to religion because it was traditional and offered an alternative source of meaning; the belief that individuals were defined and motivated by the interests of their social class; and the conviction that dangerous enemies lurked near and far, both within Soviet society and among the capitalist and fascist countries encircling the Soviet Union. All of these assumptions came to shape the revolution from above.

Collectivization of agriculture

The collectivization of agriculture was the most radical and deadly aspect of Stalin's revolution. The 1938 history of the Communist Party, which Stalin himself edited, characterized collectivization as a "profound revolution" that was accomplished *"from above*, on the initiative of the state, and directly supported *from below* by the millions of peasants, who were fighting to throw off kulak bondage and to live in freedom in the collective farms."[13] In this section, we will explore this characterization and consider what kind of "revolution" took place.

In chapter 3, we noted the difficulty of disentangling which aspects of the early Soviet state stemmed from ideological preconceptions and which from the exigencies of circumstance. The same problem applies to collectivization, which resulted from immediate economic and political problems but was shaped by beliefs about class warfare and by visions of the socialist future. Hungry urban workers posed an immediate political threat to the stability and legitimacy of a state that had been founded in the name of the proletariat. Grain was needed to feed the cities and to sell abroad in order to fund industrialization, for Stalin claimed that the inevitable future war with the capitalist world could only be won if the country had built up its industrial capacity. Trotsky's vision of international revolution had not been fulfilled, and Stalin's goal was to build and strengthen socialism in one country. Furthermore, collectivization was intended not only to facilitate grain collection, but also to bring enlightenment, modernity, mechanized agriculture, and factory-like efficiency to the backward and ignorant countryside.

Grain requisitioning began in certain regions in 1928 and by 1930 the party had launched full-scale collectivization, recruiting 25,000 urban workers and activists to go out into the countryside and establish collective farms. The poet Vladimir Mayakovsky wrote a poem extolling the revolutionary zeal of these so-called "25,000ers" (see document 5.1). Rural officials, Red Army troops, Komsomol activists, and the OGPU (political police) joined in the effort to "reconstruct the countryside historically on a factory basis," in the words of one volunteer. Collectivizers described their actions as both military campaign and civilizing mission. For example, another 25,000er asserted: "We must declare war on the old traditions and not only increase harvests but concern ourselves with the internalization of culture into the dark peasant masses."[14]

When collectivizers arrived in a village, they would start by holding a public meeting to persuade peasants to join the *kolkhoz* (collective farm), which entailed combining

Figure 5.2 A 1932 poster reads: "By the end of a five-year plan collectivization should be finished." © Heritage Image Partnership Ltd/Alamy.

Compare the imagery in this poster to that used by Mayakovsky in document 5.1. To whom was the poster meant to appeal?

their land and then working in teams to tend it. Collectivizers promised that bigger farms would allow peasants to work more efficiently, using modern technology. Instead of wooden plows, sickles, and scythes, peasants would use tractors and combines, which the state would provide. Peasants expressed doubts about giving up property, working in tandem with neighbors, and subjecting themselves to factory-like discipline. Maurice Hindus, an American journalist, returned to the Russian village of his youth in 1929 and 1930 and recorded such reactions. One peasant explained to him that "we like the feeling of independence. Today we feel like working, and we work; tomorrow we feel like lying down and we lie down; the next day we feel like going to town, and we go to town. We do as we please. But in the Kolkhoz, brother, it is do-as-you-are-told, like a horse—go this way and that, and don't dare turn off the road or you get it hard, a strike or two of the whip on bare flesh . . ."[15]

Peasants sometimes listened to the collectivizers, but sometimes argued or came up with ways to disrupt the meeting before they had to sign anything; for example, someone would interrupt the proceedings by shouting that houses had caught fire or a horse had been stolen, and the peasants would rush off to deal with the "emergency."[16] Such stalling tactics could not hold off officials for long, and when persuasion failed, they would resort to intimidation and even violence. The most powerful threat was to accuse the recalcitrant of being a *kulak* or a *podkulak* (kulak associate or sympathizer.)

The term kulak is derived from the Russian word for fist and so connotes a grasping, tight-fisted person. The Bolsheviks first applied the term to richer peasants during the Civil War, while dividing the rest of the rural population into poor and middle peasants (*bedniaks* and *seredniaks*). The notion of class conflict shaped the Bolshevik understanding of the world, so that they viewed the kulaks as exploitative class enemies and subjected them to additional taxes and other forms of discrimination. In some places, those labeled as kulaks were in fact better off than their neighbors, possessing extra livestock, an orchard, or machinery. Villagers usually attributed this relative prosperity to the kulaks' superior work ethic or sobriety. In other localities, these Bolshevik categories had little resonance among peasants, for their wealth tended to fluctuate over time according to household composition and circumstance. A village blacksmith described the artificiality of these distinctions to Hindus: "We were just neighbors in this village. We quarreled, we fooled, sometimes we cheated one another. But we were neighbors. Now we are *bedniaks, seredniaks, koolacks* . . . and we are supposed to have a class war—pull each other's hair or tickle each other on the toes, eh? One against the other, you understand? What the devil!"[17]

Regardless of how villagers understood their world, Stalin declared that class warfare must be waged in the countryside and that the elimination of the kulaks was essential for collectivization. Committees made up of local party, village soviet, and OGPU officials compiled the names of people designated as kulaks. Those they deemed the most oppositional were shot or sentenced to prison or to labor camps. Others were exiled to settlements in Kazakhstan, Siberia, or the far north, where extreme conditions and limited housing and food supplies caused intense suffering (see document 5.2). The remaining kulaks were allowed to stay in their villages, but they had no means of support because their property was confiscated and they were excluded from the collective farms. Local officials already had registries of kulaks from the previous decade, but other people were added or designated as kulak sympathizers on the basis of opposition to collectivization or local grudges. The committees were supposed to make sure that 3 (and then 5) percent of the population was "dekulaked." Sometimes people were declared kulaks at random so that officials could meet their quota or overfulfill it.

Some of the officials charged with rounding up kulaks and confiscating their possessions believed in the historical necessity of their task. They saw themselves as warriors in a struggle reminiscent of the Civil War. One such student equated dekulakization with military service:

It was not a pleasant job. But neither is going to war and shooting and throwing bombs and thrusting a bayonet into another man's flesh, yet sometimes it has to be done. And this was war and is war. The *koolack* had to be got out of the way as completely as an enemy at the front. He is the enemy at the front. He is the enemy of the *kolkhoz*.[18]

Others were not so ideologically pure and took the opportunity for looting. An OGPU police report described activists and local officials "stealing clothes and shoes, even those actually being worn; eating food they found, and drinking the alcohol. Even spectacles were stolen, and kasha eaten or smeared on ikons."[19]

Although it did not directly serve their mission, collectivizers also attacked religion. They closed churches, seized icons and other sacred objects, and deported priests, pastors, rabbis, and mullahs as kulaks. A Komsomol member at the time later recalled: "Markedly militant atheism and rowdy behavior were particularly fashionable in the Komsomol at that time." He traced these antireligious feelings to the fact that "the Revolution shook the countryside and disclosed many flaws in the ancestral order of things. The peasants' traditional ignorance was associated in our minds with their faith in God."[20] Militants reveled in offending what they saw as backward village superstition. In one village, for example, Komsomol members held a mock trial of the saints depicted in icons during which they sentenced the saints to death and then shot up the icons.[21] These actions further soured relations between urban collectivizers and the peasants and even sometimes helped to fuel rumors of an impending apocalypse.

Stalin's assertion that collectivization was supported by "millions of peasants" was belied by widespread resistance. According to security police, more than 13,000 peasant "mass actions" occurred over the course of 1930.[22] Rather than turning their livestock over to the kolkhoz, peasants slaughtered their cows, pigs, sheep, and chickens, sold the meat they could, and ate the rest, with dire consequences for the meat supply in the following years. Peasants hid kulak neighbors, publicly opposed dekulakization, beat or even killed individual party officials and 25,000ers, and burned down kolkhoz buildings. Some demonstrations became so violent and prolonged that the Red Army had to be mobilized to suppress them.

Peasant women often took the lead in protests. They would join together to pummel officials, seize livestock that had been taken for the collective farm, block the carts that were transporting grain away from the village, or stand in front of a kulak's house to prevent the confiscation of his goods.[23] Officials dismissed these incidents as *bab'i bunty*, or women's riots. The English translation does not fully capture the flavor of the original phrase, for a baba is not just a woman, but a backward and irrational one. Officials blamed these riots on the instigation of kulaks, who, they claimed, manipulated the babas' ignorance and emotional volatility. However, these women were responding to real concerns about Soviet policy and they acted strategically, for they were aware that they could get away with actions that would result in much harsher punishments for men. During one of Hindus' discussions, some of the men explained that, during collectivization meetings, they were afraid that if they objected, they would be labeled kulaks. So they "let the women do the talking . . ." A woman explained that because the men were afraid "we decided we'd do something on our account, and many of us came with our babies on purpose, because we knew that the laws about women with babies would prevent their touching us."[24]

By early 1930, the countryside was in turmoil. Stalin responded to the crises with an article in *Pravda* in March calling for a slower pace of collectivization and claiming that local officials had become "dizzy with success," and in their eagerness to transform the countryside had committed "excesses" by forcing peasants into the collective farms instead of relying on persuasion. Stalin's mendacious attempt to shift blame from central authorities to lower level officials indicates that he was genuinely worried about the extent of peasant resistance. Many soldiers heard about the upheaval from relatives in the countryside, so there was the added danger of opposition spreading to the Red Army. Some peasants took the opportunity afforded by Stalin's temporary retreat to withdraw from collective farms, but since they couldn't get their land or animals back, it was difficult for them to sustain themselves as independent farmers. In any case, by the fall the collectivization campaign had resumed.

Despite the chaos in the countryside, the 1930 grain harvest was plentiful, and the government responded by raising the amount of grain that peasants were required to provide for the following year. But the harvests fell off during the next two years, leaving the peasants unable to meet their quotas. The government sent out special brigades to seize grain and they took everything, including the families' individual supplies and seed grain for next year's crop. People in grain-growing areas, especially in Ukraine, Kazakhstan, and the Northern Caucasus were left without food. They ate bark, dandelions, grass, rats, dogs, insects, and snails. They cooked glue and old shoes and furs. There were reports of cannibalism. Between five and seven million people died of starvation and disease in the years 1932–1933, but the Soviet press did not mention the famine and roadblocks were set up to prevent starving peasants from coming into cities to beg. When some peasants found a way through anyway, they were dismissed as fakers. A man who grew up at the time recalled "Moscow being flooded with destitute, famished peasants in tatters with their hungry children wrapped in rags." When one of his classmates asked a teacher about them, she explained "that they were lazy people who did not want to work on the land and the Militia would soon clear them out of town."[25]

The famine coincided with the arrest of many Ukrainian intellectuals, officials, and professionals. This has led some scholars, and many Ukrainians, to interpret the famine as part of a larger policy intended to destroy the Ukrainian nation. This conviction became a source of bitter anti-Soviet and anti-Russian feelings among Ukrainians, and it has shaped Ukrainian national identity in the years since the breakup of the Soviet Union. Many Western historians, however, do not see the famine as genocidal in intent, since it affected many other ethnicities within Ukraine (Jews, Russians, Poles) and other areas outside of Ukraine. But there is no question that this was a man-made rather than a natural disaster. The Soviet state was culpable in causing and prolonging the famine by continuing to seize grain and even export it while peasants starved. Some of those who requisitioned grain became profoundly disillusioned; others found ways to justify their actions. One participant later recalled his mentality: "I mustn't give in to debilitating pity. We were realizing historical necessity. We were performing our revolutionary duty. We were obtaining grain for the socialist fatherland. For the five-year plan."[26]

Despite chaos, starvation, and violence, the collectivization of agriculture proceeded; by 1937, 93 percent of peasant households had been enrolled in collective farms. When the process began, there was no clear blueprint for a kolkhoz, so collectivizers improvised. Throughout the 1930s, structures and practices were gradually codified to establish a standard model. The traditional peasant commune, the mir, was abolished in 1930, and village authority shifted to the chair of the collective farm and the head of the village soviet. Most of the land and tools became the collective property of the kolkhoz members. Each household was guaranteed the right to keep a small plot, one cow, a limited number of pigs or sheep, and unlimited poultry. Peasants lived off the produce grown on their private plots, and they were permitted to sell any surplus at farmers' markets in towns and cities. These "kolkhoz markets" became an essential source of food throughout the Soviet epoch. Kolkhoz members could not concentrate all of their efforts on their personal plots, however, because they were required to work in teams on the collective farm. Despite the promises to introduce factory organization into the countryside, the collective farm workers did not receive wages as workers did. At the end of the year, after the kolkhoz had paid its taxes, the profits were divided among the members according to how many workday units they had completed. A workday unit was not synonymous with a day of work, because various kinds of work were valued differently; a day of work for a kolkhoz chairman, accountant, or tractor driver was worth more workday units than that for a field worker, milkmaid, or shepherd. While class warfare justified collectivization, the new system introduced another form of hierarchy.

To what extent did collectivization constitute a revolution? The Soviet state succeeded in introducing sweeping changes to the countryside. It amalgamated smallholdings into big farms and it eventually introduced mechanized agriculture, although shortages of machinery meant that old methods persisted. It destroyed the institutions that had shaped rural life for centuries, the peasant commune and the local church, and it replaced them with Soviet and party organizations, kolkhoz administrations, and secular schools and clubs.

However, many peasants saw collectivization not as a leap into the future, but as a return to the past and the system of serfdom that had governed the rural population until the emancipation of 1861. Collective farmers compared their required work on the kolkhoz with the serfs' obligation to work for free on their masters' estates. In tsarist Russia, serfs were heavily taxed; so were collective farmers, who had to pay individual household taxes as well as taxes assessed on the collective farms to which they belonged. Serfs were legally bound to the land. Collective farmers' mobility was limited in 1932 when the government issued internal passports to all citizens except collective farm workers. Because citizens had to show their passports when they changed jobs or residences, this policy meant that collective farm workers had to get special permission from the kolkhoz administration in order to move away from the farm or get a job in a factory. It was just this loss of autonomy that had been anticipated by some of the peasants Hindus met in 1929 and which had motivated their opposition to collectivization. One of them explained: "Now, however poor we may be, we have our own rye and our own potatoes and our own cucumbers and our own milk. We know we won't starve. But in the Kolkhoz, no more potatoes of our own no more anything of our own. Everything will be rationed out by orders; we shall be like mere batraks [hired laborers] on the landlord's estates in the old days. Serfdom—that is what it is—and who wants to be a serf?"[27]

Rapid industrialization and the First Five-Year Plan

As the Great Depression hit the United States and Europe, people across the world began to question the superiority of capitalism; perhaps socialism offered a more just and equitable path to development. In Wisconsin, a young American named John Scott dropped out of college. "Something seemed to be wrong with America," he wrote in his memoirs; after training as a welder, he set off to find work in a place with no unemployment: the Soviet Union. In 1931, he ended up in Magnitogorsk, a brand new city built to produce steel and located at the southern end of the Ural mountains, more than 800 miles from Moscow. There, Scott wrote: "I was precipitated into a battle. I was deployed on the iron and steel front. Tens of thousands of people were enduring the most intense hardships in order to build blast furnaces, and many of them did it willingly, with boundless enthusiasm . . ."[28]

The battle that Scott described was part of the First Five-Year Plan for the National Economy, initially introduced in 1928. The plan called for the rapid development of industrial capacity, which, as we have seen, was to be funded by exporting the grain produced by the collectivized peasantry. For Stalin, industrialization was crucial to the survival of the Soviet state, which was surrounded by hostile capitalist powers. In a much publicized speech in 1931, he described all of Russia's historical military defeats and declared, "We are fifty to one hundred years behind the advanced countries. We must cover this distance in ten years. Either we do this, or they will crush us."[29] The First Five-Year Plan itself was several volumes long and replete with graphs and charts that seemed to symbolize the promise that scientific management could control the economic forces that buffeted human lives under capitalism. In a capitalist economy, the mechanism of supply and demand determines the prices and quantities of commodities. In the Soviet planned economy, state agencies, staffed by experts, took the place of the market and determined what and how much should be produced in each sector of the economy.

The vision of order and rationality suggested by the First Five-Year Plan was contradicted by the extreme ways in which it was revised and enacted. The plan was rewritten several times to increase economic growth targets, and with each iteration it demanded more and more from heavy industry. For example, over the course of 1929, the quotas for pig-iron production from new factories was raised from 1.3 to 2.6 million tons and then again to 6.1 million, which was almost five times the original target.[30] The plan also included grandiose construction projects: immense factories, dams, canals, railroads, and entire cities such as Magnitogorsk. In fact, the First Five-Year Plan's goals were impossible to achieve. However, its real purpose was political; it was meant to demonstrate priorities and to inspire people with the idea that they were participating in a historic, revolutionary task. The plan resulted in substantial growth (industrial output increased by more than 50 percent), but also confusion and instability.

As the pace of industrialization intensified, workers faced cold, hunger, danger, and exhaustion. Their shifts were lengthened and their real wages fell. Factories were unsafe and turmoil in the countryside disrupted food supplies. Housing construction did not keep pace with the growing urban population, so workers were crammed into communal apartments, dorms, barracks, and even tents. John Scott described hazardous working conditions and the mentality that justified them. One day, while helping to construct a new blast furnace, he witnessed a rigger falling off the top of rickety scaffolding. He reported the incident to the foreman, who was unconcerned. "He pointed out that there was not enough planking for good scaffolds, that the riggers were mostly plowboys who had no idea of being careful, and that at thirty-five below without any breakfast in you, you did not pay as much attention as you should." Then he told Scott, "Sure people will fall. But we're building blast furnaces all the same, aren't we?"[31]

Industrial managers were compelled to meet their output targets, but the raw materials and spare parts they needed for production were often in short supply. They developed a variety of methods to cope with the situation, including hoarding supplies and using special expediters or "pushers" to procure what they needed by bartering and bargaining with suppliers and other factories. These strategies sometimes allowed individual managers to succeed, but they disrupted the planners' calculations and undermined the vision of a rational and controlled alternative to market forces.

Just as resistance to collectivization was attributed to kulak agitation, the failure to meet production goals could be blamed on sabotage by class enemies. The first such accusation occurred in 1928 and was directed against a group of engineers working in the Shakhty coal mines who had been trained under the old regime and were thus designated as "bourgeois experts." According to the OGPU, the engineers had conspired with foreign powers and Soviet émigrés to sabotage production in order to weaken the Soviet state and hasten the restoration of capitalism. The only evidence presented at the very public trial consisted of testimonies from workers and confessions extracted from the accused. Of the fifty-three men tried, four were acquitted, five were executed, and the rest were imprisoned. After the resolution of the "Shakhty affair," as it was called, Stalin warned about the continued danger of "wrecking" by such bourgeois experts, which set off a whole series of arrests of engineers and also officials in finance, planning, industry, and trade.

The persecution of engineers abated by 1931 because their expertise was still vital, but in the interval the state had begun to educate workers on a mass scale in order to produce a more politically reliable set of technicians and managers. The state expanded education on all levels, mandating compulsory elementary education for Soviet children and recruiting workers into higher education. Large numbers of working class students moved into new positions of authority as engineers, technicians, industrial managers, and Communist Party officials. Nikita Khrushchev, Leonid Brezhnev, and an entire generation of Soviet leaders, born into poverty, began their education and ascent to power in these years. This type of profound social change is one of the main reasons why scholars characterize the First Five-Year Plan as revolutionary. Just as significant was the growth of the working class and urban population that took place during this time. The number of workers more than doubled in 1928–1932 from 6.8 million to 14.5 million.[32] Most of these new workers were young and many came from the countryside; 18 million peasants moved to the cities between 1929 and 1935.[33] The Soviet state also recruited 1.6 million women into industry, many for skilled jobs that had been previously reserved for men. Activists ensured that they received training and worked to eliminate harassment and discrimination, an emancipatory agenda that only lasted through the First Five-Year Plan, although women's labor remained essential to the Soviet economy.[34]

Rapid industrialization was initiated from above, but how was it received from below? John Scott described a sense of excitement among young workers, recounting a conversation in which complaints about food shortages gave way to expressions of hope. Anya, a welder, was one of the young women who had recently entered a skilled, previously all male, trade. She predicted that in "five or ten years we won't need one single thing from the capitalist world." A rigger replied, "In five or ten years there won't be any capitalist world . . ."[35] Enthusiastic workers, labeled "shock workers," participated in shop floor competitions to see who could do the most to increase productivity, reduce costs, and overfulfill production targets.

Such fervor was not universal. Many workers expressed their disgruntlement by skipping work and switching jobs; on average, a worker lasted only eight months on a site before moving on to seek better conditions. Workers also organized slowdowns and demonstrations and wrote letters of complaint to officials and the press. In one unpublished letter sent to *Pravda* a worker compared himself to a beaten down horse: "A horse with its own strength can drag seventy-five poods, but its owner has loaded it with a hundred poods, and in addition he has fed it poorly. No matter how much he uses the whip, it still won't be able to move the cart. This is also true for the working class."[36] The most dramatic expressions of discontent took place in the textile industry, which was rocked by a series of violent demonstrations and strikes. A leaflet confiscated in one of the affected mills expressed the conviction that the government had betrayed its revolutionary promises by exploiting the workers. It read, in part: "We see what the Soviet regime has brought us to. The oppression of the workers grows more and more with each passing day. A serious hunger hangs over us. The enslavement of all the working people has intensified to the ultimate degree."[37]

The anonymous pamphleteer used the term enslavement as a rhetorical device, but in fact unfree labor played an important role in industrialization. The Gulag (an acronym for Main Administration of Corrective Labor Camps) had been established after the October Revolution, but its population rose sharply during the First Five-Year Plan from 20,000 prisoners in 1928 to one million by 1934. Kulaks, NEP men, clergy, "bourgeois wreckers," and other alleged class enemies were confined to labor camps where they were forced to mine metals and fell timber in remote regions in the far north. Prisoners built an entire 141-mile-long canal connecting the Baltic and White Sea using nothing but hand tools. Conditions were horrific and as many as 25,000 prisoners working on the canal died during the winter of 1931–1932.[38]

Maxim Gorky, the novelist, collaborated with other writers on a collection of articles celebrating the opening of the Baltic White Sea Canal, known in Russian as the Belomorkanal. Gorky had spent most of the 1920s in exile, but he returned at the end of the decade and became the dominant figure in the literary world. He and his colleagues toured the canal and produced descriptions of how honest labor had transformed criminals and kulaks into dedicated socialists. An OGPU guard at the site expressed a more ambivalent view:

> I had my doubts about the Five-Year Plan. I did not understand why we had to drive so many convicts to their deaths to finish the canal. Why did it have to be done so fast? At times it troubled me. But I justified it by the conviction that we were building something great, not just a canal, but a new society that could not have been built by volunteer means.[39]

What does this quotation suggest about the pace and methods of this "revolution from above"? What does it reveal about the mindset of the participants?

Youth and revolution

Born too late to have participated in the October Revolution and the Civil War, young activists saw collectivization and the First Five-Year Plan as their own revolutionary battleground. Komsomol newspaper articles and speeches were couched in a militarized language of struggles, fronts, and campaigns. One Komsomol member later described how an "atmosphere of undaunted struggle in a common cause . . . engaged our imagination, roused our enthusiasm, and drew us into a sort of front-line world where difficulties were overlooked or forgotten."[40]

Young people carried this militancy into cultural, political, and educational institutions during what historian Sheila Fitzpatrick has labeled as a "cultural revolution." Fitzpatrick, and many subsequent historians, use this term to encompass several connected developments that took place in the years 1928–1931: attacks on "bourgeois experts" and the recruitment of workers into management and higher education (discussed above), as well as campaigns to revolutionize culture and education.[41] What this last goal meant in practice was open to multiple interpretations. Under the slogan of cultural revolution, university students claimed the right to elect their professors and Marxist historians sought to drive noncommunist scholars out of their departments. Members of the Russian Association of Musicians tried to abolish "bourgeois" classical music and jazz, which they associated with the "spiritual degradation" of slavery, and instead promoted the creation of "mass songs" with easily recognized melodies that could be sung by untrained musicians.[42] Their literary counterparts in the Russian Association of Proletarian Writers (known by its Russian acronym of RAPP) condemned genres they deemed decadent, such as detective stories, science fiction, and fairy tales, as well as avant-garde writers whose work was incomprehensible to the average proletarian. The modernist poet Mayakovsky fell into this category despite his enthusiasm for revolution. He shot himself in 1930, an act attributed alternatively to despair over his complicated love life or to profound political disillusionment. He left a poem as a suicide note: "As they say, 'The incident is closed.'/Love boat/Smashed on convention."[43]

The cultural revolution cooled down by the end of 1931. Some professionals regained their positions and RAPP and its related proletarian arts associations were eventually disbanded. But the following year the press began to publicize a new symbol of youthful revolutionary ardor: a thirteen year old named Pavlik Morozov. According to the official version, Pavlik was an activist in the Pioneers (the junior version of the Komsomol) who lived in the remote and impoverished village of Gerasimovka in the northern Ural region. In 1932, he reported his father to the secret police for helping kulaks to hoard grain. His relatives found out about his accusation and retaliated by murdering Pavlik along with his younger brother; however, Soviet justice caught up with them and they were tried and executed. A boy named Pavel Morozov and his brother Fedor really were killed in the village of Gerasimovka in the Urals, but not much else about this story can be confirmed, despite the exhaustive efforts of an intrepid historian to uncover the truth.[44] Regardless of what actually occurred, hagiographic renditions of Pavlik's life appeared in books, songs, poems, and school curricula throughout the Soviet era and Pavlik became an example to all young people of loyalty and self-sacrifice. Maxim Gorky campaigned to get a monument to Pavlik built in Moscow, and in a speech at a Komsomol rally described "the heroic deed of Pioneer Pavel Morozov, the boy who understood that a person who is a relative by blood may well be an enemy of the spirit, and that such a person is not to be spared."[45]

While some young people were stirred by Pavlik's story, many were more inspired by his unselfish devotion than his act of denunciation. A man who had been active in the Pioneers at the time described his ambivalent reaction: "I read a serial about little Pavlik Morozov's murder and day-dreamed about unmasking kulaks myself. Once again, however, these ideas coexisted with my dislike of tattle-tales and informers, my admiration for many kinds of illegalities, and my belief in loyalty among friends."[46] While children very rarely reported their parents to the secret police, other forms of estrangement did occur. A Komsomol activist later recalled: "In my work with children

I cannot recall any instance of children being inspired to denounce their parents in the spirit of Pavlik Morozov, but I know of cases where Komsomol members left their parents because they could not reconcile themselves to their political views."[47]

Children of kulaks, clergy members, and other "enemies" were subject to discrimination and so sometimes cut themselves off from family for reasons of survival and ambition as well as political conviction. Young people wrote letters to the press renouncing their relatives or simply obscured their origins. The promising young poet Alexander Tvardovsky was one of these. The son of a blacksmith, Tvardovsky joined the Komsomol in the 1920s and then became a member of RAPP. His first published poem, which came out in 1927, criticized his father's humble prosperity. Entitled "To a Father and Rich Man," it read:

> In your home there is no shortage,
> You are rich—and I know this,
> Of all the five-walled peasant houses,
> The best is yours.[48]

Tvardovsky enrolled in teachers' college in the city and continued to publish political poems. Meanwhile, the rest of his family were condemned as kulaks and deported from their village. Alexander's parents wrote to him from a special settlement and he wrote back saying: "I cannot write to you . . . do not write to me." Later his father escaped from the settlement with his youngest son, Pavlik, and went to see Alexander, who refused to help him and then betrayed him to the police. His brother Ivan later theorized that Alexander secretly expressed remorse in poetry that was never published:

> What are you, brother?
> How are you, brother?
> Where are you, brother?
> On what Belomorkanal?"[49]

Years later, in seeking to understand his brother's actions, Ivan reflected:

> I now think that Alexander saw the revolutionary violence that swept away our parents, brothers and sisters, although unjust and mistaken, as a kind of test, to see if he could prove himself as a true member of the Komsomol . . . No doubt he rationalized it this way: "every kulak is somebody's father and his children someone's brothers and sisters. What makes my family any different? Be brave and strong, don't give in to abstract humanitarianism and other feelings outside class interests."[50]

As editor of the literary journal *Novyi mir* in the 1950s, Alexander Tvardovsky would later play an important role in publicizing the crimes of Stalinism (see chapter 9).

CONCLUSION AND FURTHER QUESTIONS

John Scott, the American who went to work in Magnitogorsk, eventually married a Russian woman whom he met there. His wife Masha exemplified the kind of upward

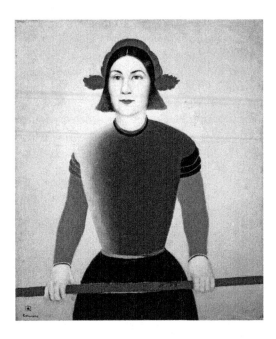

Figure 5.3 Kazimir Malevich, *A Girl with a Red Pole*, 1932–1933. © Heritage Image Partnership Ltd/Alamy.

Do you think this painting was the kind of decadent "bourgeois" art that was incomprehensible to the average proletarian? Why or why not? How do you interpret the girl's expression? Do you think she is more like Masha or Vera?

mobility made possible during this period. She grew up one of eight children in a poor peasant family that shared a one and half room hut; she didn't get her first pair of shoes until she started secondary school at age fourteen. During the 1920s the family's life grew easier and they were deeply grateful to the Soviet government for providing new opportunities for education and advancement. Masha followed an older sister to Magnitogorsk, where she enrolled in teachers' college and worked as a secretary and "was very happy . . . She felt that the world was at her feet."[51]

Masha was an ambitious career woman and, like her husband, worked and studied long hours. After their daughter was born, their lives were thrown into disarray until they hired a sixteen year old girl named Vera who shopped, cooked, and took care of the baby. Vera's father had been injured on the job and earned meager wages as a watchman, so Vera needed the housekeeping job to survive. Her family had come to Magnitogorsk in 1930 after being "dekulaked" and had spent their first winter there in a tent; conditions were harsh and one of Vera's brothers, her sister, and her mother all died. Vera worked for Scott's family for three years, and then in 1938 the police forced her and several thousand other children of kulaks to move further north and east to Chelyabinsk to build a new arms factory. According to Scott, "Vera received a mimeographed notice, and was herded off in a freight train the next night. We never saw her after that, but I am told that the plant in Chelyabinsk was constructed on schedule and went into production in 1941."[52]

The story of these two young women illustrates some of the great political and social changes of this period. The collectivization of agriculture, the First Five-Year Plan, and the cultural revolution all resulted in progress and hope for some and devastation for others. Masha was one of the beneficiaries of the era, but to what extent was her success made possible by Vera, one of the victims?

PRIMARY SOURCES

Use the questions to analyze the content, context, and significance of each primary source. Then synthesize the primary sources and the material in the chapter to formulate a response to the primary chapter question: To what extent did the policies of collectivization, rapid industrialization, and cultural revolution constitute a "revolution from above"?

Document 5.1   Excerpt from Vladimir Mayakovsky's "March of the Twenty-Five Thousand"

Questions for analysis

1   What kind of military imagery does the poet use and what meaning does it convey?
2   What is the poet's vision for the future?

> Onward, 25
> Onward 25
> Steel
> Worker thousanders.
> The enemy is advancing
> It's time to finish off
> This band
> Of priest-kulaks
> Let thousand horse-power
> tractors puff
> instead of
> worn out nags.
> The Kulak is ready—
> Look,
> Again
> With a sawn-off rifle
> Burrowed in the backwoods.
> Fall, harvest
> Under the reaping machine
> Let triple the grain
> Be harvested
> We will build sunny
> Leninist socialism
> On Soviet arable land

Source: Vladimir Maiakovskii, "Marsh dvadtsati piati tysiach," *Polnoe sobranie sochinenii, tom desiatyi* (Moscow: Khudozhestvennaia literature, 1958), 177–178. English translation adapted from Lynne Viola, *The Best Sons of the Fatherland* (Oxford: Oxford University Press, 1987), vii.

Document 5.2   The OGPU reports on letters from exiled kulaks

Questions for analysis

1   Why do you think the OGPU is reading the kulaks' mail?
2   What are living conditions like for exiled kulaks?
3   What is their attitude toward Soviet power?

In all, 16,790 communications have been processed and read. Of this total, 10,504, or 63 percent, had a negative content; 143 communications, or 0.9 percent, had a positive content; 6,143 communications, or 36.1 percent, were apolitical; and 8,871 communications, or 53 percent, were confiscated.

The most typical statements are quoted below:

. . .

"All right, we could have been allowed to suffer, but why on earth are the children with us being tormented, after all, one is eight and the other two years old, after all, how does Soviet power view children. Vania, after all, was a Young Pioneer, and we are landless laborers, and didn't have our own farm or land. The children cry bitterly because there is nothing to eat. They went to the woods and out of hunger filled themselves up with grass, but it was a kind of grass that could have poisoned them, and so people came to me and said that my children are walking around the woods and throwing up. I ran out and brought them back to the barracks, we began to take care of them, they're alive for now, but they walk around like shadows, because we get 16 kilograms of flour a month for six people . . ."

"What a wicked fate has befallen me, I still can't believe that they did this to me, and why they are tormenting me this way, as if I were a rich man or hurt somebody, they are bunglers and bloodsuckers and nothing more. We are starving here, and there's nothing to buy, nothing to eat. It's incredible how they abuse us, prisoners have it much better, they get special work clothes, three pounds of bread, but we get nothing, that's the kind of criminals we are, they'll probably torture us to death, the snakes. A lot of people are already starving to death. The damned scoundrels, I feel sorry for the people, and myself as well. What are they tormenting us for, for our property? Is it really possible the scoundrels won't come to their senses and let us live freely?"

Source: Survey by the OGPU Information Department of letters from kulaks exiled to the Northern Krai, not before 1 July 1930. Document 74 in Lynne Viola, V. P. Danilov, N. A. Ivnitskii, and Denis Kozlov, eds., *The War against the Peasantry 1927–1930* (New Haven, CT, and London: Yale University Press, 2005), 316–318. Used by permission of Yale University Press.

Document 5.3   An activist's memoirs

Questions for analysis

1   How does the author describe the young generation?
2   How does he explain his own motivation?
3   How does his viewpoint compare to those expressed in the first two documents? What accounts for the similarities and differences?

This was a new generation of young people, driven not by hatred of the enemies of the Soviet regime, but by a desire to see their country become mechanized and a wish to master technical matters themselves. In the eyes of these boys and girls one could catch the same blind stare as in the eyes of the people of my age during the Civil War. They froze their fingers, worked up to their knees in mud and got soaked by rain, but they did not walk off the job. At difficult times we set up "shock brigades" and "crash brigades" which worked from 16 to 18 hours a day.

. . .

It is true that it was not a desire for honors or rewards that caused me to do without sleep and to devote all my energy to the Party and the Komsomol. I carried out all kinds of small and large Party and Komsomol tasks in answer to some inner call. I believed that the construction of socialism in our country would radically change the future of the nation and that by a high degree of mechanization of labor and scientific achievements the doors would be flung open to cultural growth and a life free of care. I saw that the older generation, worn out after years of the war and the postwar chaos, were no longer in a position to withstand the difficulties involved in the construction of socialism. I thus came to the conclusion that success in transforming the country depended entirely on the physical exertions and the will of persons like myself. And I went among the young people to infect them with my faith and my belief in the approaching hour of the victory of socialism and to lead them to share in the most difficult parts of this construction program.

Source: Nikolai Lunev, "Blind Faith in a Bright Future," in Nikolai K. Novak-Deker, ed., *Soviet Youth: Twelve Komsomol Histories* (Munich: Institute for the Study of the USSR, 1959), 33–34.

Notes

1 D. Volkogonov, "Stalin's Mind," in Chris Ward, ed., *The Stalinist Dictatorship* (London: Arnold Publishers, 1998), 86.
2 Oleg V. Khlevniuk, *Master of the House: Stalin and His Inner Circle* (New Haven, CT: Yale University Press, 2009), 253.
3 As quoted in Hiroaki Kuromiya, *Stalin* (London: Pearson Education Ltd, 2005), 203.
4 As quoted in Kuromiya, *Stalin*, 202.
5 As quoted in Simon Sebag Montefiore, *Stalin: The Court of the Red Tsar* (London: Weidenfeld & Nicolson, 2003), 4.
6 Robert C. Tucker, *Stalin in Power: The Revolution from Above 1928–1941* (New York: W. W. Norton, 1990), 147.
7 Jan Plamper, *The Stalin Cult: A Study in the Alchemy of Power* (New Haven, CT: Yale University Press, 2012), xviii.
8 Plamper, *The Stalin Cult*, 93–94.
9 As quoted in Bruce Adams, *Tiny Revolutions in Russia: Twentieth-Century Soviet and Russian History in Anecdotes* (New York: RougledgeCurzon, 2005), 47.
10 Plamper, *Stalin Cult*, 127.
11 Sarah Davies and James Harris, "Joseph Stalin: Power and Ideas," in Sarah Davies and James Harris, eds., *Stalin: A New History* (Cambridge: Cambridge University Press, 2005), 12.
12 Mark Edele, *Stalinist Society* (Oxford: Oxford University Press, 2011), 126.
13 As quoted in Tucker, *Stalin in Power*, xiii, original emphasis.
14 As quoted in Lynne Viola, *The Best Sons of the Fatherland: Workers in the Vanguard of Soviet Collectivization* (New York: Oxford University Press, 1987), 67.
15 As quoted in Maurice Hindus, *Red Bread* (Bloomington: Indiana University Press, 1988), 25.

16 Sheila Fitzpatrick, *Stalin's Peasants* (Oxford: Oxford University Press, 1994), 51.
17 As quoted in Hindus, *Red Bread*, 22.
18 As quoted in Hindus, *Red Bread*, 181.
19 As quoted in Robert Conquest, *The Harvest of Sorrow: Soviet Collectivization and the Terror-Famine* (London: Hutchinson, 1986), 131.
20 As quoted in Nikolai Bosharov, "Off the Beaten Track," in Nikolai K. Novak-Deker, ed., *Soviet Youth: Twelve Komsomol Histories* (Munich: Institute for the Study of the USSR, 1959), 50.
21 Fitzpatrick, *Stalin's Peasants*, 61.
22 Kuromiya, *Stalin*, 91.
23 L. Viola, "Babi Bunty and Peasant Women's Protest during Collectivization," in Ward, ed., *The Stalinist Dictatorship*, 221.
24 As quoted in Hindus, *Red Bread*, 170.
25 As quoted in Oleg Krasovsky, "Early Years," in Nikolai K. Novak-Deker, ed., *Soviet Youth*, 132.
26 As quoted in Lev Kopelev, *The Education of a True Believer* (New York: Harper & Row, 1980), 235.
27 As quoted in Hindus, *Red Bread*, 24.
28 John Scott, *Behind the Urals: An American Worker in Russia's City of Steel* (Bloomington: Indiana University Press, 1989), 5–6.
29 Kuromiya, *Stalin*, 86.
30 Paul R. Gregory, *The Political Economy of Stalinism* (Cambridge: Cambridge University Press, 2004), 120.
31 Scott, *Behind the Urals*, 21.
32 M. Lewin, "Society, State and Ideology during the First Five-Year Plan," in Ward, ed., *The Stalinist Dictatorship*, 182.
33 Vladimir Andrle, *Workers in Stalin's Russia* (New York: St. Martin's Press, 1988), 32.
34 Wendy Z. Goldman, *Women at the Gates: Gender and Industry in Stalin's Russia* (Cambridge: Cambridge University Press, 2002), 281–282.
35 Scott, *Behind the Urals*, 43.
36 As quoted in Lewis Siegelbaum and Andrei Sokolov, *Stalinism as a Way of Life* (New Haven, CT: Yale University Press, 2000), 39–40.
37 As quoted in Jeffrey J. Rossman, *Worker Resistance under Stalin* (Cambridge, MA: Harvard University Press, 2005), 175.
38 Orlando Figes, *The Whisperers: Private Life in Stalin's Russia* (New York: Henry Holt, 2007), 113–114.
39 As quoted in Figes, *The Whisperers*, 111.
40 As quoted in W. I. Hryshko, "An Interloper in the Komsomol," in Novak-Deker, ed., *Soviet Youth*, 98.
41 Sheila Fitzpatrick, "Cultural Revolution as Class Warfare," in Sheila Fitzpatrick, ed., *Cultural Revolution in Russia 1928–1931* (Bloomington: Indiana University Press, 1978), 9.
42 Neil Edmunds, "Music and Politics: The Case of the Russian Association of Proletarian Musicians," *Slavonic and East European Review*, 78, no. 1 (Jan. 2000): 76.
43 As quoted in Edward J. Brown, *Russian Literature since the Revolution* (Cambridge, MA: Harvard University Press, 1982), 20.
44 Catriona Kelly, *Comrade Pavlik: The Rise and Fall of a Soviet Boy Hero* (London: Granta Books, 2005).
45 As quoted in Kelly, *Comrade Pavlik*, 144.
46 As quoted in Peter Kruzhin, "False Dawn," in Novak-Deker, ed., *Soviet Youth*, 191.
47 As quoted in N. Khvalynsky, "Life in the Countryside," in Novak-Deker, ed., *Soviet Youth*, 125.
48 Figes, *The Whisperers*, 132.
49 Figes, *The Whisperers*, 134.
50 Figes, *The Whisperers*, 135–136.
51 Scott, *Behind the Urals*, 123.
52 Scott, *Behind the Urals*, 131.

6 Making sense of Stalinism
Enthusiasm and terror

INTRODUCTION

On 1 February 1937, a crowd estimated at 200,000 paraded through Moscow, where temperatures were four degrees below zero Fahrenheit, to demand that death sentences be "pitilessly and speedily" carried out against thirteen high profile Bolshevik officials convicted of participating in a vast, fantastic (indeed fabricated) conspiracy aimed at destroying Soviet socialism. The trial, the second of three "show trials," had taken less than a week. All of the accused confessed their guilt, claiming that they had acted on orders from the exiled Lev Trotsky.[1]

Just ten days later Moscow was the scene of another spectacle as some 25,000 people crowded into the newly renamed Pushkin Square to celebrate the centenary of the great poet's death. The following day a story in the *New York Times* tried to capture the festive mood, describing the whole city, indeed the entire country, as "Pushkin-mad": "There were processions, mass meetings in public squares, gala performances of grand opera and special performances in theaters, movie houses, and workers' clubs." Alexander Pushkin, who in the first decades of Soviet power had been unceremoniously "thrown from the steamship of modernity" (in the words of the modernist poet Vladimir Mayakovsky, see chapters 2 and 5), became in 1937 a Soviet icon.

The thousands of people who braved the cold to express their hatred of Trotskyites and their love of Pushkin illustrate the paradoxes of Stalinism in the 1930s. Life in Stalin's Soviet Union encompassed on the one hand show trials, arrests, fears of espionage and sabotage, and on the other celebrations of the joyous, cultured, prosperous present and the radiant future. Arthur Koestler, a Hungarian communist who left the party in 1938, described the paradoxical climate as "darkness at noon." Historians have also called on Pushkin's metaphor for the era of Nicholas I, another dark time in Russian history: "feast in a time of plague."

CHAPTER QUESTIONS

This chapter explores the paradoxes of "darkness at noon." The early sections focus on promises of plenty that emerged in the mid-1930s. We pay particular attention to the shifting values that went along with the joyous and happy life deemed to have emerged from the industrialization drive, and ask: Did the Soviet state's apparent reversals in the spheres of family policy, nationalities policy, and foreign policy constitute "betrayals" of the revolution, efforts to defend socialism, or concessions to popular opinion?

The second half of the chapter turns to the darker side of the 1930s: the Great Terror. Here the central questions are: How did Soviet citizens and officials justify or explain the terror to themselves? To what extent and in what ways did the repressive Stalinist state cultivate and win popular support?

VOICES, MEMORIES, CONTESTED PERSPECTIVES

Promises of plenty

If 1933, a year of famine and slow industrial growth, had been the "worst year of the decade,"[2] 1934 promised abundance, comfort, and happiness. In late January the delegates to the Seventeenth Party Congress—the so-called Congress of Victors—celebrated Soviet achievements in agriculture and industry and feted Comrade Stalin. The Second Five-Year Plan was beginning to make good on the pledge to supply more consumer goods, and Soviet shoppers found—or were assured they would soon find—stores stocked not only with staples but also with luxuries such as perfume, caviar, and Soviet champagne. In 1936, a new constitution—naturally called the "Stalin Constitution"—declared the first phase of socialist construction complete, extended equal rights to all Soviet citizens, and guaranteed freedom of religion, speech, and assembly. Life was perhaps becoming, as Stalin asserted, better and more joyous.

The still scarce material rewards went first of all to the regime's new elites. The privileged included party officials; "red specialists," often upwardly mobile workers from the bench trained during the First Five-Year Plan; and the "creative intelligentsia," writers, painters, composers, architects, and other cultural workers. In the Soviet system elite status, not money, bought entry into the best vacation resorts, medical clinics, housing, and special shops that stocked hard-to-find items like sausage, eggs, shoes, and soap. So-called Stakhanovites, workers and peasants who emulated the record-breaking feats of coal miner Alexei Stakhanov, overfulfilling their norms by rationalizing production, emerged as another privileged group. They, too, received extra rations and better access to everything from housing to vacations.

At the bottom of the scale were ordinary workers and especially peasants. There was a clear geographical hierarchy: Moscow was far better supplied than provincial cities, and cities fared better than the countryside. For most people, everyday life continued to be defined by miseries large and small, from overcrowded trams to bread queues and communal apartments. All the same, many believed in the promise of a better life foreshadowed by the visible, if still limited, improvement of living standards. In a 1936 letter to the newspaper *Krestianskaia gazeta*, a seventy year old peasant affirmed, "This year my life has gotten even better; I got a piglet as a bonus, which I've never had before."[3]

A "great retreat"? Sex, gender, and family

In the mid-1930s, as life was supposedly becoming better and more joyous, the Soviet Union seemed to become less revolutionary. Declaring that socialism had been built and promising material abundance, the state increasingly promoted an image of the ideal Bolshevik as marked not by revolutionary asceticism and toughness but by "culturedness" (*kulturnost*), a term that encompassed all manner of "proper" comportment, from washing one's hands before eating to reading Pushkin in one's spare time.[4]

Notions of "proper" behavior were highly, one might say traditionally, gendered. The upwardly mobile communist man of the 1930s traded his leather jacket and Nagant revolver for a suit and tie. His wife, "with her permanent wave, fur-collared coat, and stylish cloche," likewise rejected the "plain and stern" or masculine and militarized appearance associated with earlier cohorts of communist women—a look deemed no longer appropriate in a world becoming more prosperous.[5] At the same time, Soviet social policy clearly moved away from sexual revolution. In 1934, the state recriminalized male homosexuality. In 1936, it recriminalized abortion, made divorce more costly and difficult to obtain, and cracked down on men who failed to pay family support.

In 1946, Nicholas Timasheff, a Russian émigré sociologist in the United States, explained these shifts as part of what he called a "Great Retreat" from utopian policies that also included the return of traditional schooling and adult authority over children, a resurgence of patriotic rhetoric, and the rehabilitation of prerevolutionary culture.[6] This section and those that follow raise two sets of questions about the implications of these changes for our understanding of Stalinism. First, did the Stalinist state "betray" (in Trotsky's phrase) the revolution by reinstating traditional values and prerevolutionary hierarchies of age, gender, and ethnicity? Or did Soviet leaders "incorporate traditional institutions and appeals into official culture" for the "distinctly modern" purpose of remaking and improving society?[7] Second, do these changes support the argument that Stalin ruled primarily through terror and coercion? Or did the return of "traditional values" respond to what Soviet authorities liked to call "signals from below," the concerns voiced by ordinary people?

Among the Stalinist state's earliest "retreats" was the recriminalization of sodomy (same sex relations between men), which had been decriminalized in 1922 (see chapter 4). In a September 1933 letter to Stalin, Genrikh Yagoda, then the deputy head of the political police (OGPU), urged recriminalization, deeming homosexuality a threat to state security. He wrote *after* the police had already arrested some 130 homosexual men in Moscow and Leningrad as part of a wider sweep to clear Soviet cities of "dangerous" elements, including former kulaks, beggars, prostitutes, and recidivist criminals. The new law, promulgated in March 1934, set a minimum sentence of three years for "voluntary sodomy." In May, an article by Maxim Gorky justifying the law appeared in both *Pravda* and *Izvestiia*, emphasizing an alleged linkage between fascism and homosexuality. Responding to fears generated by the Nazi rise to power, Gorky offered the chilling slogan "Destroy the homosexuals— Fascism will disappear."[8]

Here we might pause to ask how the recriminalization of homosexuality fits into narratives of "retreat" or "coercion." As justified, the legislation was not a retreat from socialism, but rather a defense of it. Deemed by its supporters a necessary means of destroying dangerous elements, the ban can also be understood as a "distinctly modern" approach to managing and sculpting the body politic. Yet as British communist Harry Whyte suggested in a lengthy letter to Stalin (see document 6.1), those affected by the ban may have experienced its enforcement of traditional notions of "natural" and "unnatural" sexuality as a betrayal of revolutionary hopes.

While the state did not publicize the recriminalization of sodomy before it occurred, in the spring of 1936 it allowed a surprisingly frank discussion in the press of a draft law that restricted divorce and outlawed abortion except in cases where the mother's life was in danger. Ending the practice of "postcard divorce," the new legislation required both spouses to appear in court and raised divorce fees from 3 to 50 rubles for a first divorce, 150 rubles for a second, and 300 for a third. To some extent recognizing the economic hardships that often led women to terminate pregnancies, the law also provided additional funding for daycare centers and stipends for women with six or more children.

The public debate suggested enthusiasm among women for disciplining men via both restrictions on divorce, almost always initiated by husbands, and harsher punishment (two years in prison) for failing to pay child support. However, the extraordinarily high rates of child support—in the final legislation up to 50 percent of wages—worried men as well as women married to men with children from previous marriages. As it turned out, the state took seriously the commitment to hold men responsible for child support but, given limited incomes, payments often came at the expense of a second wife and family.

By contrast, the public debate suggested widespread popular concerns about the abortion ban. Nearly one third of the 118 letters published in the youth-oriented *Komsomolskaia pravda* expressed some disagreement with the proposed law. While editorials emphasized that motherhood was an unparalleled joy and a civic duty, women's objections focused on material hardships and on fears that compulsory motherhood would undermine educations and careers.

Having allowed the publication of these concerns, the state proceeded to ignore them. The law went into effect in June 1936, with the addition only of an exception in the case of women with hereditary diseases. A simultaneous and secret curtailment of access to contraception further limited women's control over reproduction.

The policy succeeded only briefly in reducing the number of abortions and raising birthrates. The number of officially recorded abortions dropped precipitously in the first year of the ban from 1.9 million in 1935 to 570,000 in 1937. However, by 1939 the official number, which excluded uncounted illegal abortions, was up to 755,000. By 1940 birthrates had fallen to 1935 levels. More ominously, the number of deaths from both illegal abortions and infant mortality rose.

Did the new emphasis on motherhood and family constitute a "betrayal" of revolutionary principles? Answers varied among Soviet women who understood and experienced pronatalist policies differently. For a woman compelled by the ban to carry a pregnancy to term or to seek a dangerous illegal abortion, the law's effect—if not its intention—was to roll back concrete revolutionary gains. Such outcomes were most likely to be felt by the urban women who accounted for most abortions. In Kazakhstan, few Kazakh women availed themselves of legal abortions. Usually marrying younger and having more children than their Slavic neighbors, they experienced the pronatalist campaign primarily as financial assistance to mothers of six or more children.[9] Here pronatalism may have advanced an emancipatory agenda.

Unlike other pronatalist states in this period—notably Nazi Germany and Fascist Italy—the Soviet state continued to celebrate and support women's role in public life even as it promoted motherhood as women's greatest happiness. Propaganda and incentives such as childcare encouraged mothers to continue working or to join the industrial labor force, which by 1940 was 39 percent female. Young women participated enthusiastically in ubiquitous military training programs, becoming sharpshooters, parachutists, pilots, and medics. The public discussion of the abortion ban (see document 6.2) offers one site to assess whether the Stalinist state betrayed promises of women's emancipation or authorized the construction of gender identities in opposition to compulsory motherhood.

Soviet patriotism, national minorities, and Russian heroes

A central component of Timasheff's "Great Retreat" was the revival of nationalism, which he dated to a June 1934 law on treason that vilified "enemies of the nation" rather than "enemies of socialism."[10] The Bolsheviks, their internationalist perspective notwithstanding, had employed patriotic appeals as early as 1918 when, as the German army advanced on Petrograd, the new government tried to rally support with the slogan "The Socialist Fatherland is in danger! Long live the Socialist Fatherland!" (see chapter 3). Stalin's 1924 call to build "socialism in one country" sounded a similarly patriotic/proletarian note. What was new in the mid-1930s was the grafting of emotional evocations of the motherland (*rodina*) onto a class-based defense of socialism.

The new patriotism also blurred the line between Soviet and Russian identities, highlighting the leading role of Russian history, Russian heroes, and the Russian people in the multiethnic Soviet fatherland. On the occasion of the twentieth anniversary of the October Revolution, Stalin explained that "the Russian tsars did much that was bad. They robbed and enslaved people . . . But they did do one good thing—they put together an enormous Great Power [stretching] out to Kamchatka." The Bolsheviks, Stalin concluded, had inherited and consolidated this Russian imperial achievement but, he implied, were not imperialists because they ruled "not in the interests of landowners and capitalists, but for the toilers."[11] What does this quotation suggest about how and to what extent Stalin and Stalinist patriotism combined revolutionary and traditional appeals?

Historians have explained the revival of nationalist sentiment as grounded in a recognition of the power of nationalism to mobilize the Soviet masses. In the face of both the internal disruptions caused by industrialization and collectivization and the growing external threat posed by imperial Japan and Nazi Germany, Bolshevik leaders decided that it made sense to change course and align "the propaganda machine" with, rather than against, appeals to nationalism.[12] The 1927 war scare (chapter 4) seems to have been a key watershed. Shocked by surveillance reports that documented low levels of popular support for the regime at this moment of crisis, party leaders apparently came to the realization that socialist propaganda was "too abstract and bloodless to effectively rally the USSR's poorly educated population." Soviet patriotism and the rehabilitation of the Russian national past in new history textbooks, novels, and movies offered a "pragmatic, popular alternative." Many Russian speakers enthusiastically embraced the integration of figures like Peter the Great, the medieval Prince Alexander Nevsky, and Pushkin into the "Soviet pantheon of heroes" (see document 6.3).[13] Indeed the regime's promotion of Russian myths, heroes, and history is often credited for facilitating the mobilization of Soviet society when war finally came in June 1941.

Shifting our perspective from Russian to non-Russian speakers, however, can complicate historical generalizations. From the perspective of the peripheries, the celebration of the Russian state as a "Great Power" was hard to distinguish from a celebration of "Russian imperial domination."[14] New histories of the Soviet republics cast the Russian state (and its Soviet successor) as a wise and benevolent elder brother, a civilizer, not a conqueror.

"Nation building" (within an imperial framework) remained a vital piece of Soviet nationalities policy. The resurgence of Russian heroes and Russian patriotism did not rule out, but actually facilitated, the rehabilitation of non-Russian national heroes as long as they remained safely subordinated to the Soviet/Russian imperial state. In Ukraine, Bohdan Khmelnytskyi, who earlier Soviet histories denounced as "a feudal seigneur who sold out the Ukrainian peasants to the Russian tsar and landlords," became a "national hero who had liberated Ukraine from Polish oppression" and, most importantly, in 1654 united it with Russia.[15]

Paradoxically, even as the Soviet state in the 1930s continued to pursue policies of nation building, it also engaged in "nation destroying."[16] Resistance to collectivization was most intense in non-Russian regions (Kazakhstan, Ukraine, the North Caucasus), and Bolshevik leaders thus tended to understand it as "national" resistance. To counter resistance among nomadic Kazakhs, who responded to collectivization by slaughtering their livestock or fleeing to Chinese Turkestan, the state closed local newspapers, arrested thousands of Islamic religious leaders, and purged the Kazakh party of alleged nationalists.

The alleged national resistance in the borderlands seemed particularly threatening in the context of mounting fears of German, Polish, and Japanese aggression. In the wake of the Nazi victory in 1933, tens of thousands of Ukrainians were arrested for conspiring with the new German leadership to detach Ukraine from the Soviet Union. In 1935, the state undertook the deportation from the western borderlands of ethnic Poles, Germans, Finns, Estonians, and Latvians—Soviet citizens whom, in light of increasing international tensions, both Soviet officials and many Soviet people suspected of disloyalty. Diaspora nationalities thus became "enemy" nationalities, a threat to Soviet security.

With the Great Terror, deportations, arrests, and executions of enemy nationalities expanded to include all Soviet border areas and all diaspora nationalities, whether or not they lived in the borderlands. In 1937, all Koreans residing in the Soviet Far East, more than 170,000 people, were deported to Kazakhstan and Uzbekistan. The NKVD's "national operations" (August 1937 to April 1938) targeted alleged "espionage and sabotage contingents" made up of Poles, Latvians, Germans, Estonians, Finns, Greeks, Iranians, Chinese, Romanians, Bulgarians, Macedonians, Koreans, Afghanis, and others. These national operations constituted a major part of the Great Terror, accounting for about a fifth of the total arrests in 1937–1938 and a third of the total executions (247,157 of 681,692).[17]

The national operations clearly targeted ethnic minorities, but ostensibly not because of their ethnicity. Thus, for example, the justification for the persecution of the Kazakhs was not their national identity per se but rather their opposition to collectivization and their ties with (alleged) enemies of socialism across the border in Chinese Turkestan. Yet it seems clear that, in promoting Russians as the Union's elder brothers, the state (perhaps inadvertently) encouraged expressions of Russian chauvinism. Attitudes such as that voiced by a Russian soldier who served a Kazakh only half a bowl of borscht because "you are a Kazakh and that means half-human"[18] may not have caused the ethnic cleansing of non-Russians but may have made it easier to carry out.

Collective security and the Popular Front: a retreat from world revolution?

In March 1933, Comintern official Osip Piatnitsky confidently predicted in a letter to Stalin that the recent establishment of a Nazi dictatorship would "speed up the pace of development of Germany towards a proletarian revolution."[19] Such expectations were widespread in Moscow, where hopes for revolution in Germany died hard. Yet over the course of 1934 the realization that Nazism was unlikely to spark communist revolution and the recognition of a growing threat from Germany and Japan reshaped both the Comintern line and Soviet foreign policy.

Stalin, of course, played an important role in authorizing a less ideological, more pragmatic approach to the Nazi threat. However, the shift owed much to lesser Soviet and Comintern leaders as well as rank-and-file international communists. While the Nazi repression of the German Communist Party in the summer of 1933 elicited little response in Moscow, it rattled communist activists in France and Czechoslovakia, who proposed making common cause with socialists against fascism. A February 1934 general strike in France supported by both socialists and communists alerted the charismatic new secretary of the Comintern Georgi Dimitrov to the potential of a united front; Stalin, in turn, granted Dimitrov leeway to develop a new Comintern strategy. In August 1935, the Seventh Comintern Congress endorsed the Popular Front, deeming fascism "the bitterest enemy of all the toilers, who, without distinction of political views, have been deprived of rights and liberties."[20]

As Dimitrov reevaluated the Comintern line, the cautious and cosmopolitan Commissar of Foreign Affairs Maxim Litvinov, an Old Bolshevik who had emigrated before 1917 and was married to an Englishwoman, advocated and worked to establish a system of collective security alliances. In November 1933, Litvinov traveled to Washington, DC, and successfully negotiated American recognition of the Soviet Union; he pledged that the Soviets would refrain from disseminating seditious propaganda in the United States. The conclusion in early 1934 of a German–Polish nonaggression pact that potentially opened the way to an attack on the Soviet Union made better relationships with the Western democracies increasingly urgent. In September 1934, the Soviet Union joined the League of Nations, which the Bolsheviks had long denounced as a tool of capitalism and imperialism.

These shifts in foreign policy and the Comintern line coincided with the new emphasis on Soviet patriotism. Should they be understood as a coordinated retreat from utopian expectations of world revolution? Both collective security and the Popular Front prioritized the containment of fascism, which was clearly in the national security interest of the Soviet Union. Both required the at least temporary suspension of revolutionary appeals. Potential allies against Germany and Japan—Britain, France, the United States—hesitated to cooperate with a Soviet state loudly committed to the overthrow of capitalism and colonialism. Likewise, communist parties in France and Spain had to renounce (again, at least temporarily) their revolutionary ambitions in order to build broad, cross-party, cross-class antifascist coalitions. Was this a tactical retreat or a "betrayal" of international revolution?

To understand whether the shifts in foreign policy and the Comintern line constituted a "retreat," it is helpful to examine a central foreign policy issue of the mid-1930s: Soviet involvement in the Spanish civil war (1936–1939). The war began in July 1936 as a military coup directed against the Republic's democratically elected Popular Front government. It became a cause célèbre of the international left and a threat to Soviet security when, at the end of July, Adolf Hitler and Benito Mussolini decided to dispatch weapons, planes, and troops to the rebels. In September Stalin resolved to aid the Republic, largely because he feared a rebel victory would encourage German aggression in the east.

Once involved in the war, Stalin advised Spanish communists to focus on winning the war, not revolutionizing Spanish society. While acceptable to moderate elements in the Popular Front government, the Soviet call to prioritize the war effort (and to put revolution on the backburner) triggered a fatal confrontation between the communists and the parties to their left that ultimately shattered the Popular Front. Was the Popular Front a necessary strategic "retreat" from revolution in the face of a fascist threat to Soviet security and (as Stalin emphasized) to world peace and freedom? Was Soviet policy in Spain a "betrayal" of world revolution (as parties on the left claimed)? Or (as parties on the right claimed) was Soviet antifascism merely a cover for Soviet revolutionary ambitions?

Soviet culture and its reception

By the mid-1930s, Soviet culture had "retreated" from both the avant-garde experiments of the 1920s and the aggressive proletarian cultural revolution of the early 1930s. In 1934, the first congress of the newly established Writers' Union declared a new obligatory style: "socialist realism," which was soon applied to all the arts. Writers were to "realistically" portray not the present but the radiant future, thus becoming, in Stalin's famous phrase, "engineers of human souls." Like Stalin himself, socialist realist mass culture favored brave, uncomplicated heroes; hummable tunes; monumental buildings; and idealized portraits of the leader. It also encouraged newly literate and newly promoted proletarians to embrace Russian high culture as a badge of good taste and respectability.

The elaborate year-long celebration marking the centennial of Pushkin's death worked to Sovietize both the poet and Russian high culture. The jubilee emphasized Pushkin's accessibility, even to newly literate workers, and his friendships with early nineteenth century revolutionaries. In 1940, Mayakovsky was subjected to similar treatment. Jubilee publications presented a highly edited version of his life and work, de-emphasizing his connections to the literary avant-garde, his unconventional cohabitation with his lover Lili Brik and her poet husband Osip Brik, and his suicide.[21] Here, as in family and nationalities policy, it is worth considering how Stalinist culture balanced or combined traditional and revolutionary values.

In the Soviet Union, state censorship and official artists' unions closely policed cultural production. But state control did not necessarily mean that the resulting products were unpopular. For historians, gauging popular reception of Soviet cultural products is tricky. In the case of movies, one rough measure of reception is ticket sales, which could be quite impressive. *Chapaev*, released in 1934, was perhaps the most popular Soviet film of all. Based on Dmitry Furmanov's 1923 novel of the same name, the film told the story of the real life Civil War commander Vasily Chapaev and his men. The film drew perhaps thirty million viewers in its first year; youngsters often saw it more than once. It also won audiences and critical acclaim outside the Soviet Union.

"Socialist" popular films in the 1930s also adopted the formulas that drew so many Soviet people to Hollywood films such as *Tarzan* and *Robin Hood*. Three musicals directed by Grigory Aleksandrov that featured slapstick comedy, romance, lavish dance numbers, and catchy tunes—*Happy Guys* (1934), *Circus* (1936), and *Volga-Volga* (1938)—attracted mass audiences. They were not, however, devoid of politics. *Circus* tells the story of an American circus performer who is the mother of an interracial child. Driven out of the United States by racism, she ultimately finds a home in the Soviet Union, where the Stalin Constitution protects the equal rights of all. The number of people who saw the film suggests it was genuinely popular. What box office numbers cannot tell us is whether those who enjoyed the show learned the "correct" lessons.

Drawing on NKVD and party surveillance reports, some historians emphasize that Soviet audiences often resisted, ignored, subverted, or distorted the state's messaging. For example, Soviet people pushed back against the ubiquitous cults of Lenin and Stalin by hanging their portraits over the toilet or gossiping about their private lives. They might also repeat key slogans such as "life has become happier" with bitter irony. The NKVD, of course, was tasked with finding grumblers and enemies (which they tended to equate), so it is difficult to say how widespread such sentiments were on the basis of these sources. The larger question raised by surveillance reports is whether the dissatisfaction and apparent hostility to the regime that they reported actually "resisted" or "subverted" state propaganda. Are the cases reported by the NKVD of workers demanding that the state live up to its promises of equality and prosperity instances of people opposing state propaganda, using it for their own purposes, or perhaps believing it?

Analyzing how Soviet people participated in mass celebrations offers another way to get at the question of reception. Those who celebrated the October Revolution or other state holidays by getting drunk "may not have imbibed all of the 'culture' and political knowledge which government officials intended."[22] Yet the state itself made sure that alcohol was plentiful on such occasions. Does getting drunk on state-supplied vodka qualify as an act of resistance to or unauthorized appropriation of official rituals? A similar question could be asked about the commentaries written for the Pushkin anniversary in which critics celebrated the poet's resistance to a "terrible, merciless" government. Such texts can be and perhaps were read as referring to the contemporary terror. But, again, it was the state itself that required intellectuals to construct Pushkin as a part of the long struggle for freedom that culminated in "the victory of socialism and the Stalin Constitution."[23] Was affirming this a critique of Soviet "democracy," an effective means of working the system, or an endorsement of it?

While many historians emphasize traces of dissent, resistance, ambiguity, and non-compliance in Soviet people's responses to state propaganda, others stress that the state's language and agenda were inescapable, if also somewhat malleable. Soviet people, in Stephen Kotkin's influential phrase, "spoke Bolshevik"—used the regime's own categories to understand Soviet reality, give meaning to their lives, and even protest specific policies or leaders—both because they were drawn to its vision of the radiant future and because censorship and repression cut off access to alternatives.

Some historians emphasize that Soviet people not only spoke Bolshevik but also wanted to think Bolshevik. When Julia Piatnitskaia's husband Osip Piatnitsky (the Comintern official mentioned above) was arrested in 1937, she could not bring herself to believe in his guilt. From this inability she concluded not that the system was flawed but that she herself posed a danger to Soviet society. Thus in March 1938, as she recorded in her diary, she went to the state prosecutor and explained her unhealthy "thoughts" and suggested "that it would be expedient to remove me fully officially" from society.[24] She was arrested later that year and died in a labor camp in 1940. Should we understand these actions as Piatnitskaia's desperate effort to merge herself with the Soviet collective and overcome her own painful doubts? Or is such an interpretation of the Soviet self as driven by ideological commitment too one-dimensional?

Perhaps even more shocking from our perspective than Piatnitskaia's appeal to the NKVD for help is the reaction of her children to their father's arrest. Her eleven year old son told her, "It's too bad they didn't shoot Papa; after all, he is an enemy of the people."[25] While perhaps not typical, such a response suggests the power of Soviet propaganda, which accorded young people special importance as the chief constructors of the future, to foster identification with the Soviet cause. Children's unwavering belief may also suggest that, in the face of state violence, adults trying to protect children whose parents had been arrested "unwittingly contributed to the perpetuation of the party-state's public myths by taking personal vows of silence about the fate of the fathers and the true nature of the jealous regime that punished them"[26] (see document 6.4). At the same time, many children whose parents were often away from home on party business were raised by grandmothers, who provided clear alternatives to Bolshevik language and practices. Such was the case of Ludmilla Alexeyeva (born in 1927), who recalled in her 1990 memoir that her grandmother instilled "old values" that "directly contradicted" the "icons of the new era." Indeed

Figure 6.1 A 1936 poster by Viktor Govorkov shows Soviet children thanking "dear Stalin" for their "happy childhood." © Heritage Image Partnership Ltd/Alamy.

How might such propaganda have been understood by children whose parents were arrested?

she credited grandmothers with raising "thousands upon thousands of children" who like her—a future dissident—"could never grow up to become a cog in the machine of state."[27]

The terror from above and below

The waves of terror—or, from the official perspective, antiterrorist campaigns—that convulsed the Soviet Union in the late 1930s constitute one of the most disturbing and perplexing episodes in its history. From fall 1936 to late 1938, Nikolai Yezhov, newly appointed head of the NKVD, presided over the Great Terror (or *Yezhovshchina*), a general term that covers a range of separate but closely related campaigns to unmask and liquidate "enemies of the people." Three Moscow show trials (August 1936, January 1937, and August 1938) convicted Lenin's old comrades of treason. The Great Purges, a lethal version of the established practice of periodically "cleaning" the party of unworthy or incompetent cadres, similarly targeted privileged elites. Only in 1992 did historians discover that the terror also persecuted hundreds of thousands of ordinary workers and peasants in so-called mass operations.

All told the terror killed about 700,000 people and sentenced well over a million to exile or forced labor. As noted in chapter 5, the Gulag, the system of labor camps and so-called special settlements run by the NKVD, pre-dated the Great Terror. Throughout the 1930s, inmates performed forced labor under brutal, often deadly, conditions. Mortality rates in the camps (likely understated in official statistics) spiked during the famine of 1933 (15 percent), the second year of the Great Terror, 1938 (9 percent), and World War II (20–25 percent). As in the earlier period, the Gulag officially aimed not to exterminate or punish prisoners, but to rehabilitate them, to forge new Soviet men and women through socially useful labor. A study of the system's fourth largest camp, Karlag in Kazakhstan, concludes that the authorities took seriously the "corrective" function of their institution, although they did not consider all prisoners redeemable.[28] Other accounts emphasize the "Gulag boss's" interest in contributing to the construction of socialism by exploiting prison labor to mine gold and coal, fell trees, and build railroads and canals in remote regions of the country.[29]

The opening of the Soviet archives has provided vivid evidence to support the argument that Stalin played a central role in initiating and directing the terror. His handwriting is all over documents ordering mass arrests and approving or (less frequently) commuting thousands of death sentences. But he could not carry out an operation of such magnitude alone. Thus this section examines "not just why the terror occurred but *how* it could happen" by paying attention to the institutional, ideological, interpersonal, and international contexts in which it developed.[30] It attempts to analyze the terror both from above—the traditional or "totalitarian" emphasis on Stalin as perpetrator-in-chief—and from below, from the perspectives of those who implemented it at the local level and those (sometimes the same people) who became its victims. It asks: How did Soviet citizens and officials justify or explain the terror? How can we as historians explain the participation—coerced or enthusiastic—of millions of people in the mechanisms of terror?

Accounts of the terror often begin with the dramatic 1 December 1934 assassination of Leningrad party boss Sergei Kirov, an event that produced a shock wave comparable to that generated by the John F. Kennedy assassination. A lone gunman, a disgruntled former apparatchik, managed to gain entry to party headquarters and shoot Kirov at close range. Stalin immediately took advantage of the murder to give the political police wide-ranging powers to try and execute "terrorists." At Stalin's behest, investigators quickly announced that the murder was connected to a conspiracy organized by a shadowy "Leningrad Center" linked to Stalin's long-defeated political opponents Grigory Zinoviev and Lev Kamenev. (An alternative conspiracy theory that makes Stalin the mastermind of the murder persists, but has been largely discredited.[31])

Whatever Stalin's intentions in 1934, the murder stood out in retrospect as the prologue to the terror that followed. In January 1935, both Zinoviev and Kamenev were convicted in a closed trial of "moral responsibility" for Kirov's murder and sentenced to long prison terms. Eighteen months later, in August 1936, they along with fourteen others became defendants in an elaborately staged Moscow show trial. They now stood accused of planning Kirov's murder and of plotting to kill Stalin and a half dozen other party leaders. All but two of the defendants confessed—the NKVD had no compunctions about using torture to produce confessions—and all were shot. Their confessions, in turn, implicated other former oppositionists, notably Nikolai Bukharin, in even more far-fetched terrorist plots involving foreign intelligence services and the regime's bête noire, the exiled Lev Trotsky.

Questions about how and why the Great Terror happened—about the path from the Kirov assassination to the mass arrests of 1937—have generated often passionate and vitriolic debate largely because assessments of state violence rested on answers to more fundamental (and loaded) questions: Did Stalin govern through terror and coercion alone? Was terror the defining characteristic of the Soviet system? For many Western observers, particularly in the early years of the Cold War, pervasive, ruthless state violence appeared to be the essence of Stalinism. "Totalitarian" interpretations tended to picture the average Soviet citizen as a terrorized, brainwashed subject deprived of rights and agency by an oppressive state that controlled even the intimate spheres of home and family.

As noted above, new revelations from the Soviet archives support the argument, associated with the totalitarian interpretation, that Stalin ordered the terror. He worked closely with NKVD chief Yezhov to fabricate evidence, construct conspiracies, and put pressure on witnesses in preparation for show trials in January 1937 and March 1938 (the trial of Bukharin) as well as in the purge of Red Army commanders in June 1937. Was this cold political calculation or a reflection of Stalin's own propensity for what a biographer calls "paranoid ways of thinking"?[32] It was not necessarily paranoid to believe, as Stalin may have in the summer of 1937, that the leaders of the Red Army, like the mutinous officers who ignited the Spanish civil war, posed a threat to his power that necessitated "a policy of repression."[33] Nor, perhaps, was it unreasonable to round up "enemy" nationalities and "dangerous" elements who might prove traitorous in the event of war.

Nonetheless, it is hard to rationalize the scope of the terror Stalin actually authorized. The Red Army purge decimated the officer corps and resulted in the execution of some of the military's most experienced commanders, including Civil War hero Marshal Mikhail Tukhachevsky. The mass operations in 1937 and 1938 targeted for arrest and execution whole categories of people deemed "dangerous": former kulaks, members of the clergy, horse and cattle thieves, "enemy" nationalities, wives of enemies of the people. Over the course of sixteen months, the NKVD arrested more than 1.5 million people, convicting most and executing about 700,000 people by means of a bullet to the back of the head. At the height of the terror (August 1937 to November 1938), NKVD officers were shooting about 1,500 people per day. Given the evidence of Stalin's close personal supervision of these operations, it is difficult to ignore the leader's disturbed personality—his tendency to think in terms of conspiracies, his thirst for power, his pathological suspiciousness, his taste for revenge, his insecurity—as a source of the decision to launch a massive preemptive attack on real, potential, or imagined enemies.

In the 1970s and 1980s, Western historians, who began to investigate the Soviet Union "from below," offered a less Stalin-centric perspective on the purges. Challenging the assumption that only the actions of Stalin and the Politburo leadership mattered, "revisionist" interpretations emphasized the ways in which provincial party officials, workers, peasants, or intellectuals might evade, mitigate, distort, or even use to their own advantage directives "from above."

Although Stalin triggered the terror and ultimately halted it, it does not necessarily follow that he was able to control the way it played out across the Soviet Union. A long archival paper trail suggests that the terror was planned; however, as was clear in the industrialization and collectivization drives (chapter 5), Soviet "planning"—with its imperative to overfulfill norms, its poor allocation of resources, and its reliance on overburdened, undertrained functionaries—often resulted in quite a bit of unplanned chaos. Thus the seemingly all powerful Stalin was "constantly frustrated" by local bureaucrats who either responded to his orders with "foot-dragging and deception" or ran ahead of Moscow, exceeding centrally established "limits" on executions by as much as 25 percent.[34]

While the terror may have served Stalin as a means of disciplining or destroying (real or imagined) opponents, it can also be understood as a "populist strategy" designed to deflect discontent away from Stalin and toward local authorities.[35] The strategy seemed to work at provincial show trials of local officials, where peasants "appeared to revel in the humiliation of their former bosses." However, enthusiastic participation did not ensure that peasants learned the desired lesson. Rather than distinguishing the "good" Stalin from the bad local officials, the peasants sang, "They killed Kirov; we'll kill Stalin."[36]

Looking at the terror "from below" can also mean tracing how it spread through unions, workplaces, schools, and institutions such as the Comintern. Not wanting to be accused of lack of vigilance, many preemptively denounced their coworkers or bosses, especially ones they resented or disliked for whatever reason, although they carefully couched denunciations in the idiom of the purge, unmasking wreckers, terrorists, counterrevolutionaries, and Trotskyites (see document 6.5). In a world where the heroes of the revolution had been exposed as villains, anyone might turn out to be an enemy, and the "perpetrators of the purge often became victims of the very process they had initially promulgated."[37]

If those caught up in the purges had a sense of *how* they worked, the *why* often remained elusive. Writing during the Khrushchev years when it was possible to criticize Stalin (although her memoir was not published in the Soviet Union), Eugenia Ginzburg, a party member arrested in 1937, recalled that she struggled to understand her arrest in Bolshevik terms: "I had first to determine who these people were, who kept me imprisoned. Were they fascists in disguise?" By contrast, some party members she met in prison continued to behave as if nothing had changed. One advised her to converse as little as possible with the German communists who shared their cell, "to make sure you don't commit a crime against the Party after all." Others had never learned to speak Bolshevik to begin with, like an old peasant woman who told Ginzburg "they put me down as one of those tractorists. But as God is my witness, I never went near one of them cursed things." Ginzburg was unable to laugh at the peasant's confusion: "I was ashamed. When would I at last stop feeling responsible and ashamed for all this? After all, I was the anvil, not the hammer. But might I too have become a hammer?"[38]

CONCLUSION AND FURTHER QUESTIONS

In the decade before World War II, the threat of war loomed large in the Soviet Union, sustained both by ideology—the certainty that capitalist states would ultimately try to destroy the homeland of socialism—and by actual conflicts with Western governments. Fears took on new immediacy in 1934, when the leadership of both the state and the Comintern concluded that Nazism was not the harbinger of communist revolution in Germany.

Soviet leaders responded with policies and propaganda designed to put the country on a war footing. In the economic sphere, both collectivization and industrialization aimed to prepare for war. On the ideological front, the "retreats" of the mid-1930s— the revival of Russian nationalism, the pronatalist campaign, the turn to collective security—can be understood as efforts to mobilize popular support and mitigate external dangers. The terror, too, was justified as a necessary security measure, a preemptive strike on internal enemies. Films such as *If Tomorrow Brings War* (1938) warned that war was coming, but reassured viewers that the Soviet forces "o'er the land, in the air, and on the sea,"[39] as the popular song that came out of the film put it, would easily overpower the enemy. "Decisive victory at low cost" was not just a propaganda slogan; it reflected actual strategic planning, which proceeded on the assumption that the Red Army would immediately go on the offensive.[40]

To what extent was the "darkness at noon" that characterized the Soviet Union in the late 1930s a consequence of the regime's efforts both to stoke fears of impending war and to create a sense of inevitable Soviet victory? Did the policies implemented in the 1930s effectively prepare the Soviet Union for the war that finally came in 1941? Did Stalin and the system he built, with its amalgam of terror and enthusiasm, facilitate or hamper Soviet survival and eventual victory?

PRIMARY SOURCES

Use the questions to analyze the content, context, and significance of each primary source. Then synthesize the primary sources and the material in the chapter to formulate a response to the primary chapter questions: Did the Soviet state's apparent reversals in the spheres of family policy, nationalities policy, and foreign policy constitute "betrayals" of the revolution, efforts to defend socialism, or concessions to popular opinion? To what extent and in what ways did the repressive Stalinist state cultivate and win popular support?

Document 6.1 Letter from Harry Whyte to Joseph Stalin, May 1934

Questions for analysis

1   What does the letter suggest about Whyte's reasons for becoming a communist or moving to the Soviet Union?
2   How does he justify his opposition to the recriminalization of sodomy?
3   Does the letter support the view that Stalinist culture "retreated" from revolutionary values?

Dear Comrade Stalin!

Although I am a foreign Communist, not yet having been transferred to membership in the Soviet Communist Party, nevertheless I think that you as the leader of the world proletariat will not think it unnatural, that I am writing to you to ask you to illuminate a question that seems to me to be of great importance for a large number of Communists in the USSR and in other countries as well.

The question is: can a homosexual be considered a person worthy of becoming a member of the Communist Party?

The law just published about criminal responsibility for sodomy, confirmed by the CC [Central Committee] of the USSR on 7 March this year, obviously means that a homosexual cannot be considered worthy of bearing the name of Soviet citizen, still less, consequently, could he be considered worthy of membership in the Soviet Communist Party.

I am personally interested in this question, because I am a homosexual . . .

First of all I would like to point out that I regard the position of homosexuals belonging to the working or toiling classes in general as analogous to the position of women under capitalism, and analogous to the imperialist persecution of colored races; it is very similar in many respects to the persecution of Jews under Hitler's dictatorship, and generally it is not difficult to see the similarity with the persecution of any social group subject to exploitation and persecution in conditions of capitalist hegemony . . .

Capitalism, which requires for its flourishing an enormous labor reserve and reserve of cannon fodder, regards homosexuality as a factor threatening to lower the birthrate (as is well known capitalist countries have laws against abortion and contraception).

Regardless of the unusually strict laws about marriage in capitalist countries, perversions in the sphere of normal sexual relations are much more widespread in capitalist countries than in the USSR, where marriage legislation is the freest and most rational of any place in the world . . .

I have visited two psychiatrists to ask them if it is possible to "cure" homosexuality—you may be surprised by this. I admit that this was opportunism on my part (I could be forgiven on this occasion), but what forced me to try this was to find some way out of this damned dilemma. Least of all did I want to be in contradiction with a decision of the Soviet government . . .

One has to admit that there is such a thing as ineradicable homosexuality (I have still not found any evidence to the contrary) and as a result, I think that we must conclude by recognizing the existence of such a minority in society, regardless of whether it is capitalist or socialist. In this case there is no justification for making these people criminals on the basis of their distinguishing features, which they are in no way responsible for creating, which they cannot change, even if they wanted to . . .

With Communist greetings,

Harry Whyte [age 27, born Edinburgh, Scotland]

Source: "Letter from Harry Whyte to Iosif Stalin, May 1934," in Glennys Young, *The Communist Experience in the Twentieth Century: A Global History through Sources* (New York: Oxford University Press, 2012), 89–97. Used by permission of Oxford University Press, USA.

Document 6.2   From the discussion of the abortion ban, *Izvestiia*, 29 May 1936

Questions for analysis

1   On what basis did the letters oppose the abortion ban? To what degree and in what ways do the letter writers "speak Bolshevik" or rely on ideological arguments and phrasing?

2   Do these letters support the idea that the recriminalziation of abortion constituted part of a "Great Retreat"? Do they suggest that Soviet women continued to imagine gender identities in opposition to compulsory motherhood?

Letter signed "A Mother"

For eighteen years I went out to work and was a member of a Trade Union for fourteen years (1918–1932). Then I had a daughter. After the girl had spent a month in a nursery school and had frequently fallen ill, the doctors advised me to take her home and look after her personally. I was working at the Soyuz factory where I was released after procuring a certificate stating the reason for my absence. But after a while the Group organizer refused to mark my Trade Union card and thus annulled my standing as a worker and Trade Union member. I think this was wrong.

In the government's draft there should be included an article to run as follows: "Women who are forced to leave work to care for an ailing child do not forfeit their acquired standing as workers. The time spent in looking after the child is to be counted as outside work, for the purpose of the pension payable upon incapacitation."

Letter from "an engineer": "abortions cannot be categorically forbidden"

I am non-party, married, with a 5-year-old son. I work as an engineer and have been and still am in a responsible position. I regard myself as a good citizen of the

USSR. I cannot agree with the prohibition of abortions. And I am very glad that this law has not entered into force but has been submitted to the workers for discussion.

The prohibition of abortion means the compulsory birth of a child to a woman who does not want children. The birth of a child ties married people to each other. Not everyone will readily abandon a child, for alimony is not all that children need. Where the parents produce a child of their own free will, all is well. But where a child comes into the family against the will of the parents, a grim personal drama will be enacted which will undoubtedly lower the social value of the parents and leave its mark on the child.

A categorical prohibition of abortion will confront young people with a dilemma: either complete sexual abstinence or the risk of jeopardizing their studies and disrupting their life. To my mind any prohibition of abortion is bound to mutilate many a young life. Apart from this, the result of such a prohibition might be an increase in the death-rate from abortions because they will then be performed illegally . . . E. T.

Source: Rudolf Schlesinger, ed., *Changing Attitudes in Soviet Russia: The Family in the USSR* (London: Routledge & Kegan Paul, 1949), 254–265. Used by permission of Taylor and Francis Books UK.

Document 6.3   The response of I. A. Sudnikov, a Russian worker in Central Asia, to the film *Alexander Nevsky* (1938)

Sergei Eisenstein's 1938 film about the medieval Prince Alexander Nevsky's defeat of the invading Teutonic Knights in 1242 drew record audiences. The following reaction was sent by I. A. Sudnikov to the director and is held at the Russian State Archive of Literature and Art (RGALI 1923/1/2289/32-32ob).

Questions for analysis

1   Why did Sudnikov value films such as *Alexander Nevsky*?
2   Does the letter support the argument that the revival of Russian nationalism constituted a "retreat"?

There are lines at the ticket windows . . . Many have gone to the movie several times in order to watch this notable cinematic page from the history of our motherland's distant past again and again.

This is not coincidental. Our country's best directors have created an unusually brilliant, truthful representation of the Russian people, defending their right to independence against the Middle Ages' mongrel knight feudal lords, the relatives of today's fascists . . .

This profoundly well-thought-out historical film opens up before us the pages of the history of what was and awakens within us a feeling of pride that strengthens [our resolve] to defend our independence forever . . .

Source: David Brandenberger, *National Bolshevism: Stalinist Mass Culture and the Formation of Modern Russian National Identity, 1931–1956* (Cambridge, MA: Harvard University Press, 2002), 103–104.

Document 6.4   Olga Sliozberg's recollection of a mother in the Gulag receiving a letter from her daughter (1993)

Questions for analysis

1   Why did the mother let her daughter believe that she was guilty?
2   What does the letter suggest about why children whose parents were arrested might continue to be "true believers"?
3   What does the letter suggest about how the terror operated?

Suddenly the window in the cell door opened, and they gave Liza a letter. Its contents were not entirely ordinary.

"Dear Mama," wrote Zoia. "I am fifteen years old, and I am about to join the Komsomol. I need to know whether you are guilty or not. I keep thinking, how could you betray our Soviet power? After all, everything was so fine, after all you and Papa are workers. I remember that we lived very well. You sewed me silk dresses, you bought candies. Could you really have taken money from them? It would have been better if we had worn calico dresses. But maybe you are not guilty? Then I won't join the Komsomol, I will never forgive them for what they have done to you. And if you are guilty, then I won't write you anymore, because I love our Soviet power and will hate enemies and I will hate you. Mama, write me the truth. I want more for you not to be guilty and then I won't join the Komsomol. Your unfortunate daughter, Zoia."

Liza froze.

Out of the four pages that they had given us to write letters, she had already written on three of them. She sat like a stone figure. Then, on the fourth sheet she wrote in big letters: "Zoia, you are right. I am guilty. Join the Komsomol. This is the last time I will write you. Be happy, you and LiaLia. Mother."

She handed me Zoia's letter and her answer, and beat her head on the table, choking with sobs.

"It's better to let her hate me. How will she live without the Komsomol, an outsider? She will hate Soviet power. It is better to have her hate me."

She sent the letter, she handed in her card and never again spoke about her daughters and never received letters.

Source: Cathy A. Frierson and Semyon S. Vilensky, *Children of the Gulag* (New Haven, CT: Yale University Press, 2010), 228. Used by permission of Yale University Press.

Document 6.5   John Scott explains the mechanism of the purge in Magnitogorsk (1942)

Questions for analysis

1   What does Scott's letter suggest about how the terror operated?
2   What seems to have motivated the various denunciations he recounts?
3   How does his picture of the terror compare to Sliozberg's?

A denounces B as having said that Stalin is a son-of-a-bitch and should be shot. B, arrested, finally admits making the statement, and further asserts that C was present, and agreed with the opinion expressed. C, arrested, denies everything; then, confronted with B, admits that there was some such conversation, but insists that A was the initiator. A is arrested, like the others, for terrorist intentions against the leaders of the party and the government, but begs off on the ground that he did it all in order to expose to the authorities the counterrevolutionary activities of B and C. After six months of bantering and badgering, A, B, and C are sent for ten years to Kamchatka.

Source: John Scott, *Behind the Urals: An American Worker in Russia's City of Steel* (1942; Bloomington: Indiana University Press, 1989), 192–193.

Notes

1 On the demonstration, see Walter Duranty, "Soviet Executes 13 as Trotskyists," *New York Times*, 2 February 1937.
2 Sheila Fitzpatrick, *Everyday Stalinism: Ordinary Life in Extraordinary Times. Soviet Russia in the 1930s* (New York: Oxford University Press), 41.
3 Letter of appreciation from F. M. Postnikov to *Krest'ianskaia Gazeta*, 1936 (Document 59), in Lewis Siegelbaum and Andrei Sokolov, *Stalinism as a Way of Life: A Narrative in Documents* (New Haven, CT: Yale University Press, 2000), 173–174.
4 Vadim Volkov, "The Concept of *Kul'turnost'*: Notes on the Stalinist Civilizing Process," in Sheila Fitzpatrick, ed., *Stalinism: New Directions* (New York: Routledge, 2000), 210–230.
5 Rebecca Balmas Neary, "Mothering Socialist Society: The Wife Activists' Movement and the Soviet Culture of Daily Life, 1934–41," *Russian Review*, 58 (July 1999): 410.
6 Nicholas S. Timasheff, *The Great Retreat: The Growth and Decline of Communism in Russia* (New York: E. P. Dutton, 1946).
7 David L. Hoffman, "Was There a 'Great Retreat' from Soviet Socialism? Stalinist Culture Reconsidered," *Kritika*, 5, no. 4 (Fall 2004): 653.
8 As quoted in Dan Healey, *Homosexual Desire in Revolutionary Russia: The Regulation of Sexual and Gender Dissent* (Chicago, IL: University of Chicago Press, 2001), 189.
9 Paula A. Michaels, "Motherhood, Patriotism, and Ethnicity: Soviet Kazakhstan and the 1936 Abortion Ban," *Feminist Studies*, 27, no. 2 (Summer 2001): 324.
10 Timasheff, *Great Retreat*, 166.
11 As quoted in David Brandenberger, *National Bolshevism: Stalinist Mass Culture and the Formation of Modern Russian National Identity, 1931–1956* (Cambridge, MA: Harvard University Press, 2002), 55.
12 Timasheff, *Great Retreat*, 179.
13 Brandenberger, *National Bolshevism*, 27, 28, 100.
14 Serhy Yekelchyk, "Stalinist Patriotism as Imperial Discourse: Reconciling the Ukrainian and Russian 'Heroic Pasts,' 1939–45," *Kritika*, 3, no. 1 (Winter 2002): 56, 57.
15 Yekelchyk, "Stalinist Patriotism," 58.
16 Terry Martin, "The Origins of Soviet Ethnic Cleansing," *Journal of Modern History*, 70, no. 4 (December 1998): 816.
17 Martin, "Origins of Soviet Ethnic Cleansing," 829, 854, 855.
18 As quoted in Brandenberger, *National Bolshevism*, 107.
19 As quoted in Jonathan Haslam, "Comintern and Soviet Foreign Policy, 1919–1941," in Ronald Suny, ed., *The Cambridge History of Russia, Volume 3: The Twentieth Century* (New York: Cambridge University Press, 2006), 649.
20 "Resolution on Fascism, Working-Class Unity, and the Tasks of the Comintern, Adopted by the Seventh Congress, 20 August 1935," in Kevin McDermott and Jeremy Agnew, *The Comintern: A History of International Communism from Lenin to Stalin* (Basingstoke: Palgrave Macmillan, 1996), 243.
21 Laura Shear Urbaszewski, "Canonizing the 'Best, Most Talented' Soviet Poet: Vladimir Mayakovsky and the Soviet Literary Celebration," *Modernism/Modernity*, 9, no. 4 (November 2002): 638, 651.
22 Karen Petrone, *Life Has Become More Joyous, Comrades: Celebrations in the Time of Stalin* (Bloomington: Indiana University Press, 2000), 20.

23 E. N. Cherniavskii as quoted in Petrone, *Life Has Become More Joyous*, 143, 144.

24 As quoted in Jochen Hellbeck, *Revolution on My Mind: Writing a Diary under Stalin* (Cambridge, MA: Harvard University Press, 2006), 111.

25 As quoted in Hellbeck, *Revolution*, 97.

26 Cathy A. Frierson and Semyon S. Vilensky, *Children of the Gulag* (New Haven, CT: Yale University Press, 2010), 231–232.

27 Ludmilla Alexeyeva and Paul Goldberg, *The Thaw Generation: Coming of Age in the Post-Stalin Era* (Pittsburgh, PA: University of Pittsburgh Press, 1990), 11, 12.

28 Steven A. Barnes, *Death and Redemption: The Gulag and the Shaping of Soviet Society* (Princeton, NJ: Princeton University Press, 2011).

29 Fyodor Vasilevich Mochulsky, *Gulag Boss: A Soviet Memoir*, trans. Deborah Kaple (New York: Oxford University Press, 2011); Alan Barenberg, *Gulag Town, Company Town: Forced Labor and Its Legacy in Vorkuta* (New Haven, CT: Yale University Press, 2014).

30 Emphasis in original. Stephen Kotkin, *Magnetic Mountain: Stalinism as Civilization* (Berkeley: University of California Press, 1995), 285.

31 Matthew E. Lenoe, *The Kirov Murder and Soviet History* (New Haven, CT: Yale University Press, 2010).

32 Robert C. Tucker, *Stalin in Power: The Revolution from Above, 1928–1941* (New York: W. W. Norton, 1990), 455.

33 Oleg Khlevniuk, "The Reasons for the 'Great Terror': The Foreign-Political Aspect," in Silvo Pons and Andrea Romano, eds., *Russia in the Age of Wars, 1914–1945* (Milan: Feltrinelli, 2000), 163.

34 James Harris, "Was Stalin a Weak Dictator?" *Journal of Modern History*, 75, no. 2 (June 2003): 378, 376; J. Arch Getty, "'Excesses Are Not Permitted': Mass Terror and Stalinist Governance in the Late 1930s," *Russian Review*, 61, no. 1 (January 2002): 113–138.

35 Sarah Davies, *Popular Opinion in Stalin's Russia: Terror, Propaganda and Dissent, 1934–1941* (Cambridge: Cambridge University Press, 1997), 113.

36 Sheila Fitzpatrick, "How the Mice Buried the Cat: Scenes from the Great Purges of 1937 in the Russian Provinces," *Russian Review*, 52 (July 1993): 301, 302, 320.

37 Wendy Z. Goldman, *Terror and Democracy in the Age of Stalin: The Social Dynamics of Repression* (New York: Cambridge University Press, 2007), 7, 8.

38 Eugenia Ginzburg, *Journey into the Whirlwind* (New York: Harcourt Brace, 2002), 74, 154–155, 182.

39 "If Tomorrow Brings War," in James Von Geldern and Richard Stites, eds., *Mass Culture in Soviet Russia: Tales, Songs, Movies, Plays, and Folklore, 1917–1953* (Bloomington: Indiana University Press, 1995), 317.

40 John Erickson, *The Road to Stalingrad, Vol. 1: Stalin's War with Germany* (London: Weidenfeld and Nicolson, 1975), 27.

7 The Great Fatherland War and the origins of the Cold War

INTRODUCTION

On 27 January 1942, both *Pravda* and *Komsomolskaia pravda* (the newspaper of the Young Communist League) ran the story of a young female partisan known only by her nom de guerre, Tanya. Caught attempting to burn down stables in an occupied village about 100 kilometers (62 miles) west of Moscow, she was tortured and hanged by the Germans. Following the advancing Red Army into liberated areas of Moscow province in early 1942, *Pravda* correspondent Petr Lidov visited the village of Petrishchevo where the events occurred. He reported that Tanya did not break under torture, and that her last words had been: "It is happiness to die for one's people . . . Fight, don't be afraid! Stalin is with us! Stalin will come!" The Soviet media soon identified the unknown *partizanka* and, on 16 February 1942, the state conferred the title Hero of the Soviet Union on Zoia Kosmodemianskaia, an eighteen year old from Moscow.

Zoia Kosmodemianskaia was a real young woman who served as a partisan behind enemy lines and perhaps made a small contribution to the war effort before her capture. As such, she is emblematic of the millions of Soviet people—men, women, and children—who worked and struggled to win the war. But Zoia was an invention of the Soviet media, a heroic martyr who arguably made a more profound contribution to the war effort than the real Kosmodemianskaia, inspiring other young people to follow her example and avenge her. The Zoia "myth" may also have worked to cover up the repressive aspects of the Stalinist war effort. In the 1990s, critics claimed that there were no Germans in Petrishchevo at the time of Zoia's execution; carrying out Stalin's "scorched earth" policy, she was torching peasant huts, and the locals turned her over to the Nazis.[1]

CHAPTER QUESTIONS

This chapter focuses on the overarching question, what made it possible for the Soviet Union to survive the Nazi invasion and emerge victorious? Did victory in the war vindicate the Stalinist system, its rapid industrialization, its centralized, authoritarian institutions? Or did victory depend on fundamental (if perhaps temporary) changes in the system? What were the sources of Soviet patriotism? Was coercion more important than popular patriotism in motivating Soviet citizens to fight? How important were outside factors such as Lend Lease aid or the opening of a second front in Europe in June 1944? Why did victory fragment rather than solidify the wartime alliance?

VOICES, MEMORIES, CONTESTED PERSPECTIVES

The Nazi–Soviet Pact and the Nazi invasion

Although historians often debate the degree to which Joseph Stalin alone shaped Soviet history, most agree that what Stalin thought and did fundamentally shaped the way the Soviet Union entered World War II. By the fall of 1938, the Soviet strategy of working with the "bourgeois democracies" to contain fascism had clearly failed. In the infamous Munich Agreement, Britain and France agreed to the Nazi dismemberment of Czechoslovakia (which had a treaty of mutual assistance with France). Stalin, who was not consulted, took the move as anti-Soviet; the British and French seemed to be encouraging Hitler to sate his appetite for expansion in the east.

Under these circumstances, Stalin decided that the best way to prepare for the inevitable war was to try to turn the German war machine to the west. The result was the Nazi–Soviet Nonaggression Pact signed in August 1939. The pact's public protocols pledged the two countries to nonaggression, in essence opening the way to a Nazi attack on Poland, which came on 1 September 1939. The secret protocols divided eastern Europe into Nazi and Soviet spheres of influence. In mid-September, the Soviet army marched into eastern Poland, an invasion that the Soviet press styled a "liberation" of the Ukrainian and Belorussian nations from the oppressive Polish state.

The German invasion of Poland and the subsequent declaration of war by Britain and France marked the beginning of the second world war in twenty-five years. The Allies offered little direct military assistance to the Poles, who by early October had surrendered to the Nazis in the west and the Soviets in the east. Stalin sought to solidify his new western borderlands by the now familiar tactic of cleansing the Polish territories of potential opponents—officers, state officials, landowners, clergy, and intellectuals. At least 320,000 people were deported to Soviet Central Asia. The NKVD shot more than 20,000 Polish officers, a crime the Soviets denied for forty-six years, from 1943, when retreating Nazis found one of the mass graves in the Katyn forest near Smolensk, until 1989.

By June 1940, Germany had conquered Denmark, Norway, the Netherlands, and France. Great Britain stood alone against Germany, and Stalin apparently believed that Adolf Hitler would not turn against the Soviet Union until Britain had been dispatched. The Soviet leader refused to heed more than eighty warnings from multiple sources—British intelligence, a communist spy in Germany's Tokyo embassy, Soviet reconnaissance reports of German troops massing on the border—that all pointed to the same conclusion: A German invasion over an enormous front stretching from the Baltic to the Black Sea was set to begin on 22 June 1941.

Convinced that these disparate warnings constituted an effort to provoke war between Germany and the Soviet Union, Stalin ordered his officers to avoid any actions that might be construed as violations of the Nonaggression Pact. He neglected to bring front-line units up to strength or to put them on alert. Scrupulously adhering to the terms of the pact, the Soviet Union continued to deliver food and war materials to Germany until the very eve of the invasion. Even when reports of German bombs falling on Soviet cities began to arrive in the early morning hours of 22 June, Stalin was slow to take action. When, several hours after the invasion began, Stalin finally reacted, he ordered troops to go on the offensive, a decision that added to the disarray of units overrun by the swift Nazi advance.

Soviet losses in the first days and weeks of the German invasion were staggering. Thousands of planes were destroyed on runways. Hundreds of thousands of Soviet troops were taken prisoner. The Germans occupied Minsk, the capital of Belorussia, on 28 June. By September 1941, Axis armies rapidly advancing in a three-pronged attack had blockaded Leningrad and captured Kiev. By the end of November (when Zoia Kosmodemianskaia was hung in Petrishchevo), German forces were about thirty kilometers (18.6 miles) from Moscow. German generals reported that victory was at hand.

However, in early December, a Soviet counterattack halted the German advance toward Moscow. In retrospect, many military historians consider the German retreat from Moscow—just days before the Japanese attack on Pearl Harbor—the turning point of the war. This perspective calls into question the tendency in the West to ignore or downplay the importance of the eastern front and to focus on the US contribution to the war effort, particularly in the Asian theater. However, at the time Soviet victory hardly seemed assured.

Mobilizing for the motherland

In the radio address on 22 June 1941 announcing that war had begun, Commissar of Foreign Affairs Viacheslav Molotov emphasized that it had come without warning: The Germans attacked "without any claims having been presented to the Soviet Union, without a declaration of war."[2] But in a larger sense the invasion was hardly a surprise. For at least a decade, the Stalinist state had been preparing the country for war. Stalin's signature policies—the collectivization of agriculture and the First Five-Year Plan—aimed to develop an industrial economy that would allow the Soviet Union to survive in a world of aggressive capitalist powers. In the mid-1930s, the introduction of a school history curriculum that emphasized Russian national heroes provided a new means of mobilizing the population, particularly young people, for the expected conflict. Schools and clubs taught military skills, and thousands of Soviet schoolchildren—boys and girls—studied sharpshooting, radio communication, parachuting, and first aid. State media promoted the idea that everyone should be prepared to sacrifice "if tomorrow brings war."

These campaigns appeared to pay off when war came. In the first weeks after the invasion, hundreds of thousands volunteered for active duty in the regular army and local militias (*opolchenie*). Most of the volunteers were young, urban, and educated— the new Soviet intelligentsia. Among those clamoring to enlist were many, including men well above the draft age, women, and underage teenagers and children, whom the state, initially at least, had no interest in recruiting. In the first year of the war, the Soviet state mobilized eleven to twelve million people into the armed forces. Roughly one million women and perhaps as many as several hundred thousand youngsters under the age of eighteen, mainly boys, served over the entire course of the war.[3] Many attested that their desire to serve came from the sense of duty inculcated by prewar schools and propaganda.

For some, enlistment was less an ideological imperative than a response to the war emergency. The loss of one or more parents, the destruction and occupation of towns and villages, and hunger prompted many boys to try to attach themselves to Red Army units as *vospitanniki* (wards). The soldiers might take in boys who made their way to the front lines out of nostalgia for their own children, but the youngsters—sometimes as young as ten—were often quickly incorporated into the daily work, even combat, of the unit.

At the same time, the state and its propaganda machine had to adjust to the fact that the war was not going to be the short, glorious war the Soviet people had been led to expect—and that the military had planned for. State media promoted the importance of work in the war industry or on the collective farm (kolkhoz) for those too old or too young to serve, as well for as women. However, it also stoked the desire of young women and teenage boys to enlist. While authorities initially discouraged women who showed up at recruitment centers, the media publicized and celebrated their achievements. Young women such as the sniper Ludmilla Pavlichenko, "the girl who killed 300 fascists," became models for Soviet youth.[4] Ultimately, the state attempted to take advantage of and control young people's enthusiasm by establishing, for example, military colleges for underage boys wishing to serve in the navy and a sniper school to train female combatants.[5]

During the war, Soviet leaders and the Soviet media ratcheted up the use of the emotional term *rodina* (native place, motherland), which until the mid-1930s (see chapter 6) had been a distinctly un-Bolshevik word, as a powerful mobilizing tool. Rodina, wrote literary scholar Vera Sandomirsky in 1944, means something close to "native place," but overflows with untranslatable "emotion, with a peculiarly Russian warmth and tenderness."[6] This new tone could be heard in Stalin's first radio broadcast of the war. On 3 July 1941, with Minsk already conquered and losses mounting, Stalin addressed the Soviet people as "brothers and sisters!" Many later remembered this unexpected warmth as the most moving aspect of the speech. Neither Stalin nor the revolution disappeared from the Soviet press, but the slogans "Death to the German occupiers!" and "The motherland calls" largely supplanted the revolutionary "Workers of the world unite!" (see document 7.3). In a nod to Russian nationalism, the press dubbed the conflict the Great Fatherland War (*Velikaia Otechestvennaia voina*), a reference to the Fatherland War of 1812 against Napoleon.

The maternal figure of the motherland calling sons and daughters to avenge and protect home and family stood at the heart of the press's effort to represent the war in personal and emotionally compelling terms. Both men and women, many of whom had already experienced loss and displacement, responded (see document 7.4). In an interview recorded in the 1980s, for example, Sofia Ivanovna Sherevera, who was fifteen in 1941, recalled that after she was evacuated from the war zone, she studied by day and worked in the war industry by night. However, after "my entire group, all the girls," read about Zoia Kosmodemianskaia, she "decided to go to the front. The Party taught us that there was nothing dearer than Motherland [rodina]." At the front, Sherevera became a radio and telegraph operator.[7]

War of annihilation

From the very beginning, the Nazis approached the war against the Soviet Union as a war of annihilation, an ideological fight to destroy what they regarded as the twin evils of Bolshevism and Jewry. For the Nazis, this was a war fundamentally different from that fought in the West, a merciless war against purportedly inferior races—Jews and Slavs—fit only for slavery and death. On the eastern front German soldiers routinely engaged in rape, looting, and the summary shooting of prisoners and civilians—actions which would have led to courts-martial and a possible death sentence in France.[8]

The racial ideology that drove the invasion mandated that the German military and occupying authorities pursue a policy of extermination and ethnic cleansing. The German army and air force regularly targeted civilians, using heavy bombing raids and long-range artillery attacks on major cities as a means of sowing chaos by creating massive numbers of refugees. Millions of civilians from occupied territories were deported to Germany as forced laborers. The Germans made starvation a weapon of war. In occupied cities, the Nazis made no provision for supplying food to the local population, who often faced a choice between starvation and flight. Soviet prisoners of war were held in brutal conditions without adequate food. Some 60 to 70 percent of them died in captivity. (The corresponding mortality figure for Western Allied POWS was about 2 percent.) In the case of Leningrad, blockaded in early September 1941, German military strategists decided to destroy the city via starvation rather than risk German lives in storming it.[9] Roughly one million civilians starved to death in Leningrad during the first winter of the war, but the city held out.

As Soviet citizens died of hunger, Ukraine was to become the breadbasket of the Reich. The Soviet leadership's response, a "Scythian policy" which directed soldiers and partisans to "destroy and burn to the ground all population centers to the rear of German troops for forty to sixty kilometers behind the front and twenty to thirty kilometers on either side of the road," meant additional misery and uncertainty for the local population. The policy explains peasants' ambivalent, if not outright hostile, attitude toward partisans such as Kosmodemianskaia. Nonetheless, some historians deem the scorched earth policy a proper, if extreme, response to the "Hitlerites' stated goal of destroying the Russian state and turning any Russians who remained alive into the powerless slaves of the Aryan race."[10]

The Nazis' systematic extermination of Soviet Jews began in June 1941 with the invasion. Only later, in December 1941, did Hitler decide to exterminate German and other West European Jews.[11] In occupied cities such as Minsk, the Nazis confined Jews behind barbed wire in ghettos, where they lived under constant threat of violence and death. Before and even after the establishment of killing centers at Auschwitz and elsewhere in Poland, mass shootings constituted the primary method of genocide in the Soviet Union. In one particularly extensive two-day massacre in late September 1941, just ten days after occupying Kiev, Nazi forces shot more than thirty thousand Jewish civilians at Babi Yar ravine. Such actions were repeated on a smaller scale in thousands of towns and villages (see document 7.2). Over the course of the war, the Nazis murdered approximately 2.5 million Jews east of the Bug River (i.e., within the borders of the Soviet Union as expanded by the Nazi–Soviet Pact). This was virtually the entire Jewish population living in Soviet areas under German control; perhaps 100,000 Jews survived the Nazi occupation, as forest partisans, in hiding, or as prisoners in concentration camps.[12]

Loyalty, defeatism, and collaboration

As Sherevera's response to the Zoia myth suggests, calls to defend the motherland could motivate enlistment. But generalizing about loyalty to the regime is tricky.

Certain segments of the population—young, educated, urban, Russian—were far more likely to volunteer than others—older, non-Russian, peasants.[13] Moreover, in order to answer questions about popular attitudes, historians have to grapple with the difficult question of gauging popular sentiment in a state that severely punished any hint of dissent. During the war, almost 200,000 people were sentenced to death by military tribunals and NKVD special councils. Did patriotic actions and words reflect Soviet patriotism or fears of reprisal? What motivated Soviet people to fight?

Among much of the rural population, in particular, there was initially little enthusiasm for the Soviet cause. In Ukraine, where antireligious campaigns, collectivization, and famine had produced widespread hatred of the Stalinist state, some Soviet citizens greeted the Germans with bread and salt as liberators. In places with long histories of anti-Semitism such as recently annexed Latvia and Lithuania, as well as Ukraine, some welcomed Nazi persecution of Jews. In the occupied territories, a significant minority ultimately collaborated with the Germans in killing their Jewish neighbors. Another significant minority joined partisan units to oppose the invaders and protect their Jewish neighbors. Most, however, preferred to avoid choosing sides or switched sides (sometimes more than once) as each side's fortunes changed over the course of the war.[14]

Among city dwellers (about 33 percent of the population) support for the war effort was more visible, but hardly universal. Records of meetings held in Leningrad in the first weeks of the war suggest that "the overwhelming majority of workers maintained loyalty to the party and the Soviet state."[15] Such loyalty did not rule out hopes for a better postwar life. Sacrifice for the war effort might raise expectations of greater intellectual freedom, the end of the kolkhoz, the return of the eight-hour day, and the final collapse of the repressive system. Moreover, even in Moscow and Leningrad, state and party surveillance reports recorded pointed opposition to the regime, popular anti-Semitism, a tendency to equate communists and Jews, and the conviction that only Jews and communists would suffer under Nazi occupation (see document 7.1). Such attitudes were most likely to be voiced when the regime appeared at its weakest, for example in October 1941, when the Germans seemed on the verge of taking Moscow, and the city descended into panic and looting.[16]

Attitudes among Soviet soldiers were similarly mixed and are likewise difficult to assess. In the first six months of the war, the invaders captured more than three million Soviet troops. Some historians link the high number of prisoners to low morale among soldiers and a generalized unwillingness to fight for Stalin and his regime.[17] Others, however, argue that many of the surrenders stemmed not from "hatred of the Soviet system," but rather from "strictly military or wartime difficulties" such as the shortage of trained officers—a legacy of the purges as well as of the rapid expansion and reorganization of the Red Army in the prewar period.[18] Of course such "difficulties" can be understood as a product of the Stalinist system. Was the fact that the Soviet army was woefully unprepared for the Axis invasion a "strictly" military problem? Should shortfalls—whether the lack of trained officers or of new KV and T-34 tanks in the frontier area—be understood as the consequence of poor military planning or as a result of the "entire political, economic, and social system that fed the army"?[19] Was the soldier who surrendered to the Germans because the Red Army was unable to feed its troops in some sense a critic of the Stalinist system?

Linkages between combat behavior and political loyalties are not always straightforward or clear. Troops encircled by German armor—under heavy air attack, cut off from supplies of ammunition, food, and sometimes even water—often resisted for days. While such resistance appears to have been widespread, it tells us relatively little about soldiers' motivations. The reasons for fighting could be multiple and might, for example, have as much or more to do with love of country or hometown, a desire for revenge, fear of punishment, or a need to prove one's masculinity than loyalty to Stalin and the Soviet system. A battalion commissar who seemed to understand the multiplicity of his men's motivations appears in the front-line notebooks of Vasily Grossman, a novelist turned reporter for the Red Army newspaper *Krasnaia zvezda* (Red Star). Armed with two pistols, the commissar convinced troops "running away from the battlefield" to take up their positions again by shouting, "Where are you running, you whores, where? Go forward, for our Motherland, for Jesus Christ, motherfuckers! For Stalin, you whores!"[20] Grossman's laconic note leaves open the question of whether soldiers responded to the sanctioned battle cry "For Motherland, for Stalin," the pistols, or the curses impugning their manhood.

Overall, it seems clear that the more Soviet people learned about the behavior of the invading Germans—information they might gain from newspaper accounts, from those fleeing occupied territories, or from their own firsthand encounters—the more they came to fear the consequences of a German victory and to hate the enemy.[21] This might be the case even among those who had welcomed the Germans. In 1942, Grossman overheard a woman in a village on the road to Stalingrad reassessing the situation: "Oh this Hitler, he's a real Satan! And we used to say that the communists were Satans."[22]

Wartime Stalinism

In December 1941, the Soviet army became the first force to stop and reverse the vaunted German Blitzkrieg. Hitler and his generals had expected a lightning victory; instead they got a long, hard-fought war of attrition. The battle for Moscow in late 1941 cost the Germans more lives than all of their campaigns in the west. Moreover, by the time the Germans were halted, thousands of Soviet factories had been converted to wartime production or dismantled and evacuated beyond the Urals, and workers were turning out tanks, planes, and weapons on a vast scale. Such achievements did not mean immediate victory. During the so-called Black Summer of 1942, the Soviets again suffered massive losses as the Germans undertook an offensive in the south that brought them in August 1942 to Stalingrad on the Volga River, a strategic and symbolic prize deep in Soviet territory. The Soviet victory there in January 1943, after a brutal and much-mythologized battle fought in the ruins of the city, marked, most military historians agree, a critical turning point in the war.

For Stalin and the party, these Soviet achievements constituted a vindication of the habits, practices, and infrastructure created by the Stalinist system in the 1930s. The emphasis on heavy industry at the expense of consumer goods seemed particularly prescient, as in 1944 Soviet industry turned out 3,400 aircraft and nearly 1,800 armored fighting vehicles per month.[23] Reflecting in 1942 on what made it possible for the Russians to hold out, John Scott, an American who had helped to build the massive steel works at Magnitogorsk in the 1930s, credited the fact that: "During the last ten years the Russian people shed blood, sweat, and tears to create . . . a modern industrial base outside the reach of an invader—Stalin's Ural Stronghold—and a modern mechanized army." He also understood what we might call the repressive or coercive aspects of the regime as an essential element of its success: "The population was taught by a painful and expensive process to work efficiently, to obey orders, to mind their own business, and to take it on the chin when necessary with a minimum of complaint."[24] Scott himself had "taken it on the chin." The purges of the late 1930s forced him out of his job at Magnitogorsk, and his Russian wife Masha had to wait almost four years for an exit visa. Still, he viewed the industrialization drive of the 1930s along with its seeming excesses as keys to the Soviet ability to resist.

At the same time, the Stalinist system can be understood as the source of many of the Soviet Union's initial setbacks. In June 1941, the fear of disobeying, a lingering effect of the purge of some of the military's most prominent leaders, prevented Stalin's generals from pressing for preparations to counter a German invasion that appeared imminent.[25] While the industrialization drive clearly contributed to the Soviet ability to wage war, Scott overstates the degree to which the state built a "Ural Stronghold." Much of the new investment went to traditional industrial zones in European Russia, where plants were taken by the invaders or hastily evacuated, contributing to the chaos of the first months after the invasion.

The evacuation of machines and individuals deemed essential to the war effort— like the industrialization drive itself—occurred on a massive scale and achieved a great deal. More than sixteen million people were evacuated from the frontier zone, Moscow, and Leningrad. However, the evacuation was often carried out with great confusion, waste, and inefficiency. Although an essential part of the war effort, "the evacuation highlighted the weaknesses of the Soviet system: instead of a resolute response, the local political and managerial elite simply 'deserted' their posts, abdicating their responsibilities and defying central directives."[26]

In addition to weighing the value of Stalinist policies and methods to the war effort, historians have asked whether and to what degree winning the war required funda-mental changes in the system. Many wartime policies relied on prewar Stalinist methods of control. To maximize industrial output, the state began enforcing labor laws long on the books that prescribed draconian penalties for lateness or absentee-ism. To control access to information, authorities confiscated radio receivers. Stalin applied similar logic to military problems, declaring in August 1941 that POWs would be regarded as traitors to the motherland. In July 1942, with German troops pushing toward the Volga, Stalin issued the infamous "Not one step back" order that estab-lished "blocking battalions" (*zagradbat*) charged with shooting retreating soldiers. Perhaps as many as 13,500 soldiers were executed during the five-month battle at Stalingrad.

Coercive measures might work to maintain discipline, but they could also prove ineffective or even counterproductive at the front. Officers unwilling "to spare their best men for service in the blocking units" might simply ignore the harsh measures prescribed by the "Not one step back" order. From these officers' perspective, "it was not mere coercion that changed the fortunes of the Red Army" but rather "the emer-gence of a corps of able, self-reliant fighters."[27] In Stalingrad, General Vasily Chuikov proudly described for Grossman how, fighting house-to-house in close proximity to the enemy, "Our soldiers have become so resourceful . . . Our soldiers were on an upper floor [in a building]. Some Germans below them wound up a gramophone. Our men made a hole in the floor and fired [through it] with a flame-thrower."[28]

Although, as noted above, some 200,000 people were sentenced to death by military tribunals and the NKVD during the war, historians often describe the first catastrophic months of the war, from 22 June 1941 to the victory at Stalingrad in January 1943, as a period of "spontaneous de-Stalinization" or a "breathing space."[29] Some go further, arguing that the "extraordinary" situation created by the invasion produced a "collapse . . . of the system of repression."[30] Concrete manifestations of the "breathing space" could be found in a loosening of censorship, the revival of the Orthodox Church, and a new emphasis on merit rather than political loyalty in promotions. Among the clearest statements of the sense of freedom that accompanied the war is Boris Pasternak's well-known contention in his novel *Doctor Zhivago* that "when the war broke out, its real horrors, its real dangers, its menace of a real death were a blessing compared to the inhuman reign of the lie, and they brought relief because they broke the spell of the dead letter."[31] The poet Olga Berggolts described a similar state of liberation in one of her best-known poems from the Leningrad blockade: Amid cold, filth, and hunger, "we breathed such stormy freedom,/that our grandchildren might envy us."[32]

Expectations that such freedom might outlast the war were soon dashed. As the tide turned with the victories at Stalingrad and, in the summer of 1943, at Kursk, the largest tank battle in history, Stalin reverted to his prewar methods. In newly liberated territories, the NKVD investigated and detained tens of thousands of Soviet citizens as deserters, traitors, collaborators, and "criminal elements." Prisoners of war and forced laborers returning from Germany were often processed and sent directly to the Gulag.

Expanding on prewar precedents, entire peoples were punished. Indeed ethnic minorities may have experienced little "breathing space." In 1941, the government deported some 400,000 Volga Germans, the descendants of Germans who had settled in Russia in the eighteenth century during the time of Catherine the Great, to Central Asia and Siberia as a means of preventing their possible collaboration with the invaders. In 1943–1944, about one million members of national minorities, including Crimean Tatars, Chechens, and Kalmyks were deported from their homelands in the North Caucasus and Crimea to Central Asia.[33]

By 1943, the anti-Semitism that had been present in surveillance reports from the first days of the war became increasingly visible and tolerated. Widely circulating rumors maintained that Jews refused to fight, or were "serving" on the so-called Tashkent front—the city of Tashkent in Uzbekistan being a prime destination of those evacuated from the war zone. While a majority of the evacuees in Uzbekistan were Jews who had been evacuated not because they were Jews but because they or their spouses were important cultural or party figures, some 500,000 Jews fought in the Red Army. Nonetheless, the evacuation fueled anti-Semitism. State authorities often denied Jews who had been evacuated the right to return to their prewar homes.[34] The love of the rodina that had seemed liberating during the war remained a central feature of Soviet propaganda, but often took crueler and more exclusively Russian nationalist forms as the Soviet army began its march to Berlin.

Relations with the Western Allies

Stalin's chief demand of his allies was the opening of a second front in Europe, and his chief frustration was their slowness in delivering it. In November 1942, with the Germans holding 90 percent of the ruined city of Stalingrad, the sniper Ludmilla Pavlichenko joined a delegation of Soviet heroes who toured the US and Britain to

Figure 7.1 Russian delegates to the International Youth Assembly, Washington, DC, 1942.
Courtesy of the Library of Congress Prints and Photographs Division, Office of
War Information Photograph Collection (LC-USW3-007381-E).

*Sniper Ludmilla Pavlichenko is on the right. Why might the Soviets have sent Pavlichenko to
appeal to the American people?*

take the appeal directly to the people. At a London rally Pavlichenko said, "We
are grateful for the tanks made by British workers but we are waiting and hoping
for greater help, at least for such help that would divert from our front sixty to
seventy divisions."[35] Only in early 1943 did substantial amounts of Lend Lease aid
from the US and Britain—airplanes, tanks, artillery, jeeps, trucks, fuel, and food—
begin to reach the Soviet Union. However, even the relatively small amount of aid
delivered in 1941 and 1942 was often critical, given the heavy Soviet losses and the
disruption of production in the early months of the war.[36] Pavlichenko's appeal

stemmed from the fact that in late 1942 the Allies were facing twelve Nazi divisions in North Africa, while the Soviets faced two hundred along a 2,000 mile front, eighteen in Stalingrad alone.

The direct appeal made sense at a time when popular opinion in the West was supportive of the Soviet Union and its heroic efforts in the war. In a Gallup poll conducted in Britain in April 1943, 50 percent of respondents named the Soviets when asked which country "has so far made the greatest contribution to winning the war." The British came in at 42 percent, the Americans a paltry 3 percent.[37] The stolidly anticommunist British Prime Minister Winston Churchill and anticommunist officials in the US State Department were less enthusiastic. In late 1942, Churchill worried that "it would be a measureless disaster if Russian barbarism overlaid the culture and independence of the ancient states of Europe."[38] At the Casablanca Conference held in January 1943, Churchill and President Franklin Roosevelt agreed only to an invasion of Sicily and Italy, not the cross-Channel invasion to open a second front in France that Stalin thought necessary. (Stalin did not attend the conference.) Stalin's May 1943 dissolution of the Comintern did little to assuage Churchill's fears.

In April 1943, the German discovery of the mass graves of thousands of Polish officers in the Katyn forest near Smolensk further strained Soviet relations with the West. The Soviets, as noted earlier, denied the (accurate) German charge that the NKVD had committed the murders in the spring of 1940, following the partition of Poland authorized by the Nazi–Soviet Pact. The Polish government in exile in London doubted the Soviet denials and called for an international investigation. An indignant Stalin broke relations with the London Poles. While perhaps not fully convinced of Soviet innocence, Churchill and British Foreign Office officials put the alliance against Germany first, and treated the revelations as a case of the Nazis blaming others for what they themselves had done.[39] While the incident did not produce the fragmentation of the alliance that the Nazis hoped for, it foreshadowed the complexity and ugliness of conflicts to come over the fate of a Poland "liberated" by Soviet troops.

The matter of the second front was finally settled in November 1943 at the Teheran Conference. By the time of the meeting in Teheran, the Red Army had already won decisive victories at Stalingrad and Kursk, and had liberated Kiev. The Soviets broke the blockade of Leningrad in January 1944. The Allied landing at Normandy on D-Day, 6 June 1944, came two weeks before the opening of the massive Soviet offensive in Belorussia that on 3 July liberated Minsk. After the opening of the second front, the Allies engaged 27 German divisions in France; the Soviets faced 181 in the East.

The Soviet offensive reached the outskirts of Warsaw at the end of July 1944. On 1 August, the Polish Home Army, hoping to take the city before the Soviets arrived, rose against the Nazis. From the Soviet perspective, the uprising was both premature—the Soviet army needed time to regroup after the hard-fought battles that brought it to the Vistula River—and unwanted, as it stood to increase the postwar influence of the anti-Soviet government in exile, the London Poles. Indeed strengthening the London government against the so-called Lublin Poles, a rival group established by the Soviets, constituted a key aim of the uprising. Historians generally agree that the Soviet army could do little to aid the uprising. Whether Soviet actions, for example efforts to prevent aid from reaching the rebels, substantially changed the outcome remains a matter of historical debate.[40] In early October 1944, the Germans crushed the uprising with unimaginable ferocity, completely leveling the city—or what was left of it after the 1943 Warsaw ghetto uprising. In January 1945, the Red Army liberated the destroyed city.

Figure 7.2 Photograph taken during the Teheran Conference, 1943. Standing outside the Russian Embassy, left to right: unidentified British officer; General George C. Marshall, American chief of staff, shaking hands with Sir Archibald Clark Keer, British ambassador to the USSR; Harry Hopkins; Stalin's interpreter; Josef Stalin; Soviet foreign minister Molotov; General Voroshilov. Courtesy of the Library of Congress Prints and Photographs Division, Office of War Information Photograph Collection (LC-USZ62-132802).

What clues in the photograph suggest whether it was taken by a Soviet or Western photographer?

When Stalin, Roosevelt, and Churchill met for the second and last time in February 1945 at Yalta (see document 7.5), the Soviet army was advancing on Berlin. Crimea itself had been liberated only in May 1943, and FDR told Stalin that seeing the damage done by the Germans there made him "more bloodthirsty"; he hoped that Stalin would once again propose a toast, as he had at Teheran, "to the execution of 50,000 officers of the German Army." Even Churchill had a kind word for Stalin, noting over dinner that "the fires of war had wiped out old animosities."[41]

This mood of shared sacrifice and common purpose proved short-lived. The key questions addressed at the conference—particularly the "Polish Question"—soon became issues in the emerging Cold War. At Yalta, the Soviet Union agreed to "free and unfettered elections" in Poland. For their part, Britain and the US promised a Polish government friendly to the Soviet Union; in pursuit of that aim, the Soviets did not hesitate to arrest opposition politicians and members of the Home Army. The elections in January 1947 lacked even the appearance of freedom and fairness.

The Soviets fulfilled the commitment made at Yalta to enter the war against Japan in exchange for concessions that reversed the losses sustained by the Russian empire in the Russo-Japanese war of 1904–1905. Indeed a recent study of the end of the war in the Pacific concludes that the Soviet entry into the war, rather than the US use of atomic bombs at Hiroshima and Nagasaki, was the critical factor in the Japanese surrender.[42] Nonetheless, the new weapon, along with the "give-'em-hell" style of the new President Harry Truman, chilled relations. (Roosevelt died of a brain hemorrhage in April 1945.) Stalin dealt with the threat of the American atomic bomb both by working to develop a Soviet bomb as quickly as possible—espionage helped to make this a reality in 1949—and by behaving as if he was not intimidated by the US nuclear monopoly. This latter tactic led US Secretary of State James Byrnes to conclude that the Russians were "stubborn, obstinate, and they don't scare." The unintended result of Soviet bluster was to speed the perhaps inevitable breakdown of relations with the West. In this way "the bomb contributed to the collapse of the wartime alliance and the origins of the Cold War."[43]

Victory: costs and meanings

In 1945, World War II ended as it had begun with a paroxysm of violence against civilians. The British and Americans contributed to the destruction with massive bombing raids on German cities that killed more civilians than the fiercely resisted Soviet invasion. Soviet soldiers looted and burned what seemed to them rich German homes—even after the privations of four years of war—and raped as many as two million women in Germany alone (see document 7.6). A few looters and rapists were punished, but for the most part officers looked the other way. The lack of concern is evident in the explanation a Russian major gave British journalist Alexander Werth: "Our fellows were so sex-starved that they often raped old women of sixty, or seventy or even eighty—much to these grandmothers' surprise, if not downright delight." Perhaps not quite believing his own excuses, the major added, revealing his own racial prejudices: "But I admit it was a nasty business, and the record of the Kazaks and other Asiatic troops was particularly bad."[44]

This violence was often driven by hatred of the German invader and a (perhaps understandable) thirst for vengeance. Entering liberated Soviet territory, Soviet soldiers had encountered gruesome evidence of Nazi atrocities, including widespread rape. Many had seen the mountains of corpses in Nazi death camps liberated on the road to Berlin. Soviet posters in Germany announced: "Red Army Soldier: You are now on German soil; the hour of revenge has struck!" Rape offered a visceral and violent demonstration of the conqueror's power over both women and the men unable to protect them.

Such atrocities are rarely at the forefront of histories of the war. Across the 1991 divide, Soviet and post-Soviet accounts emphasize the Soviet people's enormous losses, their resilience and heroism, and the bitter sweetness of victory. While exact figures are difficult to establish, historians generally agree that approximately 27 million Soviet citizens—about 20 million of whom were civilians—died in the war. Death touched virtually every Soviet family; Soviet losses exceeded those suffered by all other belligerents combined. In 1945, much of the country was in ruins. In the formerly

Figure 7.3 A Letter from the Front by Aleksander Laktianov, 1947. © RIA Novosti/Alamy.
What does the painting "remember" and "forget" about the war?

occupied territories, industry and whole cities were destroyed, agriculture devastated. This was the cost, as the massive memorial built by the Soviets in defeated Berlin put it, of "saving European civilization from fascist *pogromshchiki*"—those who instigate massacres and persecution.

CONCLUSION AND FURTHER QUESTIONS

How did the Red Army overcome the disasters of 1941 and arrive triumphant in Berlin? Contemporaries offered a wide range of explanations. Nazi generals, who had dismissed the Russians as racially inferior, blamed their unexpected defeats on Hitler's mistakes or the allegedly immutable characteristics of the Russian character and land—"primitive" ferocity in battle and the devastating power of Generals Snow, Ice, and Mud. Stalin emphasized his wise prewar policies and effective wartime leadership. Later Soviet leaders blamed the purges and Stalin's incompetence as a military strategist for the early defeats, while emphasizing the leading role of the party in the "people's war." This chapter avoided such reductive, politicized, and racialized (or simply racist) explanations, instead asking how multiple factors—including popular patriotism and state coercion, local initiative and central control—interacted and shifted over the course of the war. How did the reactions and motives of Soviet people vary as they operated within the constraints of a coercive system?

In post-Soviet Russia, the Great Victory is still celebrated and, some might argue, whitewashed on Victory Day, 9 May.[45] A number of recent studies focus on the legacies of the war, asking how the post-Stalin and the post-Soviet Russian state used (or exploited) the powerful memory of the war to enhance its legitimacy.[46] We might also consider how to explain the memories of those who suffered through and won the war and who often recall it as the "best time of our lives" because "at that time we all felt closer to our government than at any other time in our lives."[47]

PRIMARY SOURCES

Use the questions to analyze the content, context, and significance of each primary source. Then synthesize the primary sources and the material in the chapter to formulate a response to the primary chapter question: What made it possible for the Soviet Union to survive the Nazi invasion and emerge victorious?

Document 7.1 Report to Leningrad party leaders on a handwritten note found in a bomb shelter, 11 October 1941

This report on the mood in Leningrad was made just over one month after the closing of the blockade, when the city was under frequent air attack.

Questions for analysis

1 How does the letter explain the current emergency? What solution does it advocate?
2 How does the letter use Bolshevik or revolutionary categories and ideas? Does the author "speak Bolshevik"? What is the author suggesting by calling for "bread and peace," the Bolshevik rallying cry in 1917?
3 What role does Russian nationalism play in this appeal? Why was Stalin identified as a Jew, Tatar, or Gypsy? (He was none of these things.)

A communist . . . brought to the VKP(b) *raikom* [the communist party's district committee] a handwritten note found in a bombshelter at 33a Karl Liebknecht Prospect, with the following content:

"Thanks to our good rulers, the evacuation has fallen apart. There are many children, women, old people, and sick here. What awaits them? If our rulers, led by the worst convict among them—the Georgian Jew, or Tatar, or Gypsy—said, 'Not one step back, we'll blow the city up, but we won't surrender it,' so you yourselves understand what's going to happen to the children, women, old people and sick. The Tatar convict is going to live, while we all perish.

"All against Stalin!!! The city should be made open, like Paris! . . .

"Down with the convict! Bread and peace! After our 20-year tribulation, we have no strength left to endure.

"Let us unite in a council of liberation for the Russian people from the convict's yoke, but know that only [Kliment] Voroshilov and [Semen] Budenny [famous Civil War commanders] are with us, and down with all the rest.

"Everyone into the street! Everyone into the battle against bolshevism!"

"Nationality of the Russian People"

This leaflet has been handed over to the district department of the NKVD, which is investigating the case.

Source: Document 57 in Richard Bidlack and Nikita Lomagin, eds., *The Leningrad Blockade, 1941–1944: A New Documentary History from the Soviet Archives* (New Haven, CT: Yale University Press, 2012), 338. Used by permission of Yale University Press.

Document 7.2   A description of the murder of Jews in Pushkin, 29 January 1945

Report of the State Extraordinary Commission for the Determination and Investigation of Nazi and their Collaborators' Atrocities in the USSR (ChGK), established in November 1942 to investigate the damage caused to civilians, public organizations, factories and state institutions in the USSR.

Questions for analysis

1   What does this source suggest about the state's priorities in collecting information on the murder of Jews?
2   What do these priorities suggest about the workings of the Stalinist system?
3   What would you look for in comparing this report to those created in other places or at other points during the war or to other types of sources (e.g., a diary)?

... On September 20, 1941, the German authorities brought 15 (fifteen) people of Jewish nationality to Dvortsovaia Square [Palace Square, Pushkin, is the site of the former imperial Summer Palace, and was a popular leisure destination for Leningraders] ... and shot them to death with sub-machineguns.

On September 21, 1941 the Germans also brought 23 Jewish children, aged five to thirteen or fourteen, and placed them in line in Pushkin's Dvortsovaia Square. They ran away in different directions, cried, but the Germans gathered them together again, beat them, and then fired at them with sub-machineguns. Thus these children were shot to death. The bodies of the fifteen adults and the 23 children remained in the square for approximately twelve days ... the corpses were buried ... at Dvortsovaia Square, but some of the corpses, five of them, were buried in ... the garden, opposite the room of Alexander II. [The corpses] were [also] buried in a trench in Ekaterininsky Park.

Besides this, I know of a lady, about 22 years old, a Jew by nationality, who used to live at 8/2 Komsomol Street, Pushkin, I do not know her exact name or patronymic [named derived from father's first name]. On October 23, 1941, the German troops brought her to Dvortsovaia Square and then took her to the park and shot her to death merely because she was Jewish ...

Source: Available at Yad Vashem Archive, www.yadvashem.org/untoldstories/database/chgkSovietReports.asp?cid=550&site_id=678 (accessed 5 March 2016).

Document 7.3   Konstantin Simonov, "Kill Him"

Originally published in *Pravda*, 1942. Simonov was a poet and war correspondent, who often wrote for the Red Army newspaper *Krasnaia zvezda*.

Questions for analysis

1   How does this poem compare to the revolutionary poetry of Mayakovsky [see document 5.1]?
2   What connections do you see between this source and the testimony regarding the murder of Jews in Pushkin?

. . . If you don't want to give away
The one you walked with together,
The one whom you didn't dare
For a long time to kiss
Because you loved her so much,
If you don't want the Germans
To take her by force, clutched in a corner,
To crucify her, three at a time,
Naked, on the floor,
If you don't want the three dogs to get
In moans, hatred, in blood
All that you so tenderly worshiped
With the strength of your masculine love . . .
If you don't want to give away to the German,
With the black gun of his,
The house where you lived, your wife, your mother,
All that we motherland call,
Know—no one will save her
Unless you save her yourself.
Know—no one will kill him
Unless you kill him yourself.
And until you kill him,
Don't talk about your love.
Do not call motherland
The place of your childhood,
The house of your own.
If your brother kills a German,
If your neighbor kills a German—
This is your brother's and neighbor's vengeance,
You—you have no excuse.
One doesn't hide behind another's back,
One doesn't avenge with the gun of another.
So kill him.

Source: Vera Sandomirsky [Dunham], "Soviet War Poetry," *Russian Review* 4 (Autumn 1944): 50. Used by permission of John Wiley & Sons Inc.

Document 7.4   Ludmilla Alexeyeva looks back on her World War II childhood

Questions for analysis

1   What does this source suggest about the effectiveness of Soviet propaganda?
2   Does the source support the argument that the war was a moment of "spontaneous de-Stalinization"?

Victory was not assured. Soviet military forces were not invincible. Everything was falling apart.

I had to act. I had to act as an individual. All of us had to. Our leaders were wrong. They needed us. They needed the public. By realizing that we became citizens.

Still, I was only fourteen, and at that age I could do little more than stand by the radio, imagining the Nazis goose-stepping down the winding Arbat [a street in central Moscow], past the house where Pushkin took his bride . . .

I vowed that if Moscow fell, I would make my way back from Kazakhstan and fight the Nazis. In those fantasies, I saw myself killing at least one of them; I wasn't sure how I would kill him or with what. Those were details that had to be worked out later.

On January 27, 1942, I opened a copy of *Komsomolskaya pravda,* the Young Communist League newspaper. On the bottom of the page there was a photograph of the corpse of a young woman in a noose. "PARTISAN TANYA [nom de guerre of Zoya Kosmodemyanskaya] TORTURED TO DEATH BY THE GERMAN FASCISTS IN THE VILLAGE OF PETRISHCHEVO," the cutline. The photo was taken by the Germans who tortured the girl.

. . . Reading the story of Tanya-the-partisan, I asked myself: How would I have behaved under torture? Would I be able to sacrifice my life with such poise and honor?

. . . That summer I worked in the kolkhoz fields. The elastic band on my pants had stretched out, so the pants were held up with a safety pin. With the bending, the pin would come undone, sticking into my side. Then with every move, the pin shifted inside the wound, and with every burst of pain, I imagined myself under torture. I was testing myself.

Source: Ludmilla Alexeyeva and Paul Goldberg, *The Thaw Generation: Coming of Age in the Post-Stalin Era* (Pittsburgh, PA: University of Pittsburgh Press, 1990), 19–21. Used by permission of the authors.

Document 7.5   Transcript from the Yalta Conference, 1945

Questions for analysis

1   Do you see changes in tone and content between the two sessions?
2   Which of the leaders seems most practical? Most ideological? Did the leaders seem to understand one another?
3   Can you find clues that suggest why the alliance didn't last? What other information would you like to have?

Third Plenary Meeting, 6 February 1945, 4 PM, Livadia Palace [Yalta]

Secret

PRESIDENT [ROOSEVELT]: I should like to bring up Poland . . . There are six or seven million Poles in the United States. As I said at Teheran, in general I am in favor of the Curzon line [border for Poland proposed after World War I by British Foreign Secretary George Curzon; it stood to the west of the 1939 border with the USSR] . . . The Poles would like East Prussia and part of Germany. It would make it easier for me at home if the Soviet Government could give something to Poland . . . Opinion in the United States is against recognition of the Lublin government on the ground that it represents a small portion of the Polish people . . . We want a Poland that will be thoroughly friendly to the Soviet for years to come. This is essential.

STALIN: (interrupting) Friendly not only to the Soviet but all three allies.

PRIME MINISTER [CHURCHILL]: I have made repeated declarations in Parliament in support of the Soviet claims to the Curzon line . . . I have always considered that after all Russia has suffered in fighting Germany and after all her efforts in liberating Poland her claim is one founded not on force but on right . . . However, I am interested more in the question of Poland's sovereign independence and freedom than in particular frontier lines . . . This is what is dear to the hearts of the nation of Britain. This is what we went to war against Germany for—that Poland should be free and sovereign . . . Great Britain has no material interest in Poland. Her interest is only one of honor because we drew the sword for Poland against Hitler's brutal attack . . .

STALIN: The Prime Minister has said that for Great Britain the question of Poland is a question of honor. For Russia it is not only a question of honor but also of security . . . because throughout history Poland has always been a corridor for attack on Russia . . . I must remind you that the Curzon line was invented not by Russians but by foreigners . . . Lenin opposed it . . . Some want us to be less Russian than Curzon and [French Prime Minister Georges] Clemenceau . . . I prefer that the war continue a little longer and give Poland compensation in the west at the expense of Germany.

Sixth Plenary Meeting, 9 February 1945, 4 PM, Livadia Palace

Top Secret

PRIME MINISTER: In Parliament I must be able to say that the elections [in Poland] will be held in a fair way. I do not much care about Poles myself.

STALIN: There are some very good people among the Poles. They are good fighters. Of course, they fight among themselves, too . . .

PRESIDENT: I want this election in Poland to be the first one beyond question. It should be like Caesar's wife. I did not know her but they said she was pure.

STALIN: They said that about her but in fact she had her sins.

Source: United States Department of State, *Foreign Relations of the United States: Conferences at Malta and Yalta, 1945* (Washington, DC: US Government Printing Office, 1945), 677–680, 853–854.

Document 7.6   A woman journalist remembers the Soviet invasion of Berlin

Questions for analysis

1   Why did the author consider mass rape a "defeat of the male sex"? Does this insight help to explain the behavior of the Soviet army in Germany?

2   How does this account compare to the testimony regarding Nazi atrocities in the Soviet Union?

I start yelling [at her neighbors]. "You pigs! Here they rape me twice in a row and you shut the door and leave me lying like a piece of dirt!" . . . At first they're quiet, then all hell breaks loose behind me, everyone talking at once, screaming, fighting, flailing about. At last a decision: "We'll all go together to the commandant and ask for protection for the night."

And so finally a small platoon of women, along with a few men, heads out into the evening twilight, into the mild air smelling of fire, over to where the commandant is said to be staying . . .

Inside the courtyard I ask to speak to the commandant . . . He looks at the pitiful group of people come to complain and laughs at my stammering. "Come on, I'm sure they didn't really hurt you. Our men are all healthy." He strolls back to the other officers. We hear them chuckling. I turn to our gray assembly. "There's no point."

. . .

These days I keep noticing how my feelings toward men—and the feelings of all the other women—are changing. We feel sorry for them; they seem so miserable and powerless. The weaker sex . . . Among the many defeats at the end of this war is the defeat of the male sex.

Source: Anonymous [since identified as journalist Marta Hillers], *A Woman in Berlin: Eight Weeks in the Conquered City. A Diary* (New York: Henry Holt, 2000), 54, 42–43. German edition: *Eine Frau in Berlin: Tagebuchaufzeichnungen vom 20. April bis 22. Juni 1945.* © 2002 Hannelore Marek. © AB – Die Andere Bibliothek GmbH & Co. KG, Berlin 2011 (first published by Eichborn Verlag, Frankfurt am Main, 2003). English language translation copyright © 2005 by Philip Boehm. Used by permission of Henry Holt and Company, LLC. All rights reserved.

Notes

1 Adrienne M. Harris, "The Lives and Deaths of a Soviet Saint in the Post-Soviet Period: The Case of Zoia Kosmodem'ianskaia," *Canadian Slavonic Papers/Revue canadienne des slavistes*, 53, no. 2–4 (June–December 2011): 287–288.

2 *Radio Address of the Vice-Chairman of the Council of People's Commissars of the USSR and People's Commissar of Foreign Affairs V. M. Molotov, June 22, 1941* (Moscow: Foreign Languages Publishing House, 1941), 1.

3 John Erickson, "Soviet Women in World War II," in John Garrard and Carol Garrard, eds., *World War 2 and the Soviet People* (New York: Palgrave Macmillan, 1993), 50–76; Olga Kucherenko, *Little Soldiers: How Soviet Children Went to War, 1941–1945* (New York: Oxford University Press, 2011), 2.

4 "Streliai, kak Liudmila Pavlichenko," *Komsomol'skaia pravda*, 2 June 1942.

5 Kucherenko, *Little Soldiers*, 231–236; Anna Krylova, *Soviet Women in Combat: A History of Violence on the Eastern Front* (New York: Cambridge University Press, 2010), 156–159.

6 Vera Sandomirsky [Dunham], "Soviet War Poetry," *Russian Review*, 4 (Autumn 1944): 47.

7 As quoted in S. Alexiyevich, *War's Unwomanly Face* (Moscow: Progress Publishers, 1988), 33.

8 Omer Bartov, *The Eastern Front, 1941–1945: German Troops and the Barbarisation of Warfare* (Basingstoke: Palgrave Macmillan, 2001), 116, 134; see also Jeffrey Burds, "Sexual Violence in Europe in World War II, 1939–1945," *Politics and Society*, 37, no. 1 (March 2009): 36.

9 Alex J. Kay, "'The Purpose of the Russian Campaign Is the Decimation of the Slavic Population by Thirty Million': The Radicalization of German Food Policy in 1941," in Alex J. Kay, Jeff Rutherford, and David Stahel, eds., *Nazi Policy on the Eastern Front, 1941: Total War, Genocide, and Radicalization* (Rochester, NY: University of Rochester Press, 2012), 101–129; Adrian E. Wettstein, "Urban Warfare Doctrine on the Eastern Front," in ibid., 60–65.

10 Quotations from M. M. Gorinov, "Zoia Kosmodem´ianskaia (1923–1941)," *Otechestvennai istoriia*, no. 1 (2003): 79, 80. On attitudes toward the partisans, see Kenneth Slepyan, *Stalin's Guerrillas: Soviet Partisans in World War II* (Lawrence: University Press of Kansas, 2006), 75–80.

11 Christian Gerlach, "The Wannsee Conference, the Fate of German Jews, and Hitler's Decision in Principle to Exterminate All European Jews," trans. Stephen Duffy, *Journal of Modern History*, 70 (December 1998): 760. More generally, see Yitzhak Arad, *The Holocaust in the Soviet Union* (Lincoln: University of Nebraska Press, 2009).

12 Hans-Heinrich Nolte, "Destruction and Resistance: The Jewish Shtetl of Slonim, 1941–44," in Robert W. Thurston and Bernd Bonwetsch, eds., *The People's War: Responses to World War II in the Soviet Union* (Urbana: University of Illinois Press, 2000), 47; Anika Walke, *Pioneers and Partisans: An Oral History of Nazi Genocide in Belorussia* (New York: Oxford University Press, 2015).

13 Roger R. Reese, *Why Stalin's Soldiers Fought: The Red Army's Military Effectiveness in World War II* (Lawrence: University Press of Kansas, 2011).

14 Oleg Budnitskii, "The Great Patriotic War and Soviet Society: Defeatism, 1941–42," *Kritika: Explorations in Russian and Eurasian History*, 15, no. 4 (Fall 2014): 783–790; Mark Edele, "'What Are We Fighting For?' Loyalty in the Soviet War Effort, 1941–1945," *International Labor and Working-Class History*, 84 (Fall 2013): 259–260.

15 Andrei R. Dzeniskevich, "The Social and Political Situation in Leningrad in the First Months of the German Invasion: The Social Psychology of the Workers," trans. Robert W. Thurston, in Thurston and Bonwetsch, eds., *The People's War*, 77.

16 Budnitskii, "Great Patriotic War," 778–783; Edele, "'What Are We,'" 262.

17 See, for example, Alexander Dallin, *German Rule in Russia, 1941–1954: A Study of Occupation Policies* (London: Macmillan, 1957), 63; George Fischer, *Soviet Opposition to Stalin: A Case Study in World War II* (Cambridge, MA: Harvard University Press, 1952), 5–6.

18 Robert W. Thurston, "Cauldrons of Loyalty and Betrayal: Soviet Soldiers' Behavior, 1941 and 1945," in Thurston and Bonwetsch, eds., *The People's War*, 237.

19 Mark Von Hagen, "Soviet Soldiers and Officers on the Eve of the German Invasion: Toward a Description of Social Psychology and Political Attitudes," in Thurston and Bonwetsch, eds., *The People's War*, 191.

20 Vasily Grossman, *A Writer at War*, ed. and trans. Antony Beevor and Luba Vinogradova (New York: Random House, 2005), 102. See also Roger R. Reese, "Motivations to Serve: The Soviet Soldier in the Second World War," *Journal of Slavic Military Studies*, 20 (2007): 263–282.

21 Budnitskii, "Great Patriotic War," 795–797.

22 Grossman, *A Writer at War*, 123.

23 John Barber and Mark Harrison, *The Soviet Home Front, 1941–1945: A Social and Economic History of the USSR in World War II* (London: Longman, 1991), 183.

24 John Scott, *Behind the Urals: An American Worker in Russia's City of Steel* (Bloomington: Indiana University Press, 1999), 265–266.

25 Admiral N. G. Kuznetsov, "At Naval Headquarters," in Seweryn Bialer, ed., *Stalin and His Generals: Soviet Military Memoirs of World War II* (New York: Pegasus, 1969), 189–200.

26 Rebecca Manley, *To the Tashkent Station: Evacuation and Survival in the Soviet Union at War* (Ithaca, NY: Cornell University Press, 2009), 63.

27 Catherine Merridale, *Ivan's War: Life and Death in the Red Army, 1939–1945* (New York: Metropolitan Books, 2006), 158, 159.

28 Grossman, *Writer at War*, 155.

29 Bernd Bonwetsch, "War as a 'Breathing Space': Soviet Intellectuals and the 'Great Patriotic War,'" in Thurston and Bonwetsch, eds., *The People's War*, 137–153; Nina Tumarkin, *The Living and the Dead: The Rise and Fall of the Cult of World War II in Russia* (New York: Basic Books, 1994), 64–65.

30 Gennadi Bordiugov, "The Popular Mood in the Unoccupied Soviet Union: Continuity and Change during the War," trans. Robert W. Thurston, in Thurston and Bonwetsch, eds., *The People's War*, 55, 61.

31 Boris Pasternak, *Doctor Zhivago*, trans. Max Hayward and Manya Harari (New York: Pantheon, 1958), 507.
32 Ol'ga Berggol'ts, "Fevral'skii dnevnik," in *Sobranie sochinenii v trekh tomakh* (Leningrad: Khudozhestvenaia literatura, 1989), vol. 2, 38.
33 Aleksander Nekrich, *The Punished Peoples: The Deportation and the Fate of Soviet Minorities at the End of the Second World War* (New York: Norton, 1978); Yaacov Ro'i, "The Transformation of Historiography on the 'Punished Peoples,'" *History and Memory*, 21, no. 2 (Fall/Winter 2009): 153–158.
34 Manley, *To the Tashkent Station*, vol. 4, 249–251.
35 "Red Anniversary Hailed in London," *New York Times*, 8 November 1942.
36 Alexander Hill, "The Allocation of Allied 'Lend-Lease' Aid to the Soviet Union Arriving with Convoy PQ-12, March 1942 – A State Defense Committee Decree," *Journal of Slavic Military Studies*, 19 (2006): 729–730.
37 George H. Gallup, ed., *The Gallup International Public Opinion Polls: Great Britain, 1937–1975* (New York: Random House, 1976), vol. 1, 76.
38 Mary E. Glantz, *FDR and the Soviet Union: The President's Battles over Foreign Policy* (Lawrence: University of Kansas Press, 2005), 144–146; Martin Gilbert, *Churchill: A Life* (New York: Henry Holt, 1991), 731.
39 P. M. H. Bell, "Censorship, Propaganda, and Public Opinion: The Case of the Katyn Graves, 1943," *Transactions of the Royal Historical Society*, Fifth Series, 39 (1989): 63–66, 71, 74; George Sanford, "The Katyn Massacre and Soviet Polish Relations, 1941–43," *Journal of Contemporary History*, 41, no. 1 (January 2006): 95–96.
40 David M. Glantz and Jonathan M. House, *When Titans Clashed: How the Red Army Stopped Hitler* (Lawrence: University of Kansas Press, 1995), 214; Irina Mukhina, "New Revelations from the Former Soviet Archives: The Kremlin, the Warsaw Uprising, and the Coming of the Cold War," *Cold War History*, 6, no. 3 (August 2006): 400–408; Geoffrey Roberts, *Stalin's Wars: From World War to Cold War, 1939–1953* (New Haven, CT: Yale University Press, 2008), 215–217; John Erickson, *The Road to Berlin* (Boulder, CO: Westview Press, 1983), 247–290.
41 United States Department of State, *Foreign Relations of the United States: Conferences at Malta and Yalta, 1945* (Washington, DC: U.S. Government Printing Office, 1945), 571, 922.
42 Tsuyoshi Hasegawa, *Racing the Enemy: Stalin, Truman, and the Surrender of Japan* (Cambridge, MA: Harvard University Press, 2005).
43 David Holloway, *Stalin and the Bomb: The Soviet Union and Atomic Energy, 1939–1945* (New Haven, CT: Yale University Press, 1994), 169.
44 Alexander Werth, *Russia at War, 1939–1945* (New York: Dutton, 1964), 964.
45 Stephen M. Norris, "Memory for Sale: Victory Day 2010 and Russian Remembrance," *Soviet and Post-Soviet Review*, 38 (2011): 201–229.
46 Tumarkin, *The Living and the Dead*; Lisa A. Kirschenbaum, *The Legacy of the Siege of Leningrad, 1941–1995: Myth, Memories, and Monuments* (New York: Cambridge University Press, 2006).
47 Hedrick Smith, *The Russians* (New York: Times Books, 1984), 403.

8   Cold War, culture, and everyday life

INTRODUCTION

In 1949, the Soviet government banned the saxophone as a symbol of American decadence. Five years later, the United States Congress amended the pledge of allegiance recited by American schoolchildren to include the phrase "one nation under God" to further distinguish Americans from godless Soviet communists. These actions were just two minor episodes in the Cold War, but they demonstrate its intensity and ubiquity.

The Cold War was a period of global struggle between the United States and the Soviet Union that, according to conventional chronologies, lasted from the end of World War II until the collapse of the Soviet Union in 1991. The Cold War spread from Europe around the world because it coincided with decolonization; European powers, exhausted by the war, could no longer fend off independence movements within their empires in Asia and Africa and, as new states took shape, the Soviet Union and the United states competed for their allegiance. The Cold War was "cold" because the US and USSR never had a direct military confrontation, although they engaged in proxy wars across the world. Despite its temperature, the Cold War was labeled a war because the two sides saw one another as the enemy. They vied with one another for both power and ideological supremacy, so that the Cold War encompassed a nuclear arms race and global violence, but also economic, cultural, and even moral competition. The Cold War was fought on military fronts around the world, in places including Korea, Vietnam, and Afghanistan, but was also waged within American and Soviet societies.

Recent scholarship has sought to complicate the depiction of the Cold War as an epic battle between two superpowers. Some historians have described the commonalities between the two sides, asserting, for example, that they shared the same essential goal of economic modernization and globalization and were thus "very distant cousins," or that ruling elites in both countries used similar techniques to manipulate popular opinion and mobilize their people.[1] Others have shifted the focus to the Third World and examined the ways in which leaders there sought to use Soviet and American intervention to fulfill their own political goals.[2] Still another recent work emphasizes international trade and argues that the Soviet Union was not the center of a separate and competing system, but rather part of a larger global economy dominated by the United States.[3] But while the image of two powerful and diametrically opposed rivals does not capture the complexity of the historical situation, it does reflect how many people at the time understood their world.

CHAPTER QUESTIONS

This chapter explores questions about the domestic front of the Cold War. As the Cold War took shape, how did Soviet leaders and ordinary people interact with Western, especially American, culture? Were certain features of late Stalinist society a result of Cold War tensions, or did they result from domestic problems? How did Cold War rivals compete in providing for their citizens? In short, what did the Cold War mean for culture and everyday life in the Soviet Union?

VOICES, MEMORIES, CONTESTED PERSPECTIVES

Origins of the Cold War

Relationships among wartime allies were never straightforward. As we saw in the previous chapter, disagreements about when and where the United States should open a second European front, conflict over the government of Poland, and then the dropping of the atomic bomb on Japan all served to further strain relations. Most historians date the beginning of the Cold War to the immediate postwar period and a series of disputes about the organization and financing of postwar reconstruction and about the future of Germany and the Eastern European countries liberated by the Soviet army at the end of the war.

Historians of the United States and the Soviet Union have engaged in a voluminous debate about the origins of the Cold War; controversies revolve around culpability and motivation. Which side is to blame? What spurred the aggressors' actions: the desire for hegemony or ideological evangelism? Traditionally, American and British scholars favored the latter explanation and attributed the start of the Cold War to the Soviet desire to spread communism to Eastern Europe and the rest of the world. Soviet historians, and later revisionists in the United States, argued that in fact the Cold War grew out of the United States' aspirations for international political and economic domination. Still others cited structural factors and cast the conflict as the inevitable result of a power vacuum left by the collapse of the German and Japanese empires in Asia and Europe.[4]

Stalin was secretive, so it was difficult for diplomats, and later scholars, to ascertain his motives and plans. However, we do know that he combined a profound distrust of his wartime allies with strategic flexibility. Evidence from archives opened up after the fall of the Soviet Union suggests that his main goals were not exclusively ideological but rather, in the words of one historian, "the USSR's security and aggrandizement." This required the establishment of a ring of allied and subordinate states surrounding the Soviet Union that could act as a buffer against future attacks from the west.[5] While the Soviet government worked to construct its own sphere of influence, leaders in the United States saw the future differently. Convinced of an inextricable link between capitalism and democracy, and peace and prosperity, they wanted a world that was open to and connected by free trade, which they claimed would reinforce democratic principles.

As each side moved to enact its vision, the other interpreted those actions as evidence of the ambition to take over the world. In some Eastern European countries, notably Czechoslovakia and Yugoslavia, communist parties could, at first, draw on genuine popular support because their wartime resistance against the Nazis endowed them with moral authority. Communists cooperated with other parties to form coalition governments, but gradually, with the backing of the Soviet Union, they pushed allied political parties out of power, often violently. By 1948, Poland, Czechoslovakia, Yugoslavia, Hungary, Romania, and Bulgaria had become communist dictatorships. Germany was divided, with the eastern part under Soviet control and the western part under Allied occupation. The city of Berlin lay in the eastern sector, but was also divided into two parts, so that West Berlin was an enclave of Western capitalism surrounded by the Soviet zone. In 1948, in one of the most dramatic episodes of the early Cold War, the Soviet government attempted to claim the entire city by blockading West Berlin. The United States responded with an airlift and, for almost a year, Berliners heard American planes constantly overhead as they flew over the city and dropped supplies in West Berlin. This episode showed how quickly wartime alliances had shifted; Americans now saw West Berliners not as former Nazis but as innocent victims of the Soviet menace, and at the same time West Germans acquired a new appreciation for the American and British occupation. In 1949, the Soviets conceded and lifted the blockade. Two separate German states were formed, the Federal Republic of Germany in the west and the German Democratic Republic in the east.

These events in Eastern and Central Europe seemed to fulfill the worst fears of the West and to confirm the warnings made by British Prime Minister Winston Churchill in his famous speech made in Fulton, Missouri, in 1946. Churchill alerted Americans to an "iron curtain" descending upon Europe, behind which Eastern European countries lay subject to Soviet domination. He warned Americans not to retreat from world affairs: "I do not believe that Soviet Russia desires war. What they desire is the fruits of war and the indefinite expansion of their power and doctrines. But what we have to consider here today while time remains, is the permanent prevention of war and the establishment of conditions of freedom and democracy as rapidly as possible in all countries."[6] This speech was interpreted in very different ways, both at the time it was given and in subsequent decades. From a British perspective, it indicated a withdrawal from world leadership and a ceding of power to the Americans. For the Soviets, it represented imperialist aspirations and ideological obfuscation. They questioned what Churchill really meant by "freedom and democracy," especially since the British still retained extensive colonies in Africa and the Middle East.

The American response to Churchill's charge took the form of two influential policies, the Truman doctrine and the Marshall Plan, both announced in 1947. For the Soviets, these policies were clear evidence of American expansionism; for the Americans, they were a sincere effort to establish the "conditions of freedom and democracy" of Churchill's speech. The Truman doctrine, formulated in response to civil war in Greece, pledged that the United States would "support free peoples who are resisting attempted subjugation by armed minorities or by outside pressures," which was understood to mean communists; the policy became the justification for American intervention in wars around the world, including Korea and Vietnam. The Marshall Plan was aimed at the economic restoration of Europe. Its goal was humanitarian and explicitly anticommunist: Building strong European economies would sap the electoral popularity of socialist and communist parties in places like France and Italy, where they had considerable strength. The United States gave almost $13 billion in aid to European countries, and to be eligible to receive aid nations had to open their markets to US exports.

For the Soviet Union, the Marshall Plan represented coerced economic integration, not "freedom and democracy." Politburo member, and close associate of Stalin, Andrei Zhdanov explained that the "purpose of this new, frankly expansionist course is to establish the world supremacy of American imperialism."[7] The Soviet Union countered the Marshall Plan with the Cominform (Communist Information Bureau), which was ostensibly founded to coordinate policy among communist parties in Eastern Europe but in reality functioned as a method of Soviet control. Eventually, in 1955, the Soviet Union would establish a formal military alliance called the Warsaw Pact with the communist countries of Eastern Europe.

In some ways, the debate about whether the Cold War sprang from ideological or more traditional territorial and hegemonic goals presents a false dichotomy. Each side was certainly interested in "security and aggrandizement" but understood these objectives ideologically, in terms of protecting the American or Soviet way of life and promoting American or Soviet values. The rest of the chapter will explore what the pursuit of territory, hegemony, and ideological supremacy meant for ordinary citizens.

The threat of Western culture and the importance of being Russian

The tense political climate at the close of the war upset many ordinary Soviet citizens. One historian has traced rumors in the postwar years by drawing on the summaries of the popular mood gathered by party and police organizations. He found that,

Figure 8.1 The main caption reads "Phrases and . . . Bases" and the American politician is shouting "Peace, Defense, Disarmament" (1952, by Viktor Ivanovich Govorkov). © Heritage Image Partnership Ltd/Alamy.

What is the poster's message about the United States?

especially after Churchill's Iron Curtain speech, many people believed in the imminence of war against Britain and the United States; some even started hoarding food and cash or making other preparations. In the Baltic regions of Latvia, Lithuania, and Estonia, and in Western Ukraine, which had all been incorporated by force into the Soviet Union during the war, people looked forward to being liberated from the Soviet Union. In Russia, they dreaded the prospect of another war.[8]

As relations between the US and the Soviet Union continued to sour, the media of both countries drew increasingly sinister portrayals of former allies. In 1949, the North Atlantic Treaty Organization (NATO) was formed as a military alliance between the United States and eleven Western European countries. The Soviet press depicted this as a ploy by American big business to compensate for the weaknesses of the US economy by fobbing off their surplus weapons onto their allies. It interpreted the Marshall Plan and NATO as indications of US aggression and depicted the US as the real heir to Nazi expansionism. Cartoons, editorials, films, and plays stressed the hypocrisy of American claims of freedom and equality, highlighting racial discrimination, crime, poverty, the persecution of leftists, and the activity of the FBI.

Given this image of American bellicosity, it is not surprising that the Soviet government began to forbid the personal contact that had taken place during the war. In Soviet Arctic ports, local women had socialized and sometimes slept with the American and British sailors stationed there to transport Lend Lease supplies. After the war, some of these women were sent to the Gulag in punishment for these relationships.[9] In 1947, marriage between Soviet citizens and foreigners was forbidden.

The Soviet government sought to limit cultural and intellectual as well as personal contact, launching a series of campaigns to ensure that Soviet minds could not be corrupted by Western influences or by anything else that seemed insufficiently Soviet in its pessimism, complexity, or eccentricity. Historians debate the motivation behind these policies. Were they a response to Cold War tensions or to concerns about restoring order and control at home? Did these campaigns achieve their goals or carry unintended consequences?

The earliest of these ideological campaigns was labeled the *zhdanovshchina*, a term derived from the name of Andrei Zhdanov, the powerful Politburo member quoted above responding to the Marshall Plan. Zhdanov began this culture war in 1946 with a speech condemning two famous writers: Zoshchenko, whose satiric stories had always annoyed Stalin, and the poet Anna Akhmatova. The party went on to criticize composers such as Shostokovich and Prokofiev for writing music that was influenced by foreign experimentalists and then various scientists for collaborating with Western colleagues. Scholars in a wide range of fields, including philosophy, physics, biology, and economics, struggled to purge foreign influence and produce work that was ideologically correct. Stalin considered himself a great intellectual authority and so he became the final arbiter of these disputes. Disagreements were not resolved simply by ideology squashing scientific discovery, for Stalin recognized the importance of science to Cold War competition in general and the effort to produce nuclear weapons in particular (the Soviet Union developed its first atomic bomb in 1949). Political relationships within the ruling circle, and the views of scientists themselves, also influenced whose views prevailed and which scientists rose to prominence and which ones lost their jobs.[10]

In addition to literature, classical music, and science, jazz became another target. The quintessentially American art form, jazz had been alternately tolerated as the music of oppressed American Negroes and despised as sexually stimulating, distracting, and decadent. During the relatively tolerant war years, Soviet jazz bands had entertained troops and helped celebrate military victories, but in the xenophobic postwar atmosphere the musical elements of jazz were suppressed. Bass players could only bow their instruments, instead of plucking them, and certain chords were forbidden. In 1949, all saxophone players in Moscow had to surrender their instruments to the State Variety Music Agency. The lucky ones were reclassified as bassoonists and oboists, but other musicians ended up in labor camps.[11] This had already happened to one of the most famous Soviet jazz musicians of the era, Eddie Rosner. A German Jew who had fled the Nazis to Poland and then the Soviet Union, where he spent the war years on tour, Rosner had an international reputation and considerable skill—he could play two trumpets at the same time. He was stopped in an attempt to immigrate back to Poland, accused of espionage, and sent to the Kolyma Gulag in 1947. The commandant of the camp was a fan, and as other jazz musicians had also been imprisoned, Rosner was able to form a top notch jazz prison band that traveled to various camps to entertain guards and prison officials. In the meantime, the government increased the production of balalaikas, encouraged folk music, and retitled popular dances so that they no longer carried foreign names. The fox trot became the "quick step" and the tango was unpoetically renamed "slow dance."[12]

As Western influences were expunged, Soviet nationality was glorified. But what did this phrase mean? Soviet citizens were not simply Soviet; they were ascribed to an official nationality, such as Russian or Uzbek, which was listed on their passports. In the postwar period, Lily Golden had an especially hard time with this process of definition. She was the daughter of two idealistic American leftists who had immigrated to the Soviet Union in 1931 to help build a more just society. Her mother was Jewish, her father African American; the couple ended up in Uzbekistan, where she was raised. Her difficulties in determining a nationality, described in document 8.2, reveal the slippery nature of this category, which was neither racial nor simply civic.

During the 1930s Russian culture, language, and history came to dominate Soviet nationality. Belonging to a non-Russian nationality could be dangerous. As we described in the previous chapter, during World War II Stalin deemed entire groups such as the Chechens disloyal and deported them from their homeland. In the postwar era, both of these developments persisted and intensified and new groups of people were targeted, especially Jews. At a victory reception in 1945, Stalin proposed a toast to the Soviet people, and, "first of all, to the health of the Russian people . . . because they are the leading nation of all the nations of the Soviet Union." Russian chauvinism "mushroomed" after this toast, according to one historian: "The Soviet media waxed rhapsodic about the Russians having always been the greatest, wisest, bravest, and most virtuous of all nations."[13] In her memoir Ludmilla Alexeyeva recalled one of the more absurd expressions of this Russo-centricism: official assertions that Russians had invented the radio, the light bulb, and the steam engine. She recounted some of the jokes that emerged to satirize these claims; for example: "A Russian, a Frenchman, and a German are asked to write books about elephants. The German writes three thick volumes titled *All about Elephants*. The Frenchman writes a novel, *Elephants and Love*. The Russian writes a pamphlet, *Russia, the Motherland of Elephants*."[14]

While Russian nationalism flourished, the party sought to stamp out any signs of non-Russian affiliation. Azeri, Turkmen, Uzbek, and Kyrgyz epic poems, which had been billed as authentic expressions of folklore, were now labeled as forgeries written by nationalist intellectuals. Scholars, novelists, and poets were denounced for works deemed too nationalistic in Armenia, Ukraine, Uzbekistan, Estonia, and even in the small autonomous republic of Tuva in southern Siberia. A scholarly institute there was criticized for not sufficiently researching "the historic friendship of Russian and Tuvinese peoples, the influence that Russian culture has had on the development of Tuvinese culture [or] the historical aid that the Russian people have provided to the Tuvinese toilers in their emancipation from the cabal of foreign occupiers and domestic feudal lords."[15] What does this mention of "foreign occupiers" suggest about the connection between Russian nationalism and the Cold War?

Histories and popular culture depicting World War II featured Russians as the most heroic combatants and all Soviet citizens as victims of German brutality, and they downplayed the military participation of non-Russians and the particular fate of the Jews as the main target of Nazi genocide. While Jews were in fact overrepresented in the armed forces, the government encouraged anti-Semitic assumptions that Jews shirked fighting, and the draft-dodging Jew became a common figure in popular fiction. At the same time, specifically Jewish suffering was erased from historical memory. The writers Ilya Ehrenburg and Vasily Grossman compiled a collection of documents and testimonies, entitled *The Black Book*, which chronicled the Nazi Holocaust in occupied areas of the Soviet Union. Publication was abruptly halted in 1947 because the book's preface had "incorrectly" asserted that the Nazis targeted Jews in particular.[16]

The final ideological crusade of this period, which began in 1949, drew on this Russian jingoism and anti-Semitism, as well as the antipathy to Western influence, and was aimed at "rootless cosmopolitans." Officials denied this term was a synonym for being Jewish, but that is how most people at the time understood the phrase. Jewish professionals were fired from their jobs, especially in academia, the media, and the arts. The Yiddish theater was closed, and its famous star was killed in an "accident" that was most likely an assassination. Jewish students found themselves denied admission to top universities. Lily Golden recalled an admissions interview at Moscow State University in which the interviewer ascertained that her mother was Jewish, after which "my documents were returned to me with the terse announcement: 'People like you are not accepted in this University.'"[17]

To make matters more confusing for people living through this period, as well as for those of us seeking to understand it, the party condemned anti-Semitism at the same time as it persecuted Jews, so that even during the anticosmopolitan campaigns overtly hateful zealots could get into trouble. Alexeyeva described a university classmate who attacked several of his Jewish professors for being too cosmopolitan, as was common. But when he was overheard discussing his desire to "strangle them all" and calling them "fucking kikes," the University Komsomol committee decided he had become an embarrassment and issued an official reprimand.[18]

Despite these ambiguities, the campaign grew more intense in the early 1950s. In 1952, members of the Jewish Anti-Fascist Committee, which had worked during the war to win support for the Soviet cause from Jews overseas, were charged with espionage and bourgeois nationalism, put on trial, and executed. In January 1953, the "Doctors' Plot" was uncovered; an article in *Pravda* accused nine physicians, six of whom had Jewish last names, of plotting to kill important Soviet officials, including Zhdanov, who had died a few years before. A Jewish teenager at the time recalled the widespread anti-Semitism that was unleashed: "It was scary to leave the classroom and go into the hallway because from all sides you heard cries of, "you Yids, you poisoned Gorky, you wanted to poison Stalin, you poisoned all our great leaders."[19]

The anticosmopolitan campaign contradicted Soviet values, since the state had, from the beginning, opposed the anti-Semitism that had been so profoundly entrenched in the government and culture of tsarist Russia. After the revolution, the government persecuted Judaism as a religion but supported secular Jewish culture, including the Yiddish language. Many Jews were thoroughly assimilated into Soviet life and some achieved prominence, although anti-Semitic attitudes persisted among certain elements of the population. After the war, the Soviet Union was the second country to recognize the state of Israel in 1948, but as Israel grew closer to the United States, Stalin grew suspicious of Zionist sentiments among Jewish citizens of the USSR; he was especially perturbed when Soviet Jews gathered, cheering, on the streets to greet the arrival of Golda Meir, the first Israeli ambassador to the Soviet Union.

Most scholars link the anticosmopolitan campaign to the Cold War. Indeed, in 1952 Stalin made an explicit connection between Jews and America, telling central committee members that "every Jew is a nationalist . . . and agent of the American secret services. The Jewish nationalists think that the United States saved their nation (there they can get rich, become bourgeois, etc.). They consider themselves indebted to the Americans."[20] Scholars have also attributed external causes to the other postwar ideological campaigns, arguing that they offered a way for the Soviet Union to project a distinctive identity to the world, one that provided an alternative to expansionist American policies and culture.[21]

By contrast, other historians emphasize the internal factors motivating the anti-cosmopolitan and other postwar ideological campaigns. According to this view, the culture wars were part of a larger effort to regain control of Soviet society after the relative freedom of the war years, distract attention from the grinding poverty and deprivation of everyday life during this period, and stamp out any possible dissent.[22] To that end, the state arrested all kinds of people, including those who had developed attachments to Western culture, science, or sailors, as we have seen, but also others suspected of disloyalty. This included Soviet soldiers who had been captured and imprisoned by the Nazis; citizens who had survived Nazi occupation; and people suspected of opposing their integration into the Soviet Union in the recently annexed territories of Latvia, Lithuania, Estonia, Finnish Karelia, Western Ukraine, and Moldavia (some of which had been former provinces of the tsarist empire). Between three and four million people were confined to labor camps during this period.

In addition to questioning whether internal or external factors are more salient in explaining the postwar ideological campaigns, historians have also pondered their impact, which raises wider questions about the nature of Soviet power. To what extent did policy shape the way that people thought about culture? How effective was Soviet propaganda? Scholars focusing on culture tend to disagree with the idea that a totalitarian Soviet state succeeded in monopolizing meaning and identity. They describe the ways in which, for example, readers and audiences could impose their own meanings on the literature and histories that were produced at this time, and they emphasize the strategies developed to evade or mitigate the impact of state policies.[23] For example, the prominent band leader Leonid Utesov retained a very jazzy piece in his repertoire that he was permitted to play because it was entitled "Song of the Unemployed American" and its lyrics mocked the hypocrisy of the United States. It became very popular and was often requested at gigs.[24]

Other scholars take a differentiated approach to answering these questions and try to uncover the variety of responses to ideological campaigns. For example, one historian points out that Russo-centric propaganda during and after the war did result in a heightened sense of Russian national identity, but only, of course, for Russians. Another suggests that the terms of the ideological campaigns, including phrases such as "decadence" and "cosmopolitan," simply did not mean very much for many people, and this confusion dulled their impact among much of the general population. By contrast, victims were deeply affected. A daughter of loyal and high ranking Jewish communist officials described in her memoirs how, in response to the anticosmopolitan campaigns, "my sense of belonging to the Jewish nation was different to what it had been before. I felt my affinity with the downtrodden. I sympathized with them and could not see their guilt."[25] Persecution alienated intellectuals, strengthened Jewish identity, and caused some to question the Soviet system.[26]

The allure of Western style

Vassily Aksyonov was the son of Eugenia Ginzburg, whom we encountered in chapter 6. His parents were communist officials who had been arrested and sent to the Gulag in 1937. Young Vassily was confined to an orphanage, a fate common to the children of detainees, before being rescued by an uncle. When his mother was released from prison into Siberian exile, he went to join her, before moving to Kazan and then Leningrad for medical school. In 1952, he was a young man from the provinces who found himself at a party in Moscow. Most of the guests were the children of diplomats who were wearing fashionable clothes, listening to jazz, smoking American cigarettes, and calling each other English endearments like "baby" and "darling." The daughter of a top KGB officer was dancing with such abandon that her skirt flew up in the air and he could see underneath it. Aksyonov was astounded by this display of sexy sophistication and later marveled that "at the height of the cold war America had such devoted allies among the Soviet elites."[27] In this section, we will explore the allure of Western style. What form did the devotion take? And what did it mean? Should it be seen as subversive or as a form of apolitical youthful rebellion?

Clearly, despite the anti-Western campaigns, young people managed to find ways to learn about foreign music, dance moves, and fashion. Red Army officers stationed in East Berlin acquired new American records in West Berlin, and the BBC and Voice of America had started broadcasting music into the Soviet Union. Enthusiasts made illegal copies of Western recordings on old x-ray film or plate; this was given the hip name of "jazz on bones." In addition to music, returning veterans brought home glossy magazines and clothing, which was sold on the black market or in legal second-hand stores. Movies were another source of information about style, dance, and music. The Soviet film industry had been devastated by the war and, in order to profit from the pent-up demand for films, the government authorized screenings of so-called "trophy films," which were European and American films that the Soviet army had seized during their victorious march across Germany. The films were given new titles in order to avoid paying royalties to the American producers. Aksyonov recalled that the famous western *Stagecoach* was called "The Journey Will Be Dangerous;" instead of credits, a politically correct introduction was inserted explaining that the film "treats the heroic struggle of the Indians against Yankee imperialism." Aksyonov saw *Stagecoach* ten times and recalled "a period when we spoke to our friends almost entirely in quotes from American movies."[28] Tarzan was also intensely popular, as it had been in the 1930s, and young men adopted the longish hairstyle of its star and took to imitating the ape-man yodel.

In 1949, the satirical magazine *Krokodil* came up with a derogatory nickname for the most dedicated fans of Western fashion: *stiliag* (plural, *stiliagi*), from the Russian word for style. While Aksyonov described upper class stiliagi, the trend included young people from a variety of backgrounds.[29] Drawing inspiration from films and magazines, stiliagi obtained foreign goods, or altered or created clothing and accessories in order to adopt what they saw as Western styles. They wore wide trousers and big-shouldered jackets similar to the zoot suits popular among African American and Mexican American youths; later, the fashions shifted to pants that were tight at the top and then flared. At first ties were fat and decorated with cacti, cowboys, or girls in bathing suits, and then they became thin and sleek. Thick soled shoes and colored socks were part of the outfit, so stiliagi had to casually rest their feet up on park benches and barriers to display them. Although stiliagi danced and socialized with girls in makeup and tight blouses, in the immediate postwar years the subculture was male-dominated. In addition to fashion, stiliagi defined themselves through music, dance moves, slang made up of English words and jazz jargon, and the claiming of certain urban spaces. Gorky Street in Moscow and the lower half of Nevsky Prospekt in Leningrad were favorite hangouts and dubbed "Broadway" or "Brod" for short.

In recalling the late 1940s from the vantage point of an American exile several decades later, Aksyonov mused: "When you think about it, stiliagi were the first dissidents."[30] Did love of Western fashion and popular culture indicate disloyalty to the Soviet Union? Was the Iron Curtain being subverted from within by lindy-hopping zoot-suiters? Some historians question this assumption, pointing out that even the intensely suspicious Stalinist government did not seem to regard the stiliagi as dangerous. Some stiliagi were expelled from the Komsomol or from university, and they often experienced vocal criticism from parents, teachers, and the general public. One stiliag remembered walking into a tram and hearing people say: "Young man, aren't you ashamed of yourself, walking around looking like a parakeet?"[31] But surprisingly enough, there was no widespread campaign against stiliagi in the late 1940s; an expert on the period notes that out of 20,000 legal cases in the years 1945–1953, he found only one example of a stiliagi circle being prosecuted.[32] In fact, official criticism of stiliagi intensified only after Stalin's death, in a different political context that will be discussed further in the next chapter.

In contradicting the notion that stiliagi were dissidents, one scholar explained that tough and macho war veterans dominated Soviet life during this period so that, for men too young to have served in the war, being stiliagi provided an alternative form of masculinity. The subculture was a nonpolitical way for young people to develop their own identities.[33] A compatible interpretation holds that most young people at the time neither totally adopted nor resisted official identities; they saw themselves as both good Soviet citizens and fans of jazz or Hollywood films. One jazz aficionado described his taste in terms of aesthetics, not politics: "The music was attractive. I was a pretty 'red' person, or pink. At any rate I believed in socialism."[34] Another scholar who concurs with these evaluations of stiliagi nonetheless notes that there was something "undeniably oppositional" about them. "They denied some of the most cherished tenets of socialist life: rather than being equal, they wanted to be different; rather than demure, they wanted to be shrill; rather than self-improvement, they craved pleasure."[35] This rowdy and hedonistic individualism seems anti-Soviet, and perhaps even quintessentially American. Yet adults in Western Europe and the United States also worried about the overt sexuality and frivolousness of the music and dances popular among youth, such as boogie woogie and the jitterbug. Were stiliagi, like their international peers, just looking for fun? Or, given the ideological dimensions of the Cold War struggle, was the pursuit of apolitical pleasures a political act?

The competition for the good life

Both the United States and the Soviet Union saw ensuring a good life for more people as an expression of the fairness and moral superiority of their respective political and economic system; thus the Cold War included a race for higher living standards for all citizens. The US had a huge head start, because World War II had desolated the Soviet Union, and the immediate postwar years were a time of hardship, grief, and struggle. In 1946, bad weather struck and crop failures and starvation spread across Europe. The Soviet Union kept grain in reserve rather than distributing it to the hungry population, resulting in the third great famine of the Soviet epoch. At least 1–1.5 million people starved to death.

Life was particularly harsh in the countryside. Collective farms lacked workers, electricity, and machinery, and agricultural policies exacerbated desperate rural poverty. The prices paid for agricultural goods were so low that they did not even meet production costs, and pay for collective farm work sunk below prewar levels. As a result, peasants continued to concentrate their efforts on their private plots, as they had during the war; in some places they had actually augmented these plots by taking over kolkhoz land. Even after the government began to reverse this practice and restore collective farms, farmers formulated strategies to minimize kolkhoz work and maximize private acreage. For example, since private plots were allotted by household, some households pretended to split up so that they could claim extra land.[36] In its tug of war with the peasants, the government did its best to wring more revenue out of private plots by requiring households to deliver some of the vegetables and dairy products produced there and by levying a tax on households based on the value of their private plots.[37] Peasants were further disadvantaged when, in an effort to combat inflation, the government devalued the currency in 1947. This meant that the money peasants had saved from the sale of produce abruptly lost most of its purchasing power. A joke from the period describes a peasant who comes to the city with a sack of money after the currency reform. "He puts the sack in a corner and goes to find out where he can exchange the old money for new. When he returns, he finds the money strewn on the floor and the sack gone: the thieves have taken everything of value."[38]

In factories, plants, and mines, workers endured dangerous conditions, long hours, harsh discipline, and low wages. Housing was overcrowded and lacked basic services and adequate sanitation in the immediate postwar years. Outside of Moscow the majority of the population had no indoor running water and so people used outhouses and water from pumps or wells. In such conditions, it was hard to keep clean, which resulted in the spread of infectious diseases.[39] Even in Moscow, people struggled to get by. Lily Golden recalled her university years: "Though peace had come seven or eight years before, many of us were still hungry. We dressed modestly and in poor taste. Through all my five years at University, I only owned one dress."[40]

Amidst this acute poverty, a life of comfort and pleasure was unattainable for most people, but promised to a privileged few who were participants in what scholar Vera Dunham described as the "Big Deal." Starting from the premise that the Soviet state could not maintain power through repression alone, Dunham suggested that it cultivated the support of the middle class by striking an implicit agreement. The engineers, factory managers, and officials who made up this group were allowed to pursue a comfortable and contented life in return for political acquiescence and the diligent application of their professional skills. In chapter 3 we saw the revolutionary poet Mayakovsky railing against *meshchanstvo*, a concept encompassing pettiness, materialism, and the pursuit of self-interest; the Big Deal reversed this type of revolutionary idealism and sanctioned the values of *meshchanstvo*, albeit tacitly.

Dunham wrote her book in the 1970s, at a time when archival records were closed, but even if this had not been the case, direct evidence to support her thesis would have been difficult to obtain. The Big Deal could not be stated outright, since it contradicted the revolutionary promise of equality that was the ideological basis of the Soviet state. In fact, most societies are held together by social agreements that are understood implicitly rather than being described explicitly. Dunham developed an imaginative method to support her argument through the analysis of popular fiction. Unlike works with serious literary ambitions, these novels and stories reflected official values in a straightforward manner. Reading them, discussing them, and writing letters about them to the press were among the few ways for people to talk publicly about social issues, and the Big Deal was conveyed through their plots, characters, and descriptions. For example, protagonists were no longer glorified for the single-minded, ascetic devotion to work, as they had been in the 1930s; now they were supposed to have stable and devoted families. In a ballad entitled "The District Boss Bids Farewell," the eponymous boss amazes his subordinate by expressing interest in his personal life and then giving advice about it: "He hears the old stern chief of the district/Say to him: 'Take care of your beloved.'"[41] Objects, furniture, and the kind of ornaments scorned by Mayakovsky in the 1920s were described approvingly as symbols of domestic happiness and comfort. One novel detailed the heroine's ornaments: on "an intricate series of shelves [she] arranged a display of baby dolls with large bows, bright cologne bottles and little seashell boxes. And tea was served under an orange lampshade in red, polka-dotted cups. In this small, gay, and bright paradise, everybody was pleased with life."[42]

Dunham's work has been very influential, although more recently historians have dated the inception of the Big Deal to the mid-1930s and the special privileges accorded to Stakhanovites. Scholars have expanded upon the idea of the Big Deal in various ways. For example, one historian described what she called a "darker big deal" during this period that allowed party elites to engage in illegal activities without fear of reprisals. While ordinary people were punished harshly for breaking laws, those who were well connected got away with enriching themselves by embezzling state goods, the kind of corruption usually associated with a later era in Soviet history (see chapter 10).[43] Scholar Kate Brown has found that the Big Deal was extended to an entire city, Ozersk, built to house the staff at a plant producing plutonium for nuclear weapons. The head of the facility, writes Brown, offered "nothing less than a nuclear Big Deal: middle-class urban affluence for working class operators in exchange for the risks of plutonium production."[44]

After Stalin's death in 1953, his eventual successor Nikita Khrushchev eased relations with the West, positing the possibility of "peaceful coexistence" between the Soviet Union and the US. In subsequent decades, competition was focused on global influence, especially in newly independent nations, but also on culture and sports, scientific achievements, such as space exploration, and the provision of a comfortable everyday life for all citizens, not just the elites. In 1957, Khrushchev initiated a massive housing construction program that eventually moved millions of people from dorms, communal apartments, and barracks into individual family apartments. His economic plans called for increased production of consumer goods. At the Twenty-Second Party Congress in 1961, the party program set the goal of achieving a higher living standard than that of any capitalist country. A joke from this period mocks Khrushchev's physique as well as his grandiose promises to overtake the United States in per capita consumption. One student says to the other, "Do you know we've already beaten America in the production of meat?" The other student responds, "How do you figure that?" "Well," says the first, "doesn't Khrushchev weigh twenty kilos more than Eisenhower?"[45]

Many Americans saw commodities as an effective Cold War weapon. In 1951, the critic David Riesman published an essay called "The Nylon War" which described a fictional campaign in which the US bombed the Soviet Union with cigarettes, wrist watches, nylon stockings, permanent wave kits, sanitary napkins, toys, and domestic appliances. Once exposed to the bounty of American capitalism, the Soviet people, especially women, began to protest and pressure their government to produce consumer goods instead of weaponry. In an epilogue written in 1962, Riesman wrote

Figure 8.2 A Soviet exhibit in Moscow, 1959. Courtesy of the Library of Congress Prints and Photographs Division (LC-U9- 2870-9).

Why are these items on display? Why are the visitors so interested?

with dismay that the "combination of fright and self-righteousness of many Americans" meant that readers took his essay literally, rather than recognizing it as satire.[46] But in fact, the idea behind "The Nylon War" became the basis for official policy, as the US Information Agency and Commerce departments sponsored international exhibits of American goods and sent entrepreneurs on trade missions abroad. In a comment that revealed the aspirations, as well as gendered assumptions, behind such efforts, Ida Rosenthal, the founder of Maidenform bras, told a newspaper reporter: "I'd like the Russian women to wear Maidenform bras. They'll look better, they'll feel better, and maybe we'll get along better."[47]

Like the United States, the Soviet Union promoted a version of the good life that rested on notions of plenty. As Khrushchev explained in an interview, the eventual transition from socialism to full communism would bring "abundance." He continued, in his characteristically earthy and rambling style: "If communism is proclaimed where there is, say only one pair of pants to ten people, and that pair of pants is divided equally into ten parts, then everyone will be going around without pants altogether. We reject this sort of trouser-less communism. It would be a perversion."[48] Soviet ideals of prosperity were cast in opposition to the anxious and acquisitive pursuit of commodities characteristic of capitalism and the selfishness symbolized by the stiliagi. The Soviet good life was made possible by social services: free healthcare, day care, education, the right to work. Consumer objects were not meant to satisfy women's greed, but to liberate them from domestic burdens.[49] This vision of prosperity without greed became an important theme of propaganda aimed at the developing countries. For example, a radio broadcast to Vietnam in 1964 explained that "the capitalists have only one dream—the dream to gain more profit." Whereas in the Soviet Union economic development occurred "so that children can live even better . . . Not only in our country, but in all the world."[50]

Despite assertions of difference, Soviet and US ideals sometimes converged. For example, the Soviet city Ozersk, discussed above in the context of the Big Deal, shared fundamental characteristics with the American city of Richland in Washington State. Both were built from the ground up to house workers at plants producing plutonium for nuclear weapons. In both places, citizens were given good housing and schools, pleasant neighborhoods, and were isolated from the poverty and crime that afflicted nearby areas; historian Kate Brown calls these communities "plutopia." Living in plutopia entailed working with extremely hazardous materials under dangerous conditions, the health risks of which were not openly disclosed. It also required sacrificing political rights in return for material comfort. In Richland, General Electric owned all the housing, subsidized and controlled the city newspaper, and administered the town in lieu of an elected government; as in Ozersk, there was no free press or private property. Many of plutopia's inhabitants saw their cities as "the materialization of the American dream or Communist utopia, an affirmation that their national ideology was correct."[51] The good life looked the same in both plutopias: affluence for a chosen few at the cost of political freedom, social equality, and, eventually, the health of citizens and the environment.

CONCLUSION AND FURTHER QUESTIONS

The Cold War spanned the globe and lasted decades. In considering some of the ways in which it affected Soviet society and culture, this chapter has brought up broader questions: What is the political meaning of popular culture? How do international and domestic policies influence one another? And, despite its distinctiveness, what characteristics did the Soviet Union share with other contemporary societies?

These questions can be applied to other topics covered in this book, but the issue of comparability is especially interesting when considering the Cold War because starkly polarized rhetoric disguised similarities between the US and USSR. For example, in 1949, the secretary of the Komsomol gave a speech condemning American policy, explaining: "Blackmail, extortion, economic and political pressure, bribery, trickery and lies—these are all characteristics of thieving, imperialistic politics." Five years later, the Chaplain for the US Senate warned that "atheistic world communism" was "the most monstrous mass of organized evil that history has known."[52] As these quotations make clear, these two Cold War combatants defined one another in opposition to their own highest ideals. Yet they did so in very similar terms and for some of the same reasons: to ensure power abroad and the good life at home.

PRIMARY SOURCES

Use the questions to analyze the content, context, and significance of each primary source. Then synthesize the primary sources and the material in the chapter to formulate a response to the primary chapter question: What did the Cold War mean for culture and everyday life in the Soviet Union?

Document 8.1   A Soviet criticism of jazz

Questions for analysis

1   What do you think the author means by describing jazz as "cosmopolitan"?
2   Why does he invoke lynching and the Ku Klux Klan?
3   How does he interpret the Marshall Plan? (See the reference to "Marshallized countries.")
4   How would you describe the tone of this article?

Bourgeois musicologists at one time built up a legend of the folk nature of jazz. The jazz band was presented as a genuine native Negro orchestra. Actually this was the most shameless lie, a malicious calumny of "White" lovers of "Black exotica." Present-day jazz contains nothing of a genuine Negro folk quality. It is typical cosmopolitan art. When they took motifs from Negro folklore for restaurant jazz, these motifs not only lost all their national folk flavor but were utterly distorted, "lynched" and mocked by the American musical Ku-Klux Klans-men. This barbaric gangster treatment of the art of the Negro people cannot but call forth the indignation of Soviet people, who love and cherish the folk art of all nationalities. Those who know and prize the marvelous art of Paul Robeson, of the splendid Negro woman singer Marian Anderson and of many other great Negro singers scorn and despise jazz, that "American way of art!"

Need one mention too that jazz in the USA is not just "art," but, like the Hollywood "industry," a business, an article of export. They call jazz there "the music of big business." The USA "bestows upon" the Marshallized countries tens of millions of jazz records, along with Hollywood's trash. There is double profit and a double purpose in this: to dispose of unsold stocks and by the scrunch and squeal and roar of senseless, stupefying jazz "music" to deafen, to kill the man in men, to turn them into cannon fodder. Jazz is the music of enslavement of the spirit . . .

Source: M. Sokolsky, "Why Jazz Is Not for Soviet Ears," *Sovetskoye iskusstvo*, 16 Feb. 1952, p. 3. Translated in *Current Digest of the Russian Press*, 4, no. 9, (12 April 1952), 5–6. Used by permission of East View Press.

Document 8.2   A Soviet Negro applies for a passport

Questions for analysis

1   Why is it so difficult to determine Golden's nationality? What does this indicate about what the category actually means?
2   Why does she want to be classified as Negro and why is the official so reluctant to do so?
3   What views of America become evident in this conversation?

I am 16 and I must get my Soviet passport. I went to the police, who gave me a passport that recorded my nationality as "American." I told them that "American" was a term of citizenship, while I was "Soviet." The officer explained that "Soviet" did not mean nationality. After that complaint, they gave me another passport that stated that I was "Uzbek." Again I complained that I had no Uzbek blood in my veins. Then they wrote that I was "Russian." By this time, when I refused to take this passport, the policeman was impatient with me and asked: "What do you want me to write?" I answered: "I was born in the Soviet Union. So I should be Soviet, but you explained that there is no such nationality. I think you must write that I am a 'Negro,' which I am indeed . . ." At that time, Black people in the United States were fighting for the right to be called "Negro" with a capital "N"—and I was influenced by their struggle. Again, the policeman explained that there was no such nationality as "Negro." Negro was not a nationality, but rather a race. I insisted that, whether or not it was a race, I am "Negro."

The officer, attempting a reasoned argument, asked: "How will you prove that you are a Negro? One can come and say that he is a Negro. Others will come and say that they are something else. Must I believe everybody? Then anybody can come and say that he is a Negro. You think that, by stating you are a Negro, you will be able to leave the country." I had to go home to search for a newspaper article from *Amsterdam News*, in which my father was mentioned as Negro, and bring it back to the police. At last I could prove my point, and it was written, in black and white, that he was a Negro. Thus I became the only person in the world with a passport in which it was written that I was "Negro." The Uzbek policeman was a kind person.

Source: Lily Golden, *My Long Journey Home* (Chicago, IL: Third World Press, 2002), 37–38.

Document 8.3   The "Kitchen Debate": Khrushchev and Vice President Richard Nixon in the model kitchen at the American National Exhibit, 1959

Questions for analysis

1   What is the difference between how Nixon and Khrushchev see the roles of women in society?
2   How does each leader critique the other's system and defend his own?
3   Compare this document to document 8.1. How have the Soviet views of the United States changed in tone and substance? What remains the same?

[Both men enter kitchen in the American exhibit.]
Nixon: I want to show you this kitchen. It is like those of our houses in California.
[Nixon points to dishwasher.]
Khrushchev: We have such things.
Nixon: This is our newest model. This is the kind which is built in thousands of units for direct installations in the houses. In America, we like to make life easier for women . . .
Khrushchev: Your capitalistic attitude toward women does not occur under Communism.
Nixon: I think that this attitude toward women is universal. What we want to do, is make life more easy for our housewives . . .

Nixon:	This house can be bought for $14,000, and most American [veterans from World War II] can buy a home in the bracket of $10,000 to $15,000. Let me give you an example that you can appreciate. Our steel workers, as you know, are now on strike. But any steel worker could buy this house. They earn $3 an hour. This house costs about $100 a month to buy on a contract running 25 to 30 years.
Khrushchev:	We have steel workers and peasants who can afford to spend $14,000 for a house. Your American houses are built to last only 20 years so builders could sell new houses at the end. We build firmly. We build for our children and grandchildren.
Nixon:	American houses last for more than 20 years, but, even so, after 20 years, many Americans want a new house or a new kitchen. Their kitchen is obsolete by that time . . . The American system is designed to take advantage of new inventions and new techniques.
. . .	
Khrushchev:	In Russia, all you have to do to get a house is to be born in the Soviet Union. You are entitled to housing . . . In America, if you don't have a dollar you have a right to choose between sleeping in a house or on the pavement. Yet you say we are the slave to Communism.
. . .	
Nixon:	If you were in the Senate, we would call you a filibusterer! You— [Khrushchev interrupts]—do all the talking and don't let anyone else talk. This exhibit was not designed to astound but to interest. Diversity,

Figure 8.3 Khrushchev and then Vice President Richard Nixon, live on American television at the American National Exhibit in 1959. Courtesy of the Library of Congress Prints and Photographs Division (LC-U9- 2808-33).

What does their body language convey?

the right to choose, the fact that we have 1,000 builders building 1,000 different houses is the most important thing. We don't have one decision made at the top by one government official. This is the difference.

Khrushchev: On politics, we will never agree with you. For instance, Mikoyan likes very peppery soup. I do not. But this does not mean that we do not get along.

Nixon: You can learn from us, and we can learn from you. There must be a free exchange. Let the people choose the kind of house, the kind of soup, the kind of ideas that they want.

Source: http://teachingamericanhistory.org/library/document/the-kitchen-debate/.

Notes

1 Vladislav M. Zubok, *A Failed Empire: The Soviet Union in the Cold War from Stalin to Gorbachev* (Chapel Hill: University of North Carolina Press, 2007); Margaret Peacock, *Innocent Weapons: The Soviet and American Politics of Childhood in the Cold War* (Chapel Hill: University of North Carolina Press, 2014).
2 Odd Arne Westad, *The Global Cold War: Third World Interventions and the Making of Our Times* (Cambridge: Cambridge University Press, 2005).
3 Oscar Sanchez-Sibony, *Red Globalization: The Political Economy of the Soviet Cold War from Stalin to Khrushchev* (Cambridge: Cambridge University Press, 2014).
4 Ralph B. Levering, Vladimir O. Pechatnov, Verna Botzenkhart-Viehe, and C. Earl Edmonson, *Debating the Origins of the Cold War* (Lanham, MD: Rowman & Littlefield, 2001), 24.
5 Zubok, *A Failed Empire*, 19–20.
6 Available at www.winstonchurchill.org/learn/biography/in-opposition/qiron-curtainq-fulton-missouri-1946/120-the-sinews-of-peace (accessed 7 January 2016).
7 As quoted in Max Beloff, *The Great Power: Essays in Twentieth Century Politics*, Routledge Revivals (New York, Routledge, 2009), 78.
8 Timothy Johnston, *Being Soviet: Identity, Rumour, and Everyday Life under Stalin, 1939–53* (Oxford: Oxford University Press, 2011), 134–135.
9 Johnston, *Being Soviet*, 116.
10 Ethan Pollack, *Stalin and the Soviet Science Wars* (Princeton, NJ: Princeton University Press, 2006), 214.
11 S. Frederick Starr, *Red and Hot: The Fate of Jazz in the Soviet Union* (New York: Limelight, 1994), 216.
12 Richard Stites, *Russian Popular Culture: Entertainment and Society since 1900* (Cambridge: Cambridge University Press, 1992), 119; David Caute, *The Dancer Defects: The Struggle for Cultural Supremacy during the Cold War* (Oxford: Oxford University Press, 2003), 442.
13 Serhey Yekelchyk, *Stalin's Empire of Memory: Russian Ukrainian Relations in the Soviet Historical Imagination* (Toronto: University of Toronto Press, 2004), 88.
14 Ludmilla Alexeyeva and Paul Goldberg, *The Thaw Generation: Coming of Age in the Post-Stalin Era* (Pittsburgh, PA: University of Pittsburgh Press, 1990), 39.
15 As quoted in David Brandenberger, *National Bolshevism: Stalinist Mass Culture and the Formation of Modern Russian National Identity, 1931–1956* (Cambridge, MA: Harvard University Press, 2002), 188.
16 Amir Weiner, *Making Sense of War: The Second World War and the Fate of the Bolshevik Revolution* (Princeton, NJ: Princeton University Press, 2002), 216.
17 Lily Golden, *My Long Journey Home* (Chicago, IL: Third World Press, 2002), 41.
18 Alexeyeva and Goldberg, *The Thaw Generation*, 44.
19 As quoted in Juliane Fürst, *Stalin's Last Generation: Soviet Post-War Youth and the Emergence of Mature Socialism* (Oxford: Oxford University Press, 2010), 85.
20 As quoted in Weiner, *Making Sense*, 197.

21 Johnston, *Being Soviet*, 168.
22 Stites, *Russian Popular Culture*, 116, 119.
23 Yekelchyk, *Stalin's Empire of Memory*, 12.
24 Johnston, *Being Soviet*, 88.
25 As quoted in Fürst, *Stalin's Last Generation*, 79.
26 Fürst, *Stalin's Last Generation*, 92–93.
27 Vassily Aksyonov, *In Search of Melancholy Baby* (New York: Random House, 1985), 14.
28 Aksyonov, *In Search*, 18.
29 Fürst, *Stalin's Last Generation*, 220.
30 Aksyonov, *In Search*, 18.
31 As quoted in Mark Edele, "Strange Young Men in Stalin's Moscow: The Birth and Life of the Stiliagi, 1945–1953," *Jahrbücher für Geschichte Osteuropas*, Neue Folge, 50, no. 1 (2002): 43, available at article stable URL: http://ezproxy.adrian.edu:2051/stable/41050842 (accessed 6 May 2014).
32 Johnston, *Being Soviet*, 203.
33 Edele, "Strange Young Men," 61.
34 As quoted in Johnston, *Being Soviet*, 203.
35 Fürst, *Stalin's Last Generation*, 232.
36 Jean Levesque, "'Into the Grey Zone': Sham Peasants and the Limits of the Kolkhoz Order in the Post-war Russian Village, 1945–1953," in Juliane Fürst, ed., *Late Stalinist Russia: Society between Reconstruction and Reinvention* (New York: Routledge, 2006), 105.
37 Shelia Fitzpatrick, "Postwar Soviet Society: The 'Return to Normalcy,' 1945–1953," in Susan J. Linz, ed., *The Impact of World War II on the Soviet Union* (Totowa, NJ: Rowman & Allanheld, 1985), 146.
38 James Von Geldern and Richard Stites, eds., *Mass Culture in Soviet Russia* (Bloomington: Indiana University Press, 1995), 488.
39 Donald Filtzer, "Standards of Living vs. Quality of Life: Struggling with the Urban Environment in Russia during the Early Years of Post-war Reconstruction," in Fürst, ed., *Late Stalinist Russia*, 83–89.
40 Golden, *My Long Journey Home*, 51.
41 As quoted in Vera Dunham, *In Stalin's Time* (Durham, NC: Duke University Press, 1990), 79.
42 Dunham, *In Stalin's Time*, 43.
43 Cynthia Hooper, "A Darker 'Big Deal:' Concealing Party Crimes in the Post Second World War Era," in Fürst, ed., *Late Stalinist Russia*, 157.
44 Kate Brown, *Plutopia* (Oxford: Oxford University Press, 2013), 135.
45 As quoted in Susan E. Reid, "Cold War in the Kitchen: Gender and the De-Stalinization of Consumer Taste in the Soviet Union under Khrushchev," *Slavic Review*, 61, no. 2 (Summer 2002): 221. Article DOI: 10.2307/2697116.
46 David Riesman, "The Nylon War," reprinted in *Abundance for What?* (New Brunswick, NJ: Transaction Publishers, 1964), 76.
47 As quoted in Emily S. Rosenberg, "Another Mission to Moscow: Ida Rosenthal and Consumer Dreams," in Choi Chatterjee and Beth Holmgren, eds., *Americans Experience Russia: Encountering the Enigma, 1917 to the present* (New York: Routledge, 2012), 135.
48 As quoted in Jerome M. Gilison, *The Soviet Image of Utopia* (Baltimore, MD: Johns Hopkins University Press, 1975), 124.
49 Reid, "Cold War in the Kitchen," 225.
50 Quoted in Margaret Peacock, "Broadcasting Benevolence: Images of the Child in American, Soviet and NLF Propaganda in Vietnam, 1964–1973," *Journal of the History of Childhood and Youth*, 3, no. 1 (Winter 2010): 25.
51 Brown, *Plutopia*, 335.
52 Peacock, *Innocent Weapons*, 71–72.

9 Paradoxes of the Thaw

INTRODUCTION

In 1954, the writer Ilya Ehrenburg published a novel called *The Thaw*. It was set during the very last years of Stalin's life and evoked some of the unsavory aspects of those years. Characters included a Jewish physician worried by reports of the "Doctors' Plot"; an artist who refused to compromise his principles by creating falsely cheerful art and thus lived in dire poverty; and a narrow-minded factory manager who invested funds earmarked for workers' living quarters back into the factory, sacrificing the well-being of his workers in order to increase output. At the end of the novel, injustices were righted, and some of the sympathetic characters strolled through a park in springtime, where they saw trees budding and a symbolically significant flower pushing through the ice.

In his memoirs, Ehrenburg described his aspirations for the work: "I wanted to depict how historical events of tremendous importance affect the lives of people in a small town and to impart my feeling about the Thaw and my hopes." Many critics condemned the book but Ehrenburg himself reported receiving "thousands of letters standing up for it."[1] Ludmilla Alexeyeva was not impressed. She dismissed the novel's literary merits, describing it as "a book I read then forgot all about. I had no inkling that it would give the name to an era."[2]

CHAPTER QUESTIONS

The period from Stalin's death in 1953 to approximately the mid-1960s is named after this novel because it is traditionally seen as an era of change, honesty, and hope. However, more recently historians have emphasized the limitations of this new freedom and the intrusiveness of the party as it attempted to shed the hypocrisy of late Stalinism in order to infuse communism into everyday life. An influential scholar has argued that citizens actually experienced more repression during the Thaw because the Khrushchevian state was so ambitious about regulating new areas of life in order to turn citizens into true communists.[3] This chapter raises questions about the meaning of the Thaw period: Did the Thaw constitute a fundamental break with Stalinism? How did the Soviet system change and in what ways did it remain the same? To what extent did the Thaw bring about more freedom? How did the greater openness of the period impact how Soviet people thought about their place in the world? How did the government's desire to reanimate sincere communism bring new restrictions to people's lives?

VOICES, MEMORIES, CONTESTED PERSPECTIVES

Khrushchev's critique

Stalin died of a cerebral hemorrhage on 5 March 1953. Ilya Ehrenburg was astonished to hear the news. "I tried to think out what would happen to us all now but was quite unable to. Like so many of my compatriots at that moment, I was in a state of shock."[4] Many people expressed intense grief mixed with fear. Decades later, one woman told an historian: "Anyone who says they did not cry when they heard about Stalin's death is lying. Everyone was in tears. We did not know what was going to happen next. We had never known anything different."[5] Mikhail Gorbachev, leader of the Soviet Union from 1985 to 1991, was a university student at the time of Stalin's death. Although both of his grandfathers had been arrested during the 1930s, he remembered that the "overwhelming majority of the students were . . . deeply and sincerely moved by Stalin's death, perceiving it as a tragedy for the country. A similar feeling, and I won't deny it, welled up in me then."[6] Those who welcomed Stalin's death rejoiced discreetly, behind locked doors and with trusted friends or family. In the Gulag, inmates celebrated what they hoped would be their imminent release.

Like Lenin, Stalin died without naming an heir. Publicly, Politburo members resolved to lead collectively, while maneuvering for dominance behind the scenes. Lavrenti Beria, the head of the secret police, was the first to be eliminated by his former allies, who arrested him for treason and sentenced him to death in 1953. After this, the power struggle became less deadly and the losers were relieved of their jobs in the capital rather than their lives. What does this shift suggest about how Soviet politics changed during the Thaw?

The man who eventually assumed control was the impulsive yet shrewd Nikita Sergeevich Khrushchev. Khrushchev was born in 1894 into a family of poor peasants in southern Russia. As a teenager, he went to work in the mines of a nearby town, joined the Bolsheviks in 1918, and served as a commissar in the Red Army during the Civil War. After the war, he studied at a technical institute and began to rise through the party ranks, a beneficiary of the immense social mobility afforded during the First Five-Year Plan (see chapter 5). After serving in Moscow and Ukraine, he joined the Politburo in 1939. Khrushchev became general secretary of the party in 1953, and assumed leadership of the government as well in 1958, but he never possessed the dictatorial powers that Stalin had exercised. He was always compelled to work with or against other powerful politicians, and they eventually ousted him in 1964. Nor did Khrushchev project a remote, god-like persona as Stalin had; he was gregarious, with a jovial and sometimes crude manner and a colorful way of speaking that reflected his humble origins. Gorbachev was a provincial Komsomol official when he first met Khrushchev in 1958. He recalled "his open and frank ways, his peculiar folksy manner and his desire to establish contact with everyone."[7]

Khrushchev was imaginative and ambitious, with grand visions for the future of communism. One of the defining moments of his leadership came in 1956 at the Twentieth Communist Party Congress. After the regular proceedings had ended, the delegates received a message that they should return to the Kremlin. At about midnight, Khrushchev began a speech that lasted until four in the morning. Although it was called the secret speech, its contents were soon widely known: It consisted largely of criticisms of Stalin that were shockingly honest, though incomplete. Khrushchev read from Lenin's testament damning Stalin for "rudeness" (see chapter 4). He then went on to denounce Stalin's construction of a personality cult and compared this self-glorification unfavorably to Lenin's personal modesty. Khrushchev condemned the terror, saying that Stalin had "discarded the Leninist method of convincing and educating, he abandoned the method of ideological struggle for that of administrative violence, mass repressions and terror. He acted on an increasingly larger scale and more stubbornly through punitive organs, at the same time often violating all existing norms of morality and of Soviet laws." He also blamed Stalin for Russia's unpreparedness for World War II and for the military disasters that resulted from it.[8] However, Khrushchev praised as necessary the suppression of the left and right opposition during the 1920s and mentioned neither the Shakhty trial, nor the upheaval and violence incurred by the collectivization of agriculture. Khrushchev blamed the great injustices he described on Stalin and the heads of the secret police, thus exculpating by implication other Soviet leaders, including himself. What do these inclusions and omissions indicate about the parameters of reform?

Some loyal communists welcomed Khrushchev's speech because it allowed them to maintain their faith in the system despite Stalinist repressions. An Old Bolshevik who spent seven years in prison wrote: "The cult of personality of Stalin was created not by the people, but by Stalin and his lackeys ... Though the Soviet people lived in forced silence, they never lost faith in tomorrow. That's why the whole Soviet people rejoiced when it was told the truth about Stalin and his abuse of power."[9] However, most people experienced Khrushchev's speech as less reassuring than disorienting. A man serving in the military recalled that when it was read aloud, it "produced a certain shock among the soldiers in our company. 'How can that be?' they would say in bewilderment. 'If Stalin did harm with his power, then nothing that was done under Stalin was right either.' Discussions and arguments started."[10] Gorbachev spent weeks leading discussions of the speech among Komsomol members, as described in this passage from his memoir:

> Some of the people to whom I talked—especially the younger and better-educated ones and those who themselves had in some way been victims of Stalinist repression—applauded the condemnation of the personality cult. Others refused to believe the facts stated in Khrushchev's report and rejected his assessment of Stalin's role and activities. A third, fairly large group did not doubt for a moment the veracity of the stated facts, but kept asking the same question: "What for? What is the point of washing one's dirty linen in public, speaking publicly about these things and fuelling unrest among the people?"[11]

Uncertainty about the recent past was reflected in controversies about what to do with the ubiquitous portraits of Stalin. Party, government, and factory leaders were told to remove the images and while some people resisted, others tore them down, defaced them, or burnt them.[12] One old communist arose from his sickbed to take down the picture of Stalin and, according to the report, "warned his wife never to hang the portrait again."[13]

The secret speech also had unexpected ramifications in the Eastern European countries that by this time had developed their own Stalinist systems. In Poland and Hungary, it sparked demonstrations by workers and intellectuals that eventually resulted in new reform governments. The Hungarian leadership, under pressure from crowds of protestors, grew more radical and announced the country's withdrawal from the Warsaw Pact, the Soviet military alliance. If this were permitted, Khrushchev said, the "West would say we are either stupid or weak, and that's one and the same thing. We cannot possibly permit it . . . We would have capitalists at the frontiers of the Soviet Union."[14] The Soviet army attacked the capital, Budapest, crushed the Hungarian resistance, and installed a more compliant government. Twenty thousand Hungarians and fifteen hundred Soviet soldiers were killed in the violence.[15] What does this event suggest about the extent to which Khrushchev had left behind Stalinist methods and policies?

Liberation from the Gulag

Even before Khrushchev's secret speech, party leaders had begun to rein in the state terror apparatus that had, at times, threatened their own personal security. Within weeks after Stalin's death, they released the surviving physicians arrested as part of the alleged "Doctors' Plot" and announced an amnesty for various categories of prisoners, including ordinary, nonpolitical criminals serving short sentences, mothers with children, and elderly people. This policy was extended, especially after 1956, so that eventually as many as five million people were freed from the Gulag over the course of the decade.[16]

Both pragmatic and ideological factors lay behind the mass liberation. The Gulag system had become a drag on postwar economic recovery, for although enslaved workers received no pay, they were too malnourished and poorly motivated to constitute a productive labor force. Operating prison camps was complicated and costly, and a series of camp protests starting in the late 1940s made it even more expensive to maintain discipline. Khrushchev's genuine idealism was also an important factor. He saw freeing prisoners as part of a larger campaign to establish communism on the basis of legality and enthusiasm rather than coercion and terror, and this aspiration marks one of his most important departures from Stalinism.

Liberation brought joy, but uncertainty too. A poem written by a former prisoner to celebrate his release expressed these mixed emotions. It began with happiness: "I walk—and do not believe: / alone, / without guards? / And there is joy, / and tenderness, / and shyness in me." Yet the conclusion of the poem hinted at the difficulties inherent in the transition to freedom: "But my hands / out of habit / I hold behind my back."[17]

Indeed, the *zeks* (Russian slang for prisoners) were liberated under disparate conditions. A privileged minority were officially rehabilitated, which meant public acknowledgment that their convictions were unfair and a restoration of property, positions, and party membership. Others received no compensation but were permitted to live where they chose; another group found themselves restricted to areas outside of the capitals. Not surprisingly, ex-prisoners' ability to find jobs and homes varied. Many suffered physical and psychological scars. Like combat veterans and other trauma victims, they felt isolated because friends and family could not understand what they had been through and may have treated them as guilty. A woman who returned home after twenty years reflected: "What could I tell them? . . . However much detail I described, it would still be incomprehensible to them. Nobody can understand what we went through. Only those who know what it was like can understand and sympathize."[18] Some prisoners chose to rebuild their lives away from their home towns, in the cities where their prison camps had been located. There they could draw on a social network of former *zeks* who could help them find work and housing and provide emotional support.[19]

Some communist ex-*zeks* maintained faith in the ideology that had provided their lives with purpose and meaning. According to one: "My moral-ideological state never wavered from the beginning to the end, despite the undeserved insult visited upon me with the label of 'enemy of the people.' And despite having endured a severe prison regime and interrogations."[20] For many others, imprisonment was profoundly alienating, and some returned from the camps with oppositional attitudes that were expressed in songs, poems, leaflets, tattoos, and verbal outbursts. One ex-convict got drunk and caused a ruckus, shouting at the police who came to arrest him: "Down with Soviet Power!" and "Long live capitalism." Another warned that "Grandpa Truman" would come hang all the communists.[21]

Law enforcement agencies worried about the influence of violent and subversive ex-*zeks* on the general population, especially impressionable young people. Ordinary people were concerned about the growing crime rate and some blamed it on ex-prisoners. One letter of complaint declared that people "return from the campus and begin their dark deeds again." Another suggested that criminals should "be sent off only to the north, and after the end of their sentences, be made to stay there forever."[22] What do such opinions reveal about the perils of freedom and the tensions between maintaining order and advancing liberation?

Opening to the world: tourists and students

In addition to its social and political dimensions, the Thaw also reconfigured international relations. Khrushchev denied the inevitability of war between the capitalist and communist worlds, for in the age of nuclear weapons, he stated, the two sides had to develop "peaceful coexistence" or risk total devastation. Soviet leaders were suspicious of the West, as was made clear during the Hungarian uprising, but also interested in establishing better diplomatic and economic relations. As a symbol of this intention, Khrushchev himself visited the United States in 1959, stopping in California, New York, and the corn fields of Iowa. In 1955, the Soviet Union passed a new law allowing citizens to travel abroad, and in subsequent years cultural exchange agreements brought foreign films, art, music, and literature to the Soviet Union. In 1957, an international youth festival attracted visitors from around the world to Moscow, and the government began to encourage students from the developing world to study in the Soviet Union. All of these developments allowed Soviet citizens to experience foreign cultures and ideas, yet in the context of the Cold War this opening to the world brought with it official concern about the corrupting potential of cultural exchange.

As international tourism developed during this period, carefully selected Soviet tourists were sent abroad to both Eastern and Western Europe with the goals of representing Soviet achievements, reconfirming Soviet superiority, and also learning about other societies. The state allowed only politically trustworthy people to travel, and for many of these privileged citizens admiration for European culture coexisted with confidence and optimism in the Soviet future. At other times, contradictions emerged to disturb official narratives. For example, while Soviet tourists were supposed to see Eastern Europeans as junior members of the socialist family, some couldn't help but notice both the superior consumer goods and the sometimes hostile attitudes of their "socialist younger brother[s]."[23] In Romania, a train conductor made a group of Soviet tourists give up their seats to Romanians, telling them, "It's our territory, our power."[24]

Even as Soviet citizens began to explore the world, in 1957 the world came to the Soviet Union when an international youth festival was held in Moscow that summer. The government spent months in preparation, painting and repairing buildings and arresting people for public drunkenness and suspected prostitution to get them off the streets; after all, the festival was supposed to show off the capital, increase international prestige, and reassure communists from other countries. About 34,000 young people from 131 different nations attended. They were communists and anticommunists, peace activists, left wingers, and those just seeking a cheap and novel vacation. Once in Moscow, they attended a huge array of organized activities: parades, carnivals, concerts, athletic events, exhibits, dances. There were meetings among professional groups (young miners, steel workers, architects, sailors, law students) and among hobbyists and fans (stamp collectors, photographers). For young Soviet citizens, the festival offered new experiences: They could see abstract paintings in the art exhibits, listen to jazz, and dance with foreigners.[25] Many of them remember the festival as a giddily joyful time; in the area around Moscow University, for example, a journalist laughingly recalled many decades later that "there was dancing and so on in every corner, in the squares, on the staircases, in the fountain . . . How we romped. How Moscow frisked about. It was all awesome, from the heart. This really was fun and exciting."[26]

Although some foreign participants complained that there were too many events crammed into the schedule, young people did have the opportunity to strike up spontaneous conversations in the parks and streets of Moscow. They discussed serious topics such as the Hungarian uprising of the previous year, but also fashion, jazz, and rock 'n' roll. And they flirted, or at least tried to. One group of students from the Sorbonne were interrupted in their attempts to chat up some Russian girls and taken to the police station, where officers checked their papers and told them that "Moscow was not Paris."[27] On the other hand, the poet Yevtushenko (the author of document 9.2) recalled, years later, that during the festival: "For the first time in my life, my socialist lips touched so-called 'capitalist' lip(s) because I kissed one American girl, breaking any Cold War rules."[28] Many jokes and rumors about promiscuous behavior and "festival babies" emerged after the event, reflecting larger concerns about the corrupting influence of the West.

One of the goals of the festival was to impress visitors from newly independent nations of Asia, Africa, the Middle East, and Latin America, although perhaps not in the manner witnessed by Lily Golden. Golden, the "Russian Negro" discussed in the previous chapter, was put in charge of the delegations from African countries, and she recalled that when walking with a friend from Guinea: "Young women sidled by and pushed notes with phone numbers into his pockets or followed him for miles."[29]

In more official acts of diplomacy, the Khrushchev government increased military and economic aid to developing nations in order to further the spread of communism. As part of this outreach effort, the Soviet government offered university scholarships to students from the Third World. In 1960, it established a university especially for them called the People's Friendship University, later renamed Patrice Lumumba University in honor of the first democratically elected prime minister of Congo, who

Figure 9.1 Students outside Patrice Lumumba University in 1961. © Bettmann/CORBIS.

What aspects of the Thaw are conveyed in this photo?

was assassinated shortly after taking office with the connivance of the US and Belgium. The number of students from developing countries enrolled in Soviet universities grew rapidly during this period, from 46 in 1956–1957 to 1,667 by 1961. By the mid-1960s, there were about 4,000 students from sub-Saharan Africa alone.[30]

For many students from Africa, in particular, the decision to study in the Soviet Union was a practical, rather than political, one; the free tuition, housing, and stipend made higher education very affordable.[31] And while many of them appreciated the educational opportunities the Soviet Union offered them, dissatisfactions also emerged. One Nigerian complained that there were "No cars, no cafes, no good clothes or good food, nothing to buy or inspect in the stores, no splash of colour to relieve Moscow's damp gray. Nothing but shortages and restrictions."[32]

More serious were the accusations of racial discrimination. The Soviet Union had long portrayed itself as the champion of downtrodden peoples and favorably contrasted its commitment to equality with the racial injustice and hypocrisy that plagued the United States, and so African students were disillusioned to find themselves getting harassed or even beaten up. Because the vast majority of foreign students were men, interracial dating was a particular point of tension (see document 9.1). In 1963, a Ghanaian medical student who had been engaged to a Russian woman died in mysterious circumstances. The authorities explained that he had drunk too much, passed out outside, and froze to death, but African students suspected his death was a racially motivated murder. They organized the first recorded political protest in Moscow's Red Square since the 1920s. Hundreds of people marched through the square carrying signs reading "Stop Killing Africans" and "Moscow, a second Alabama."[33] Historians have argued that foreign students' complaints and protests inspired their Soviet contemporaries by providing them with examples of free expression and democratic action, concepts that, for many intellectuals and artists, lay at the heart of the Thaw.

Warming up? Arts and the Thaw

In many ways, the Thaw began with the arts. Within months after Stalin's death, some writers and artists had begun to complain about the constraints that Stalinist literary policies and the doctrine of socialist realism had placed upon their work. They called for honesty, a truthful account of the past, and a more realistic portrayal of human beings. In the summer of 1953, before starting *The Thaw*, Ehrenburg wrote an essay on literature that discussed some of these themes. He asked: "Why does one so seldom find stories with any mention of love, or family dissensions, or illness, or the death of dear ones, or even of bad weather? . . . Some critics still cling to the naive view that our philosophic optimism and the portrayal of our people's achievements are incompatible with descriptions of unrequited love or the loss of someone dear."[34] A film student published a similar critique of the depiction of love in the cinema. Mocking the wooden dialogue typical in Soviet films of the time, she wrote: "One does not say to one's beloved, 'fulfill the quota 100% and I shall love you.'" She insisted that "Our artists' object of attention should become not man 'in general,' not an abstract being, but living concrete man with all his passions, thoughts, behavior, dreams, merits and defects, in things big and small, 'private' and public."[35]

Alexander Tvardovsky, the poet whose family had been "dekulaked" in the 1930s (see chapter 5), became a key figure in the exploration of artistic honesty. By this time he had become an eminent literary figure and the editor of the literary journal *Novyi mir* (New world). In December 1953, he oversaw the publication of an essay by Vladimir Pomerantsev entitled "On Sincerity." Pomerantsev criticized contemporary literature for "varnishing" over reality and advocated, instead, realistic depictions of actual living conditions, contemporary problems, and human emotions and relationships.

Ludmilla Alexeyeva remembered reading the essay and discussing it with the other students and scholars who hung around the smoking lounge in Moscow's main scholarly library: "I agreed with every one of Pomerantsev's points, as did everyone else in the smoking room."[36] The essay sparked widespread interest across the Soviet Union. In a letter to *Novyi mir*, a reader described how, while waiting two months to get a copy of the journal from the library, he kept hearing discussions of the essay: "And everywhere . . . the verdict was the same: 'Great! What a punch! What a knockout! That's where the truth is told!'"[37] This enthusiasm was not universal, and some literary critics and party officials attacked the piece, accusing Pomerantsev of ignoring the importance of ideology in literature, of disrespecting socialist realism, and of expressing "anti-Marxist and anti-Leninist ideas."[38] As result of the controversy, the Writers' Union removed Tvardovsky from his editorship in 1954.

The Khrushchev government wanted to encourage the creation of more engaging literature, while at the same time maintaining control over it and making sure it did not present fundamental or overarching criticisms of the Soviet system, just as Khrushchev's secret speech had sought to uncover some of Stalin's crimes while limiting the extent of the revelations. This approach to literature resulted in both lighter censorship and periodic crackdowns, such as Tvardovsky's dismissal. The government's inconsistency was made especially conspicuous when Tvardovsky was restored to his post as editor of *Novyi mir* in 1958. He continued to publish work nobody else was willing or able to, and Alexeyeva recalled how influential *Novyi mir* became for intellectuals: "The May issue could come in July, but no one complained. The delay meant that Tvardovsky had a battle to fight and that the material was worth fighting for. Hence, it was also worth waiting for . . . A stranger spotted reading *Novyi mir* on a bus could no longer be regarded as a stranger. It was natural to ask him if the new issue had finally come out. If you talked for a few minutes, you discovered you had mutual friends."[39]

Tvardovsky's most important achievement as editor was the 1962 publication of Alexander Solzhenitsyn's chronicle of daily life in the Gulag, *One Day in the Life of Ivan Denisovich*. Hundreds of people wrote letters responding to the novella, many of them recounting their own experiences in the Gulag. Tvardovsky could not publish most of these memoirs, but he assured his correspondents that he would keep them in the journals' archives so that historians and writers could use them in the future, a promise that he kept. Some readers were furious at Solzhenitsyn's use of camp slang and his refusal to distinguish between guilty and innocent prisoners, but many others confirmed the essential truthfulness of this fictional account, which compelled readers to grapple with the meaning of the terror for their society and their individual lives. One critical letter ended by acknowledging that, despite its faults, "I cannot but sense the power of this work."[40]

Like Thaw era writers, some film directors were preoccupied by sincerity and innovation. Movies were subject to stricter censorship than literature, since they reached a wider audience, but in the late 1950s film makers were no longer required to submit scripts to the central authorities for approval, and they took advantage of this opportunity to explore new themes and techniques. (This policy, however, was eventually reversed under Brezhnev.)[41]

Poets, too, began to experiment, and young poets in particular enjoyed intense popularity. In 1958, hundreds of young Muscovites began to congregate in front of a new statue of the poet Mayakovsky to hear poems read aloud (see document 9.2 for an example of this work). Vladimir Bukovsky became a regular participant at these gatherings and later described how "Young people, mainly students, assembled almost every evening to read the poems of forgotten or repressed writers, and also their own work, and sometimes there were discussions of art and literature. A kind of open-air club came into being. But the authorities could not tolerate the danger of these spontaneous performances for long and eventually stopped the gatherings."[42] Similar gatherings in 1960 were also broken up by the police.

In a society in which culture had always been politicized, poets and party members alike took literary critiques of Soviet society and calls for honesty and independent thinking very seriously. The Soviet state's concern was not misplaced. Both Alexeyeva and Bukovsky later became dissidents who undertook illegal activities in order to campaign for human rights, and they both dated their political awakening to Thaw era literature.[43] Alexeyeva connected new ideas about art to new ideas about freedom, writing in her memoir that: "Without asking permission from the party or the government, we asserted that writers had a right to write what they wanted; that readers had the right to choose what they read; and that each of us had a right to say what he thought."[44] In fact, Alexeyeva's first dissident actions were connected to reading. She recalled that "*Novyi mir*, for all its good points, published only a small fraction of what we wanted to read."[45] So she and her fiends developed *samizdat*, or self-publishing, which involved typing out and then distributing to trusted friends copies of handwritten manuscripts: prison camp memoirs, poetry, and translations of American and European literature. What does the inception of samizdat, as well as the new "sincerity" in literature, suggest about the Thaw era freedom and its limits?

Sexuality: how much honesty?

Many of the novels famous for their exposés of Stalinist injustice, including *The Thaw*, also depicted love triangles or adultery. For example, in Galina Nikolaevna's 1957 novel *Running Battle*, the married hero and his lover finally consummate their love after almost five hundred pages of restraint. The hero says: "I have never loved another woman but you. I have never fallen in love with anybody but you. But I . . . will never leave my family." The heroine replies sadly that she would not have fallen in love with him if he had been a man who could leave his children.[46] The novel ends unhappily with the couple separating to preserve the hero's family.

In other works, however, lovers do not give up their extramarital relationships; instead, they become more honest and authentic by freeing themselves from the hypocrisy of their marriages. In the play *Alone (Odna)*, the party representative comes to warn the hero to end or at least hide his adulterous affair, or else risk being expelled from the party. The hero replies: "I earned my card at the front. And I'll manage to defend it. The party doesn't want me to lie. The party wants me to be an honest man. It wants me to work honestly. It wants my family to be founded on love."[47] These explorations of morality, love, and duty seemed more "sincere" to people because they acknowledged the complexities of emotion and also hinted at the power of sexuality.

Under Stalin, the government had silenced the wide-ranging literary and medical conversations about sex that had taken place during the 1920s, but the relative openness of the Thaw brought new public attention to issues of sexuality and, for the first time in decades, physicians and educators could openly discuss formerly forbidden topics such as masturbation, premarital sex, and contraception. While these professionals drew on medical materials from the 1920s, public discourse lacked the candid considerations of sexual freedom and pleasure found in Alexandra Kollontai's fiction from that period (see chapter 4); Thaw era discussions of sexuality were more circumscribed.

Public consideration of sexuality was sparked in part by the decriminalization of abortion in 1955 (abortion was first legalized in 1920 and then prohibited again in 1936). The decision to reverse the abortion ban was motivated (as it had been in 1920) by concern about the serious public health problem posed by widespread illegal abortions. And as in the 1920s, health officials legalized abortion and simultaneously launched educational efforts to discourage it because they believed it had injurious mental and physical consequences, especially for young people. Physicians and health officials were also worried about what they saw as sexual immorality, which included any sexual activity outside of marriage. They argued that adultery destroyed family stability and distracted people from work and that premarital sex deprived young people of vital energy, leaving them undisciplined and irresponsible. Masturbators were antisocial; in the words of one physician they "often diverge from the collective and from collective interests, they become reserved, individualistically disposed, they easily fall into despondency and pessimism."[48] Such warnings about various forms of "sexual immorality" coexisted with sympathetic literary depictions of romantic love triangles and conscience-stricken adulterers. What does this suggest about the conflicting ideals of this period?

The problems of abortion and sexual morality were both supposed to be solved by sex education and, following a 1956 decision by the USSR Ministry of Health, physicians began to produce books, pamphlets, and magazine articles that discussed masturbation, premarital sex, and abortion. They also explained, with varying degrees of thoroughness, the various forms of contraceptives that were supposed to be available: condoms, rubber diaphragms, cervical caps made out of aluminum or silver, and spermicidal cream. However, there were persistent shortages of educational materials and especially contraceptive devices throughout the Soviet era. Despite the repeated urgings of physicians, the production of contraceptives was never made a national priority, so that even as late as the early 1990s abortion remained the most common form of birth control in the former USSR.[49]

Furthermore, there was no consensus about the content or parameters of formal sex education. Some officials advocated a purely moral form of instruction and feared that providing any physiological information to adolescents would arouse a precocious interest in sexuality. Others argued that if sex education was not included in school curricula, young people would get their information, or misinformation, from one another. For example, during a 1955 discussion within the Ministry of Education about a new physiology textbook, one education official argued that the language in the text should be less explicit because a "detailed description of sexual cells [and] the process of fertilization might lead to a whole series of additional questions in class, [and] these questions are completely superfluous and undesirable." Another countered by warning against leaving the task of sex education "to the street, [to] everyday life."[50] This controversy might sound familiar to students in the United States with knowledge of the debates about abstinence-only sex education curricula. In the Soviet case, where decision making was highly centralized, it resulted in institutional procrastination, and sex education was not included in the Soviet high school curriculum until 1983.[51]

Creating and instilling communist morality

Concern about sexual masturbation and extramarital sex was part of a larger effort to instill communist morality, a set of principles that demanded devotion to communism, hard work, collectivism, and the proper conduct of private life and family relations (see document 9.3). Communist morality was part of the Khrushchev government's attempt to formulate a source of political legitimacy that would not depend upon wide-scale terror or Stalin's personality cult, but on consent and persuasion. If people lived according to communist morality, they would be hard workers, loyal citizens, conscientious parents, and considerate neighbors. In a utopian vision of the future that harked back to the 1920s, party leaders believed that under fully developed communism morality, rather than coercion or law, would eventually govern all relations between individuals. People would no longer experience conflict between desires and morals, between private interests and the public good. In the meantime, however, in cases where conflicts arose, personal needs were to be sacrificed to public goals.

Starting in the mid-1950s, Soviet citizens encountered an outpouring of books, articles, and speeches detailing how to live a properly communist life. The revolutionary poet Mayakovsky, whose statue became the site of poetry readings, experienced another kind of ghostly resurgence as authors frequently quoted his verses from the 1920s to illustrate the necessity of unity in public and private life: "Communism / is not only / on the land / at the plant in the sweat / it is also at home / at the table / in the relations / in the family / In everyday life."[52] How do we interpret this invocation of Mayakovsky and this concern with transforming *byt* (everyday life)? To what extent does it suggest a break with Stalinism and a return to the utopian Bolshevik aspirations of the 1920s?

Trade union, party, Komsomol, and a host of new voluntary organizations were charged with instilling and enforcing communist morality. Some historians point to this development as evidence that the Khrushchev government brought not new freedoms but new forms of control, since all kinds of personal behavior were now subject to scrutiny and correction. Communist Party members, for example, were supposed to serve as role models, and the party widened its definition of what constituted unacceptable behavior. Party members were censured not just for failing to pay child support, as in the past, but also for behavior that had previously been mostly ignored: ineffective or neglectful parenting and extramarital affairs. Furthermore, the party adopted new methods of punishment. Rather than expelling wayward spouses and parents, the party employed various techniques of public shaming with the goal of educating and correcting party members' behavior. The party was, in one scholar's phrase, "less repressive but more intrusive."[53] A joke from this period made fun of the party's intervention in intimate matters by describing how women from various countries retained their husbands' interest, the "German by being a good housewife, the Spaniard by being passionate, the Frenchwoman by her elegance and refined caresses . . . and the Russian by the Party committee."[54]

In addition to self-discipline, party members were also supposed to help the general public by giving lectures and interceding in family problems. A pamphlet, appropriately entitled 'Everyday Life [*byt*] Is Not a Private Matter', described this type of intervention. A factory party committee became concerned about the behavior of the son of one of the factory's engineers. They held a meeting to discuss the matter, and when the engineer tried to excuse himself by explaining how busy he and his wife were building their careers, the party members responded by scolding him: "We want your son to grow up to be a real person. Understand, Vovka isn't just your delight, but our future, and yours and mine and all of ours. And concern for the future is a very important matter. That is why this conversation is occurring at a party meeting." The engineer repented and began to pay more attention to his son, whose conduct improved.[55] This story was written as an ideal scenario for use by professional propagandists; in real life, the father might have responded differently, perhaps with defiance or indifference.

Instilling communist morality was not just the responsibility of the party elite. Ordinary people were also supposed to get involved through a series of new and newly revived community organizations. These included the street patrol teams empowered to arrest those disturbing public order; apartment house committees; various parent/school organizations; and comrades' courts. Most of these groups dated from the early years of the Soviet Union and were originally intended to facilitate self-government. During the Thaw period, however, these organizations were run from above by party, factory, and local government officials, and their goal was to monitor and improve citizens' conduct. Comrades' courts, for example, empowered elected citizen-judges to hear cases concerning work discipline, drunkenness, and bad behavior in public; "unworthy" attitudes toward women or parents; neglect of children; insult, damage to housing and communal property; violation of common living rules; quarrels between tenants about living space and payment of utility bills; and other antisocial but not criminal behavior. The courts could apply sanctions ranging from stern warnings to the initiation of eviction proceedings, and their sessions were public so that violators could serve as examples of the consequences of bad behavior.[56]

The police and court systems also intensified their scrutiny of everyday behavior. New laws criminalized "petty hooliganism," a broadly and variably defined category of offenses that included some of the same acts targeted by comrades' courts: swearing, public drunkenness, loud quarrels with neighbors and family, harassing women, and urinating in public. Millions of Soviet citizens were arrested as hooligans and subject to short jail sentences and mandatory physical labor. Honest work, such as street cleaning and snow shoveling, was supposed to rehabilitate hooligans, and the fact that this work was public added an element of humiliation to their punishment. However, these "hooligans" weren't always adequately supervised, and sometimes they dragged their feet, shirked their assigned tasks, and left their worksites.[57]

The fact that convicted hooligans sometimes abandoned their court-mandated public service complicates our attempts to evaluate the repressiveness of Thaw era policy. It suggests that the government initiated new efforts to monitor and control everyday life and private behavior, but did not always implement them effectively. For example, while some house committees and comrades' courts were very busy, others were disorganized, ineffective, or moribund. Activists sometimes encountered obstacles to their efforts to instill collectivism and social responsibility. After an organizer scolded a group of tenants for failing to repair the playground, a man responded by expressing complaints about the building and a negative attitude unconducive to activism: "The questions of equipment, of planting greenery, of areas for children are raised, but when plaster flakes off on your head, when everything around is rotten and you await an accident, it could drive you to drink."[58]

The Soviet state's inconsistency adds still another layer of complexity. Even as the government attempted to regulate private life, it also introduced other reforms that allowed for more autonomy. Divorce became increasingly easy to obtain, and, as we discussed above, abortion was legalized. Most fundamentally, Khrushchev's massive housing construction program, mentioned in the previous chapter, allowed families to move into their very own small but separate apartments, where they could escape the constant scrutiny of communal apartment neighbors.

CONCLUSION AND FURTHER QUESTIONS

Khrushchev hoped that young members of the Thaw generation would emulate their zealous predecessors who came of age during the First Five-Year Plan (described in chapter 5). He encouraged urban youth to give up the comforts and distractions of city life and to volunteer for large-scale construction projects in remote areas or for the Virgin Lands, a campaign to grow grain on previously uncultivated steppe lands in Central Asia. While some young people took up this challenge, others did not, and the press developed a whole vocabulary of critical terms for those who evaded self-sacrifice. They were loiterers, no-gooders, parasites, fungus, lazybones, and *stiliagi* (fashion fans).[59]

The style-obsessed stiliagi first appeared in the immediate postwar years, and, as described in the previous chapter, the Stalinist state paid them little attention. Under Khrushchev, however, they came under much more intense criticism because their frivolity was an affront to communist morality. Citizen patrols and Komsomol groups sometimes attacked them, clipping off their florid neckties, cutting their hair, or even beating them up. An activist who participated in such raids explained why the stiliagi offended him: "Against our high ideals they placed tight trousers and shrill ties."[60] The press released a barrage of articles and cartoons condemning the shallowness of the stiliagi and detailing examples of their tasteless accessories; however, this coverage inadvertently publicized fashion trends and inspired new stiliagi, thus broadening the subculture. At the same time, improved relations with the West and greater access to foreign visitors and culture brought more diverse sources of inspiration for the fashionable; for example, ponytails became popular among female stiliagi after a traveling exhibition featured a Picasso painting of women wearing that style.[61] Thus, during the Thaw era, stiliagi were subject to greater persecution and criticism than previously, but were also more numerous, diverse, and visible.

This paradox is characteristic of the period. Recent historical works characterize the Thaw as an amalgam of apparent opposites: It was both "optimistic and . . . anxiously authoritarian," "exhilarating and treacherous," and "full of hope . . . but disorienting and potentially unsettling."[62] In describing her own experience of this era, Alexeyeva concluded by emphasizing its temporary and uncertain quality: "A Thaw was not quite spring. The spring is cyclical and irreversible, and it turns to summer as surely as night turns to day. But a Thaw is tenuous. A frost could strike any minute."[63]

PRIMARY SOURCES

Use the questions to analyze the content, context, and significance of each primary source. Then synthesize the primary sources and the material in the chapter to formulate a response to the primary chapter question: To what extent did the Thaw bring about more freedom?

Document 9.1   A Nigerian student recalls life in Moscow

Questions for analysis

1   What does this document tell you about the role of Komsomol activists?
2   What does this document tell you about the range of students' attitudes toward political authority?
3   What does it tell you about the politics of popular culture during this period?

If we managed to invite some Russian friends to the University, to the room of one of our fellow students who lived there, we could be sure of a visit from at least one Komsomol activist. They would simply "barge" into the room and listen and join in the conversation without so much as a by-your leave. They would be particularly assiduous if there were Russian girls present as guests. In that case they would try to befriend our guests and even invite them to their rooms. Only when this bad-mannered behaviour led to protests, even from other Russian students, would they desist from these tactics. They then resorted to another method of preventing Russians, and especially Russian girls, from keeping up their friendships with us. Every guest who comes into the University is compelled to surrender his or her internal passport, which every Russian is compelled to carry, to the office on the ground floor. They then have to declare whom they are visiting and receive a pass for that room. The Komsomol's task was easy. They simply went to the office, got the details of the visitors from their passports and either accosted them on their way out, or simply wrote a letter to their factory or their house warden . . .

   . . .

   I would not like to leave the impression that we were suspicious of all the Russian students at the University. On the contrary, most of us had very good friends among them. Many of our Russian friends and colleagues would get into trouble because of us. Suddenly they would try to avoid meeting you. And then in a less-public place they would come up to us and confess that they had been warned off by the Komsomol from associating with foreigners. Many of the Russian students, too, showed a healthily independent turn of mind. For example, when they were being persuaded to go and meet Mr. Khrushchev in the streets on his return from his triumphant tours they would often simply ignore the summons and show that they saw the propaganda.
   One of the things which often brought us together with the Russian students was listening to modern jazz music. Large numbers of them appreciated the better kind of jazz and also realized and acknowledged that it had developed from the folk music of the African people . . . It was really the popularity that this type of music gained among Russian students, thus bringing them into close contact and friendship with American and African students, that really decided the Soviet authorities to condemn

this kind of music. In other words, as we saw quite obviously rock-'n'-roll was condemned by Khrushchev and the authorities not on aesthetic, but mainly on political, grounds.

Source: Andrew Richard Amar, *A Student in Moscow* (London: Ampersand, 1960), 33–34 and 62–63.

Document 9.2   "Freshness"

Questions for analysis

1   What do you think the poet means by "Freshness"?
2   Who is the "we"?
3   Why do you think the poet laid the poem out on the page in such short lines? What impression is conveyed?

Freshness!
        Freshness!
We want freshness!
Pure nuptial snow,
and no old tracks,
freshness of muscle,
brain,
        brush stroke,
freshness in music
and language!
May all things long-lain,
crusted with dust,
crumble away,
and not stay there stale.
May freshness
with all inevitability
very simply
            and quickly
displace
        all this.
What's the use
their making
            a fuss—
those
    who object
to fresh air?
Who will maintain it?
It won't be sustained!
Freshness!
        Freshness!
We want freshness!

Source: Yevgeny Yevtushenko, "Freshness," 1960. From George Reavey, trans. and ed., *The New Russian Poets, 1953–1966: An Anthology* (New York: October House, 1966), 77.

Document 9.3   *Pravda* explains communist morality

Questions for analysis

1   How does the author explain violations against communist morality?
2   What responsibilities does he assign to party, Komsomol, and other organizations?
3   What is the proper relationship between public and private?
4   How would this author respond to the first two documents?

The political and moral qualities of the Soviet individual are indissolubly united. Every conscious citizen understands that each action of his personal or public life must correspond to the interests of socialist society . . . However, we must not forget that remnants of capitalism, survivals of the old, bourgeois ideology and morality are still alive in the minds of certain Soviet people, and individual traces of bourgeois ideology are still met. Private interests are opposed to public interests. There are people ensnared in the tenets of private-property psychology-self-seekers, grabbers, idlers, plunderers of state property, careerists, humbugs . . .

The main reason for the presence in people's minds of remnants of capitalism is the fact that the development of people's minds lags behind social reality. Soviet people destroyed the exploitative structure long ago, but the old concepts, ideas and habits engendered by it still litter the minds of a certain part of the working people, the peasants and the intelligentsia.

Another reason for the tenacity of the remnants of the old morality is the influence of the hostile capitalist world. The imperialists, who hate socialism, try to revive the remnants of the old and implant corrupting views and norms of bourgeois morality among unstable people.

One of the cornerstones of communist morality is the unity of principles and norms of conduct in a person's public and personal life, in political and everyday life . . .

Some leaders of the Party, Young Communist League and other organizations verbally acknowledge the inseparability of public and private life but actually evaluate the conduct of employees solely on how they behave at work, without looking into their daily life, although there may be grave reasons for doing so.

For example, there are well-known cases where an employee's drunkenness, polygamy, depravity or other amoral acts are not promptly and decisively condemned. It is also well known that Party organizations do not always properly judge a communist who displays moral instability and sometimes have a liberal attitude toward violations of socialist norms of conduct in everyday life.

Such organizations and their leaders do not understand that a person's conduct in everyday life and at work should be subordinated to unified principles, that a person's amorality and lack of discipline in everyday life inevitably will sooner or later affect his work and public activity and will lead to his political downfall.

Source: M. Zhurakov, "Communist Morality," *Pravda*, 10 April 1955. Translated in *Current Digest of the Soviet Press*, 7, no. 11 (1955): 3–4. Used by permission of East View Press.

Notes

1 Ilya Ehrenburg, *Post-War Years: 1945–1954* (Cleveland, OH: The World Publishing Company, 1967), 326–327.

2 Ludmilla Alexeyeva and Paul Goldberg, *The Thaw Generation: Coming of Age in the Post-Stalin Era* (Pittsburgh, PA: University of Pittsburgh Press, 1990), 74.
3 O. Kharkhordin, *The Collective and the Individual in Russia: A Study of Practices* (Berkeley: University of California Press, 1999), 279–280, 302–303.
4 Ehrenburg, *Post-War Years*, 300.
5 Catherine Merridale, *Night of Stone: Death and Memory in Twentieth-Century Russia* (New York: Viking, 2000), 259.
6 Mikhail Gorbachev, *Memoirs* (New York: Doubleday, 1996), 47.
7 Gorbachev, *Memoirs*, 67.
8 The entire text of the speech is available in translation at www.marxists.org/archive/khrushchev/1956/02/24.htm (accessed 7 January 2016).
9 As quoted in Nanci Adler, *Keeping Faith with the Party: Communist Believers Return from the Gulag* (Bloomington: Indiana University Press, 2012), 79.
10 As quoted in N. Dubovin, "For the Sake of a Furlough," in Nikolai K. Novak-Deker, ed., *Soviet Youth: Twelve Komsomol Histories* (Munich: Institute for the Study of the USSR, 1959), 255.
11 Gorbachev, *Memoirs*, 62.
12 Miriam Dobson, *Khrushchev's Cold Summer: Gulag Returnees, Crime, and the Fate of Reform after Stalin* (Ithaca, NY: Cornell University Press, 2009), 98.
13 As quoted in Polly Jones, "From the Secret Speech to the Burial of Stalin: Real and Ideal Responses to De-Stalinization," in Polly Jones, ed., *The Dilemmas of Destalinization* (London: Routledge, 2006), 48.
14 As quoted in Ronald Grigor Suny, *The Soviet Experiment* (Oxford: Oxford University Press, 2011), 427.
15 William Taubman, *Khrushchev: The Man and His Era* (New York: Norton, 2003), 299.
16 Adler, *Keeping Faith*, 4.
17 As quoted in Alan Barenberg, "From Prisoners to Citizens? Ex-prisoners in Vorkuta during the Thaw," in Denis Kozlov and Eleonory Gilburd, eds., *The Thaw: Soviet Society and Culture during the 1950s and 1960s* (Toronto: University of Toronto Press, 2013), 147.
18 As quoted in Orlando Figes, *The Whisperers: Private Life in Stalin's Russia* (New York: Henry Holt, 2007), 565.
19 Barenberg, "From Prisoners to Citizens?," 166.
20 As quoted in Adler, *Keeping Faith*, 65.
21 Dobson, *Khrushchev's Cold Summer*, 117–118.
22 As quoted in Dobson, *Khrushchev's Cold Summer*, 165, 168.
23 Anne E. Gorsuch, *All This Is Your World: Soviet Tourism at Home and Abroad after Stalin* (Oxford: Oxford University Press, 2011), 105.
24 Gorsuch, *All This*, 91.
25 *Courtship of Young Minds: A Case Study of the Moscow Youth Festival* (New York: East European Student and Youth Service Inc., 1959).
26 As quoted in Eleonory Gilburd, "The Revival of Soviet Internationalism," in Kozlov and Gilburd, eds., *The Thaw*, 388.
27 *Courtship of Young Minds*, 17.
28 As quoted in Roth-Ey, "Loose Girls on the Loose?: Sex, Propaganda and the 1957 Youth Festival," in Melanie Ilic, Lynne Attwood, and Susan Reid, eds., *Women in the Khrushchev Era* (Basingstoke: Palgrave Press, 2004), p. 81.
29 Lily Golden, *The Long Journey Home* (Chicago, IL: Third World Press, 2002), 63.
30 Roger E. Kanet, "African Youth: The Target of Soviet African Policy," *Russian Review*, 27, no. 2 (April 1968): 167, available at stable URL: www.jstor.org/stable/127025 (accessed 7 January 2016).
31 Maxim Matsusevich, "An Exotic Subversive: Africa, Africans and the Soviet Everyday," *Race and Class*, 49, no. 57 (2008): 69.
32 As quoted in Matusevich, "An Exotic Subversive," 71.
33 Julie Hessler, "Death of an African Student in Moscow: Race, Politics and the Cold War," *Cahiers du monde russe*, 47, no. 1 (2006): 33.
34 Ehrenburg, *Post-War Years*, 325.

35 As quoted in Deborah A. Field, *Private Life and Communist Morality in Khrushchev's Russia* (New York: Peter Lang, 2007), 44. Some of the material in the following sections appeared in this book; I thank the publisher for permission to reprint it.

36 Alexeyeva and Goldberg, *The Thaw Generation*, 73.

37 As quoted in Denis Kozlov, *Readers of Novyi Mir: Coming to Terms with the Stalinist Past* (Cambridge, MA: Harvard University Press, 2013), 59.

38 Kozlov, *Readers*, 73.

39 Alexeyeva and Goldberg, *The Thaw Generation*, 96.

40 As quoted in Kozlov, *Readers*, 195, 211.

41 Lynne Attwood, *Red Women on the Silver Screen* (London: Pandora, 1993), 74; Richard Stites, *Russian Popular Culture* (Cambridge: Cambridge University Press, 1992), 139.

42 Vladimir Bukovsky, *To Build a Castle: My Life as a Dissenter* (New York: Viking Press, 1979), 142.

43 Bukovsky, *To Build a Castle*, 147.

44 Alexeyeva and Goldberg, *The Thaw Generation*, 4.

45 Alexeyeva and Goldberg, *The Thaw Generation*, 98.

46 As quoted in Field, *Private Life*, 46.

47 S. Alyoshin, "Alone," in Hugh McLean, ed., *The Year of Protest* (New York: Vintage, 1961), 92.

48 As quoted in Field, *Private Life*, 53.

49 Larissa I. Remennick, "Patterns of Birth Control," in Igor Kon and James Riordan, eds., *Sex and Russian Society* (Bloomington: Indiana University Press, 1993), 45.

50 As quoted in Field, *Private Life*, 56.

51 Lev Shcheglov, "Medical Sexology," in Kon and Riordan, eds., *Sex and Russian Society*, 154–158.

52 Field, *Private Life*, 13.

53 Edward D. Cohn, "Sex and the Married Communist: Family Troubles, Marital Infidelity, and Party Discipline in the Postwar USSR, 1945–1964," *Russian Review*, 68 (July 2009): 430.

54 Igor S. Kon, *The Sexual Revolution in Russia* (New York: Free Press, 1995), 83.

55 As quoted in Field, *Private Life*, 18.

56 Field, *Private Life*, 19.

57 Brian Lapierre, "Making Hooliganism on a Mass Scale: The Campaign against Petty Hooliganism in the Soviet Union, 1956–1964," *Cahiers du monde russe*, 47, no. 1/2 (Jan.–Jun. 2006): 368–370.

58 As quoted in Field, *Private Life*, 32.

59 Juliane Fürst, "The Arrival of Spring? Changes and Continuities in Soviet Youth Culture and Policy between Stalin and Khrushchev," in Jones, ed., *The Dilemmas of Destalinization*, 144.

60 Fürst, "The Arrival of Spring?" 147.

61 Juliane Fürst, *Stalin's Last Generation: Soviet Post-War Youth and the Emergence of Mature Socialism* (Oxford: Oxford University Press, 2010), 225.

62 Gorsuch, *All This*, 4; Stephen V. Bittner, *The Many Lives of Khrushchev's Thaw* (Ithaca, NY: Cornell University Press, 2008), 26; Dobson, *Khrushchev's Cold Summer*, 15.

63 Alexeyeva and Goldberg, *The Thaw Generation*, 74.

10 An era of stagnation?

INTRODUCTION

The three Soviet leaders Stalin, Khrushchev, and Brezhnev are all traveling in the same train compartment. All of a sudden, the train lurches to a halt. Stalin leans out of the window and shouts "Shoot the driver." The train doesn't move; then Khrushchev says, "Rehabilitate the driver," but the train still doesn't move. So Brezhnev says, "I know, let's pull the compartment curtains closed, rock back and forth, and pretend we're moving." This well-known joke illustrates a common perception of Leonid Brezhnev, who became the first secretary of the Communist Party of the USSR in 1964 and retained his power until he died in 1982. This period was deemed an "era of stagnation," but only after it was over. Mikhail Gorbachev and other reformers, along with Western observers, described the Soviet Union of this time as complacent, corrupt, and, as the joke indicates, both dishonest and immobile. They emphasized the tenacity of bureaucrats who held on to their positions for decades, the slowdown of the economy, and the curbing of cultural expression (the "frost" described by Alexeyeva in the quotation that ended the previous chapter).

The notion of "stagnation" also includes a negative moral and aesthetic assessment, a sense that late socialism was both repressive and drab. In the United States, this image was publicized in part by Yakov Smirnoff, a comedian from Odessa who immigrated to America in the late 1970s and is best known for inventing the "Russian reversal." The Russian reversal is a play on words that contrasts life in Soviet Russia and the United States by reversing subject and object; for example in a beer commercial that aired on US television, Smirnoff proclaimed in heavily accented English: "In America, you can always find a party. In Russia, Party always finds you." Smirnoff's popularity has waned since its high point in the 1980s, but the Russian reversal enjoys a vibrant second act as an internet meme, and it has shaped an image of late Soviet life as harsh and impoverished, especially among Americans too young to remember the Cold War.

CHAPTER QUESTIONS

Over the past ten years, scholars have begun to challenge the notion of stagnation. They point out that the Soviet Union's disintegration, less than a decade after Brezhnev's death, suggests that important changes were taking place despite the impression of immutability. Furthermore, the difficulties of post-Soviet life have engendered nostalgia for late socialism. In fact, polls conducted in the late 1990s and early 2000s revealed that many Russians remembered this era fondly, rating it as the most positive in the twentieth century.[1] In this chapter, we consider the question of whether the Brezhnev period was an "era of stagnation." What aspects of life stayed the same and what changed? Were people disillusioned with their society or by and large content?

VOICES, MEMORIES, CONTESTED PERSPECTIVES

The politics of stability and the problem of foreign policy

Khrushchev was removed from office in October 1964. He was granted a pension and the right to his country house outside of Moscow. He spent the rest of his life puttering in his garden and dictating his memoirs and died of a heart attack in 1971. Newspaper accounts explained that he had resigned because of ill health and advanced age, but subsequent editorials in *Pravda* hinted at the real reasons for his ouster by condemning such Khrushchevian phenomena as harebrained schemes, bossiness, bragging, and half-baked conclusions. Khrushchev had not succeeded in fulfilling his promises of huge economic growth, and the various agricultural reforms he instituted met with mixed results. Peaceful coexistence with the US suffered major setbacks, most terrifyingly during the Cuban missile crisis of 1962, when the Soviet government's attempt to install missiles in Cuba almost precipitated a nuclear war between the US and USSR. Finally, Khrushchev had reorganized the party and state apparatus, which threatened the careers and comfort of the party elite. When he assumed power, Brezhnev brought an end to this, saying: "Under Stalin people were afraid of repression, under Khrushchev of reorganizations and rearrangements ... Soviet people should receive a peaceful life so that they can work normally."[2]

Brezhnev's slogan was "Trust in Cadres," which meant that the people who held positions in the party, government, and management got to keep them. In contrast to earlier eras, the Central Committee of the Communist Party and the Politburo showed very little turnover, which meant that by the early 1980s the average age of Poliburo members was over 70.[3] Brezhnev himself steadily gained power over the course of the 1960s. After Khrushchev's ouster, authority was shared among Brezhnev, Nikolai Podgornyi, who became head of state (Chairman of the Supreme Soviet), and Alexei Kosygin, who was prime minister (Chairman of the Presidium of the Council of Ministers), but Brezhnev gradually used his position as Communist Party leader to assume prominence. As he aged, he attempted to institute a personality cult, which never gained the popularity of the Stalin cult (described in chapter 5). Brezhnev's self-aggrandizing predilection, manifested in the many honors, prizes, and medals he awarded himself, became the subject of numerous jokes. One, for example, asked: Did you hear about the crocodile that ate Brezhnev? Yes, the poor thing has been pooping out medals for weeks.

During this period, the Communist Party shifted expectations about the future. Theorists no longer wrote about the imminence of communism; instead they acknowledged that the utopian vision formulated in the 1920s and partially revived during the Thaw would occur far in the distant future, so that the withering away of the state was still a long way off. Contemporary society was in a newly conceived historical stage called "Developed Socialism," a long epoch during which science and technology would be used to perfect socialism.[4]

Scholars have debated whether or not Brezhnev fully deserves his reputation for dimwitted conservatism but, regardless of his efforts to ensure stability at home, the continuation of the Cold War meant that international relations remained volatile. Considering foreign policy thus complicates our understanding of "stagnation." Brezhnev's first major foreign policy crisis occurred in 1968, during the "Prague Spring," when the government of Czechoslovakia began a series of radical reforms aimed at establishing a more open and democratic form of socialism. The Soviet Union regarded the possibility of open elections and the lifting of press censorship (and subsequent public criticism of Soviet power) as a danger for all socialist nations and launched a military invasion that forced the reform Czech government out of power. Some Soviet intellectuals reacted with despair to what they saw as despotism; some became dissidents (see below). But from the Soviet government's point of view, it was vital to maintain control over the countries of central Europe that made up the Warsaw Pact. Brezhnev issued a statement that came to be known as the Brezhnev doctrine: The Soviet Union had the obligation to intervene wherever socialism was threatened. The Brezhnev doctrine mirrored the Truman doctrine, and in many ways Soviet and American leaders held identical assumptions. The Americans subscribed to a domino theory, which motivated US involvement in Vietnam by positing that Asian countries were like dominos lined up; if one fell to the communists, it would push the rest of them down. Soviet leaders saw a similar danger in Eastern Europe.[5] For both Cold War rivals, military actions abroad seemed necessary for maintaining domestic strength and protecting the Soviet (or American) way of life; the politics of stability required foreign intervention.

Brezhnev proved his toughness to the other Soviet leaders by suppressing the Prague Spring, and this allowed him sufficient credibility to seek better relations with the United States. Throughout the 1970s, the Soviet Union and the United States pursued a policy of reduced tension, called détente, which involved limiting the proliferation of nuclear weapons, increasing trade, and, as part of an international agreement called the Helsinki Final Act of 1975, agreeing to protect basic human rights. Détente produced a precarious peace that was rendered vulnerable by the increased presence of both superpowers in the developing world. As we saw in previous chapters, the Cold War coincided with the destruction of the great European overseas empires, and both the Soviet Union and the United States deployed various methods to gain the alliance of newly independent countries in Asia and Africa. Soviet involvement and influence in the developing world reached its apex in the 1970s , with pro-Soviet governments taking power in Southeast Asia, the Middle East, and Latin America (specifically in Vietnam, Laos, Cambodia , Afghanistan, South Yemen, Angola, Ethiopia, Nicaragua, Grenada).[6] As in the Khrushchev period, the Soviet Union provided aid to countries around the world, but in the 1970s the emphasis shifted from providing economic loans and initiating construction projects to supplying military aid and weapons.

For some anticolonial leaders, the Soviet Union was both a model of successful modernization and an alternative to the capitalist exploitation and racism of the West. Alex La Guma, a South African antiapartheid activist, saw the Soviet Union as a successful example of how to unify a multinational, multiracial country and establish policies to allow "once backward peoples to catch up quickly with the advanced."[7] For Ali Sultan Issa, of Zanzibar, socialism represented a method of development, a way to create modern, disciplined citizens: "I wanted to instill socialist morality in Zanzibar and to fight against the corruption bred by capitalism . . . I wanted to build factories and heavy industry not only to produce tractors and guns but also because an individual cannot remain lazy if he is working on an assembly line."[8]

The interplay between independence struggles and Cold War rivalry resulted in tumult in Africa, Asia, and Latin America. Lily Golden, discussed in the previous two chapters, found her life changed by these events. After finishing college, she worked at Moscow's Institute of African Studies, where she met a student from Zanzibar named Abdulla Kassim Hanga. During their first meeting, Lily Golden was impressed by his dedication to the independence struggle, determination, intelligence, and good looks. Toward the end of their conversation he announced, "I am the general secretary of the Afro-Shirazi Party. Our revolutionary council has decided that, when we win independence, I will be president of Zanzibar." This assertion amused Golden, since many of the African students she knew proclaimed their presidential destinies, but she was startled when he added that the council had also proposed that he marry her.[9] Although she was skeptical at first, eventually Abdulla Hanga won her over, they married, and then he returned to Zanzibar to foment revolution while she stayed in Moscow to pursue her studies in African music and give birth to their daughter. In 1964, much to Golden's pride and astonishment, Hanga was successful and became prime minister of Zanzibar; later that year Tanganyika and Zanzibar merged to form the new nation of Tanzania, and Hanga led an official delegation to Moscow, where the couple reunited. But Golden began to wonder if her husband's policy ideas, such as nationalizing all business, were too radical, even as his gender standards became increasingly conservative. He began to demand that she change her behavior to conform to his idea of a Muslim leader's wife and she was no longer allowed to sit at the table with male guests or to leave the house without permission. Eventually, Hanga went back to Tanzania and a long, frightening silence ensued. Golden eventually found out in the 1970s that her husband had been assassinated.[10]

Lily Golden's account illustrates the revolutionary dreams of independence leaders as well as some of the dangers they faced: Radical economic transformation sparked controversy; socialist and religious ideals clashed; and violence and even civil war erupted.[11] All of these problems were present in Afghanistan, with devastating consequences. When the communist People's Democratic Party of Afghanistan launched a successful coup in 1978, it came as a surprise to the Soviet government, which had serious reservations about the party leadership. The PDPA was split into two irreconcilable factions and didn't have strong support in many parts of the country, where people were alienated by its program of radical reform.[12] During a secret meeting between the new prime minister of Afghanistan, Nur Mohammad Taraki, and the top Soviet leaders, Kosygin drew an analogy with the United States' struggle in Vietnam and warned Taraki that he needed to develop the loyalty of his own people and not rely solely on Soviet aid to prop up his government. With the example of Vietnam before them, many of the Soviet leaders opposed committing troops to Afghanistan in order to support an increasingly unpopular government.[13]

Yet, the following year the Soviet Union ended up invading Afghanistan despite these apprehensions. Taraki's main ally, an admirer of Stalin named Hafizullah Amin, had turned on Taraki, arrested him, and then had him strangled in his prison cell. The Soviet leadership was horrified and began to debate how they should react. Yuri Andropov, head of the KGB, Minister of Foreign Affairs Andrei Gromyko, and

Minister of Defense Dmitry Ustinov all pushed for an invasion. They feared the growing strength of militant Islam both within Afghanistan and among its neighbors (especially Iran) and worried that it might influence Central Asian Muslims within the Soviet Union. Furthermore, the KGB believed that Amin was secretly seeking support from the United States (a report that turned out to be based on dubious evidence). The Soviet Union's top military leaders argued against direct intervention, pointing out that an invasion would worsen relationships with Islamic countries and threaten détente, and that fighting on difficult terrain would endanger Soviet soldiers. They were overruled and the Soviet Union attacked Afghanistan in order to oust Amin, replace him with a more amenable leader, and stabilize the government.[14] A Russian who worked in Afghanistan in the 1980s asserted in an oral history interview that the invasion was "far more legal than America's going into Iraq. America felt it had to, so it invaded, although there was absolutely no grounds for doing so . . . But in Afghanistan, they overthrew the ruler. We invaded on legal grounds, yet then got drawn in deeper for nothing."[15]

Soviet success in Afghanistan proved elusive. Radical Islamists, calling themselves Mujahedin, or holy warriors, used guerilla tactics to resist the Soviet army. President of the United States Jimmy Carter interpreted the invasion as evidence of a Soviet plan to expand control to the Persian Gulf region and threaten American access to oil. Under his leadership, the CIA supplied weapons and communications equipment to the Mujahedin. The resulting war lasted almost ten years and led to the deaths of fifteen thousand Soviet soldiers and many more Afghanis (estimates of casualties range from 876,825 to 1.71 million).[16] In the view of many scholars, the war in Afghanistan undermined confidence in the Soviet government and military, strained resources, and thus ultimately contributed to the collapse of the Soviet Union.[17] Citizens who initially supported the war gradually became disillusioned and those who served in the war grew alienated from civilian life (see document 10.1) After the Soviet Union withdrew in 1989, civil war ravaged Afghanistan until 1996, when a radical fundamentalist Muslim party called the Taliban eventually emerged to claim victory and establish the militant Islamic Emirate of Afghanistan.

In the post-Soviet years, many Russians mourned and resented their country's loss of superpower status, but it is worth questioning the relationship between international hegemony and domestic stability. During the Cold War, both the United States and the Soviet Union sought influence in areas around the world that they saw as vital to their national interests. Did the pursuit of that influence result in security and stability? For how long and for whom?

Economic slowdown

The Soviet economy grew rapidly in the postwar years, but then began to slow down in the early to mid-1970s; this is one of the main reasons why this period is characterized as stagnant. In previous decades, rapid economic growth had resulted from exploiting natural resources in new ways and moving workers out of agriculture and into more productive forms of labor through industrialization. By the late 1960s, the Soviet Union had succeeded in becoming an industrial power and was running out of new resources to mobilize. The government began to shift spending to defense and agriculture, two areas which did not yield as much profit as heavy industry. Demographic changes meant that the labor force wasn't growing as fast as it had previously.

Furthermore, the increased complexity of the economy exacerbated problems with central planning, especially in the areas of prices and incentives. Prices were set by economic planners and were problematic because they did not reflect demand or production cost. There was no incentive for a plant or factory to produce more than required by the quota set by the economic plan; if they did so, they would just get a higher target set in the future. If the enterprise was not profitable, it would still be subsidized and workers would keep their jobs. Economic planners proposed a series of reforms aimed at ameliorating these problems, but these were never fully implemented and were gradually abandoned by the end of the 1960s.[18]

While economic growth was decelerating, people's aspirations for consumer goods rose and living standards continued to improve. As a result of Khrushchev's housing program, more and more Soviet citizens moved out of communal apartments and into their own places, and they started to buy appliances to fill them: televisions, washing machines, radios, tape recorders. The percentage of households owning such items rose throughout the Brezhnev period. In 1966, 11 percent of households owned a refrigerator; this had risen to 85 percent in 1980. Diets improved as well, shifting from the heavy reliance on grain and potatoes to increasing proportions of fish, meat, vegetables, and fruits.[19] But while the supply of consumer goods grew, it never met demand; nor were commodities equally accessible, especially outside of the capital cities of Moscow and Leningrad. Residents of Saratov, about 450 miles southwest of Moscow, recalled going to Moscow to shop: "We'd go to Moscow for meat, sausages, delicacies, smoked fish, and for clothing, of course, and shoes and everything;" so many people made the journey that they referred to "so called sausage trains to Moscow."[20]

The sausage trains provide an example of how people formulated strategies to deal with scarcity. In a much-cited article, James R. Millar discussed such adaptions and drew a contrast between this microlevel creativity and macrolevel economic immobility. He posited a "Little Deal," between government and people, similar to the "Big Deal" described by Vera Dunham and discussed in chapter 8. In return for political acquiescence, the government tolerated private economic transactions.[21] Some of these activities were in fact lawful, notably the sale of food at kolkhoz markets. The government did not control prices there most of the time, and the markets remained an important source of food for the population throughout the Soviet era.[22] Other forms of private enterprise were illegal, such as participating in the "black market" of forbidden items or speculation, defined as the purchase and resale of goods at a profit.[23] Many other economic transactions fell into a more ambiguous category. Small-scale, privately run businesses, including automobile and appliance repair, house-cleaning, hair cutting, and tutoring services, were permitted, but they often relied on the illegal use of state resources such as tools and other supplies taken from work. Millar describes, for example, the chauffeurs of Soviet officials moonlighting as taxi services by making use of state-owned cars and gasoline.

Perhaps the most common private economic transactions were those conducted through reciprocal personal networks, or *blat* in Russian. Economist Alena Ledeneva defines *blat* as a nonmonetary system of exchange among a circle of people with personal ties: family, friends, and acquaintances. The object of exchange was not necessarily things, but access to state resources.[24] *Blat* was present throughout the Soviet epoch, but became particularly ubiquitous during the Brezhnev era. People used it for a number of purposes. For some, it was a way to acquire goods. As one of

Ledeneva's informants explained: "If you had an acquaintance working in a shop, you were able to buy products in short supply. You paid the same price, but an acquaintance meant that you knew when to come, could buy more, or even jump the queue."[25] People also used *blat* to improve upon the basic medical care, housing, and education guaranteed by the state. *Blat* helped people to get rare medicines or appointments with specialists, to find apartments in good locations or receive permits for building garages or dachas (summer cottages), or to ensure their children's entrance into specialized high schools and universities. *Blat* was also important for fun. It was needed, according to one informant, to obtain a "ticket to interesting events or slots in tourists groups to popular places. All of this was mostly done through unofficial ties. Without them, there's little you'd be able to do."[26]

Many scholars group *blat,* semi-legal, and illegal black market activities together under the rubric of a "second" or "parallel" economy. Millar rejects this terminology because he sees these transactions not as separate but as fundamental to the overall operation of the Soviet system. Ledeneva concurs, arguing that *blat* allowed the Soviet economy to function, but ultimately subverted it. However, she criticizes Millar's notion of a "Little Deal" between government and people because such a metaphor implies that both sides in some way accepted *blat*, albeit tacitly. She asserts that in fact neither the state nor people approved of *blat*. The government either ignored it or condemned it, explaining it as the result not of systemic economic problems but of the greed of selfish, anti-Soviet individuals. People resented *blat* because it was a result of inequitable access to privilege. As one informant recalled in an oral history interview: "There was inequality associated with *blat, blat* and more *blat*, the need to acquire things through *blat*, to get in somewhere, to go somewhere, to eat somewhere. It was repugnant."[27] But, according to Ledeneva, while people criticized others' use of *blat*, they often "misrecognized" it in their own lives, perceiving the favors they traded as an outgrowth of friendship and expression of their warmth, helpfulness, unselfishness. One of her subjects, a physician explained:

> There was a number of families where everything was solved through me. Not only health problems but everything—quarrels with husbands, troubles with daughters. I had to help with everything: tickets to Yalta, booking places in health resorts. My dedication was strong, and of course those people sought to express gratitude. They treasured me. The word blat in this case I wouldn't apply.[28]

People who were successful in using *blat* to improve their lives, the so-called *blatniki*, had to have good people skills and a lot of energy; thus it is not surprising that at the end of the 1980s they became the earliest entrepreneurs.[29] The creativity, adaptability, and activity of *blatniki* suggest that assessments about the nature of economic stagnation depend on whether we look at aggregate trends or zoom in on individuals. As Millar pointed out: "Ironically, the Little Deal afforded the individual increased freedom to wheel and deal at the microlevel of Soviet society, while at the macrolevel managerial discretion was restrained, overt political dissent was persecuted and generally repressed and a gray, conservative pallor overspread the regime."[30] According to Millar, the Soviet leaders made a conscious decision that maintaining political and social stability required forgoing the large-scale reforms that would render private economic transactions unnecessary. In the next chapter of this book, we will consider whether they miscalculated.

Dissent and repression

The political dissent that Millar mentions in the quotation above became the life's work of Ludmilla Alexeyeva. In 1965, two of Alexeyeva's friends, Yuli Daniel and Andrei Sinyavsky, were arrested for publishing materials in the West that were critical of the Soviet Union. They were charged under Article 70 of the Criminal Code of the Russian Republic, which prohibited anti-Soviet propaganda, and were sentenced to prison. For Alexeyeva, this was the "beginning of the twenty year war waged by the Brezhnev government against the intelligentsia."[31] She and her circle of friends participated in a demonstration to protest the decision and then began to gather food, money, and clothing for their imprisoned friends. Soon Alexeyeva's group had formed what they called the "Red Cross" to send parcels to other political prisoners and provide support for their families, and this charitable effort evolved into a human rights organization aimed in part at instituting *glasnost*. Glasnost, Alexeyeva explained "was an ordinary, hardworking, nondescript word that was used to refer to a process, any process of justice or governance being conducted in the open."[32] She and other dissidents sought to compel the Soviet government to adhere to its own constitution and later the international human rights standards the Soviet government had agreed to under the Helsinki Final Act of 1975, mentioned above. They wrote letters and signed petitions objecting to the arrest and trial of critics of the Soviet system, and they produced and distributed samizdat.

Several internationally famous figures became dissidents, notably Andrei Sakharov, a physicist who helped build the Soviet atomic bomb, and the writer Alexander Solzhenitsyn, and this raised the public profile of the movement. Foreign reporters played an important role in publicizing dissident activism and, in doing so, helped pressure the Soviet government to improve the treatment of political prisoners. Journalists also provided jobs and material support for dissidents. In addition, the Voice of America, Radio Liberty, the BBC, and other Western radio stations broadcast information about political trials and dissident activity back into the Soviet Union, which helped keep Soviet citizens informed.

In 1968, Alexeyeva began work on a samizdat journal called the *Chronicle of Current Events*, which described human rights abuses throughout the Soviet Union. She and her Moscow colleagues made contact with a wide variety of protesters: Baltic and Ukrainian activists seeking greater cultural and political autonomy; Crimean Tatars, who had been dispossessed by Stalin during the World War II and sought restitution of their homeland; persecuted religious minorities such as Pentecostals, Baptists, and Seventh Day Adventists; and Jews who had been refused permission to emigrate to Israel but were punished for the attempt (the so-called refuseniks). As this diversity makes clear, Soviet dissidents never formed a unified movement and their analyses, goals, and priorities diverged radically. While liberals like Alexeyeva fought for the rule of law, conservatives, most notably Solzhenitsyn, rejected not just Marxism but all Western values and ideologies; Solzhenitsyn sought a return to what he saw as pure Russian values, and this nationalist and anti-Western stance has proved influential in post-Soviet years.[33]

Dissidents valued friendship and altruism. According to one scholar, their activism was a form of spiritual purification, a way to cleanse themselves from what they saw as the hypocrisy of a system which professed humane values but was built on violence.[34] Alexeyeva certainly made sacrifices for her convictions. She was expelled from the

Communist Party, fired from her job, and struggled to make ends meet, subsisting on freelance editing, typing, and ghostwriting jobs. She was called into the KGB office for interrogations so many times that she developed a routine. She would bring a particularly delicious lunch and during the interrogation she would eat it slowly, saving the pastry for last. "I have no doubt that by the time I got to the éclair, the interrogator had to strain to control his salivary glands. That, of course, put me in the position of strength. There was also the matter of the bathroom; the good Lord had given me a remarkably strong bladder, thereby undermining my interrogator's gambit of restricting my access to the toilet."[35]

This description suggests that the Soviet secret police had mellowed since Stalinist times, as pastry could be used as an effective weapon of resistance. Nonetheless, despite the bravado of Alexeyeva's account, the Soviet government undertook harsh measures to silence the dissidents and by the early 1980s many of them had been exiled, imprisoned, or committed to mental hospitals under vague and bogus diagnoses. The mental illness of one was described as "nervous exhaustion brought on by her search for justice." Another suffered from "delusional ideas of reformism and struggle with the existing social political system in the USSR;" still another was diagnosed with a "mania for reconstructing society."[36]

Some of Alexeyeva's former friends might have agreed with such characterizations, for they found her activism a little crazy and they severed their relationship with her. Others negotiated awkward compromises. For example, one woman helped Alexeyeva to find jobs but had difficulty maintaining a friendship. In Alexeyeva's analysis: "She and her husband were on the way up; I was on the way out. Without actually saying it, she made it clear that she didn't want me to talk to her about my other friends, political trials, and political prisoners. Her views weren't different from mine. She just couldn't afford to act on them."[37]

Many Soviet citizens were uneasy with the dissidents and saw them, in the words of one scholar, as "irrelevant or potentially dangerous."[38] Others were convinced by government accusations that dissidents were motivated by greed for the attention, favors, and material goods they received from Western journalists, so that despite their pretense of moral purity they were simply engaged in obtaining an exotic variety of *blat*.[39] Still others expressed a sense that the dissidents were a courageous but tiny minority. According to one Muscovite: "Only a very small number of people got involved. I believe they're heroes. They challenged the system. My acquaintances and I supported them, but we ourselves did not take part in demonstrations."[40]

Dissidents led lives replete with danger, sacrifice, and meaning, and they formulated new ideas about politics, society, history, and literature. Does the existence of their movement contradict the notion that they were living during an "era of stagnation"? Or does the fact that they were a tiny, isolated, and ultimately repressed minority render them irrelevant?

Social change and women's dilemmas

While scholars offer differing assessments of the dissident movement and debate the extent to which the politics and economics of the Brezhnev period stagnated, they agree that modernization brought profound social change. By the 1960s, the Soviet Union was no longer the largely peasant country described in the first half of this volume, for it had been transformed into an industrialized, predominantly urban nation. As in other countries, these large-scale changes resulted in shifting ideas about marriage and divorce. Marriage was no longer primarily an economic institution; instead its purpose was companionship and emotional fulfillment. If the point of marriage was happiness, unhappy spouses no longer felt compelled to stay married. It is not surprising, therefore, that, starting in the 1950s when judges became more lenient about granting divorce, the divorce rate rose dramatically. By the 1970s, there was one divorce for every three marriages, on average. The divorce rate was similar in the United States during this period, although the US divorce rate grew even more rapidly until it peaked in 1980.[41] The most common reasons given in court for divorce were incompatibility, adultery, and, at the top of the list, husbands' drunkenness; Soviet sociological studies from the 1970s and 1980s indicate that alcoholism was becoming a major problem.[42]

Figure 10.1 A 1972 poster that reads: Make sure that serious boozers can't get to your construction site!
© Heritage Image Partnership Ltd/Alamy.

What is the message and purpose of this poster?

Another source of marital tension was women's double shift, that is their responsibility for both work and household. Most Soviet women had jobs, but they made less money than men because they held lower-ranked positions or worked in professions that were both feminized and low paid, which in the Soviet Union included not only teaching but also medicine. At the same time, much sociological data compiled in the 1960s and 1970s showed that women spent two to three times more time doing housework than men did.[43] Soviet journalists and sociologists started to recognize this as a problem in the 1950s, and in the 1960s several popular works of fiction illuminated the dilemmas of women's everyday lives. The most famous example was Natalya Baranskaya's novella entitled *A Week Like Any Other*, which appeared in the journal *Novyi mir* in 1969 and garnered much attention. It describes the quotidian details in the life of Olga, a harried scientific researcher and mother who rushes around going to work, standing in long lines for food, cooking, cleaning, doing laundry, getting her children to bed. Her boss lectures her for tardiness; she worries about missing too much work to take care of her sick children; her husband resents having to pick up the children at daycare; and she is constantly exhausted. Demographers distribute a time-management questionnaire to the women in her laboratory asking how many hours they spend on various activities, but she is too busy and exhausted to fill it out.

One result of this "double burden" was the increased divorce rate and another was the declining birthrate. In urban areas, most women had only one or two children and the birthrates in most parts of the Soviet Union started to sink. Although contraception was not widely available, urban women married later than rural ones and relied on abortions to limit family size. By contrast, in Central Asia (the Kazakh, Uzbek, Kyrgyz, and Tajik republics), birthrates were much higher because many families there lived more traditional lifestyles and valued large families. These demographic trends raised much concern for Soviet leaders for a variety of reasons. They worried about future labor shortages and there was also a sense of unease among some leaders of European descent that they could find themselves in the minority one day. They were also concerned about the potential conflict between a growing Islamic population and the atheism of the Soviet government. Consequently, starting in the 1970s, Soviet officials began campaigns to encourage urban, educated women to stay home and have more babies; these met with little success. In Baranskaya's novella, Olga's colleagues discuss the time-management questionnaire and one of them explains: "What they really want to know is why women don't want to have babies."[44] A spirited debate ensues among the women in the laboratory about whether childbirth is a social obligation or personal choice and why it is so difficult for working women to raise children. In some ways the Soviet discussions resemble the current American preoccupation with whether women can "have it all" by achieving professional success and happy family lives, or whether they should "drop out" and devote themselves to raising families. And, as in the case of the United States of our own time, most women wanted or needed to work, and also wanted families, and struggled to satisfy both sets of demands. One Russian woman explained that "although I think women obtain fulfillment from their family, their children, and their husbands, work also means a lot to them. I'm always trying to find some balance between the two. It's really hard." Another concurred: "I enjoy being a woman, but have always had it harder than men, be they in Russia or America. There's work, the home, the need to at least try to look nice."[45] Olga, the heroine of *A Week Like Any Other*, argues against her husband's suggestion that she quit her job (see document 10.2).

Leisure and the politics of rock 'n' roll

In addition to altering family life, modernization brought other changes to the every-day life of Soviet citizens, including new opportunities for fun. After Khrushchev's ouster, the Soviet government retreated from the collectivist, self-sacrificing ideals of communist morality and instead began to promote, in the words of one scholar, "individuality, self-reliance, and privatism." The government encouraged the development of both educational hobbies and consumerism, and this became an era of serious amateurs.[46] People practiced yoga, participated in community theater, built shortwave radios, watched their favorite football (soccer) team at the stadium and on TV, and, especially if they were young, listened to rock 'n' roll music.

For Soviet rock 'n' roll fans, it all began with the Beatles. In one exuberant recollection:

> A friend came to me and asked if I'd heard about the new sensation, The Beatles, and put on a tape recorded from a BBC broadcast. It was something heavenly. I felt blissful and invincible. All the depression and fear ingrained over the years disappeared. I understood that everything other than The Beatles had been oppression.[47]

Young fans got access to rock 'n' roll music in a variety of ways. The same Western radio stations that broadcast information about dissident activities to the Soviet Union also played jazz and then rock music as part of their Cold War efforts to influence public opinion in the communist world. As with jazz in the 1940s, rock 'n' roll fans made illegal recordings on used x-ray plates, but in the late 1950s several new technologies made it easier for people to acquire recordings. Small cassette tape recorders became increasingly available and the government also opened up what were called music studios or salons, where people could record holiday messages or other greetings with songs in the background, or just make copies of popular songs onto small records.[48] There was also an active black market trade in records and cassettes, as exemplified in the career of one young fan turned mogul. Arnold (nee Aron) Gurevich began his career by recording a copy of the Beatles' 1964 album *A Hard Day's Night* from some family friends. Then he started traveling from his native Ukrainian city of Dnepropetrovsk to Moscow, where he forged connections with the important black marketers who provided him with more records to copy and sell. He ended up providing rock music to the children of all the most important people in his home town (party and government officials, KGB officers, industrial managers) and, by maintaining good relations with this elite, ensured his personal safety. He made enough money to expand operations to other towns, hire several employees, pay bribes to the local police and government officials so that they would ignore his business, and still enjoy considerable profit.[49] In many ways Gurevich personifies the innovative, if illegal, entrepreneurship that Millar described and that complicates notions of economic stagnation.

Party and Komsomol officials disapproved of rock 'n' roll and criticized its bourgeois character and the hyper-sexuality and violence of the lyrics. But as its popularity grew, the government made accommodations. Professional Soviet pop bands, called Vocal Instrumental Ensembles (VIAs for short), were formed and produced cheerful, safe, melodic songs as an alternative to the rougher-edged music of British and American bands. In the mid-1970s, the state-owned record label Melodiia released several compilations of Western rock 'n' roll, although it neglected to get permission from the companies who held the rights to the songs. Rather than listing the names of the bands or songwriters, songs were given innocuous titles such as "folk song" or "English people's song" or "protest song."[50]

Some scholars, journalists, and memoirists emphasize the political significance of rock 'n' roll. They argue that it provided young fans with a vision of the freedom and glamor of the West that made their own everyday reality seem dull and oppressive; their resulting disillusionment with communism helped hasten the demise of the Soviet Union. One memoirist wrote that "when you multiplied the Beatles youthful vitality by the forbidden-fruit factor, it was more than a breath of fresh air—it was a hurricane, a release, the true voice of freedom. We paraphrased Mayakovsky's line, 'I'd learn Russian just because it was spoken by Lenin,' to read: 'I'd learn English just because it was spoken by Lennon.'"[51] In the late 1960s, amateur and unofficial Russian rock musicians began to write songs in Russian, which some scholars see as another form of countercultural opposition to the Soviet system. The first band to do so, Time Machine, was criticized for being decadent and pessimistic (see document 10.3).

Other scholars disagree with the notion that playing and listening to rock music was a form of political rebellion. Alexei Yurchak described how Komsomol leaders helped organize music festivals and performances and argues that they integrated their love of rock 'n' roll music with their own version of communist values. He also pointed out the ways in which Soviet policies inadvertently created conditions favorable to rock music. The increased production of radios and tape recordings allowed people to make and distribute music, and the government promoted certain values that were conducive to this kind of creative production: "creativity, internationalism, cultural erudition, science, and technology."[52] In fact, rock 'n' roll music seems to have had a very diverse set of effects. One scholar describes how some of the rock fans of Dnepropetrovsk became increasingly estranged from Ukrainian language and identity because Soviet rock music was almost always sung in Russian; rock 'n' roll thus aided Russification. But in other cases, rock 'n' roll led to religion. Some fans were inspired by George Harrison of the Beatles to study Hinduism, Krishnaism, and Buddhism. Others were influenced by the rock opera *Jesus Christ Superstar* to try to learn more about Christianity. A fifteen year old described in his diary how he and his friends translated the lyrics into Russian to understand the story of the opera and tried to research Jesus Christ. And then one day they made a great discovery: "My neighbor, Vasia, brought an Old Russian Bible he found in his grandmother's room and we read the Gospels and compared them to the opera lyrics."[53]

CONCLUSION AND FURTHER QUESTIONS

In this chapter, we have described politics, economics, dissidence, social change, and popular culture. The evidence presented in this chapter and the primary source documents should enable you to consider which aspects of life during this period were stable, and which were changing. Is the notion of stagnation useful in understanding this era? Why or why not?

Pondering the question of whether this was an era of pessimism or contentment demonstrates the slipperiness of the past and how the present inevitably influences our understanding of it. An influential scholarly article published in 1980 traced the sources of what the author saw as a growing pessimism of the Soviet middle class: perceptions of economic decline, the government's failure to meet rising expectations for consumer goods, unfavorable comparisons with living standards in the "near abroad" of Eastern Europe.[54] However, studying intangibles such as moods and emotions is very challenging for historians because we cannot know how people felt; we can only know how they expressed how they felt, and this tends to change over time and be based in part on unspoken comparisons with past and future. The pessimism described in 1980 was in contrast to the greater optimism of the Thaw era, during which living standards were lower but there was more widespread hope and confidence for future improvement. But in the late twentieth and early twenty-first century, when the collapse of the Soviet Union brought rapid change and a great deal of uncertainty to people's lives, they grew nostalgic for the stability and more leisurely pace of the Brezhnev period and remembered the happiness and ease of the time.

In evaluating the "era of stagnation," this chapter also gives you an opportunity to reflect on the multiple meanings of freedom. Soviet citizens did not possess freedom of speech or assembly. But unless they were dissidents, they were free from fear of unemployment and homelessness and they were free to explore their interests and pursue pleasure. As one man later recalled, people "had a stable, normal life. Everyone did his own thing. There were no illusions, no changes. We lived, we worked, we rested, we read, we went to the movies. Our life didn't change, but it was predictable, it was stable, and there was no fear."[55] The next chapter will explore when and why this was no longer enough.

PRIMARY SOURCES

Use the questions to analyze the content, context, and significance of each primary source. Then synthesize the primary sources and the material in the chapter to formulate a response to the primary chapter question: Was the Brezhnev period really an "era of stagnation"?

Document 10.1   A nurse's reflection on her tour in Afghanistan

Questions for analysis

1   What were the nurse's original expectations about the war in Afghanistan?
2   Why and how did she change her mind?
3   Why does she say the impact of the war was worse for men than for women? What are her assumptions about gender roles?

We were told that this was a just war, that we were helping the Afghan people to put an end to feudalism and build a wonderful socialist society. There was a conspiracy of silence about our causalities . . .

    . . .

Gradually we began to ask ourselves what we were all here for. Such questions were unpopular with authorities, of course. There were no slippers or pajamas, but plenty of banners and posters with political slogans, all brought from back home. Behind the slogans were our boys' skinny, miserable faces. I'll never forget them . . .

Twice a week we attended a political "seminar" where we were continually told that we were doing our sacred duty to help make the border totally secure. The nastiest thing about army life was the informing: our boss actually ordered us to inform. Every detail, about every sick and wounded patient, had to be reported . . . it was called "knowing the mood." The army must keep healthy and we must banish pity from our minds. But we didn't, it was only pity which kept the whole show going.

We went to save lives, to help, to show our love, but after a while I realized that it was hatred I was feeling. Hate for that soft light sand which burnt like fire, hate for the village huts from which we might be fired on at any moment. I hated the locals, walking with their baskets of melons or just standing by their doors. What had they been doing the night before? They killed one young officer I knew from hospital, carved up two tents full of soldiers and poisoned the water supply. One guy picked up a smart cigarette-lighter and it exploded in his hands.

    . . .

After all that—well, I saw my own country with different eyes. Coming home was terribly difficult and very strange. I felt I'd had my skin ripped off. I couldn't stop crying, I could bear to be only with people who'd been there themselves. I spent my days—and nights—with them. Talking to anybody else seemed a futile waste of time. That phase lasted six months. Now I have rows in the meat queue like everybody else.

You try and live a normal life, the way you lived before. But you can't. I didn't give a damn about myself or life in general. I just felt my life was over. And this whole process was much worse for the men. A woman can forget herself in her child—the men had nothing to lose themselves in. They came home, fell in love, had kids—but none of it really helped, Afghanistan was more important than anything else. I too wish I could understand what it was all about, and what it was all for. Over there we had to force such questions back inside us, but at home they just come out and have to be answered.

Source: Svetlana Alexievich, *Zinky Boys: Soviet Voices from the Afghanistan War* (New York and London: W. W. Norton, 1990), 22–23, 26. Introduction by Larry Heinemann, translated by Julia and Robin Whitby. Copyright © 1990 by Svetlana Alexievich. Translation copyright © 1992 by Julia and Robin Whitby. Used by permission of W. W. Norton & Company, Inc.

Document 10.2   A domestic quarrel

Questions for analysis

1   What is the quarrel about?
2   Who do you think is right and why?
3   Compare the ideas about women's roles in this document to those expressed in the previous one.

"Well, Olya, maybe it's better to give up work altogether. You spend nearly half the year at home as it is."

"And you want me to spend all of it here? Anyway, we couldn't possibly live on what you earn."

Dima looks around the kitchen, at the rucksack and the iron. "If I didn't have all this to bother about I could probably earn more, 200–220 roubles. And, in actual fact, if you add up all the days you don't get paid, you probably only earn about sixty roubles a month. It's not worth it."

No, no! "Dima," I say, "You want me to do all the routine stuff, while you do your interesting work, because you think my work isn't worth it. You're just a rotten capitalist."

"Maybe I am," says Dima with an unfriendly smile, "but it's just a question of money. It would be better for the children as well. The kindergarten is bad enough, but the crèche is even worse. Gulka hardly gets out at all in the winter, and she's always got a cold."

"Dima, do you really think I don't want what's best for the children? You know I do, but what you're suggesting would kill me. What about my five years at university, my degree, my seniority, my research? It's easy enough for you to dismiss it all, but if I didn't work, I'd go mad, I'd become impossible to live with. Anyway, there's no point in talking about it. There's no way we would live on your salary and at the moment you really haven't been offered anything else."

Source: Natalya Baranskaya, *A Week Like Any Other*, trans. Peita Monks (Emeryville, CA: Seal Press, 1990), 59–60.

Document 10.3   Criticism of the Russian rock band Time Machine

Questions for analysis

1   What kinds of feelings and ideas do the Time Machine lyrics express?
2   Why does the author of this piece object to them?
3   What are the author's criticisms of Time Machine's singing style? What assumptions about gender underlie those criticisms?

Today we're talking not just about tour appearances in Krasnoyarsk, and not just about the laws of poetry, which Time Machine ignores. We're talking about the position taken by a group that every evening gives thousands of listeners dangerous injections of highly dubious ideas:

> Wear masks,
> Wear masks!
> Only under a mask
> Can you be yourself.
> And if trouble
> Befalls your friend,
> You can sometimes put on
> The mask of a friend,
> The mask of sympathy.

After such a confession, if you'll pardon the term, it's not hard to answer the question:

> Tell me, why are you happy?
> Stop, look back!
> Stop, look back,
> And you'll see the autumn waning
> And the crows circling
> Where once the orchard bloomed.

The last line is accompanied by such cheerful chords that the "ditty" about carrion crows conveys pleasure instead of pain. And, quite frankly, the bluebird that each of us cherishes is turned into a "carrion crow":

> They say that in these years
> The bluebird's last trace has vanished,
> That in the annals of our country's nature
> The creature's not so much as mentioned.

In all times, there have been unabashed versifiers who have lived outside their time. However, it's only a step from tasteless mannered writing to cynicism.

Even entertainment-oriented Western groups can't overlook such acute topics – and, for any normal person, not just acute but overriding topics – as the struggle for peace or the question of what you've done to help reason triumph. But this group gives us murky, bilious reveries and a deliberate escape into pointless grumbling . . .

In conclusion, we would like to mention one more detail that is vividly manifest in Time Machine. Mainly, it's an infantile, "childlike" intonation, which at any moment may break into midvoice or falsetto. Taken together with the performers' mustaches, and sometimes even beards, this style of singing completely negates the masculine principle, both in their performance and in their artistic position. It's become a problem to hear a normal male voice in groups such as this. Men! Sing like men!

Source: *Komsomolskaia pravda*, 11 April. From: *Current Digest of the Russian Press*, 34, no. 38, (20 October 1982): 5–6. Used by permission of East View Press.

Notes

1 Cited in Edwin Bacon, "Reconsidering Brezhnev," in Edwin Bacon and Mark Sandle, eds., *Brezhnev Reconsidered* (Basingstoke: Palgrave Macmillan, 2002), 4–5.
2 As quoted in Ian D. Thatcher, "Brezhnev as Leader," in Bacon and Sandle, eds., *Brezhnev Reconsidered*, 26.
3 Bacon, "Reconsidering Brezhnev," 2.
4 Mark Sandle, "Brezhnev and Developed Socialism: The Ideology of Zastoi?" in Bacon and Sandle, eds., *Brezhnev Reconsidered*, 182.
5 Vladislav M. Zubok, *A Failed Empire: The Soviet Union in the Cold War from Stalin to Gorbachev* (Chapel Hill: University of North Carolina Press, 2007), 207.
6 Mark Webber, "'Out of Area' Operations: The Third World," in Bacon and Sandle, eds., *Brezhnev Reconsidered*, 111–112.
7 As quoted in Christoper J. Lee, "'Only he who has no friends cannot say goodbye': Alex La Guma's *A Soviet Journey* (1978) and the Contingent History of Covert Travel to the USSR in South African Politics," in Maxim Matusevich, ed., *Africa in Russia, Russia in Africa: Three Centuries of Encounters* (Trenton, NJ: Africa World Press, Inc., 2007), 247.
8 As quoted in Thomas Burgess, "A Socialist Diaspora: Ali Sultan Issa, the Soviet Union, and the Zanzibari Revolution," in Matusevich, ed., *Africa in Russia*, 284.
9 Lily Golden, *The Long Journey Home* (Chicago, IL: Third World Press, 2002), 92.
10 Golden, *Long Journey Home*, 101–104, 107–112.
11 Webber, "'Out of Area' Operations", 121.
12 Odd Arne Westad, "Prelude to Invasion: The Soviet Union and the Afghan Communists, 1978–1979," *International History Review*, 16, no. 1 (Feb. 1994), 51.
13 Westad, "Prelude to Invasion," 58; Zubok, *A Failed Empire*, 260.
14 Zubok, *A Failed Empire*, 262–263.
15 As quoted in Donald J. Raleigh, *Soviet Baby Boomers: An Oral History of Russia's Cold War Generation* (Oxford: Oxford University Press, 2012), 264.
16 Imtiyaz Gul Khan, "Afghanistan: Human Cost of Armed Conflict since the Soviet Invasion," *Perceptions: Journal of International Affairs*, 17, no. 4 (2012): 212–213.
17 Rafael Reuveny and Aseem Prakash, "The Afghanistan War and the Breakdown of the Soviet Union," *Review of International Studies*, 25, no. 4 (Oct. 1999): 693–708, available at stable URL: www.jstor.org/stable/20097629 (accessed 2 February 2016).
18 Mark Harrison, "Economic Growth and Slowdown," in Bacon and Sandle, eds., *Brezhnev Reconsidered*, 52–55; James R. Millar, "The Little Deal: Brezhnev's Contribution to Acquisitive Socialism," *Slavic Review*, 44, no. 4 (Winter 1985): 695, available at stable URL: www.jstor.org/stable/2498542 (accessed 7 January 2016).
19 William J. Tompson, *The Soviet Union under Brezhnev* (Edinburgh: Pearson Longman, 2003), 84.
20 As quoted in Raleigh, *Soviet Baby Boomers*, 225–226.
21 Millar, "The Little Deal," 694–706.
22 Alec Nove, "Soviet Agriculture: New Data," *Soviet Studies*, 34, no. 1 (Jan. 1982): 118.
23 Gregory Grossman, "The 'Second Economy' of the USSR," in Alexander Dallin, ed., *The Khrushchev and Brezhnev Years* (New York: Garland Publishing, Inc., 1992), 476.
24 Alena V. Ledeneva, *Russia's Economy of Favours: Blat, Networking and Informal Exchange* (Cambridge: Cambridge University Press, 1998), 37.
25 As quoted in Ledeneva, *Russia's Economy of Favours*, 28.
26 As quoted in Raleigh, *Soviet Baby Boomers*, 229.

27 As quoted in Raleigh, *Soviet Baby Boomers*, 229.
28 Ledeneva, *Russia's Economy of Favours*, 65.
29 Ledeneva, *Russia's Economy of Favours*, 184.
30 Millar, "The Little Deal," 697.
31 Ludmilla Alexeyeva and Paul Goldberg, *The Thaw Generation: Coming of Age in the Post-Stalin Era* (Pittsburgh, PA: University of Pittsburgh Press, 1990), 138.
32 Alexeyeva and Goldberg, *The Thaw Generation*, 109.
33 Michael Confino, "Solzhenitsyn, the West, and the New Russian Nationalism," *Journal of Contemporary History*, 26, no. 3/4 (Sep. 1991): 611–636, available at stable URL: www.jstor.org/stable/260663 (accessed 7 January 2016).
34 Barbara Walker, "Pollution and Purification in the Moscow Human Rights Networks of the 1960s and 1970s," *Slavic Review*, 68, no. 2 (Summer 2009): 376–395, available at stable URL: www.jstor.org/stable/27697964 (accessed 7 January 2016).
35 Alexeyeva and Goldberg, *The Thaw Generation*, 267.
36 "Abuse of Psychiatry against Dissenters," *Economic and Political Weekly*, 16, no. 6 (7 Feb. 1981): 187, available at stable URL: www.jstor.org/stable/4369508 (accessed 7 January 2016).
37 Alexeyeva and Goldberg, *The Thaw Generation*, 197.
38 Alexei Yurchak, *Everything Was Forever until It Was No More: The Last Soviet Generation* (Princeton, NJ: Princeton University Press, 2005), 106.
39 Barbara Walker, "The Moscow Correspondents, Soviet Human Rights Activists, and the Problem of the Western Gift," in Choi Chatterjee and Beth Holmgren, eds., *Americans Experience Russia: Encountering the Enigma, 1917 to the Present* (New York: Routledge, 2013), 139.
40 As quoted in Raleigh, *Soviet Baby Boomers*, 245.
41 Available at http://nces.ed.gov/pubs98/yi/yi05.pdf (accessed 7 January 2016).
42 Peter H. Juviler, "The Soviet Family in Post-Stalin Perspective," in Stephen F. Cohen, Alexander Rabinowitch, and Robert Sharlet, eds., *The Soviet Union since Stalin* (Bloomington: Indiana University Press), 246–247.
43 Juviler, "The Soviet Family," 238.
44 Natalya Baranskaya, *A Week Like Any Other*, trans. Peita Monks (Emeryville, CA: Seal Press, 1990), 8.
45 As quoted in Raleigh, *Soviet Baby Boomers*, 260.
46 Anna Paretskaya, "A Middle Class without Capitalism?" in Neringa Klumbyte and Gulnaz Sharafutdinova, eds., *Soviet Society in the Era of Late Socialism, 1964–1985* (Lanham, MD: Lexington Books, 2013), 45.
47 As quoted in Artemy Troitsky, *Back in the USSR: The True Story of Rock in Russia* (London: Faber and Faber, 1988), 13.
48 Sergei Zhuk, *Rock and Roll in the Rocket City: The West, Identity, and Ideology in Soviet Dniepropetrovsk, 1960–1985* (Washington, DC: Woodrow Wilson Center Press, 2010), 82–83, 96.
49 Zhuk, *Rock and Roll*, 98–101.
50 Zhuk, *Rock and Roll*, 96; Yurchak, *Everything Was Forever*, 190–191.
51 As quoted in Zhuk, *Rock and Roll*, 79.
52 Yurchak, *Everything Was Forever*, 209, 192.
53 Zhuk, *Rock and Roll*, 1–2; on Eastern religion, 200.
54 John Bushnell, "The 'New Soviet Man' Turns Pessimist," in Cohen, Rabinowitch, and Sharlet, eds., *The Soviet Union since Stalin*, 179–199.
55 As quoted in Raleigh, *Soviet Baby Boomers*, 237.

11 Gorbachev and the truth paradox

INTRODUCTION

On 11 March 1985, after the death of three elderly Soviet leaders in a space of three short years, a telegenic and forceful personality stepped onto the Soviet and by extension the world stage; his name was Mikhail Sergeevich Gorbachev. He assumed the office of the General Secretary of the Communist Party of the Soviet Union. After a decade of stagnation, the military stalemate in Afghanistan, and the repression of civil society, hopes ran high that the relatively youthful Gorbachev, and his stylish and highly educated wife Raisa Maximovna, would reform the economy, loosen the levers of control that were exercised by the party and the KGB, and present a more humane Soviet face to the world. On 25 December 1991, barely six years after taking office, Gorbachev, in a public address to the people, announced the death of the Soviet Union. At 7:25 pm that evening the Soviet flag was lowered and at 7:32 pm the prerevolutionary Russian flag was run up the pole. Few noticed the new flag fluttering in the Kremlin on this otherwise unremarkable and cold winter evening.

Nobody cheered, and fewer still protested as the chimes from the Spassky Tower Clock rang for several minutes to mark the historic occasion. Around the world political leaders, foreign policy makers, academics, and professional Kremlin watchers were amazed at the turn of events. Nobody had predicted the end of the Soviet Union, and in fact President George Bush's administration had quietly worked behind the scenes to prolong the life of the Soviet Union even as they encouraged Gorbachev to press forward with his democratizing reforms.[1] But 25 December 1991 would prove to be as significant a date in world history as 7 November 1917 had been. If the collapse of the tsarist empire had redefined the world order in the twentieth century, then the collapse of the Soviet Union would prove to be a catalyzing event for twenty-first century globalization.

CHAPTER QUESTIONS

In this chapter we will propose some answers to the paradoxical nature of the reforms that Gorbachev instituted and analyze their consequences for post-Soviet Russia. What did Gorbachev mean by the terms *perestroika* and *glasnost*? Why did his vision of socialism with a human face, which raised so much hope among the Soviet intelligentsia at home and social democrats abroad, founder on the shoals of a steadily declining economy? Did the Soviet Union die from an excess of truth telling? Finally,

Figure 11.1 Gorbachev's calendar image from 1990. © Heritage Image Partnership Ltd/Alamy.

What image does the artist present of the Soviet leader? How does this differ from the image of Stalin in chapter 7?

why did progressive foreign policies that led to the end of the Cold War, the peaceful liberation of Eastern Europe, and the secession of the fifteen socialist republics that had comprised the USSR, lead to so much grief and unhappiness among Gorbachev's domestic audiences?

VOICES, MEMORIES, CONTESTED PERSPECTIVES

The Soviet revolution

The October Revolution of 1917 started with the dissatisfaction of broad sections of the imperial citizenry in the capital, fed up with the inability of the tsarist state to supply bread and coal to St. Petersburg, or to end Russia's disastrous involvement in

World War I. Peasants, workers, and soldiers responded to Lenin's call for "Land, Bread and Peace" with enthusiasm, convinced that the *burzhui* or capitalists were evil and that their property, whether in the form of banks, factories, mansions, or agricultural land, should be expropriated and redistributed throughout society. Subsequently, through many false starts and deviations, as we saw in chapters 3 and 4, the Soviet state in the 1930s instituted a new model of state-sponsored modernization that threatened and challenged capitalist societies worldwide. Developing nations such as India, China, Mexico, and Tanzania, among others, appropriated selectively from the Soviet model and used central planning by experts and politicians to build a base of heavy industry and thus ameliorate the endemic rural poverty that afflicted these nations. Countries throughout the world borrowed Soviet innovations in public welfare and created pensions for the elderly, subsidized public education, housing, and healthcare. During the course of the twentieth century the world witnessed a global cross-pollination of state practices from both sides of the Iron Curtain.

Paradoxically, however, the adoption of socialist policies within the Soviet Union created a vast class of consumers and property owners located in urban areas whose aspirations became increasingly individualistic and market oriented with time. According to many experts, a modern Soviet civil society produced Gorbachev and made his reforms both necessary and possible.[2] The Soviet middle class, a sizable section of society that was led by the cultural aspirations and economic predilections of a professional, scientific, and cultural intelligentsia, refused to countenance the decline in living standards in the 1980s as they had done so uncomplainingly in the past. Open and trenchant criticism of the poor quality of goods and services in the Soviet Union became increasingly commonplace, even while cultural and political leaders worried that the Soviet youth were becoming materialistic and losing faith in the values of socialism.

As we have seen in the last chapter, accustomed to steady increases in the standards of living during and after the Khrushchev era, and schooled into new modes of consumption by the acquisition of state-subsidized private apartments and cars, a generation of Soviet citizens developed expectations that the state was unable to fulfill. They were exposed to modern lifestyles that they viewed on their televisions sets,[3] and those of tourists and foreign students frequenting Moscow and St. Petersburg. Travels to Western Europe, Eastern Europe, and the United States, and also to parts of Asia, Africa, and Latin America where Soviet technical experts and military personnel labored to institute their model of economic development, convinced the intelligentsia, legions of party apparatchiks, as well as sections of the party elite, that the fabled market, the communist's worst nightmare, was perhaps not as evil as state media had represented it to be.[4]

According to Stephen Kotkin, the collapse of the Soviet Union was neither natural nor the inevitable end to the unnatural socialist system that was doomed to decay; instead it was caused by intentional policies adopted at the highest levels of government.[5] Mikhail Gorbachev undertook to leaven state socialism by the gradual introduction of a socialist market, and to galvanize citizen participation in the society and economy by the policies of perestroika and glasnost (restructuring and openness). He optimistically hoped to democratize the sclerotic and gargantuan Communist Party, and change the labyrinthine system of patronage that helped elevate Gorbachev himself to the highest office in the land by introducing elections and an elected legislature. Gorbachev, a firm believer in the European identity of Russia, wanted to end the stalemate in Afghanistan, lift the Soviet military control of Eastern Europe, and end the disastrous arms race with the United States that had nearly bankrupted the Soviet Union.

Unfortunately, Gorbachev decided to simultaneously implement these four ultra-revolutionary policies at a time when Soviet growth rates had slowed precipitously, a reality that was compounded by the falling international price of oil, the Soviet Union's premier export. His tenure also coincided with two major tragedies: the Chernobyl nuclear disaster of 1986 that led to widespread contamination and a public health catastrophe, and the earthquake in Armenia in 1988 that led to the deaths of many thousands. However, it is important to disentangle the intentions of the reformists surrounding Gorbachev from the many unintended consequences that ensued during the 1980s.

In many ways, Gorbachev's biography exemplifies the achievements and failures of the Soviet Union.[6] Born into a middling peasant family in Stavropol, in the multiethnic Kuban province in the Caucasus, Gorbachev experienced both the impact of Stalinist terror, during the course of which both his grandfathers suffered greatly, as well as incredible personal success. The Communist Party created conduits of upward mobility in every corner of the Soviet Union through its commitment to education and vast subsidies of the arts, humanities, and sciences. Young Mikhail soon found himself at the center of the power nexus as he graduated from the prestigious Moscow University with a law degree. Gorbachev returned to Stavropol where he served as the secretary for agriculture and tried to link agricultural worker performance to cash payments. He was brought back to Moscow through his friendship with Yuri Andropov, another native of the Kuban and chairman of the KGB. Gorbachev rose steadily through the ranks of the party to become one of the youngest members of the Politburo.

As a consummate insider, a member of the privileged nomenklatura that numbered almost a million members, Gorbachev saw firsthand how the monopoly of power had vitiated the Communist Party. Cut off from vital contact with the people, the source of its strength and legitimacy, the party had become a monument to the deficiencies of socialism. Gorbachev was a member of the student generation that rebelled world-wide during the 1960s, calling for an end to patriarchy, capitalism, imperialism, and destruction of the environment. While he was neither a dissident nor a human rights activist, Gorbachev had absorbed some of the idealism of this era and he tried to rein-terpret the canon of leftist thought for the modern era.

The youth festivals of the 1950s and 1960s in the Soviet Union and the Eastern bloc countries showed the Soviet intelligentsia that there were many young people throughout the world who longed to reform socialism. They dreamed of shearing it of its vulgar Stalinist accretions, and reinfusing it with its original idealism of economic equality, peaceful coexistence, and democracy.[7] Although Soviet tanks rolled into Hungary in 1956, and then again into Prague in 1968, to end seditious talk of "socialism with a human face," it could not contain the spread of ideas within its own borders. Gorbachev's college room-mate in Moscow was the future Czech dissident and ideologue for the Prague Spring Zdeněk Mlynář, and they discussed the possibility of creating real socialism in their dormitory. Gorbachev, like the generation of idealists in the Soviet Union in the 1960s called the *shestidesiatniki*, turned to the works of Lenin to unearth the original promises of socialism that they believed had been distorted beyond recognition by Stalin. During his trip through Western Europe in

1970, Gorbachev saw that the living standards even in the poorer parts of rural Italy and France were considerably higher than those in Soviet cities, and he struggled to connect the promises of socialism with their actual institution.

While acknowledging the many deficiencies of the Soviet economy, Gorbachev, however, had no intention of surrendering wholesale to the free market. He wanted to preserve the gains that the economy had made under socialist modernization, while reducing the role of central planning and the system of price controls that had distorted the value of products and labor. He, and other reformers such as Alexander Yakovlev, Abel Aganbegian, and Tatiana Zaslavskaia, wanted to force industrial establishments to turn a profit, upgrade investments in science and technology rather than buy and borrow wholesale from the West, and increase worker productivity exponentially. In his book on perestroika, Gorbachev laid out a powerful vision of socialist renewal, hoping to convince many that there was a genuine alternative to the free market and unregulated capitalism. At the same time, Gorbachev also opposed the many Soviet conservatives who wanted to preserve the existing system by using terror to compel workers to be more productive and managers and party members to be less corrupt and self-seeking.[8]

Like Khrushchev (see chapter 9) he believed that, rather than motivate people by fear or the promise of material gain, he would inspire them by harking back to the days of revolutionary promise, when Soviet citizens, especially the youth, were committed to altruism, patriotism, and internationalism. Perhaps Gorbachev was naive in his understanding of human nature, but Marxist philosophy is predicated on the notion that the needs of the individual have to be subordinated to the needs of the community.

Economy

The black market economy of goods and services had always existed in Soviet cities despite the best efforts of the party and the KGB to control it. Private enterprise in the countryside, where peasants produced fruit and vegetables for cities on their private garden plots, had already brought a modified form of retail practices to the Soviet Union for several decades. But while people used their savings to shop in these private markets and longed for more choices at state run stores, at the same time they were very critical of large-scale private traders who brought in fresh produce from the Caucasus and Central Asia, the mafia that controlled illegal mining, timber, and oil operations, and servicemen who made millions from the illegal trade in armaments and army supplies. Ruble millionaires who bribed members of the party and secret police to turn a blind eye to their covert operations were universally despised by the intelligentsia.

Most people in the Soviet Union believed that socioeconomic inequality was immoral and that the accumulation of wealth was not the product of hard work and enterprise alone, but also the result of cronyism and corruption at the highest levels. And, as we saw in the previous chapter, many people misrecognized their own use of *blat*. At one level the anticapitalist propaganda of the Party was very successful, and most citizens had internalized this deep-seated suspicion of profit-making and commerce. Thus when Gorbachev decided to harness the productivity of an imagined socialist market to revitalize a moribund state socialism, he had to confront his own and Soviet citizens' deep ambivalence about the workings of the market and capitalism.

It is important to remember, however, that most people in the Soviet Union, specialist and lay people alike, had little idea about the true nature of unbridled capitalism. Many believed, like Gorbachev, that it was possible to combine the guaranteed employment, pensions, subsidized healthcare, education, and housing, and the array of welfare benefits that the Soviet system provided, with the abundance of goods and vastly improved services that capitalist societies offered. Many also chose to willingly ignore the booms and busts that lie at the heart of the business cycle: unemployment, high personal indebtedness, the existence of a permanent underclass, and the vast socioeconomic inequalities of capitalist societies. The belief that it was possible to have the best of both worlds of socialism and capitalism, or to pursue a European-style social democratic system, underlay much of the pro-market rhetoric that issued from the Party during the decade of the 1980s.

Gorbachev's biggest challenge was the gargantuan Soviet economy. While the Soviet growth rate had astonished the world in the 1930s, and then again in the aftermath of World War II when it recovered from Nazi depredations within record time with little help from the international community, it was beginning to decline at a precipitous rate by the 1980s. The low international oil prices, the Soviet Union's premier export, and the costs of war in Afghanistan and of maintaining peace in the empire and in Eastern Europe compounded a larger problem of the socialist economy that promised too much to too many. Rather than tackle the economy first, like the communist leaders in China, Gorbachev's well-meaning but intemperate policies that tried to achieve too much too soon were bewildering and maddening to many at home who saw living standards drop precipitously during the course of perestroika.

In China, by contrast, Deng Xiaoping and the authoritarian Chinese Communist Party were gradually introducing free market principles and foreign investment in select urban and rural areas in a bid to revive the moribund economy after the depredations of the Cultural Revolution. Hundreds and millions were raised out of poverty in China in the 1990s and the first decade of the twenty-first century, and many Russians compared Gorbachev and his reformers unfavorably to the Chinese leadership that led their country to great power status. A contemporary joke asked: What are the prospects of perestroika? The answer: There are two possible scenarios. The first scenario is realistic: Martians will come to the Earth and do everything for us. The second scenario is out of science fiction: We will achieve the goals of perestroika on our own.

But it must be remembered that while China has moved from a desperately poor and overwhelmingly peasant society to a middle income country during the last two decades, Gorbachev had the harder task of increasing standards of living in a middle income country that lacked the vast reserves of cheap labor that attracted so many foreign investors to China. Moreover, while massive infusions of capital from an extremely wealthy diaspora helped jumpstart the Chinese economy, Russia witnessed a steady outflow of both capital and human resources during the same period.[9]

As Gorbachev candidly admitted, the Soviet economy built to respond to the threat of 1930s fascism and the subsequent Cold War never really transitioned to a peacetime economy. The economy was controlled for the most part by gigantic ministries that allocated production orders based on a plan that owed as much to economists as it did to the personal predilections of party leaders. The Soviet economy, structured around the production of heavy industry, oil and gas, chemicals, timber, and mineral resources, never really developed light industry that was geared to the production of consumer

goods. While the Soviet Union excelled in the fields of laser physics and space technology and had the largest number of people with advanced graduate degrees in the
world, in the more mundane realms of everyday life Soviet television sets, cars, and
washing machines broke down frequently and the quality left much to be desired.
Gorbachev hoped to wean industries from guaranteed state subsidies and guaranteed
orders for products, no matter how poor the quality, and introduce a socialist market
where industries would manage their accounting, be accountable for profits and losses,
and produce goods of a quality that both the state and the consumer would desire.

The agricultural sector that consumed a substantial portion of the budget was
notoriously inefficient, forcing the Soviet Union to import expensive food from the
United States and Canada. As in other modernizing parts of the globe, young people
fled the collective farms despite rising wages under Khrushchev and Brezhnev, while
elderly people concentrated their energy on growing produce on private plots, knowing
that state subsidies would offset production losses. Gorbachev hoped to reverse this
trend by giving agricultural workers the monetary incentive to raise production by
introducing collective contracts and family contracts on collective farms. He wanted
to introduce wage differentials on the farm, reward productive workers, and increase
food supplies to the cities. Gorbachev introduced laws between 1986 and 1988 that
made it easier to create small-scale family-owned businesses, cooperatives, and joint
stock companies with employees. But on the one hand suspicious bureaucrats withheld
supplies of raw materials and supplies from these private operations, and on the other
hand criminal mafia groups demanded bribes in return for "protection." Restaurants,
street vendors, and owners of small businesses found it very difficult to succeed in
these perilous times.

Many ridiculed Gorbachev as an impractical dreamer and thought that the socialist
system was unredeemable,[10] based as it was on the unproductive socialist worker and
a political system that had disregarded civil society, stifled popular initiative, and
derided the spirit of entrepreneurship. Under Stalin, fear of the secret police had motivated people to work for the state, but under the conditions of late socialism while
there were few punishments for workers who were drunk at the factory sites, there
were even fewer incentives for them to sober up and turn in a hard day's work. Yuri
Andropov, Gorbachev's predecessor, had waged a war against drunkenness and one of
Gorbachev's first acts was to raise the costs of hard liquor and restrict the times when
it was sold. He encouraged Russians to turn to wine and beer, and drunkenness and
absenteeism were punished by the state. Unfortunately, the antialcohol campaign,
instead of reducing alcoholism, reduced the state's income from taxes on liquor
at a time when it could least afford it and led to a huge increase in the production of
illegal alcohol.

While under capitalism poor work is punished by dismissal and good work rewarded
by monetary incentives, under the conditions of late socialism both the system of
rewards and punishments seemed to be in jeopardy as an increase in wages under both
Khrushchev and Brezhnev in both the agricultural and the industrial sector was
matched by declining labor productivity. Mirroring the work ethic of the workers,
Soviet management, cushioned by unending state subsidies, had little incentive to
increase productivity in the farms and factories, or increase quality and choice.
Gorbachev realized that while enterprises could be forced to move to a capitalistic
system of accounting by investing in technology, sound management practices, and
shrinking financial federal allocations, it was going to be harder to motivate millions

in the Soviet Union to work for the principles of socialism, the welfare of the community as well as individual gain.

Gorbachev's biggest failure and that of the economists who supported him was their inability to devise a practical system of social democracy, one that would motivate entrepreneurs to create wealth not just for themselves but also for the welfare of the community. The Soviet Union was not alone in its failure, as economists are yet to devise an economic system where profits are distributed on a more equitable basis rather than being concentrated in the hands of the few, and where private enterprise does not destroy the natural environment that it is based on.

Glasnost

Gorbachev penitently admitted that the Communist Party, by cutting itself off from its own constituencies, had fostered a culture of secrecy and subservience where people were both cynical and afraid to take responsibility. Gorbachev believed that glasnost, or open democratic debate, would inspire people to once again believe in the ideals of communism, to seek ownership of their workplace, and to work to create an equitable, productive, and open society. He said many times that the Soviet Union had to confront its Stalinist past and fill in the blank spots of history that had been created by the oppressive policies of the party and the secret police. The reduction of censorship in the late 1980s led to a dramatic upsurge in the publication of novels, memoirs, works of history, and accounts of imprisonment in the Gulag that had lain hidden for many decades.[11]

Weeklies such as *Ogonek* and *Moskovskie novosti*, and literary journals such as *Novyi mir*, redefined notions of censorship and press freedom, as did television programs such as *Vzgliad* (Point of View) that covered the many drawbacks of life under socialism in excruciating detail. Rock music that had survived in the underground as a dissident and subversive phenomenon, its musicians subject to periodic repression and even jail time, suddenly was legalized. Bands such as Time Machine, Kino, and Aquarium were allowed to catapult to stardom and hold mega-concerts. While some musicians such as Alla Pugacheva mastered the commercial music scene quickly, many were unable to transition from being dissidents under socialism and producers of music with subversive meaning to being vendors of music under capitalism.

Banned literature started appearing in the pages of the Soviet press, including the novels and poetry of famous writers, such as Alexander Solzhenitsyn, Anna Akhmatova, Boris Pasternak, Vasily Grossman, Andrei Platonov, Eugenia Ginzburg, Marina Tsvetaeva, and Joseph Brodsky to name only a few, who had been either sent into exile or silenced in the past. The 1980s represented an unprecedented renaissance in art, literature, and poetry. People bought books and periodicals in massive quantities, amazed to find texts that had long circulated only in samizdat forms being sold openly in book stores, kiosks, and pavement displays. In large cities, the members of the intelligentsia watched films, attended art exhibitions of conceptual and sots art that mocked the pomposity of socialist realism. Students discussed the popular histories of the eighteenth and nineteenth centuries written by Natan Eidelman that challenged Soviet versions of the prerevolutionary past. People wrote hundreds and thousands of letters to the press expressing their honest opinion about their country and the Communist Party, airing their grievances and uncovering bitter memories of past repression.[12]

The period of glasnost represented an unprecedented intellectual ferment when the entire nation was suddenly talking and arguing about the Russian past, the Soviet present, and the yet unnamed future.[13] Gorbachev reached out to the towering intellectual and moral figures to legitimize his revolution, and while Solzhenitsyn refused to come back to the Soviet Union, eminent physicist turned dissident and human rights activist Andrei Sakharov came back to Moscow from exile in Gorky to participate in the reconstruction of the Union. While he challenged a visibly irritated Gorbachev in the Congress of People's Deputies by insisting that the Communist Party cede its monopoly on political power, Sakharov, like Gorbachev, believed that the Soviet Union should transition to a social democratic order where the government would take responsibility for the poorest sections of society.[14]

The film *Repentance*, directed by the Georgian Tengiz Abuladze, captured the zeitgeist of the time. Initially, after the film was made, it was not released because of the incendiary subject matter. But by 1987 it was being screened at movie theaters around the Soviet Union to great acclaim. The subject of the film was the death of a dictator, Varlam, and his mysterious dead body that refuses to stay buried underground. The dictator is a composite rendition of Stalin, Mussolini, and Hitler, with elements of Charlie Chaplin's Great Dictator, but the fact that the film was set in Georgia led many to believe that the film was about Stalin. As the film unfolds, viewers learn that Ketevan Baratelli, the female protagonist, refuses to allow the dictator to rest in peace and insists that there be a public accounting of the terror that he inflicted on the population. The brilliant cinematography, aided by a powerful script, highlighted the original sin of the Soviet revolution: the use of massive and unjustified force against both elites and ordinary workers and peasants. The film ends when the son, in an act of patricide, hurls the dead body of the dictator from a cliff. But it was going to be harder for Gorbachev to jettison the ballast of the past quite so easily. Gorbachev believed that the democratic debate engendered by glasnost would afford moral respite and therapy to a people traumatized by events that they had experienced and witnessed but had been unable to either represent or even discuss with their loved ones.

But unfortunately Gorbachev's hope that the national catharsis would lead to a renewed commitment to the original principles of socialism was unfounded. While the reevaluation of Stalinism after decades of silence was morally exhilarating to many, others were disturbed by the media's depiction of problems within Soviet society. Juris Podniek's documentary *Is It Easy to Be Young?* (1987) revealed youth in Latvia that were addicted to drugs and violence, and completely alienated from Soviet society. While the screening of the film represented a triumph for Gorbachev's policy of openness, the main message of the film was extremely depressing to generations of Soviet citizens who believed that life should have meaning, work should have value, and that the welfare of the community was more important than individualism and consumerism. Other popular films such as *Little Vera* (1988) and *Adam's Rib* (1990) presented to a bemused Soviet society young women bedeviled by the problems of drug addiction, alcoholism, and casual sex.

To a people accustomed to pious platitudes from state propagandists about unending Soviet progress and happy Soviet people, it was shocking to learn about the poor conditions of the economy and agriculture, about corruption within the party, and the repression of the intelligentsia. Returning veterans from Afghanistan undid the last source of legitimacy for the Soviet Union.[15] The armed forces that had fought so gloriously against the Nazis were greatly admired among the general public. But like the Vietnam veterans in the United States, the Afghantsy spoke a new banal language of war: of a bruised and corrupt masculinity. There was little heroism on the battlefields of Afghanistan; it was a sad tale of botched imperialism, of brutalized soldiers inflicting horrendous violence on an Afghan enemy, and rendering millions homeless in the process. Veterans spoke of drug addiction, gun running, prostitution, brutal hazing of young recruits, and of illegal fortunes made from a brisk trade in consumer goods acquired in Afghanistan. The Afghantsy were not heroes and they did not come back to a hero's welcome. People scrambling to make ends meet in times of inflation had little time for the drug-addicted and badly damaged collateral of war.

Gorbachev and his idealistic cohort realized to their bitter cost that truth telling was neither sufficiently therapeutic nor politically expedient. The crimes of Stalinism ultimately delegitimized the party and the Soviet state beyond redemption. Instead of creating a renewed commitment to socialism, the media stories about corrupt bureaucrats, failing enterprises, the horrendous state of healthcare, rural poverty, shortages of goods, poor Soviet leadership during World War II that led to millions of excess deaths,[16] and the extensive nature of the Gulag, engendered even more cynicism and confusion among the general public about socialist ideals.

The intelligentsia demanded more and more facts about the crimes of Stalinism as many of them sincerely believed that without truth, moral freedom, and a code of legality a new edifice could not be erected on socialist foundations. But history shows us that the success of any political system is based to a large degree on a widely shared subscription to a version of the past that valorizes certain foundational events and suppresses inconvenient facts about slavery, colonialism, caste systems, genocide, land appropriation, environmental degradation, ethnic conflict, and war. Democratic states and dictatorships alike depend on the public support of the creative and intellectual class to create a usable past that shores up the legitimacy of the present. Artists that glorify the current social order, novelists, poets, and film makers who can imagine no viable alternatives to the present system, are an integral part of a stable society. But during glasnost the Soviet intelligentsia, inspired by universal notions of truth and unmoved by the political impact of their truth telling, vied with each other to unearth the skeletons from the Soviet past.

The existence of the Gulag or forced labor camps was perhaps the hardest part of the Stalinist legacy to come to terms with and, as we have seen in the previous chapters, post-Stalinist administrations tried a variety of tactics to deal with this accursed problem. Khrushchev tried to institute a milder form of de-Stalinization during the Thaw, only to see such attempts falter under Brezhnev. Gorbachev, while he was committed to uncovering the truths about the Stalinist past, realized belatedly that the battle for truth had to be balanced with the needs of political pragmatism, a position that sections of the democratic intelligentsia were not prepared to either understand or entertain.

The gulf that grew between Gorbachev and the intelligentsia over the limits of glasnost can best be illustrated by the dispute that arose over Alexander Solzhenitsyn, author of perhaps the best known book of the twentieth century, *The Gulag Archipelago*, a searing account of the Stalinist system of labor camps. A historian and a novelist who received the Nobel Prize, Solzhenitsyn also served in World War II with distinction and was decorated for his services. However, he was arrested for writing derogatory comments about Stalin in a letter and sentenced to hard labor for eight years and exile thereafter. As we described in chapter 9, Solzhenitsyn's brilliant novella *One Day in the Life of Ivan Denisovich*, about the everyday experiences in a labor camp, was published under Khrushchev in 1962 to great acclaim. But *The Gulag Archipelago*, a three volume compendium on the camp system, could not be published in the Soviet Union for political reasons.

Solzhenitsyn was exiled from the country in 1974. Under glasnost, most members of the intelligentsia campaigned to publish the work, but Gorbachev refused as he was incensed with Solzhenitsyn's attacks on Lenin, the founder of the Soviet system, and his wholesale condemnation of Soviet history and communist ideology. Nationalists were angry when Solzhenitsyn called for the breakup of the Soviet Union in the name of Slavic unity. Gorbachev's initial decision to keep Solzhenitsyn's works unpublished in Russia alienated large numbers of the liberal intelligentsia, including Andrei Sakharov, but by 1989 the work appeared in a Russian edition. By then it was considered to be too little and too late, and many began to doubt the genuineness of Gorbachev's reformist credentials.[17]

On the other side of the spectrum, former Gorbachev protégés such as Yegor Ligachev, a member of the Politburo who felt that *The Gulag Archipelago* should not be published, along with Victor Chebrikov, head of the KGB, worried that an excess of truth telling would sap the ideological foundations of the state.[18] The discussion about crimes from the Stalinist era deeply offended sections of the party elite who believed that, despite the mistakes that had been made, Stalinism represented the high point of Soviet strength and glory.

In March 1988, Nina Andreyeva, an unknown chemistry teacher, published a letter in *Sovetskaia Rossiia* with the tacit support of high ranking members of the Central Committee; it was entitled "I Cannot Forsake My Principles." She charged the media and irresponsible intellectuals with creating nihilism and disorientation among the youth by desecrating the entirety of the seventy-year communist history and salvaging nothing from the past. It was ironic that the Bolsheviks, who had done their best to destroy the tsarist heritage, were now claiming the past as a source of salvation.[19]

Foreign policy and the end of the Union

The quagmire of Afghanistan had another unintended consequence; it showed the Soviet armed forces the cost of imperialism. Although the Soviet army had invaded Hungary in 1956 and Czechoslovakia in 1968 and put down the solidarity movement in Poland in 1980, by the late 1980s neither the armed nor the security forces had the appetite to keep Soviet control over Eastern Europe, where countries were increasingly looking toward the European Union for integration and salvation.[20]

Gorbachev's vision of a democratic-socialist "common European home" and refusal to use force against democratic movements in Eastern Europe horrified Erich Honecker, the neo-Stalinist leader of East Germany, and Todor Zhivkov of Bulgaria. Gorbachev acquiesced in the destruction of the Berlin Wall by the people and the reunification of Germany. The year 1989 became "a carnival of revolution"[21] as mass movements toppled Soviet-inspired regimes in Poland, Czechoslovakia, Hungary, Bulgaria, and even Romania, where the dreaded dictator Ceaucescu was hounded out of office and finally shot by a firing squad in 1989.

The Soviets, despite their military strength and overwhelming nuclear capability, stood aside as country after country in Eastern Europe declared independence. Perhaps the American disaster in Vietnam and the Soviet one in Afghanistan convinced the superpowers that land-based empires were a thing of the past even if imperialism was not. In Beijing, to the contrary, the military crushed the massive student demonstrations in Tiananmen Square in early June of 1989. They arrested thousands in the aftermath, making it abundantly clear that the accommodation with the forces of capitalism did not include a loosening of the Communist Party's grip on power.

Thanks to the efficiency of the KGB in controlling nationalist movements in the fifteen socialist republics and the acquiescence of the ruling elites installed by Moscow, there were few full-scale independence movements within the Soviet Union comparable to those in Algeria, India, Kenya, Angola, Indonesia, and Vietnam among other colonized countries in Asia and Africa that received their freedom in the twentieth century. In the Baltic states of Estonia, Latvia, and Lithuania, where the elites had been very recently repressed in the 1940s, there were full-throated cries for independence. But in Ukraine, dependent as they were on cheap Russian energy and investments in the coal industry, there was considerable ambiguity about what a post-Soviet future would look like. While nationalists in Western Ukraine wanted integration into the European Union, in the eastern parts of the state, with almost eleven million ethnic Russians and many more families of mixed origin, integration with the Soviet Union seemed a safer option.

In Central Asia the tensions played out mostly among ethnic minorities within the states. The independent states of Uzbekistan, Turkmenistan, Kyrgyzstan, and Tajikistan continued to have close ties with Russia after 1991 under the umbrella of the CIS, Commonwealth of Independent States, that was formed after the collapse of the Soviet Union. Even though the oil-rich provinces of Kazakhstan and Azerbaijan signed deals with Western oil companies, the significant Russian diaspora centered near Astana, the capital of Kazakhstan, proved crucial for the success of the oil industry as they provided the necessary technical and scientific skills. Of the 25 million strong Russian diaspora scattered throughout the various republics, only 25 percent came back to the motherland.

In the Caucasus, war broke out between Armenia and Azerbaijan over the control of Nagorno-Karabakh, an Armenian majority territory within Azerbaijan. There were anti-Soviet protests in Tbilisi, the capital of Georgia, but the northern parts of Georgia, Abkhazia, and Ossetia were pro-Russian and demanded independence from Georgia. While no one lifted a finger in defense of the Soviet Union and the Russian empire between 1989 and 1991, many Russian nationalists bitterly regretted the loss of prestige that accompanied the loss of empire and superpower status. These feelings were going to resurface and profoundly shape post-Soviet Russia.

Ultimately, it was the Russian Republic under the leadership of Boris Yeltsin that broke up the Soviet Union by seceding from it. Gorbachev feared that the conservative Stalinists would end perestroika, but in the end the threat came from Yeltsin, an outspoken and charismatic populist from the Urals who worked the crowds in the best traditions of democratic elections. He became a thorn in Gorbachev's side, urging him to move faster toward a free market economy. In the first ever multiparty elections held in the Soviet Union in 1989, Yeltsin was elected to the newly formed legislature, the Congress of Deputies, with an overwhelming number of votes. In August 1991, there was a half-hearted coup by members of Gorbachev's cabinet who were afraid that events were spinning out of control too fast. This quickly failed due to the ineptitude of the ring leaders and the inaction of the armed and security forces that refused to engage in mass repression. Gorbachev himself was briefly put under house arrest, but later released and the ring leaders themselves arrested.

Images of Yeltsin, heroically defending the Russian White House from military tanks during the August coup of 1991, stayed in popular memory and his political stock climbed in proportion to the widening economic debacle caused by Gorbachev's reforms. On 25 December 1991, the Soviet flag over the Kremlin was hauled down, seventy-three years after the Bolshevik revolution. Gorbachev, a widely admired figure in the West for peacefully dissolving the Soviet empire, pulling out of Eastern Europe, and ending the Cold War, was the hated president of a country that ceased to exist as the Russian Federation broke away from the former USSR.

CONCLUSION AND FURTHER QUESTIONS

Russia entered the twentieth century as the first communist society in the history of the world, but by the 1990s a hyper and predatory capitalism had made a triumphant reentry, orchestrated by a class of violent and corrupt oligarchs and their patrons in the Kremlin. The socialist dreams of the 1960s were finally over; more than anything 1991 represented the victory of capitalism and consumerism worldwide, including in communist China! It is ironic that it was the policies of Mikhail Gorbachev, an ardent Leninist and true believer in the redemptive powers of a revitalized and democratic socialism, that led to the dissolution of state ownership, the deregulation of state control of the market, and a rollback of the welfare state in post-Soviet Russia and subsequently in much of the world.

PRIMARY SOURCES

Use the questions to analyze the content, context, and significance of each primary source. Then synthesize the primary sources and the material in the chapter to formulate a response to the primary chapter question: What did Gorbachev mean by the terms "perestroika" and "glasnost"?

Document 11.1   Excerpts from "I Cannot Waive Principles" by Nina Andreyeva, published in *Sovetskaia Rossiia*, 13 March 1988

Questions for analysis

1   Do you believe that this letter was written by a simple schoolteacher, or was it a political exercise by Gorbachev's enemies?
2   Is Nina Andreyeva justified in her defense of the Soviet past?
3   Can any political formation survive in the aftermath of complete truth telling?

I decided to write this letter after lengthy deliberation. I am a chemist, and I lecture at Leningrad's Lensovet Technology Institute. Like many others, I also look after a student group. Students nowadays, following the period of social apathy and intellectual dependence, are gradually becoming charged with the energy of revolutionary changes. Naturally, discussions develop about the ways of restructuring and its economic and ideological aspects. Glasnost, openness, the disappearance of zones where criticism is taboo, and the emotional heat of mass consciousness (especially among young people) often result in the raising of problems that are, to a greater or lesser extent, "prompted" either by Western radio voices or by those of our compatriots who are shaky in their conceptions of the essence of socialism. And what a variety of topics that are being discussed! A multiparty system, freedom of religious propaganda, emigration to live abroad, the right to broad discussion of sexual problems in the press, the need to decentralize the leadership of culture, abolition of compulsory military service. There are particularly numerous arguments among students about the country's past . . .

In the numerous discussions now taking place on literally all questions of the social sciences, as a college lecturer I am primarily interested in the questions that have a direct effect on young people's ideological and political education, their moral health, and their social optimism. Conversing with students and deliberating with them on controversial problems, I cannot help concluding that our country has accumulated quite a few anomalies and one-sided interpretations that clearly need to be corrected. I would like to dwell on some of them in particular . . .

Take, for example, the question of Joseph Stalin's place in our country's history. The whole obsession with critical attacks is linked with his name, and in my opinion this obsession centers not so much on the historical individual himself as on the entire highly complex epoch of transition, an epoch linked with unprecedented feats by a whole generation of Soviet people who are today gradually withdrawing from active participation in political and social work. The industrialization, collectivization, and Cultural Revolution which brought our country to the ranks of the great world powers are being forcibly squeezed into the "personality cult" formula. All of this is being questioned. Matters have gone so far that persistent demands for "repentance" are being made of "Stalinists" (and this category can be taken to include anyone you like) . . .

Let me say right away that neither I nor any members of my family were in any way involved with Stalin, his retinue, his associates, or his extollers. My father was a worker at Leningrad's port, my mother was a fitter at the Kirov plant. My elder brother also worked there. My brother, my father, and my sister died in battles against Hitler's forces. One of my relatives was repressed and then rehabilitated after the 20th Party Congress. I share all of the Soviet people's anger and indignation about the mass repressions that occurred in the 1930s and 1940s and with the party–state leadership of the time, which is to blame. But common sense resolutely protests against the monochrome depiction of contradictory events that now dominates in some press organs...

It is the champions of "left-wing liberal socialism" who shape the tendency toward falsifying the history of socialism. They try to make us believe that the country's past was nothing but mistakes and crimes, keeping silent about the greatest achievements of the past and the present . . .

Source: Available at Isaac J. Tarasulo, ed., *Gorbachev and Glasnost: Viewpoints from the Soviet Press* (Wilmington, DE: Scholarly Resources Inc., 1989), 277–290. SR Books is an imprint of Rowman & Littlefield Publishers, Inc. Used by permission of Rowman & Littlefield Publishers, Inc.

Document 11.2   Excerpts from the transcript of Mikhail S. Gorbachev's resignation speech in Moscow on 26 December 1991

Questions for analysis

1   Are Gorbachev's achievements validated by the arguments contained in this chapter?
2   If Gorbachev had achieved all his goals, why did the citizens of Russia hate and resent him?
3   What would Nina Andreyeva say to Gorbachev if she had a chance to meet him? Would she ask him to repent for his sins?

Dear compatriots, fellow citizens, as a result of the newly formed situation, creation of the Commonwealth of Independent States, I cease my activities in the post of the U.S.S.R. president. I am taking this decision out of considerations based on principle. I have firmly stood for independence, self-rule of nations, for the sovereignty of the republics, but at the same time for preservation of the union state, the unity of the country . . .

Yet, I will continue to do everything in my power so that agreements signed there should lead to real accord in the society, [and] facilitate the escape from the crisis and the reform process. Addressing you for the last time in the capacity of president of the U.S.S.R., I consider it necessary to express my evaluation of the road we have traveled since 1985, especially as there are a lot of contradictory, superficial and subjective judgments on that matter.

Fate had it that when I found myself at the head of the state it was already clear that all was not well in the country. There is plenty of everything: land, oil and gas, other natural riches, and God gave us lots of intelligence and talent, yet we lived much worse than developed countries and keep falling behind them more and more.

The reason could already be seen: The society was suffocating in the vise of the command-bureaucratic system, doomed to serve ideology and bear the terrible burden of the arms race. It had reached the limit of its possibilities. All attempts at partial reform, and there had been many, had suffered defeat, one after another. The country was losing perspective. We could not go on living like that. Everything had to be changed radically.

The process of renovating the country and radical changes in the world turned out to be far more complicated than could be expected. However, what has been done ought to be given its due. This society acquired freedom, liberated itself politically and spiritually, and this is the foremost achievement which we have not yet understood completely, because we have not learned to use freedom.

However, work of historic significance has been accomplished. The totalitarian system which deprived the country of an opportunity to become successful and prosperous long ago has been eliminated. A breakthrough has been achieved on the way to democratic changes. Free elections, freedom of the press, religious freedoms, representative organs of power, a multiparty [system] became a reality; human rights are recognized as the supreme principle.

The movement to a diverse economy has started, equality of all forms of property is becoming established, people who work on the land are coming to life again in the framework of land reform, farmers have appeared, millions of acres of land are being given over to people who live in the countryside and in towns.

Economic freedom of the producer has been legalized, and entrepreneurship, share-holding, privatization are gaining momentum. In turning the economy toward a market, it is important to remember that all this is done for the sake of the individual. At this difficult time, all should be done for his social protection, especially for senior citizens and children.

We live in a new world. The Cold War has ended, the arms race has stopped, as has the insane militarization which mutilated our economy, public psyche and morals. The threat of a world war has been removed. Once again I want to stress that on my part everything was done during the transition period to preserve reliable control of the nuclear weapons.

We opened ourselves to the world, gave up interference into other people's affairs, the use of troops beyond the borders of the country, and trust, solidarity and respect came in response.

The nations and peoples of this country gained real freedom to choose the way of their self-determination. The search for a democratic reformation of the multinational state brought us to the threshold of concluding a new Union Treaty. All these changes demanded immense strain. They were carried out with sharp struggle, with growing resistance from the old, the obsolete forces.

The old system collapsed before the new one had time to begin working, and the crisis in the society became even more acute . . .

Some mistakes could surely have been avoided, many things could have been done better, but I am convinced that sooner or later our common efforts will bear fruit, our nations will live in a prosperous and democratic society . . .

Source: Available at www.publicpurpose.com/lib-gorb911225.htm (accessed 5 November 2015).

Document 11.3   Excerpts from Andrei Sakharov's essay "Inevitability of Perestroika," translated by Edward Kline

Questions for analysis:

1   How does Sakharov define freedom and what does he mean by the moral atmosphere of the country? Do we have an equivalent for this phrase?
2   How can truth telling improve the moral atmosphere of a nation? What are the most important changes that Sakharov would like to bring about in his country?
3   Does Sakharov trust the Gorbachev government to bring about meaningful change in the country?

. . . First of all, I want to emphasize that I am convinced of the absolute historical necessity of perestroika. And like war—victory is a must! But serious economic, psychological, and organizational difficulties and obstacles are inevitable. For many years, the people (and here I include the intelligentsia) have been schooled in pretending to work, in hypocrisy, lies, and egoism, in adapting to a corrupt system. Have they preserved within themselves adequate moral force? If this force is insufficient, then our progress will be slow and contradictory, with backsliding and reverses. But I believe that among the people, and among the young especially, a vital fire burns beneath their outer shell. It must make itself known. This depends on us all. Moral and material motivation is needed for perestroika. Each of us must be interested in its success. However, the sense of a great common cause cannot be instilled by decree or conjured up by pep talks, and yet, without it, everything will remain up in the air. The people have to believe that they are being told the truth. This requires our leaders to speak only the truth and the whole truth, and always to back up their words with deeds. Even in the most favorable circumstances, there will still be great difficulties. Already, the transition to enterprise self-sufficiency and self-financing, to new systems of supply, to cooperatives, has cost many people part of their income, and some have even lost their jobs. And this is only the beginning of our difficult transition. It would be better, of course, if we can make fewer foolish mistakes and proceed in a more rational and responsible manner. The main obstacles to perestroika are the ossification of the bureaucratic administrative system, which has grown with time, and its millions of employees at all levels, who have no interest in an efficient, self-regulating system. This creates the danger that some of them will actively, or passively, through lack of understanding or ability, hinder perestroika, will pervert it, will ridicule it, or will represent its temporary difficulties as its final collapse. We will have to get through all of this . . .

As I have mentioned, dissidents were subject to harsh persecution in the 1970s and 1980s. In the course of 1987 the majority of "prisoners of conscience"—persons imprisoned for their opinions or for nonviolent actions in support of their beliefs according to Amnesty International's definition—were released. Some, including Anatoly Shcharansky, Yuri Orlov, my wife and myself, were released even earlier. However, about twenty persons sentenced under Article 70 of the RSFSR Criminal Code [Anti-Soviet agitation and propaganda] remain in prison, labor camp, or internal exile, as well as some prisoners of conscience sentenced under other articles of the Criminal Code, or confined in psychiatric hospitals. All of them should be freed.

This is critical for improving the moral atmosphere in our country and for overcoming "The Inertia of Fear" (title of a samizdat book). It is psychologically important that all prisoners of conscience should be rehabilitated, and not simply pardoned and quietly released. It is past time to end the practice of rehabilitating innocent people posthumously instead of during their lifetime. Furthermore, the 1987 demand that prisoners of conscience should formally request a pardon was clearly improper from a moral and legal standpoint . . .

And, of course, the penal system should be made more humane and brought into line with international standards. The complete abolition of the death penalty is also necessary. Beccaria, Hugo, Tolstoy and other writers and humanists of earlier times opened people's eyes to the extreme psychological cruelty of capital punishment. Besides, errors in court proceedings are inevitable, and they cannot be corrected after a defendant has been executed. The abolition of capital punishment would be a step toward the humanization of our society. Unfortunately, many people are not convinced of this, and, appalled by certain crimes, continue to campaign for its retention. I hope that their opinion will not prevail. Perestroika should promote the openness of our society as a fundamental prerequisite for the moral and economic health of our country and for international trust and security. The concept of "openness" should include: monitoring by society of key government decisions (repetition of a mistake such as the invasion of Afghanistan must be made impossible), freedom of opinion, freedom to receive and impart information, and freedom to choose one's country of residence and one's domicile within that country . . . The right to return is an important adjunct to the right to emigrate.

Source: Available at http://users.physics.harvard.edu/~wilson/sakharovconference/ Suggested_Reading/The%20Inevitability%20of%20Perestroika.pdf (accessed 10 May 2014). Used by permission of Edward Kline.

Notes

1 Serhii Plokhy, *The Last Empire: The Final Days of the Soviet Union* (New York: Basic Books, 2014).
2 Moshe Lewin, *The Gorbachev Phenomenon: A Historical Interpretation* (Berkeley: University of California Press, 1988).
3 Kristin Roth-Ey, *Moscow Prime Time: How the Soviet Union Built the Empire That Lost the Cold War* (Ithaca, NY: Cornell University Press, 2011).
4 Anne Gorsuch, *All This Is Your World: Soviet Tourism at Home and Abroad after Stalin* (New York: Oxford University Press, 2011); Maxim Matsuevich, ed., *Africa in Russia, Russia in Africa: Three Centuries of Encounters* (Trenton, NJ: Africa World Press, Inc., 2007).
5 Stephen Kotkin, *Armageddon Averted: The Soviet Collapse 1970–2000* (New York: Oxford University Press, 2001).
6 Archie Brown, *Seven Years That Changed the World* (New York: Oxford University Press, 2007); Archie Brown, *The Gorbachev Factor* (New York: Oxford University Press, 1996); Robert English, *Russia and the Idea of the West: Gorbachev, Intellectuals and the End of the Cold War* (New York: Columbia University Press, 2000).
7 Anne Gorsuch and Diane Koenker, *The Socialist Sixties: Crossing Borders in the Second World* (Bloomington: Indiana University Press, 2013); Rossen Djagalov, "The People's Republic of Letters: Towards a Media History of Twentieth Century Socialist Internationalism," PhD diss., Yale University, 2012.
8 Mikhail Gorbachev, *Perestroika, New Thinking for Our Country and the World* (New York: Harper and Row, 1987).
9 Christopher Marsh, *China's Rise, Russia's Fall and the Interdependence of Transition* (Lanham, MD: Lexington Books, 2005).

10 Martin Malia, *The Soviet Tragedy: A History of Socialism in Russia, 1917–1991* (New York: Free Press, 1991).
11 Anton Antonov-Ovseenko, *Time of Stalin: Portrait of a Tyranny* (New York: Harper and Row, 1981).
12 Kathleen Smith, *Remembering Stalin's Victims: Popular Memory and the End of the USSR* (Ithaca, NY: Cornell University Press, 1996).
13 Leon Aron, *Road to the Temple: Truth, Memory, Ideas and Ideals in the Making of the Russian Revolution, 1987–1991* (New Haven, CT: Yale University Press, 2012).
14 Andrei Sakharov, *Memoirs* (New York: Alfred Knopf, 1990).
15 Svetlana Alexievich, *Zinky Boys: Soviet Voices from the Afghanistan War* (New York: W. W. Norton and Co., 1992).
16 Alexander Nekrich and Vadim Petrov, *"June 22 1941." Soviet Historians and the German Invasion* (Columbia: University of South Carolina Press, 1968).
17 Robert Horvath, *Dissidents, Democratization, and Radical Nationalism in Russia* (New York: Routledge, 2005), 220.
18 Yegor Ligachev, *Inside Gorbachev's Kremlin: The Memoir of Yegor Ligachev* (Boulder, CO: Westview Press, 1996).
19 Archie Brown, *Rise and Fall of Communism* (New York: Oxford University Press, 2009), 504.
20 Vladislav Zubok, *A Failed Empire: The Soviet Union in the Cold War from Stalin to Gorbachev* (Chapel Hill: University of North Carolina Press, 2007).
21 Padraic Kenny, *Carnival of Revolution: Central Europe, 1989* (Princeton, NJ: Princeton University Press, 2003).

12 Russia after 1991

Change and continuity

INTRODUCTION

The Cathedral of Christ the Savior, originally built in 1885 and then dismantled in 1931 (see chapter 5), was rebuilt and reconsecrated in the city of Moscow on 19 August 2000, the Day of Transfiguration.[1] With monies donated by the faithful, and supplemented by sizable contributions from the state and rich donors, the giant construction project was conceived by the Yeltsin administration and spearheaded by the energetic and ambitious mayor of Moscow, Yuri Luzhkov. In the 1980s, groups of Soviet intellectuals and members of the Orthodox Church had conceived of rebuilding the church as they were concerned with preserving the architectural and religious legacy of the Russian past. But their ideas were quickly hijacked by the Yeltsin administration. Supported by Alexei II, Patriarch of the Russian Orthodox Church, both Yeltsin and Luzhkov believed that the reconstruction of the cathedral was a way to restore the Russian national and cultural identity that had been disrupted by the Soviet experience and the collapse of the Soviet Union. The monumental cathedral, built at a cost of an estimated 400 to 500 million dollars, was to serve as a symbol of resurrection: of Moscow, the heart of the Russian nation, and its cultural essence, the Russian Orthodox Church.

On 21 February 2012, members of a feminist punk rock collective called Pussy Riot staged a brief rock performance at the altar of the cathedral to protest the authoritarianism of the Putin regime, only to be forcibly interrupted by irate church officials. With their faces covered with balaclavas and clad in loose dresses and neon tights, the members of the band danced and sang with electric guitars. But by the evening an enhanced video of their performance entitled "Punk Prayer—Mother of God, Chase Putin Away" had gone viral on the internet. The members of the group were soon arrested and two of them sentenced to a period of incarceration. If the Russian Orthodox Church had survived many years of antireligious propaganda under the Soviet regime and made a triumphal comeback after the collapse of the Soviet Union, then the Pussy Riot performance showed that reports of the death of the Russian intelligentsia had been widely exaggerated.[2] The Russian intelligentsia, artists, intellectuals, and academics, who believed that they had a moral mission to criticize and lampoon the excesses of state authority, had also reemerged in the postcommunist order, determined to offer alternative visions for Russia's future.

CHAPTER QUESTIONS

In the two decades after the collapse of the Soviet Union, Russia, shorn of its many imperial acquisitions from the Baltics to the Caucasus and from Eastern Europe to Central Asia, tried to chart a new economic course, create a new state structure and political ideology, and craft a foreign policy that was commensurate with the global realities of the postimperial order, which was increasingly dominated by a coalition of Western Europe and the United States, and a rising new power: China. In this chapter we will review the major economic, social, and political trends in post-Soviet Russia and also consider the impact of these epochal transitions through the lives of three Russian women: Viktoria Ivanovna, geologist turned entrepreneur, Anna Politkovskaya, famed journalist and human rights activist, and Nadezhda Tolokonnikova, member of Pussy Riot. What does it mean to be Russia without an empire? How are Russian leaders attempting to formulate new political, economic, and social structures? How are they reimagining a Russian cultural identity that addresses its links with both Europe and Asia? And what are the diverse ways that Russian citizens are reacting to these efforts?

VOICES, MEMORIES, CONTESTED PERSPECTIVES

Transition to a representative political system

Since the introduction of multiparty electoral politics in Russia in 1991 we have seen the classic tug of war between the executive, the office of the president, and the legislature, the bicameral federal assembly, that accompanies the political transition from a centralized authoritarian structure to a polity where there is more than one locus of authority. In 1993, after an armed standoff with the members of the legislature who were determined to limit presidential power, Boris Yeltsin, the new president of Russia, ushered in a constitution that gave more power to the Kremlin than to the legislature. Although Yeltsin engineered a centralized political system, he became increasingly powerless and infirm in his second term of office and overtly dependent on the power and purse of a group of oligarchs or influential businessmen who bankrolled his electoral campaigns. Between 1998 and 2000, Russia had five prime ministers, until in 2000 Vladimir Putin, Yeltsin's protégé, took power as president in May of that year.[3]

In Russia, in addition to the elected offices of the presidency and the prime minister, who is appointed by the president with the approval of the legislature, power is also vested in a judiciary. Since the 2000s, the Russian judicial system has been brought into line with that of Western Europe by reducing terms of detention for those in pre-trial incarceration and adopting trial by jury in certain criminal cases. But political control in the upper echelons of the judicial order is still pervasive, and this has been demonstrated repeatedly by the high profile trials of billionaire Mikhail Khodarkovsky, members of Pussy Riot, political activist Alexei Navalny, and others who have publicly opposed the Putin administration.

Within the federal structure of Russia there are eighty-five provincial administrations that range from republics such as Kalmykia, which is predominantly Buddhist, to ethnically denoted areas such as the Jewish Autonomous Oblast, Birobidzhan, in the

Russian Far East. Many of these units claimed substantial autonomy under Yeltsin, especially the elected governors of the provinces. The third ring of power in Russia comprises the newly formed class of capitalists, who after 1991 acquired state-owned factories, natural resources, and property at prices substantially below market levels. This appropriation of state property was made possible because of their collusion with key members from the upper ranks of the Communist Party, high ranking members of the Soviet bureaucracy, and directors of state-run factories and enterprises.

It is important to remember that, even after the collapse of the Soviet Union, Russia, with its 142 million people, its vast territories, geostrategic location, and substantial reserves of coal, natural gas, oil, and nonferrous metals, remains a major world power supported by a significant diaspora located both in the "near abroad" in former Soviet republics and in Israel, the European Union, and the United States. In the wake of the imperial collapse, Russians now compose 80 percent of the population. However, it still remains a multiethnic society, with almost 10 percent of the population belonging to the Muslim faith in addition to significant Buddhist and Jewish communities. This multiethnic character of post-Soviet Russia complicates attempts to found an exclusively Russia-centric national identity.

Transition to a market economy

By the 1980s, multinational corporations, the World Bank and the International Monetary Fund, and heads of states had concluded that socialist economics led to stagnation and stasis that inhibited economic growth and productivity. Influential economists around the world, trained in the philosophy of Friedrich Hayek and Milton Friedman, preached that only deregulated and unregulated markets could jumpstart the slowing socialist economies, eliminate the state from the process of development, and usher in an era of unprecedented prosperity that would trickle down to the lowest rungs of society. Individualism and hard work, and private enterprise freed from the oversight of the state and society, would create wealth, opportunity, and creativity. Lazy and irresponsible workers, coddled by the cradle-to-grave welfare system, would be schooled by the market to work hard, to consume endlessly, and to provide for their families.[4] But how did this transition to a market-based economy affect everyday lives?

Belief in neoliberal ideologies of individualism and private material gain were not restricted to the upper echelons of Russia; as Olga Shevchenko has shown, many in Moscow believed that people should take personal responsibility for their own well-being instead of depending on a corrupt and hapless socialist state. Among the widespread cynicism and fear that Shevchenko encountered during her anthropological fieldwork in the 1990s, she also noted the range of strategies that people adopted to make ends meet, pay their bills, privatize living space, and secure consumer goods for themselves and their children in a vain attempt to insulate their lives from the crisis of transition. Unfortunately, many also lost all hope in the power of collective political action and social protest as a means to make the ruling class more responsible to its constituents.[5]

The Yeltsin administration was committed to incorporating the Russian economy into an increasingly globalized world that took shape after the collapse of the Soviet bloc. While the transition from a state owned and managed economy to one controlled by the market and international capital seemed easy enough on paper and promised substantial increases in wages and living standards, in reality the process was horrendously complicated and protracted. In the absence of the Soviet state and the Communist Party, who really owned the rusting factories, the limitless mineral wealth, the collective farms, the banks and financial institutions, the transportation systems, the apartment complexes, the resorts, the commercial places, and the public spaces of this staggeringly vast empire? Could the citizens of the country claim legitimate ownership of public resources? Finally, would state subsidies for housing, staples of daily life, education, healthcare, and energy instituted under socialism have to be abolished in order to allow prices for goods and services to seek a "natural" correlation between demand and supply?

Under the guidance of Yegor Gaidar and Anatoly Chubais, the Yeltsin administration implemented the "shock therapy" of privatization and the "discipline" of the market to stem the decline of the Soviet economy that centered on rusting and technologically obsolete factories and plants. Russians joked that there was too much shock and not enough therapy. Vital sections of the Russian economy, especially oil and gas resources, were sold at below market prices to powerful individuals and conglomerates of Soviet elites in the party, state, and bureaucracy. The lightning speed of the transactions hid the intrinsic illegality of this process of turning state-owned resources into private property. Deregulation of markets and the privatization of former state-owned industries and assets such as mines, energy sectors, media, and telecommunications were global phenomena after 1991, creating a class of newly minted billionaires worldwide.[6]

Russians realized that the onset of capitalism led to dramatically lower standards of living for the vast majority and enormous concentrations of wealth in the hands of the few, who alone seemed to benefit from the new market order. People suffered greatly during the 1990s, especially in the small towns and villages of provincial Russia where there were few new employment opportunities to compensate for ailing state-run enterprises that could barely afford to pay their workers. Hyperinflation ate away at savings accumulated over decades, and the random privatization of property ate away at the public places such as forests, parks, recreation centers, and clubs that the Soviet state had previously provided for its citizens. As the legendary Soviet welfare state shrank, most Russians could not afford the consumer goods on display in stores and kiosks in metropolitan areas, nor avail of services in the new private hospitals, banks, and educational institutions. In the 1990s, visitors to Russia could see elderly pensioners selling their meager possessions on the streets and boulevards to cope with the depredations of hyperinflation. Teachers, professors, doctors, and other professionals lost the middle class status that they had acquired during late socialism and took on second and third jobs in order to make ends meet. According to Caroline Humphrey, the "unmaking" of socialism was traumatic and painful not only because it required economic readjustments to a market economy, but also because it forced people to rethink their personal identities and values, and find new class and cohort affiliations.[7] Past practices such as corruption, nepotism, and bribe taking referred to as *blat*, which were considered to be peculiarly socialist phenomena, took on new meaning in a market economy where they grew at an astronomical rate.[8]

At the other end of the spectrum, the most powerful members of Russia's nascent capitalist class, the oligarchs, exercised considerable influence in the Kremlin. Boris Berezovsky, Mikhail Khodarkovsky, and Vladimir Gusinsky became household names because of their enormous wealth, proclivity for self-promotion, and the media empires that they built and controlled. Russia witnessed vast outflows of capital cannibalized from former state-owned enterprises, which was stashed away in overseas accounts, properties, and business investments in Cyprus, Israel, the United Kingdom, France, Italy, the United States, Dubai, and Switzerland to name only a few countries of destination. Russians also had to deal with organized crime, as private armies of businessmen fought each other to acquire state-owned property.[9] Mafia organizations, many of which had been incubated in the Soviet Gulag, and members of the armed forces and the state security services provided protection and muscle for new Russian businesses. Films, books, and journalism from the 1980s and 1990s chronicled the seamy side of life in Russia. Stories of trafficked women and children, rape, murder, gang wars, corruption, and general decline in norms of morality and civility were so ubiquitous that the term "chernukha," derived from the Russian word *chernyi* (black), was coined to describe its prevalence in popular culture. The immensely popular film *Tycoon, a New Russian* (2002), a thinly fictionalized account of Boris Berezovsky's accumulation of his legendary wealth, showed the corruption, political networking, and violence that accompanied the creation of private fortunes.

The everyday lives of the Russian *nouveaux riches* were chronicled in a best-selling novel called *Ca$ual* by Oksana Robski, published in 2005. Describing the residents of the affluent suburb of Rublevka near Moscow, Robski offered her readers an insider view of the ways of the post-Soviet elite. Surrounded by an army of personal attendants, the women in the novel, mostly wives, lovers, and occasional business partners of wealthy and powerful men, were groomed to an inch of their lives during the day in order to socialize in expensive night clubs, restaurants, and the occasional male strip bar at night. The novel chronicled the rise of an exuberant and sophisticated club scene in Moscow. The ostentatious lifestyles of the 1 percent in Russia were curiously similar to those of their global counterparts, as they skied in Courcheval, summered at St. Tropez and the Cap d'Antibes in the south of France, and sailed their yachts in the Mediterranean and the Caribbean. They owned luxurious homes in London and New York, drove Aston Martins and Lamborghinis, and displayed their wealth through acts of unimaginative but conspicuous consumption.

In the 1990s, Yeltsin's Russia was floundering from too much freedom and too much unregulated capitalism. As Stephen Kotkin and others have argued, a successful market economy needs the state and a legal system to uphold the laws of private property.[10] To a people accustomed to strong patrimonial rule from the center, the antics of a drunken and increasingly feeble Yeltsin seemed distasteful. Russians were humiliated by their loss of world stature and resented being reduced from a superpower to an ex-empire with a shrunken economy, shrunken borders, and a demoralized military. Vladimir Putin, who came to power in 2000, has described the 1990s as a "Time of Troubles" in order to emphasize the achievements of his own administration, which brought internal peace, prosperity, and a small measure of imperial glory back to Russia.

The Putin phenomenon

An ex-KGB man who witnessed the collapse of Soviet power from a ringside seat in East Germany, Vladimir Putin drew valuable lessons about the construction and deconstruction of state power. Putin has been soundly reviled and criticized by well-known Russian intellectuals such as Masha Gessen, Anna Politkovskaya, Boris Nemtsov, Ludmilla Alexeyeva, Dmitry Bykov, Vladimir Pastukhov, and Alexei Navalny, to name only a few. After the arrest of the members of Pussy Riot in 2012, the criticisms of Putin reached a global crescendo that continued to rise because of the Ukrainian crisis that started in 2014. Even the successful American television series *House of Cards* featured a belligerent and ruthless Putin during its third season.

Putin has been accused of every crime in the book, from money laundering, stealing state assets, diverting government funds to pet projects, awarding favorable contracts to crony capitalists to receive kickbacks, to using his political office to build a personal fortune valued at 20 to 40 billion dollars. He has also been accused of turning Russia away from its natural home in a democratic Western Europe toward a more authoritarian Eurasian identity. According to critics, Putin has muzzled the media, destroyed democracy by monopolizing political power by alternating between the post of president and prime minister for too long, promoted homophobia and gay-bashing, conducted genocide in Chechnya, and turned Russia into an incipient fascist state with help from his ex-KGB partners, right-wing nationalist groups, and the leaders of the Russian Orthodox Church. Finally, Putin's publicly stated desire to revitalize Russia through a muscular and interventionist foreign policy and reclaim its "rightful" place in the world order has unleashed a torrent of vituperation from journalists, scholars, and foreign policy experts at home and abroad that is very reminiscent of the heated interchanges during the Cold War.[11]

Is Putin really the "Man without a Face," as the title of one of his many antibiographies claims, or does he represent a return to the time-tested Russian model of a patrimonial and imperial power, or is he, to use his own words, simply a pragmatist? It is too soon to arrive at a definitive historical judgment about Putin, but it is important to note that he is enormously popular within Russia, and in the section that follows we will consider the reasons for Putin's high approval ratings at home. Vladimir Putin was lucky in that his time in office coincided with high oil, gas, and metal prices, Russia's premier exports.[12] Putin also decided to reassert state control over the energy sector and use the proceeds to strengthen his government. Oil magnates such as Mikhail Khodarkovsky and Boris Berezovsky witnessed the sequestration of their property by the state. While Khodarkovsky was jailed for an extended period following a very public trial, Berezovsky went into exile to the United Kingdom where he died under mysterious circumstances. Under Alex Kudrin, Putin's minister of finance, the administration, while reasserting state control over key sectors of the economy, also followed pro-business and pro-market policies. Inflation was brought under control, Russian banks were stabilized, and laws were instituted that guaranteed the stability of private property and capital investment. Russia boasted that it levied one of the lowest income tax rates in Europe, at 13 percent. Profits from the energy sector not only stabilized the Russian economy, but also allowed Russia to pay off its foreign debts incurred during the 1990s. Russia established a substantial foreign currency reserve called the Stabilization Fund, modeled after the sovereign wealth funds of other resource-rich countries such as Norway and Saudi Arabia, and this has allowed it to weather the 2008 recession and the decline in oil prices that started in 2014. Economists, however, believe that Russia is too dependent on the export of natural resources and should diversify the economy by encouraging the creation of private businesses, especially in the agricultural, services, and technological sectors.[13]

The privatization of the housing market that had started under Yeltsin, when the state gave de facto ownership of the housing to former tenants and residents with few fees and taxes, gathered pace under Putin. Almost 85 percent of Russia's housing stock is now privately owned.[14] While poorer residents dwelling in communal apartments in central Moscow and St. Petersburg were "relieved" of their property rights by a newly formed class of realtors and property developers, it is important to note that large numbers of citizens received apartments practically free as both the Yeltsin and the Putin administrations believed that home ownership is the key to the building of a stable middle class society. While home ownership has grown significantly in Russia, the capitalization of the housing market has led to huge inequalities that we now see in cities around the world. In Russia, this phenomenon is compounded by inflated property values and lack of low interest mortgage loans or a well-developed credit system. Currency fluctuations also affect the housing market and Russians, after being accustomed to the stable monetary policies of the Soviet era, are learning to cope with the booms and busts of the capitalist business cycle.

In 2005, Putin's United Party announced four National Projects with much fanfare. These included increased investment in healthcare, education, housing, and the development of agro-industrial complexes that would provide for employment in the rural sectors. Putin tackled the growing demographic crisis in Russia that had started in the 1980s when rising mortality rates among Russian men became an issue of international concern among demographers and foreign policy analysts. In 2007, a fund for maternal capital was created similar to that adopted in Quebec and Australia, and mothers who had a second child or adopted a second one received a fixed sum of money from the state. After 2010, fertility rates began to rise and concerns about the "dying" Russian population have begun to ebb in the media. Other welfare measures included investment in healthcare that had deteriorated badly during the 1990s, and the state has started to spend significantly more on pre- and postnatal care and the construction of hospitals and medical centers, especially in rural areas. However, in these areas Russia has yet to reach parity with standards of living in Western Europe and the United States.

During the 2000s, Russia tried to break with its Soviet past by reviving its pre-revolutionary past in terms of art, architecture, and a narrative of a continuous Russian civilization that lay beneath the Soviet veneer. Under Mayor Luzhkov, Moscow was transformed by the addition of giant malls, shopping centers, chic hotels and restaurants, art galleries, museums, and renovated church buildings. Beautiful art nouveau buildings in areas such as Ostazhenka in Moscow, also known as the Golden Mile, were revitalized and renovated. Ancient provincial cities such as Tver, Yaroslavl, and Novgorod, with their wealth of Orthodox churches and neoclassical buildings, were also upgraded to meet the needs of a growing international and domestic tourist presence. Leningrad changed its name back to St. Petersburg, and the historic center of the city, composed of neoclassical and baroque buildings, was recognized by UNESCO as a World Heritage Site in 1990.

While many of the tsarist era palaces, buildings, and noble mansions have been restored, preservationists and residents have been alarmed by the spate of constructions and land grabs by various highly connected officials and businessmen. The new mansions in the leafy parks that surround the old estates in St. Petersburg threaten its architectural heritage. Matters came to a head in 2005 when Gazprom, Russia's biggest natural gas company, decided to build the gigantic Okhta Center, the company headquarters, close to the historic downtown of St. Petersburg.[15] Vociferous protests by civic organizations and enraged citizens forced Gazprom to relocate the gigantic and futuristic complex, billed as Europe's tallest building complex, to the city outskirts, and it was renamed the Lakhta Center. This marked a rare victory for an engaged citizenry, but many are still divided about the aesthetic impact of this building on the St. Petersburg skyline.

While economists argue about the size and depth of the Russian middle class, in the last twenty years or so there has been a significant reduction in real poverty rates, accompanied by an increase in the purchasing power of a class that has benefited greatly from the growing Russian economy. The Russian middle class, like its counterparts in the rest of the world, defines itself by its education, home and car ownership, leisure practices, including trips to Turkey, Egypt, Thailand, and Malaysia, modest consumerism, and consumption of popular fiction, movies, and television. Science fiction, fantasy, romances, detective novels, crime thrillers, and Western popular fiction in translation can be found in bookstores throughout Russia, and Russians are avid and savvy consumers of media and digital technologies.

Foreign policy

While few would disagree with the considerable achievements of the Putin administration in stabilizing the economy, his foreign policy has been more controversial, and in the section that follows we will analyze the global repercussions of Russia regaining what it deems to be its rightful place in the world order. Gorbachev had hoped that with the abolition of the Soviet empire in Eastern Europe, and especially the reunification of Germany, NATO, a military coalition aimed at containing the Soviet Union, would also cease to exist. But since 1991 we have seen an increase in the size and composition of NATO, and Russia continues to feel aggrieved that Western promises of the demilitarization of Europe were not kept after 1991. As we have seen, Russia has always been insecure about its western borders, from where historically the enemies of Russia have waged murderous campaigns.

Like other decolonizing powers in Europe, Russians keenly felt their loss of status after the imperial collapse of 1991. Russian nationalism is often presented in terms of nostalgia for the greater Russian empire expressed by both extreme right and left wing parties. Ardent nationalists such as Alexander Dugin, one of the prominent ideologues affiliated with the Putin administration, often talk about the concept of Eurasianism: Russia's natural destiny in creating a traditional Eurasian society that includes Turkic and Slavic races in opposition to the liberal materialist order led by the United States and based on the Atlantic world. Dugin claims that maritime civilizations enshrine selfish individualism and the denial of history, whereas Eurasian societies believe in a larger notion of humanity or community buttressed by indigenous traditions. Dugin, who has two doctorates and until recently held a professorship at the Moscow University, is very prominent in the far-right political circles of Europe. He has been an outspoken advocate of Russian imperialism and called for the reannexation of the former Soviet republics, military expansion into Inner Asia and the Balkans, an alliance with Germany, Iran, and Japan, and the expansion of the Russian empire to the Indian Ocean! Dugin has on several occasions chided Putin publicly for being insufficiently militaristic and aggressive in his foreign policy.[16]

Putin, characteristically pragmatic, and despite his many links to Dugin's extremist National Bolshevik Party, has followed a more realistic foreign policy in line with Russia's diminished military capabilities. Putin and his foreign minister, Sergei Lavrov, have repeatedly accused the West of militarism on its borders, of drawing Poland, the Czech Republic, and Hungary into NATO, the military alliance between the United States and European countries, and of erecting missile sites aimed at Russia in these countries. The entry of the Baltic states of Latvia, Estonia, and Lithuania into the European Union in 2004 outraged the Putin administration, and sections of the Russian populations living within the borders of these states are very receptive to ideas of a future reunification with Russia. The expansion of the European Union into the Balkans is considered by Russia to be a direct affront. Moscow sees the former republics as the natural Russian sphere of influence and resents Western interference in the political affairs of countries in Central Asia, Georgia, and Ukraine. For the most part, Russia has used the media and foreign office to express its displeasure over what it views as Western infiltration through philanthropy, aid, religious missions, and the funding of civil society and pro-democracy projects. It is interesting that, despite the nominal independence of the former republics, Moscow has followed a foreign policy of drawing these countries back within its imperial orbit, whether through trade, political agreements, or acts of military intervention. As Jane Burbank and Frederick Cooper have argued, empires have been a constant presence in world history and it is useful to put Russian foreign policy in a comparative perspective of decolonization in the twentieth and twenty-first century.[17]

France fought a bitter fight in both Indo-China and North Africa, leading to the deaths of millions of civilians, before the sovereign nations of Vietnam and Algeria were formed from the detritus of the French empire. Similarly, the British settler colonies in Kenya and Rhodesia responded with brutal violence and erected concentration camps when indigenous peoples demanded freedom from colonial oversight. The repeated incursions of Western powers into the modern Middle East, led by the United States during the war on terror, show that the boundaries of nation states offer no real defense against imperial incursions, and Russia is following a time honored script of imperial intervention in areas that it considers to be within its sphere of influence.

Putin ascended to power by playing an important role in the Second Chechen War that started in 1999.[18] Chechnya, a Muslim majority republic led by a highly decorated general from the Russian army, Dzhokhar Dudaev, tried to break away from Russian control, leading to the First Chechen War between 1994 and 1996. The demoralized Russian army performed poorly against Chechen fighters who fought brilliantly on their own mountainous territory. Composed of only a million people and with deep oil reserves, Chechnya lies in a significant geo-political location as it is the conduit to Moscow's control of the Southern Caucasus, especially Georgia and Armenia.

The Russian empire spent many decades between the 1780s and the formal incorporation of the region in 1862 in fighting the mountainous and independent peoples that lived in isolated villages in this difficult terrain. During the revolution of 1917 the area briefly gained independence, only to be reincorporated by military force in 1921. During World War II almost half a million Chechens were deported to labor camps in Central Asia because of their purported sympathy with the Nazi army. They were only allowed to return in 1957, when the Chechen-Ingush Autonomous Soviet Republic was reestablished.

The Second Chechen War broke out in 1999 when, under the leadership of Shamil Basaev, an Islamic-based force attacked Dagestan, a neighboring province, in order to build the Islamic caliphate. Putin used this act to frame his war in Chechnya as a response to Islamic terrorism, and in many ways the Russian state anticipated the US response to terrorism after the bombings of 11 September 2001. Like the United States and India, who were also engaged in conflict with Islamic fundamentalists, Russia declared the right to respond to teroristic acts, such as the Moscow apartment bombings in 1999, the hostage crisis at the Nord-Ost Theater in Moscow in 2002, the hostage crisis involving schoolchildren in Beslan in 2004, and the bombings at the Moscow metro in 2010 and the airport in 2011, with unilateral military measures often unconstrained by the rule of constitutional law. The war in Chechnya took a bizarre turn after the initial military invasion, when the Russian government chose the strong man Akhmet Kadyrov and, after his death, his son Ramzan Kadyrov to attack Islamic fundamentalists in the North Caucasus. Subsequently, the Russian army used Chechnya as a springboard to control Islamic movements in neighboring Ingushetia and Dagestan. The Kadyrov family benefited greatly from their alliance with Moscow both economically and militarily, and Chechnya emerged as a profitable center of arms trafficking, oil smuggling, and the drug trade.

Ramzan Kadyrov lives an ostentatious lifestyle, engaging publicly with celebrities and actors such as Jean-Claude Van Damme and Gerard Depardieu. In 2011, the famed violinist Vanessa Mae performed at Kadyrov's birthday celebrations in Grozny. Despite his playboy image, Kadyrov has supported a return to the traditional form of a decentralized Sufi Islam in Chechnya that is based on individual charismatic leaders and their communities in order to dismantle the appeal of a transnational Sunni ideology that seeks to resurrect the Islamic caliphate in Eurasia. While Kadyrov has been criticized for following socially conservative policies toward women as a way to increase birthrates, Chechnya has recovered economically from the two devastating wars that caused enormous destruction. During the last decade there has been a building boom in this war-torn country, and the Kadyrov administration has carried out extensive restorations in the badly damaged capital, Grozny. At the same time, Kadyrov has used Moscow's largesse to enormously strengthen his personal power: to build a private militia and silence opposition by intimidation, arrests, and extra-judicial torture and killings.

The Putin administration has followed a muscular and interventionist foreign policy on its borders, one that it can ill afford. In 2008, upset by the fact that Georgia and Ukraine were seeking to join the NATO military alliance, the Putin administration backed an uprising in Southern Ossetia and Abkhazia and militarily prevented Georgia's attempts to restore control over this territory. However, the biggest crisis to engulf the Putin presidency has been the issue of Ukraine. In 2014, Russia unilaterally reannexed the Crimean Peninsula from Ukraine. Crimea, home originally to the ethnic Tatars, the warlords of Russia in the distant past, had been annexed by Russia in 1783 and only temporarily transferred to Ukraine in 1954, when it was still a part of the Soviet Union. During World War II, like the Chechens, the Tatars were deported by Stalin for suspected collaboration with the Nazis and only allowed to return after 1991. By then the area held a sizable Russian and Ukrainian population, and Tatars became a minority in their own land.

As Russia's only warm water port and home to the Black Sea Fleet, Crimea is of immense geo-strategic importance as it serves to connect Russia to the Middle East,

West Asia, and Eastern Europe through the Black Sea. The incorporation of Crimea triggered a separatist movement in Eastern Ukraine, where a significant ethnic Russian population is demanding a reunion with Russia. Russia for its part needs the industrial and agricultural resources of Ukraine to bolster its economic status, and it is really in the interests of both sides to find an amicable solution as Ukraine is dangerously reliant on cheap oil and gas from Russia for its energy needs, as well as monetary remittances from its guest workers in Russia. Backed by Moscow's arms and money, the insurgency has turned into a proxy war against Western Ukraine, which is seeking integration into the European Union, helped by arms and money from the West. While critics have denounced Moscow's imperial policies, and international sanctions have been levied on the Russian economy, many within Russia believe that they have the right to defend their borders against Western encirclement. Despite the havoc wreaked by economic sanctions coupled with falling oil prices, most Russians have publicly expressed support for the separatists in Eastern Ukraine, and Putin's attempts to reestablish Russia's influence over its former republics and allies have increased his popularity at home.[19]

To offset Russia's increasingly contentious relations with Western Europe and the United States, Putin's administration has nurtured close relations with Asian countries. It has maintained close ties with the former republics in Central Asia, especially the oil-rich state of Kazakhstan where Russian engineering and technical personnel have played a key role in the development of the vast energy sector. China and Russia have signed long-term agreements in the energy sector and the arms trade. China is interested in buying oil and gas at reduced prices as well as fighter jets, surface-to-air missiles, and submarines from Russia, and both have a vested interest in controlling Islamic fundamentalism in Central Asia, the Caucasus, and South Asia. China has sided with Russia's policies in the Middle East, especially its support of the Syrian dictator Bashar al-Assad, whose country has been engulfed in a civil war since 2010, and has been noticeably silent about Russia's military incursions into Ukraine. Russia also enjoys excellent relations with its former client India and is a significant supplier of arms to this emerging nation.

Everyday lives in post-Soviet Russia: Viktoria Ivanovna, Anna Politkovskaya, and Pussy Riot

In the section that follows we will examine the history of post-Soviet Russia through the eyes of women and analyze the changes and continuities in their lives. Viktoria Ivanovna (last name omitted for reasons of privacy) is a trained geologist from the prestigious Moscow University. Her parents divorced early, and Viktoria was raised by a redoubtable grandmother, Valentina. Valentina believed in the Soviet Union and was proud of the major accomplishments of the Stalinist revolution. Born to a poor peasant family in a historic town not far from Moscow, Valentina came of age in the 1930s and enthusiastically supported the processes of collectivization. The Communist Party, recognizing her considerable talents, enrolled her in a school of agricultural technology, and she soon rose to a position of responsibility in her collective farm. Valentina, when questioned about Stalin's reign of terror, always admitted the excesses that had been committed during the 1930s and 1940s, but she blamed these on corrupt and morally degraded individuals. Valentina believed that the collectivization of agriculture and the industrial revolution of the 1930s transformed a poor and backward Russia into a modern superpower.

Viktoria was raised in relative comfort as during the Khrushchev era her grandmother was one of the first to receive a modest two-roomed private apartment with running water and electricity for her untiring service to the state. Viktoria was a gifted student and after a short stint in a factory, on her grandmother's advice to increase her competitiveness, she was accepted into the Department of Geology in the highly prestigious Moscow University. Viktoria graduated in 1989 when glasnost was at its height. The mixed messages of the Gorbachev regime about market socialism confused many in Gorbachev's audience, and for young people these were difficult times as the old ways of upward mobility were becoming unavailable, and new ones were yet to emerge. Rather than seek employment with the state, Viktoria enrolled in a course on book-keeping, hoping to understand the new market economy. During the 1990s, she dabbled in a series of businesses and then decided to become an importer of Indian goods, mainly clothing. Viktoria, like thousands of other street traders, sold her cheap Indian goods at hastily improvised stalls on the streets of Moscow during the 1990s. Since it was not possible to succeed without mafia protection, she paid her dues and at work even packed a gun for her own safety.

However, Viktoria kept setting aside her profits from this precarious business and continued to live modestly in her rented apartment, afraid to show her wealth in the uncertain political atmosphere. In the early 2000s, after Putin came to power, she opened a store that specialized in imported linen from Italy. She also bought a fashionable apartment in a block of Khrushchev apartments that had been renovated with an Italian marble foyer and a futuristic German kitchen. Her two children were enrolled in a private school, and Viktoria takes a vacation every year in an exotic foreign destination. Many family members have criticized her for her wholehearted embrace of capitalism and for wasting her university education, but Viktoria remains proud of her many achievements. She also remains a fervent supporter of Putin's policies. Do people prize their economic security and place personal achievements over the transgressions of their country?

Politkovskaya, like Viktoria, came of age during the collapse of the Soviet Union. Born to a Ukrainian family of diplomats in New York, Politkovskaya identified herself as Soviet/Russian. Despite her university education, Politkovskaya focused on raising their two children while her husband Sasha Politkovsky, host of the famous television talk show *Vzgliad* (Point of View), played a crucial role during glasnost in covering the nuclear disaster in Chernobyl, among his other pioneering exposés. In the 1990s, Politkovskaya turned to investigative journalism and over time became a star reporter for the *Novaia gazeta*, one of Russia's most liberal newspapers. Politkovskaya found her voice reporting on the two Chechen wars and the brutality of the Russian army in this war-torn region of Europe. She wrote about the *zachistkas*, or cleaning operations, an antiterrorist strategy followed by the Russian army. Villages would be blockaded for days on end and young men arrested, tortured, and killed with little or no evidence. Villagers wishing to leave the village would be forced to pay enormous bribes. Politkovskaya also uncovered a brisk trade in dead bodies where Chechen relatives paid outrageous sums for the mutilated bodies of kidnapped men in order to give them a decent burial.

To Politkovskaya's credit, she was an impartial witness; while she excoriated the genocidal violence of the Russian army, she had little sympathy for the Chechen nationalists and separatists and their brutal policies. Politkovskaya reserved her special ire for Ramzan Kadyrov and accused him of becoming a Chechen Stalin. Politkovskaya went into dangerous places to retrieve information on the war in Chechnya and to interview the families of survivors. She was kidnapped by Chechen authorities, beaten up by Russian armed forces, and poisoned, but nothing deterred her in her quest for truth. In numerous hard hitting books and articles, Politkovskaya listed the collateral damage of the two wars in Chechnya: the hungry and traumatized children, grieving mothers and widows who wept over the mutilated and tortured bodies of dead sons and husbands, burning schools, the bombed hospitals, the devastated farms, the houses in which normal people presumably once lived normal lives flattened to rubble. She also recounted the brutalization of young Russian conscripts and soldiers in the Russian army who were forced to fight a war that they did not choose.

Politkovskaya's life was cut short on 7 October 2006, when she was shot dead in front of her apartment by armed gunmen. Politkovskaya's raw courage and refusal to make compromises with Putin's regime have made her a veritable icon of resistance. Family members, friends, colleagues, and legions of admirers worldwide have kept her ideas alive through films, awards established in her name, and the publication of her works.[20] Politkovskaya's inability to understand that compromise lies at the heart of politics reminds us of the fearlessness of Russia's nineteenth century heroines, such as Ekaterina Breshkovskaia, Vera Figner, and Sofia Perovskaia, who also condemned government sponsored oppression.

While Viktoria and Politkovskaya represent the transitional generation connecting the two eras before and after socialism, members of the punk rock group Pussy Riot are an entirely post-Soviet phenomenon. The leading members of Pussy Riot, who were imprisoned for their performance in the Cathedral of Christ the Savior, Maria Alyokhina and Nadezhda Tolokonnikova, grew up in the world described in this chapter. They saw state structures crumbling, only to be replaced by more authoritarian ones. But they also grew up in a world where revolution was still a possibility, and where street theater and collective social action could shake the political establishment. Their activism is based on their fundamental conviction that space, whether a church, a street, a museum, or a bus stop, is a public resource. Shocking punk performances only highlight the illegality of the authorities that seek to privatize such commons or mandate norms of public behavior.

The members of Pussy Riot are articulate and very well versed in literature, philosophy, and Western feminism. Nadezhda Tolokonnikova, a student of philosophy at the prestigious Moscow State University, in an interview with *Spiegel* that was conducted from prison on 3 September 2013, claimed: "we're part of the global anticapitalist movement, which consists of anarchists, Trotskyists, feminists and autonomists. Our anti-capitalism is not anti-Western or anti-European."[21] In keeping with their antimaterialist philosophy, Pussy Riot refused to perform with Madonna, as their performances are intended for political and not commercial effect. Prior to their show in the cathedral, members of Pussy Riot had performed in various public spaces such as a scaffold on the subway, trolley buses, Timiryazev State Biology Museum in Moscow, on top of Moscow Detention Center Number 1 Prison, where, among others, Alexei Navalny, a lawyer turned political activist, was being held. On 20 January 2012, on Lobnoe Mesto, in front of St. Basil's Cathedral in Red Square in Moscow, Pussy Riot performed their legendary and perhaps most infamous song

Figure 12.1 Members of Pussy Riot awaiting trial, 3 August 2012. © epa european
pressphoto agency b.v./Alamy.

Why do you think this photo generated so much media attention?

"Putin Zassal," roughly translated as "Putin Chickened Out" or more infamously
"Putin Wet himself," while setting off a smoke bomb. While the members were briefly
detained and fined for their unsanctioned performances, few either in Russia
or abroad knew about the group's existence or their aims. Their iconoclastic act in
the Cathedral of Christ the Savior might have also gone unnoticed by history but for
the fact that the Russian government imprisoned three of the members and charged
them with a criminal offense.

In late October 2012, after a spectacularly mismanaged trial, Nadezhda
Tolokonnikova (22) and Maria Alyokhina (24) were separated and sent to prison in
labor camps in Mordovia and Perm Oblast respectively. A third member of Pussy
Riot, Yekaterina Samsuevich (29), was freed on probation, while two other members
of the group fled Russia fearing arrest. To be sentenced to two years of imprisonment
at a labor camp on charges of "hooliganism motivated by religious hatred," in
addition to their pre-trial imprisonment for five months, seemed to be a heavy price to
pay for a punk performance. Russian religious leaders across the country, including
Patriarch Kirill I and the Chief Rabbi of Moscow, Berel Lazar, called on the members
of Pussy Riot to repent for their devilish deeds and apologize.[22]

However, according to Russian opinion polls, many believed that their sentence
was disproportionate to the crime. Academics, journalists, feminist groups, Amnesty

International, and media celebrities such as Yoko Ono and Paul McCartney all protested about the incarceration of Maria and Nadezhda.[23] Both used their trial to protest the suppression of civil and political liberties in Russia and continued to protest against conditions in prison, conducting interviews and smuggling out letters that reached a worldwide audience. Nadezhda Tolokonnikova and Maria Alyokhina were freed from jail in December 2013, and they have continued to criticize the attrition of democratic liberties in Russia.

CONCLUSION AND FURTHER QUESTIONS

As the Pussy Riot trial has shown, since 1991 Russia has become a part of the rapidly globalizing world, and the government is unable to insulate internal affairs from international media commentary. Like China, Russia has made significant improvements in living conditions for many and developed a middle class whose consumer tastes and aspirations are very similar to ours. It is also, like ours, an unequal society with extreme concentrations of wealth and power at the very top. Russia has a patriotic population that has strong memories of being a former superpower, a people that is willing to make sacrifices at home in order to regain influence over former Soviet territories and in select areas in Eastern Europe. Putin has ruled Russia since 2000, guiding the country out of the Time of Troubles, but it remains to be seen whether or not he will yield power to a younger and more democratically inclined and materialistic generation, or whether he will continue to increase his political hold over Russia and use isolation to increase its geo-political and military strength at the cost of living standards for the many.

PRIMARY SOURCES

Use the questions to analyze the content, context, and significance of each primary source. Then synthesize the primary sources and the material in the chapter to formulate a response to the primary chapter questions: What does it mean to be Russia without an empire? How are Russian leaders attempting to formulate new political, economic, and social structures?

Document 12.1   Selections from the last article published in the *Novaia gazeta* newspaper by Anna Politkovskaya on 12 October 2006

Questions for analysis

1 Provide examples of human rights abuses committed in the Republic of Chechnya from the text.
2 Do you think that Anna Politkovskaya is an objective and impartial reporter?
3 Do you think that the state has the right to apprehend and torture potential terrorists in order to prevent terrorist crimes from being committed?

WE ARE DESIGNATING YOU A TERRORIST

Dozens of files come my way every day which contain copies of materials from criminal cases against people jailed, imprisoned or under investigation in Russia for "terrorism."

Why put "terrorism" in quotes? Because the overwhelming majority of these suspects have been designated terrorists. Now in 2006, this habit of designating people has not only displaced any genuine attempt to combat terrorism, but is of itself producing potential terrorists thirsting for revenge. When the Prosecutor-General's Office and the courts fail to uphold the law and punish the guilty, and instead merely act on political instructions and connive in producing anti-terrorist statistics to please the Kremlin, then criminal cases get cooked up like pancakes.

A conveyer belt for mass producing "voluntary confessions" works faultlessly to ensure targets are met in the so-called struggle against "terrorists" in the North Caucasus . . .

Do we combat lawlessness with the law? Or do we try to bash their lawlessness with our own? . . .

Ukraine recently extradited to Russia, Beslan Gadayev, a Chechen arrested in early August when documents were being checked in the Crimea. These lines are from a letter he wrote on August 29, 2006.

"When I was extradited from Ukraine to Grozny, I was immediately taken to an office and asked whether I had killed a member of the Salikhov family, Anzor and his friend, a Russian truck driver. I swore I had shed no one's blood, neither Russian, nor Chechen. They stated as a fact, 'No, you killed them.' I started denying it again, and when I repeated that I had never killed anyone they immediately started beating me. First they punched me twice in the right eye. While I was recovering my senses, they pushed me down and handcuffed me. They pushed a pipe between my legs so that I could not move my hands, even though I was already handcuffed. Then they grabbed me, or more precisely this pipe they had attached to me, and suspended me from two nearby cabinets, which were about a metre high.

"As soon as they had done that, they attached wires to the little fingers of both my hands. A couple of seconds later they turned on the current and started beating me with rubber truncheons wherever they could." . . .

The defence lawyer has lodged a formal complaint about these gross violations of human rights with the Prosecutor's Office of the Chechen Republic.

Source: Reprinted in Anna Politkovskaya's collection of articles *Is Journalism Worth Dying For?* (Brooklyn, 2011) and translated by Arch Tait. Used by permission of Melville House Publishing, LLC, USA.

Document 12.2   Selections from Putin's speech on the annexation of Crimea on 18 March 2014

Questions for analysis

1   Can a state use reasons from the historical past to reannex a part of its former territory?
2   Is Putin elaborating an aggressive or a defensive foreign policy? Provide evidence for your answer.
3   Should Russian foreign policy be studied in isolation or in comparison to that of other states? Or what is the Russian view of US foreign policy?
4   Does this speech reflect the right of the peoples of Ukraine to self-determination? If not, provide reasons for your answer. How might Ukrainians view this speech?

. . . Everything in Crimea speaks of our shared history and pride. This is the location of ancient Khersones, where Prince Vladimir was baptized. His spiritual feat of adopting Orthodoxy predetermined the overall basis of the culture, civilization and human values that unite the peoples of Russia, Ukraine and Belarus. The graves of Russian soldiers whose bravery brought Crimea into the Russian empire are also in Crimea. There is also Sevastopol—a legendary city with an outstanding history, a fortress that serves as the birthplace of Russia's Black Sea Fleet. Crimea is Balaklava and Kerch, Malakhov Kurgan and Sapun Ridge. Each one of these places is dear to our hearts, symbolizing Russian military glory and outstanding valor . . .

Incidentally, the total population of the Crimean Peninsula today is 2.2 million people, of whom almost 1.5 million are Russians, 350,000 are Ukrainians who predominantly consider Russian their native language, and about 290,000–300,000 are Crimean Tatars, who, as the referendum has shown, also lean towards Russia . . .

Unfortunately, what seemed impossible became a reality. The USSR fell apart. Things developed so swiftly that few people realized how truly dramatic those events and their consequences would be. Many people, both in Russia and in Ukraine, as well as in other republics, hoped that the Commonwealth of Independent States that was created at the time would become the new common form of statehood. They were told that there would be a single currency, a single economic space, joint armed forces; however, all this remained empty promises, while the big country was gone. It was only when Crimea ended up as part of a different country that Russia realized that it was not simply robbed, it was plundered . . .

I understand why Ukrainian people wanted change. They have had enough of the authorities in power during the years of Ukraine's independence . . . They did not wonder why it was that millions of Ukrainian citizens saw no prospects at home and went to other countries to work as day laborers. I would like to stress this: it was not some Silicon Valley they fled to, but to become day laborers. Last year alone almost 3 million people found such jobs in Russia. According to some sources, in 2013 their earnings in Russia totaled over $20 billion, which is about 12% of Ukraine's GDP . . .

Our western partners, led by the United States of America, prefer not to be guided by international law in their practical policies, but by the rule of the gun. They have come to believe in their exclusivity and exceptionalism, that they can decide the destinies of the world, that only they can ever be right. They act as they please: here and there, they use force against sovereign states, building coalitions based on the principle "If you are not with us, you are against us." To make this aggression look legitimate, they force the necessary resolutions from international organizations, and if for some reason this does not work, they simply ignore the UN Security Council and the UN overall . . .

Source: Translated text was made available by the *Prague Post*, http://praguepost. com/eu-news/37854-full-text-of-putin-s-speech-on-crimea#ixzz3ZTfUqUaj (accessed 6 May 2015).

Notes

1 Ekaterina V. Haskins, "Russia's Post-Communist Past," *History and Memory*, 21, no. 1 (Spring/Summer 2009): 25–62.
2 Masha Gessen, *Dead Again: Russian Intelligentsia after Communism* (London: Verso, 1997).
3 Timothy Colton, *Yeltsin: A Life* (New York: Basic Books, 2008).
4 For opposing points of view see Anders Åslund, *How Capitalism Was Built: The Transformation of Central and Eastern Europe, Russia and Central Asia* (New York: Cambridge University Press, 2007); Peter Reddaway and Dmitri Glinskii, *The Tragedy of Russia's Reforms: Market Bolshevism and Against Democracy* (Washington, DC: United States Institute of Peace Press, 2001).
5 Olga Shevchenko, *Crisis and the Everyday in Postsocialist Moscow* (Bloomington: Indiana University Press, 2009).
6 Padma Desai, *Going Global: The Transition from Plan to Market in the World Economy* (Cambridge, MA: MIT Press, 1997); Joseph Stiglitz, *Globalization and Its Discontents* (New York: Basic Books, 2001).
7 Caroline Humphrey, *Unmaking of Soviet Life: Everyday Economies after Socialism* (Ithaca, NY: Cornell University Press, 2002).
8 Alena Ledeneva, *Russia's Economy of Favors: Blat, Networking, and Informal Exchange* (Cambridge: Cambridge University Press, 1998).
9 David Hoffman, *Oligarchs: Wealth and Power in the New Russia* (New York: Public Affairs, 2001).
10 Stephen Kotkin, *Armageddon Averted: The Soviet Collapse, 1970–2000* (Oxford: Oxford University Press, 2001).
11 Masha Gessen, *The Man without a Face: The Unlikely Rise of Vladimir Putin* (New York: Riverhead Books, 2012); Lilia Shevtsova, *Putin's Russia* (Washington, DC: Carnegie Endowment for International Peace, 2005); Anna Politkovskaya, *A Russian Diary: A Journalist's Final Account of Life, Corruption, and Death in Putin's Russia* (New York: Random House, 2007); Vladimir Putin, *First Person: An Astonishingly Frank Self-Portrait by Russia's President* (New York: Public Affairs, 2000).
12 Marshall Goldman, *Petrostate: Putin, Power, and New Russia* (New York: Oxford University Press, 2008).

13 For opposing viewpoints on Putin see Karin Dawisha, *Putin's Kleptocracy: Who Owns Russia?* (New York: Simon and Schuster, 2014), and Richard Sakwa, *Putin: Russia's Choice* (New York: Routledge, 2nd ed., 2008).
14 Jane Zavisca, *Housing the New Russia* (Ithaca, NY: Cornell University Press, 2012).
15 Stephen Wegren and Dale Herspring, eds., *After Putin's Russia: Past Imperfect, Future Uncertain* (Lanham, MD: Rowman and Littlefield Publishers, 2010).
16 Marlène Laruelle, *Russian Eurasianism: An Ideology of Empire* (Baltimore, MD: Johns Hopkins University Press, 2008).
17 Jane Burbank and Frederick Cooper, *Empires in World History: Power and Politics of Difference* (Princeton, NJ: Princeton University Press, 2010).
18 Thomas Remington, *Politics in Russia* (New York: Pearson/Longman, 2008); Emma Gilligan, *Terror in Chechnya: Russia and the Tragedy of Civilians* (Princeton, NJ: Princeton University Press, 2010).
19 Richard Sakwa, *Frontline Ukraine: Crisis in the Borderlands* (London: I.B. Tauris, 2015).
20 See Marina Goldovskaya's brilliant documentary on Politkovskaya, *A Bitter Taste of Freedom* (2011).
21 "Interview with Pussy Riot Leader: I Love Russia, but I Hate Putin," *Der Spiegel*, 3 September 2012, available at www.spiegel.de/international/world/spiegel-interview-with-pussy-riot-activist-nadezhda-tolokonnikova-a-853546.html (accessed 5 July 2013).
22 "If Pussy Riot Not Punished, Thousands Could Have Followed Them—Russian Chief Rabbi." By Interfax, Russia and FSU General News, 5 March 2013, p. 1, available at http://mimas.calstatela.edu/login?url=http://search.ebscohost.com.mimas.calstatela.edu/login.aspx?direct=true&db=bwh&AN=85912810&site=ehost-live (accessed 21 July 2013).

Maps

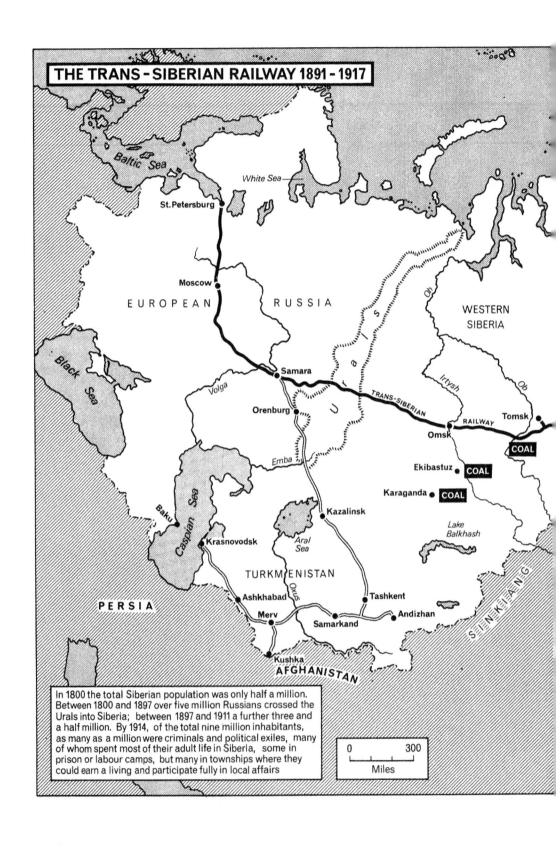

THE TRANS-SIBERIAN RAILWAY 1891-1917

Baltic Sea

White Sea

St.Petersburg

Moscow

EUROPEAN   RUSSIA

WESTERN
SIBERIA

Black Sea

Samara

Volga

Orenburg

Irtysh

Ob

TRANS-SIBERIAN

Tomsk

RAILWAY

Omsk

COAL

Emba

Ekibastuz

COAL

Karaganda

COAL

Baku

Caspian Sea

Kazalinsk

*Lake
Balkhash*

Krasnovodsk

*Aral
Sea*

TURKMENISTAN

Oxus

S I N K I A N G

PERSIA

Ashkhabad

Merv

Tashkent

Andizhan

Samarkand

Kushka

AFGHANISTAN

In 1800 the total Siberian population was only half a million.
Between 1800 and 1897 over five million Russians crossed the
Urals into Siberia; between 1897 and 1911 a further three and
a half million. By 1914, of the total nine million inhabitants,
as many as a million were criminals and political exiles, many
of whom spent most of their adult life in Siberia, some in
prison or labour camps, but many in townships where they
could earn a living and participate fully in local affairs

0   300
Miles

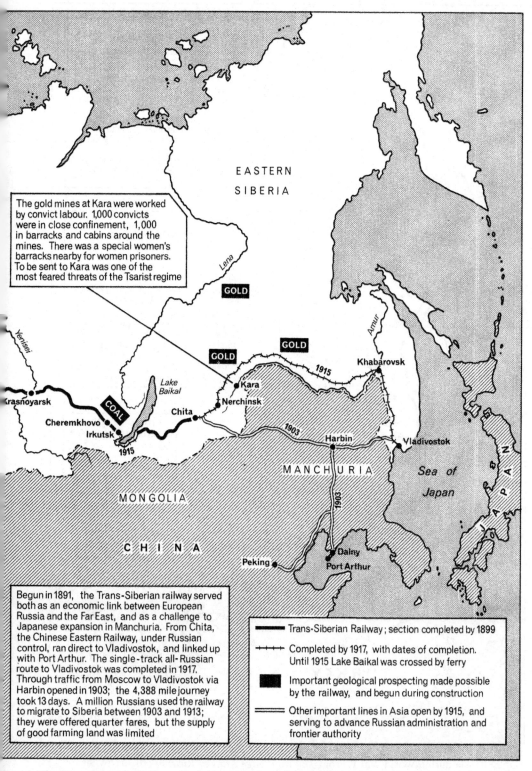

The gold mines at Kara were worked by convict labour. 1,000 convicts were in close confinement, 1,000 in barracks and cabins around the mines. There was a special women's barracks nearby for women prisoners. To be sent to Kara was one of the most feared threats of the Tsarist regime

EASTERN
SIBERIA

GOLD

Lena

Amur

GOLD

GOLD

1915

Khabarovsk

Lake
Baikal

Kara

Krasnoyarsk

COAL

Nerchinsk

Chita

Cheremkhovo

Irkutsk

1903

Harbin

Vladivostok

1915

MANCHURIA

Sea of
Japan

MONGOLIA

1903

CHINA

Peking

Dalny
Port Arthur

Yenisei

J A P A N

Begun in 1891, the Trans-Siberian railway served both as an economic link between European Russia and the Far East, and as a challenge to Japanese expansion in Manchuria. From Chita, the Chinese Eastern Railway, under Russian control, ran direct to Vladivostok, and linked up with Port Arthur. The single-track all-Russian route to Vladivostok was completed in 1917. Through traffic from Moscow to Vladivostok via Harbin opened in 1903; the 4,388 mile journey took 13 days. A million Russians used the railway to migrate to Siberia between 1903 and 1913; they were offered quarter fares, but the supply of good farming land was limited

Trans-Siberian Railway; section completed by 1899

Completed by 1917, with dates of completion. Until 1915 Lake Baikal was crossed by ferry

Important geological prospecting made possible by the railway, and begun during construction

Other important lines in Asia open by 1915, and serving to advance Russian administration and frontier authority

Map 1 The Trans-Siberian Railway and the expansion of the Russian empire from Muscovy to 1917. From *The Routledge Atlas of Russian History* by Sir Martin Gilbert, © 2006, Routledge, reproduced by permission of Taylor & Francis Books UK. www.martingilbert.com

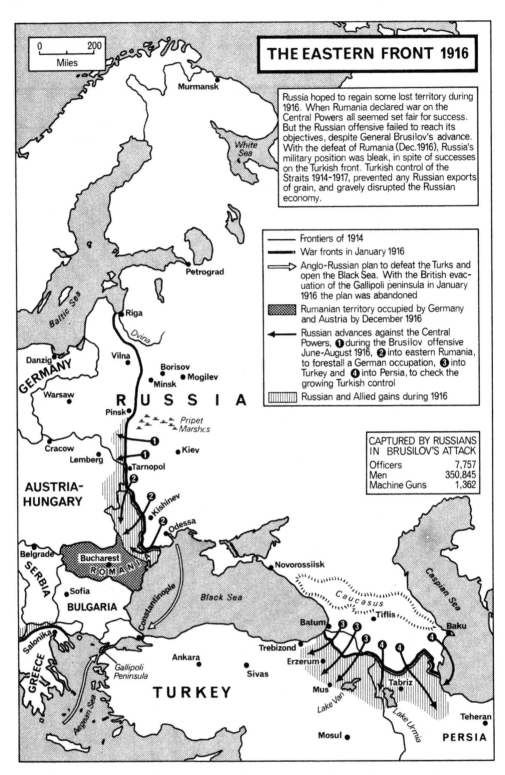

THE EASTERN FRONT 1916

Russia hoped to regain some lost territory during 1916. When Rumania declared war on the Central Powers all seemed set fair for success. But the Russian offensive failed to reach its objectives, despite General Brusilov's advance. With the defeat of Rumania (Dec.1916), Russia's military position was bleak, in spite of successes on the Turkish front. Turkish control of the Straits 1914-1917, prevented any Russian exports of grain, and gravely disrupted the Russian economy.

Frontiers of 1914

War fronts in January 1916

Anglo-Russian plan to defeat the Turks and open the Black Sea. With the British evacuation of the Gallipoli peninsula in January 1916 the plan was abandoned

Rumanian territory occupied by Germany and Austria by December 1916

Russian advances against the Central Powers, ❶ during the Brusilov offensive June-August 1916, ❷ into eastern Rumania, to forestall a German occupation, ❸ into Turkey and ❹ into Persia, to check the growing Turkish control

Russian and Allied gains during 1916

CAPTURED BY RUSSIANS IN BRUSILOV'S ATTACK

Officers	7,757
Men	350,845
Machine Guns	1,362

Map 2 Russia during World War I. From *The Routledge Atlas of Russian History* by Sir Martin Gilbert, © 2006, Routledge, reproduced by permission of Taylor & Francis Books UK. www.martingilbert.com

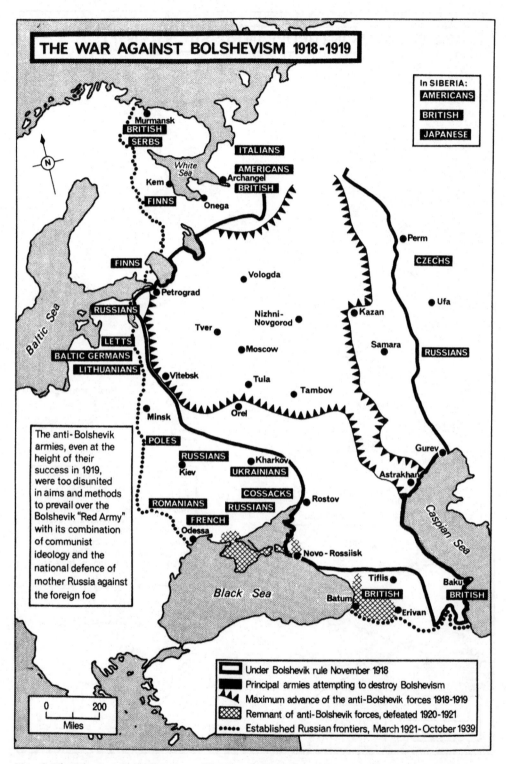

Map 3 The Russian Civil War. From *The Routledge Atlas of Russian History* by Sir Martin Gilbert, © 2006, Routledge, reproduced by permission of Taylor & Francis Books UK. www.martingilbert.com

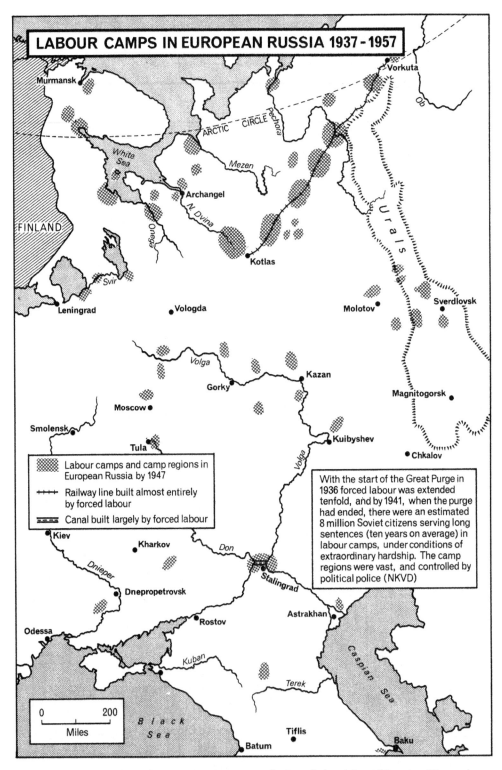

LABOUR CAMPS IN EUROPEAN RUSSIA 1937-1957

Murmansk

Vorkuta

ARCTIC CIRCLE

Pechora

Ob

White Sea

Mezen

Archangel

N. Dvina

FINLAND

Onega

Svir

Kotlas

Urals

Leningrad

Vologda

Molotov

Sverdlovsk

Volga

Kazan

Gorky

Magnitogorsk

Moscow

Smolensk

Kuibyshev

Tula

Chkalov

> Labour camps and camp regions in European Russia by 1947
>
> Railway line built almost entirely by forced labour
>
> Canal built largely by forced labour

Kiev

Kharkov

Don

Dnieper

Dnepropetrovsk

Stalingrad

With the start of the Great Purge in 1936 forced labour was extended tenfold, and by 1941, when the purge had ended, there were an estimated 8 million Soviet citizens serving long sentences (ten years on average) in labour camps, under conditions of extraordinary hardship. The camp regions were vast, and controlled by political police (NKVD)

Rostov

Astrakhan

Odessa

Kuban

Caspian Sea

Terek

0   200
Miles

Black Sea

Tiflis

Baku

Batum

Map 4 Labour camps in European Russia. From *The Routledge Atlas of Russian History* by Sir Martin Gilbert, © 2006, Routledge, reproduced by permission of Taylor & Francis Books UK. www.martingilbert.com

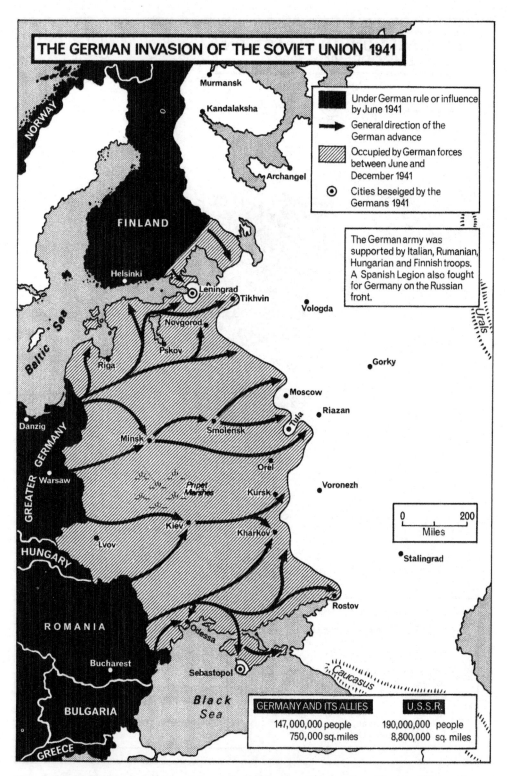

Map 5 World War II on the eastern front. From *The Routledge Atlas of Russian History* by Sir Martin Gilbert, © 2006, Routledge, reproduced by permission of Taylor & Francis Books UK. www.martingilbert.com

THE SOVIET UNION IN EASTERN EUROPE 1949-1968

0 — 200
Miles

FINLAND
Vyborg
Leningrad
Tallin (Reval)

SWEDEN

Riga

North Sea

Baltic Sea

Klaypeda (Memel)

Kaliningrad

SOVIET
UNION

Rostock
East Berlin
Szczecin
Gdansk
EAST GERMANY
Posnan
POLAND
Warsaw
Halle
Dresden
Lodz
WEST GERMANY
Wroclaw
Prague
CZECHOSLOVAKIA
Lublin
Cracow
Przemysl
Kiev

FRANCE
Brno
Kosice
Lvov

Bratislava

SWITZ.
AUSTRIA
Debrecen
Györ
Budapest
HUNGARY
Jassy
Odessa

Zagreb
Pécs
Cluj
Rijeka
Arad
ROMANIA

Belgrade
Constanza
YUGOSLAVIA
Split
Bucharest
ITALY
Adriatic Sea
Nish
Varna
Kotor
BULGARIA
Black Sea
ALBANIA
Sofia
Burgas
Tirana
Durres
Vlone

GREECE

TURKEY

Aegean Sea

— Frontiers of communist states since 1945

▨ Only European communist state entirely free from Soviet direction of foreign, economic and domestic policy since 1949

▧ Only communist state within the Soviet bloc pursuing a relatively independent foreign policy since 1968

▨ Only communist state in Europe aligned with China and refusing all contact with the Soviet Union since 1961

☐ Only European communist state to accept Soviet guidance with equanimity

■ Principal areas of anti-Soviet protest and revolt 1953–1968, crushed by Soviet military intervention (East Germany, Hungary, Czechoslovakia) and by strong political pressure (Poland)

Map 6 The Soviet Union in Eastern Europe 1949–1968. From *The Routledge Atlas of Russian History* by Sir Martin Gilbert, © 2006, Routledge, reproduced by permission of Taylor & Francis Books UK. www.martingilbert.com

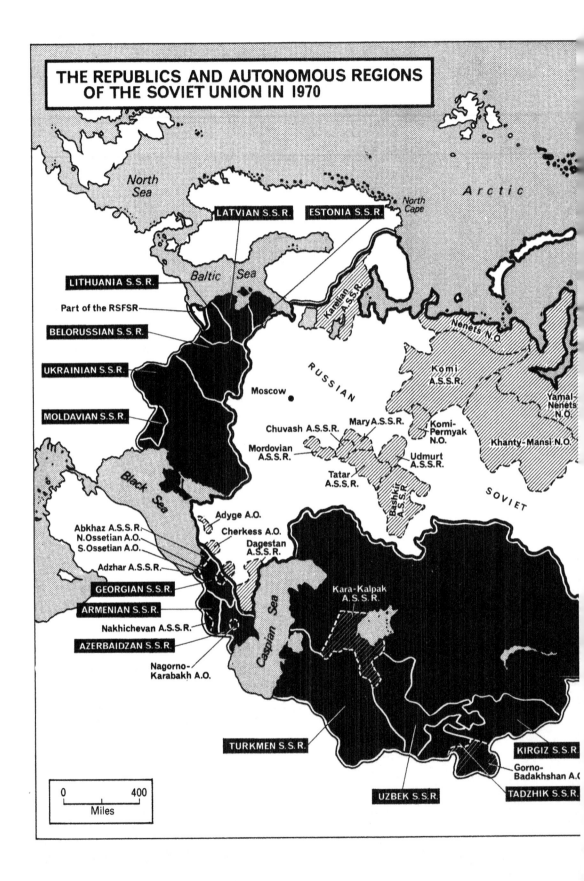

THE REPUBLICS AND AUTONOMOUS REGIONS OF THE SOVIET UNION IN 1970

North Sea

Arctic

North Cape

LATVIAN S.S.R.

ESTONIA S.S.R.

Baltic Sea

LITHUANIA S.S.R.

Part of the RSFSR

BELORUSSIAN S.S.R.

UKRAINIAN S.S.R.

MOLDAVIAN S.S.R.

Karelian A.S.S.R.

Nenets N.O.

Komi A.S.S.R.

RUSSIAN

Moscow

Yamal-Nenets N.O.

Mary A.S.S.R.

Komi-Permyak N.O.

Khanty-Mansi N.O.

Chuvash A.S.S.R.

Mordovian A.S.S.R.

Udmurt A.S.S.R.

Tatar A.S.S.R.

Bashkir A.S.S.R.

SOVIET

Black Sea

Adyge A.O.

Abkhaz A.S.S.R.
N.Ossetian A.O.
S.Ossetian A.O.

Cherkess A.O.

Dagestan A.S.S.R.

Adzhar A.S.S.R.

GEORGIAN S.S.R.

ARMENIAN S.S.R.

Nakhichevan A.S.S.R.

AZERBAIDZAN S.S.R.

Nagorno-Karabakh A.O.

Kara-Kalpak A.S.S.R.

Caspian Sea

TURKMEN S.S.R.

KIRGIZ S.S.R.

Gorno-Badakhshan A.O.

TADZHIK S.S.R.

UZBEK S.S.R.

0   400
Miles

Map 7 The republics and autonomous regions of the Soviet Union in 1970. From *The Routledge Atlas of Russian History* by Sir Martin Gilbert, © 2006, Routledge, reproduced by permission of Taylor & Francis Books UK. www.martingilbert.com

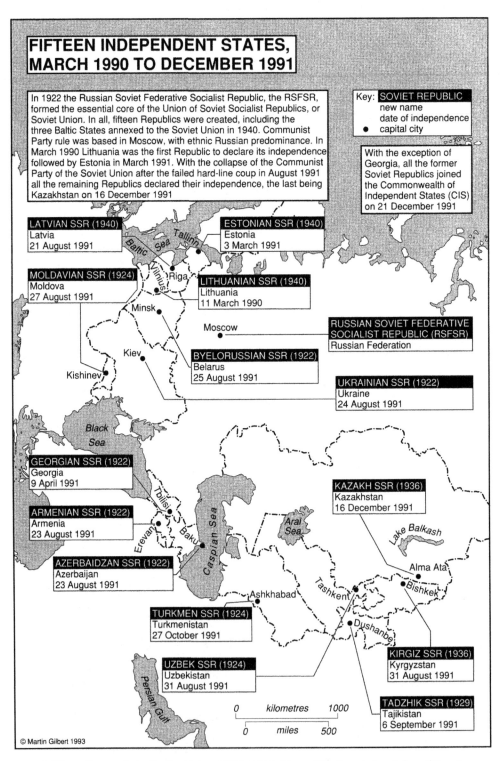

Map 8 The collapse of the Soviet Union 1990–1991. From *The Routledge Atlas of Russian History* by Sir Martin Gilbert, © 2006, Routledge, reproduced by permission of Taylor & Francis Books UK. www.martingilbert.com

Index

Christianity 6, 7, 8, 19, 32, 98, 208; *see also* atheism, Orthodox Church, religion
Chubais, Anatoly 238
Chuikov, Vasily 138
Churchill, Winston 141–42, 150–51, 157, 159
cinema; *see* film
Circassians 7
Circus (film) 119
civil rights 10, 23, 31, 37, 249
civil society 10, 19, 37, 216, 218, 222, 243
Civil War 44, 47, 48, 50, 51, 53–61, 65–66, 74, 80, 82, 95, 97, 103, 109, 118, 122, 147, 177, 259; *see also* Red Army
Clemenceau, Georges 151
clothing 17, 32, 35, 57, 61, 66, 81, 82, 87, 98, 108, 113, 128, 163–64, 165, 182, 201, 203, 235, 246; *see also* fashion, *stiliagi*
Cold War 3, 40, 55, 70, 122, 142–43, 155–69, 171–74, 180, 181, 196, 198, 199, 200, 207, 217, 221, 228, 231, 240
collectivization, collective farms; *see under* agriculture
colonialism; *see* empire
Comintern 45, 65, 71–74, 85–86, 117, 119, 123, 124, 141
Commissariat of Education; *see* education
Commissariat of Food Supply; *see* food
Commissariat of Foreign Affairs 49, 117
Commissariat of Health 78
Commissariat of Justice 78
Commissariat of Labor 49
Commissariat of War 56
Commonwealth of Independent States 227, 230, 252
communal apartments; *see under* housing
communism 3, 34, 45, 47, 56–61, 69, 71, 72, 73, 82, 86, 87–88, 92, 104, 113, 117–18, 125–26, 136, 137, 141, 157, 34, 60, 72, 73, 87, 88, 117, 155, 156, 168, 169, 172–73, 176, 177, 179, 181, 186–87, 208, 223, 226
Communist Manifesto 75
Communist Party 47, 48, 49–51, 52, 57, 59, 60, 61, 63, 69, 72, 73, 75, 78, 79, 92, 93, 94, 95, 97, 98, 100, 102, 109, 111, 112, 115, 116, 119, 120, 121, 122, 123, 124, 125–26, 134, 136, 137, 139, 145, 147, 158, 159, 160, 162, 166, 167, 176, 177, 178, 179, 183, 184, 185, 187–88, 193, 198, 197, 199, 204, 207, 216, 218, 219, 220, 221, 223–26, 227, 237, 238, 245; Party Congresses 59, 60, 112, 167, 230
Congress of People's Deputies 224, 227
Congress of Soviets 40, 41, 47, 49, 51, 54
Constantinople 37
Constituent Assembly 39, 49, 50–51, 52, 54, 56

consumption 17, 18, 29, 32, 61, 82, 112, 137, 167–68, 181, 201, 207, 209, 218, 221–22, 224, 225, 228, 237, 238, 239, 242, 249; *see also* shopping
Cooper, Frederick 243
Cossacks 15, 33, 38, 53
Council of People's Commissars; *see* Sovnarkom
Courland 52
Crimea 15, 139, 142, 203, 244, 245, 251, 252–53
Crimean War 8, 9
Cuban missile crises 197
cultural revolution 104, 106, 107, 118, 229; *see also under* China
Curzon line 150–51
Czechoslovak Legion 53, 56
Czechoslovakia 53, 117, 132, 156, 157, 198, 226, 243

D-Day 141
Dagestan 244
dance 13, 76, 119, 160, 163, 164, 165, 181, 235
Daniel, Yuli 203
Davis, Richard Harding 5
decolonization 70, 155, 242, 243
Decree on Land 49
Decree on Peace 49
Deng Xiaoping 221
Denikin, Anton 55, 58
de-Stalinization 139, 149
détente 198, 200
Dimitrov, Georgi 117
dissidents 121, 164, 184–85, 198, 203–204, 207–209, 219, 223, 224, 232
divorce; *see under* marriage
Dnepropetrovsk 66, 207, 208
Doctor Zhivago (novel) 139
Doctors' Plot 161–62, 176, 179
Donbass 66
Dostoevsky, Fedor 17, 35
dual power 39, 40
Dudaev, Dzhokar 243
Dugin, Alexander 242–43
Duma 19, 23–24, 26, 38, 39, 43
Dunham, Vera (née Sandomirsky) 134, 166, 201

education 1, 7, 8, 9, 13, 14, 15, 17, 18, 19, 22, 28, 29, 34, 35, 36, 37, 80–81, 83, 87–88, 100, 102, 104, 106, 113, 114, 161, 168, 182, 186, 191–92, 202, 212, 218, 219, 221, 238, 241, 242; Commissariat of Education 81; ideological education 47, 48, 55, 60, 63, 81, 102, 104, 133, 178, 187, 188, 229–30;